KAPLAN
PUBLISHING

GW01471466

NOW THIS EXAM KIT COMES WITH
FREE ONLINE ACCESS
TO EXTRA RESOURCES AIMED AT HELPING YOU PASS YOUR EXAMS

IN ADDITION TO THE OFFICIAL QUESTIONS AND ANSWERS IN THIS BOOK, GO ONLINE AND EN-gage WITH:

- Fixed Tests
- Interim Assessments
- Exam paper Guides
- Latest Official ACCA exam questions
- Answers updated to include legislation relevant to next exam
- Frequent and varied new additions to these resources – watch this space!

And you can access all of these extra resources anytime, anywhere using your EN-gage account.

How to access your online resources

If you are a Kaplan Financial tuition, full-time or distance learning student	You will already have an EN-gage account and these extra resources will be available to you online. You do not need to register again, as this process was completed when you enrolled. If having problems accessing online materials, please ask your course administrator.
If you purchased through Kaplan Flexible Learning or via the Kaplan Publishing website	You will automatically receive an e-mail invitation to EN-gage online. Please register your details using this e-mail to gain access to your content. If you do not receive the e-mail or book content, please contact Kaplan Flexible Learning.
If you are already a registered EN-gage user	Go to www.EN-gage.co.uk and log in. Select the 'add a book' feature and enter the ISBN number of this book and the unique pass key at the bottom of this card. Then click 'finished' or 'add another book'. You may add as many books as you have purchased from this screen.
If you are a new EN-gage user	Register at www.EN-gage.co.uk and click on the link contained in the e-mail we sent you to activate your account. Then select the 'add a book' feature, enter the ISBN number of this book and the unique pass key at the bottom of this card. Then click 'finished' or 'add another book'.

Your Code and Information

This code can only be used once for the registration of one book online. This registration will expire when the final sittings for the examinations covered by this book have taken place. Please allow one hour from the time you submitted your book details for us to process your request.

EN-gage

feE1-tY5Q-fm2v-blmD

For technical support, please visit www.EN-gage.co.uk

Paper F7

FINANCIAL REPORTING (UK)

EXAM KIT

ACCA
OFFICIAL PUBLISHER

KAPLAN

PUBLISHING

British Library Cataloguing-in-Publication Data

A catalogue record for this book is available from the British Library.

Published by:

Kaplan Publishing UK

Unit 2 The Business Centre

Molly Millar's Lane

Wokingham

Berkshire

RG41 2QZ

978-1-84710-772-5

© Kaplan Financial Limited, 2009.

Printed and bound in Great Britain.

Acknowledgements

The past ACCA examination questions are the copyright of the Association of Chartered Certified Accountants. The original answers to the questions from June 1994 onwards were produced by the examiners themselves and have been adapted by Kaplan Publishing.

We are grateful to the Chartered Institute of Management Accountants and the Institute of Chartered Accountants in England and Wales for permission to reproduce past examination questions. The answers have been prepared by Kaplan Publishing.

CONTENTS

Section

[NEW] **New features in this edition**

In addition to providing a wide ranging bank of real past exam questions, we have also included in this edition:

- An analysis of all of the recent new syllabus examination papers.

- Paper specific information and advice on exam technique.

- Our recommended approach to make your revision for this particular subject as effective as possible.

  This includes step by step guidance on how best to use our Kaplan material (Complete text, pocket notes and exam kit) at this stage in your studies.

- Enhanced tutorial answers packed with specific key answer tips, technical tutorial notes and exam technique tips from our experienced tutors.

- Complementary online resources including full tutor debriefs and question assistance to point you in the right direction when you get stuck.

December 2009 – Real examination questions with enhanced tutorial answers

The real December 2009 exam questions with enhanced "walk through answers" and full "tutor debriefs", updated in line with legislation relevant to your exam sitting, is available on Kaplan EN-gage at:

www.EN-gage.co.uk

You will find a wealth of other resources to help you with your studies on the following sites:

www.EN-gage.co.uk

www.**acca**global.com/students/

INDEX TO QUESTIONS AND ANSWERS

INTRODUCTION

The pilot paper is included at the end of the kit.

KEY TO THE INDEX

PAPER ENHANCEMENTS

We have added the following enhancements to the answers in this exam kit:

Key answer tips

All answers include key answer tips to help your understanding of each question.

Tutorial note

All answers include more tutorial notes to explain some of the technical points in more detail.

Top tutor tips

For selected questions, we "walk through the answer" giving guidance on how to approach the questions with helpful 'tips from a top tutor', together with technical tutor notes.

These answers are indicated with the "footsteps" icon in the index.

ONLINE ENHANCEMENTS

    Timed question with Online tutor debrief

For selected questions, we recommend that they are to be completed in full exam conditions (i.e. properly timed in a closed book environment).

In addition to the examiner's technical answer, enhanced with key answer tips and tutorial notes in this exam kit, online you can find an answer debrief by a top tutor that:

- works through the question in full

- points out how to approach the question

- how to ensure that the easy marks are obtained as quickly as possible, and

- emphasises how to tackle exam questions and exam technique.

These questions are indicated with the "clock" icon in the index.

    Online question assistance

Have you ever looked at a question and not know where to start, or got stuck part way through?

For selected questions, we have produced "Online question assistance" offering different levels of guidance, such as:

- ensuring that you understand the question requirements fully, highlighting key terms and the meaning of the verbs used

- how to read the question proactively, with knowledge of the requirements, to identify the topic areas covered

- assessing the detail content of the question body, pointing out key information and explaining why it is important

- help in devising a plan of attack

With this assistance, you should then be able to attempt your answer confident that you know what is expected of you.

These questions are indicated with the "signpost" icon in the index.

Online question enhancements and answer debriefs will be available from Spring 2010 on Kaplan EN-gage at:

www.EN-gage.co.uk

A CONCEPTUAL FRAMEWORK FOR FINANCIAL REPORTING

A REGULATORY FRAMEWORK FOR FINANCIAL REPORTING

FINANCIAL STATEMENTS

BUSINESS COMBINATIONS

ANALYSING AND INTERPRETING FINANCIAL STATEMENTS

ANALYSIS OF PAST PAPERS

The table below summarises the key topics that have been tested in the new syllabus examinations to date.

Note that the references are to the number of the question in this edition of the exam kit, but the Pilot Paper is produced in its original form at the end of the kit and therefore these questions have retained their original numbering in the paper itself.

	Pilot 07	Dec 07	Jun 08	Dec 08	Jun 09
Group financial statements					
Consolidated profit and loss			✓		
Consolidated balance sheet	✓	✓			✓
Consolidated P&L and B/S				✓	
Associates	✓	✓	✓		✓
Non-group financial statements					
From trial balance	✓	✓		✓	✓
Redraft			✓		
STRGL/ movement on reserves	✓		✓	✓	
Performance appraisal					
Ratios	✓	✓		✓	
Cash flow statement			✓		
Ratios and cash flow statement					✓
Mixed transactional					
Statement of principles	✓	✓		✓	
Accounting principles / FRS 5		✓	✓		
SSAP 4					
SSAP 5 / FRS 16 / FRS 19					
SSAP 9	✓		✓		
SSAP 13 / FRS10		✓			
SSAP 19					
SSAP 21		✓			
FRS 3		✓			
FRS 11					
FRS 12				✓	
FRS 15				✓	✓
FRS 18		✓			
FRS 21					✓
FRS 22					
FRS 25 / 26 / 28 / 29			✓		

KAPLAN PUBLISHING

EXAM TECHNIQUE

- Use the allocated **15 minutes reading and planning time** at the beginning of the exam:
  - read the questions and examination requirements carefully, and
  - begin planning your answers.

  See the Paper Specific Information for advice on how to use this time for this paper.

- **Divide the time** you spend on questions in proportion to the marks on offer:
  - there are 1.8 minutes available per mark in the examination
  - within that, try to allow time at the end of each question to review your answer and address any obvious issues

  Whatever happens, always keep your eye on the clock and **do not over run on any part of any question!**

- Spend the last **five minutes** of the examination:
  - reading through your answers, and
  - **making any additions or corrections**.

- If you **get completely stuck** with a question:
  - leave space in your answer book, and
  - **return to it later.**

- Stick to the question and **tailor your answer** to what you are asked.
  - pay particular attention to the verbs in the question.

- If you do not understand what a question is asking, **state your assumptions**.

  Even if you do not answer in precisely the way the examiner hoped, you should be given some credit, if your assumptions are reasonable.

- You should do everything you can to make things easy for the marker.

  The marker will find it easier to identify the points you have made if your **answers are legible**.

- **Written questions**:

  Your answer should have:
  - a clear structure
  - a brief introduction, a main section and a conclusion.

  Be concise.

  It is better to write a little about a lot of different points than a great deal about one or two points.

- **Computations**:

  It is essential to include all your workings in your answers.

  Many computational questions require the use of a standard format:

  e.g. profit & loss account, balance sheet and cash flow statement.

  Be sure you know these formats thoroughly before the exam and use the layouts that you see in the answers given in this book and in model answers.

PAPER SPECIFIC INFORMATION

THE EXAM

FORMAT OF THE EXAM

Number of marks

5 compulsory questions which will be **predominantly computational**:

Question 1:	Group financial statements	25
Question 2:	Non-group financial statements	25
Question 3:	Performance appraisal	25
Question 4:	Any area of the syllabus	15
Question 5:	Any area of the syllabus	10
		100

Total time allowed: 3 hours plus 15 minutes reading and planning time.

Note that:

- Question 1 will focus on the preparation of group accounts which could include up to a five mark written element. Question 1 will always include a subsidiary company and sometimes an associate as well. You will either be required to prepare a consolidated balance sheet a consolidated profit and loss account or both

- Question 2 will always require the preparation of non-group financial statements either from a trial balance or a re-draft of financial statements Knowledge for this question is required from many areas of the syllabus but common topics are depreciation, revaluations of fixed assets, substance over form and revenue recognition

- Question 3 will require the preparation of a cash flow statement, accounting ratios or both. This question generally requires some performance appraisal and you will be assessed on your ability to interpret the underlying information from the financial statements and ratios that you have prepared.

- Questions 4 and 5 will cover the reminder of the syllabus. It is important that you are familiar with the conceptual and regulatory framework, accounting concepts and the accounting standards outline in the list of examinable documents available on the ACCA website.

PASS MARK

The pass mark for all ACCA Qualification examination papers is 50%.

READING AND PLANNING TIME

Remember that all three hour paper based examinations have an additional 15 minutes reading and planning time.

ACCA GUIDANCE

ACCA guidance on the use of this time is as follows:

This additional time is allowed at the beginning of the examination to allow candidates to read the questions and to begin planning their answers before they start to write in their answer books.

This time should be used to ensure that all the information and, in particular, the exam requirements are properly read and understood.

During this time, candidates may only annotate their question paper. They may not write anything in their answer booklets until told to do so by the invigilator.

KAPLAN GUIDANCE

As all questions are compulsory, there are no decisions to be made about choice of questions, other than in which order you would like to tackle them.

Therefore, in relation to F7, we recommend that you take the following approach with your reading and planning time:

- **Skim through the whole paper**, assessing the level of difficulty of each question.

- **Write down** on the question paper next to the mark allocation **the amount of time you should spend on each part.** Do this for each part of every question.

- **Decide the order** in which you think you will attempt each question:

  This is a personal choice and you have time on the revision phase to try out different approaches, for example, if you sit mock exams.

  A common approach is to tackle the question you think is the easiest and you are most comfortable with first.

  Others may prefer to tackle the longest questions first, or conversely leave them to the last.

  Psychologists believe that you usually perform at your best on the second and third question you attempt, once you have settled into the exam.

  It is usual however that student tackle their least favourite topic and/or the most difficult question in their opinion last.

  Whatever your approach, you must make sure that you leave enough time to attempt all questions fully and be very strict with yourself in timing each question.

- **For each question** in turn, read the requirements and then the detail of the question carefully.

  Always read the requirement first as this enables you to **focus on the detail of the question with the specific task in mind**.

  For computational questions:

  Highlight key numbers / information and key words in the question, scribble notes to yourself on the question paper to remember key points in your answer.

  Jot down proformas required if applicable.

  For written questions:

  Take notice of the format required (e.g. letter, memo, notes) and identify the recipient of the answer . You need to do this to judge the level of financial sophistication required in your answer and whether the use of a formal reply or informal bullet points would be satisfactory.

  Plan your beginning, middle and end and the key areas to be addressed and your use of titles and sub-titles to enhance your answer.

  For all questions:

  Spot the easy marks to be gained in a question and parts which can be performed independently of the rest of the question. For example laying out basic proformas correctly, answer written elements not related to the scenario etc.

  Make sure that you do these parts first when you tackle the question.

  Don't go overboard in terms of planning time on any one question – you need a good measure of the whole paper and a plan for all of the questions at the end of the 15 minutes.

  By covering all questions you can often help yourself as you may find that facts in one question may remind you of things you should put into your answer relating to a different question.

- With your plan of attack in mind, **start answering your chosen question** with your plan to hand, as soon as you are allowed to start.

Always keep your eye on the clock and do not over run on any part of any question!

DETAILED SYLLABUS

The detailed syllabus and study guide written by the ACCA can be found at:

www.accaglobal.com/students/

KAPLAN'S RECOMMENDED REVISION APPROACH

QUESTION PRACTICE IS THE KEY TO SUCCESS

Success in professional examinations relies upon you acquiring a firm grasp of the required knowledge at the tuition phase. In order to be able to do the questions, knowledge is essential.

However, the difference between success and failure often hinges on your exam technique on the day and making the most of the revision phase of your studies.

The **Kaplan complete text** is the starting point, designed to provide the underpinning knowledge to tackle all questions. However, in the revision phase, pouring over text books is not the answer.

Kaplan Online fixed tests help you consolidate your knowledge and understanding and are a useful tool to check whether you can remember key topic areas.

Kaplan pocket notes are designed to help you quickly revise a topic area, however you then need to practice questions. There is a need to progress to full exam standard questions as soon as possible, and to tie your exam technique and technical knowledge together.

The importance of question practice cannot be over-emphasised.

The recommended approach below is designed by expert tutors in the field, in conjunction with their knowledge of the examiner and their recent real exams.

The approach taken for the fundamental papers is to revise by topic area. However, with the professional stage papers, a multi topic approach is required to answer the scenario based questions.

You need to practice as many questions as possible in the time you have left.

OUR AIM

Our aim is to get you to the stage where you can attempt exam standard questions confidently, to time, in a closed book environment, with no supplementary help (i.e. to simulate the real examination experience).

Practising your exam technique on real past examination questions, in timed conditions, is also vitally important for you to assess your progress and identify areas of weakness that may need more attention in the final run up to the examination.

In order to achieve this we recognise that initially you may feel the need to practice some questions with open book help and exceed the required time.

The approach below shows you which questions you should use to build up to coping with exam standard question practice, and references to the sources of information available should you need to revisit a topic area in more detail.

Remember that in the real examination, all you have to do is:

- attempt all questions required by the exam

- only spend the allotted time on each question, and

- get them at least 50% right!

Try and practice this approach on every question you attempt from now to the real exam.

EXAMINER COMMENTS

We have included some of the examiners comments to the specific new syllabus examination questions in this kit for you to see the main pitfalls that students fall into with regard to technical content.

However, too many times in the general section of the report, the examiner comments that students had failed due to:

- "misallocation of time"

- "running out of time" and

- showing signs of "spending too much time on an earlier question and clearly rushing the answer to a subsequent question".

Good exam technique is vital.

THE KAPLAN PAPER F7 REVISION PLAN

Stage 1: Assess areas of strengths and weaknesses

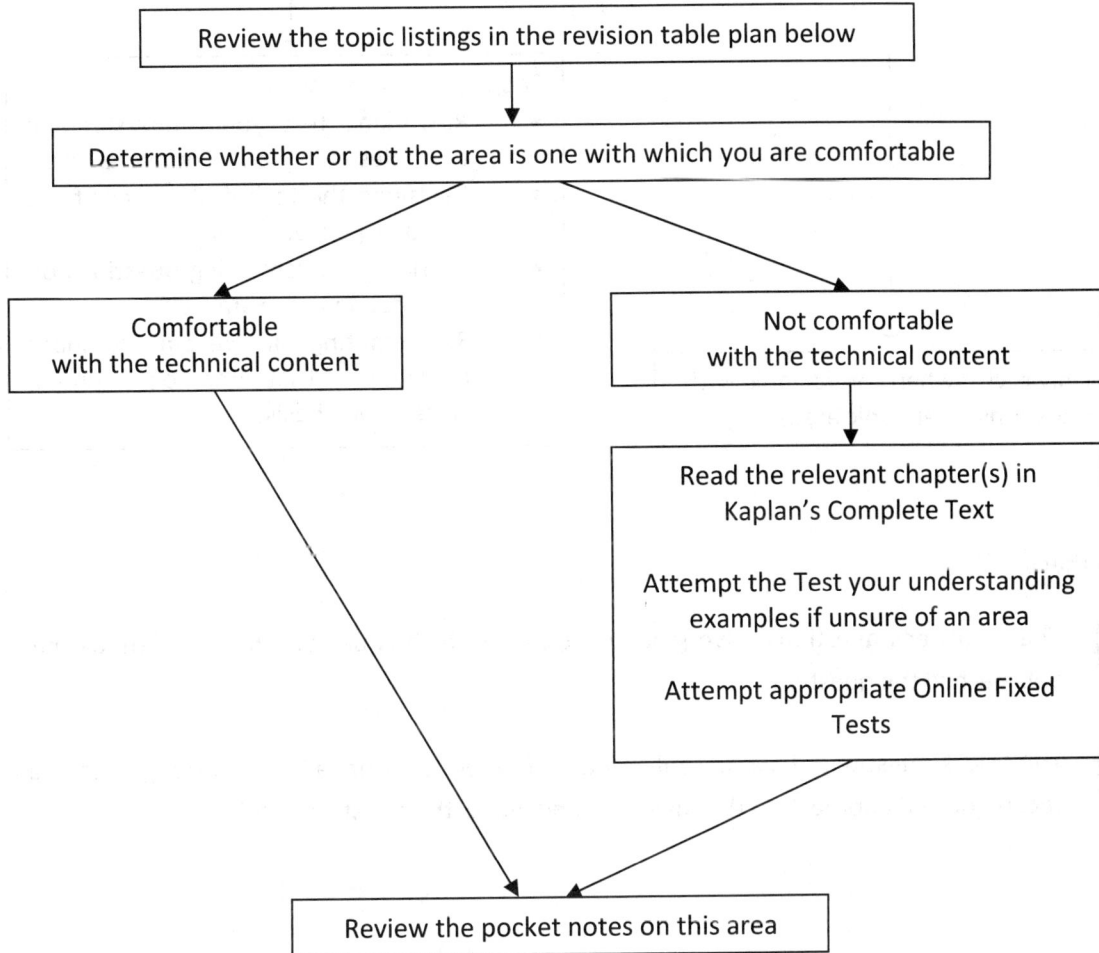

Review the topic listings in the revision table plan below

Determine whether or not the area is one with which you are comfortable

Comfortable
with the technical content

Not comfortable
with the technical content

Read the relevant chapter(s) in
Kaplan's Complete Text

Attempt the Test your understanding
examples if unsure of an area

Attempt appropriate Online Fixed
Tests

Review the pocket notes on this area

Stage 2: Practice questions

Follow the order of revision of topics as recommended in the revision table plan below and attempt the questions in the order suggested.

Try to avoid referring to text books and notes and the model answer until you have completed your attempt.

Try to answer the question in the allotted time.

Review your attempt with the model answer and assess how much of the answer you achieved in the allocated exam time.

Fill in the self-assessment box below and decide on your best course of action.

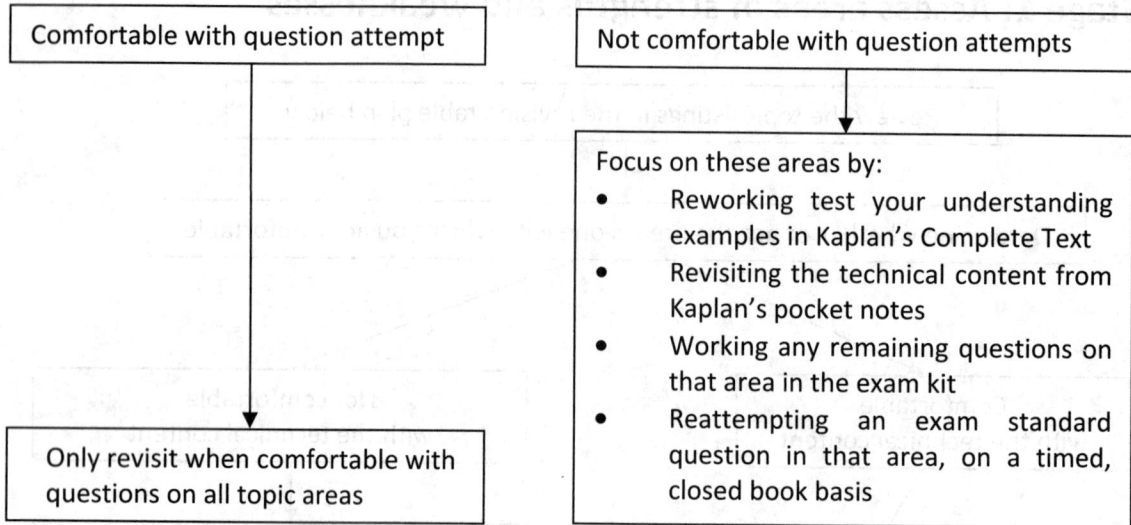

Comfortable with question attempt

Not comfortable with question attempts

Focus on these areas by:
- Reworking test your understanding examples in Kaplan's Complete Text
- Revisiting the technical content from Kaplan's pocket notes
- Working any remaining questions on that area in the exam kit
- Reattempting an exam standard question in that area, on a timed, closed book basis

Only revisit when comfortable with questions on all topic areas

Note that :

The "footsteps questions" give guidance on exam techniques and how you should have approached the question.

The "clock questions" have an online debrief where a tutor talks you through the exam technique and approach to that question and works the question in full.

Stage 3: Final pre-exam revision

We recommend that you **attempt at least one three hour mock examination** containing a set of previously unseen exam standard questions.

It is important that you get a feel for the breadth of coverage of a real exam without advanced knowledge of the topic areas covered – just as you will expect to see on the real exam day.

Ideally this mock should be sat in timed, closed book, real exam conditions and could be:

- a mock examination offered by your tuition provider, and/or

- the pilot paper in the back of this exam kit, and/or

- the last real examination paper (available shortly afterwards on Kaplan EN-gage with "enhanced walk through answers" and a full "tutor debrief").

THE DETAILED REVISION PLAN

Topic	Complete Text Chapter	Pocket note Chapter	Questions to attempt	Tutor guidance	Date attempted	Self assessment
Consolidated balance sheet	5 / 7	5 / 7	44 46	Practice the Kaplan 5 working approach. Ensure you get the easy marks available in the question from adding the parent and subsidiary assets and liabilities together.		
Consolidated profit and loss account	6 / 7	6 / 7	48 52	Watch the dates carefully – is there a mid-year acquisition? If so you have to time apportion the subsidiary company results when adding the parent and subsidiary together.		
Consolidated profit and loss and balance sheet			45 53	Set up your proforma's first and get the easy marks by adding the parent and subsidiary results together – then complete the 5 standard balance sheet workings before moving on to complete the profit and loss account.		
Accounting standards:						
FRS 15	8	8	14 27	Be clear on initial recognition rules, subsequent measurement and component depreciation.		
FRS 11	10	10	15 18 (part b)	Learn the impairment test proforma and the income generating unit write down rules.		
SSAP 21	13	13	10	Be sure you can identify the		

			17 (part b)	differences between an operating and a finance lease.
FRS 12	15	15	1 (part c (i)) 26	For FRS 12 the recognition rules are very clear – learn the 3 recognition rules.
FRS 21	15	15	28	Learn the differences between adjusting and non-adjusting events.
SSAP 9	11	11	16 18 (part d)	The measurement of stock is key and plenty of practice on long-term contracts is recommended.
FRS 25 / 26	12	12	1 (PART C (iii)) 18 (part a) 21 22	Amortised cost is the core area here. Make sure you can deal with loans issued at a discount & redeemed at a premium. You will also need an awareness of the four financial asset categories and the accounting treatment for them.
FRS 18	3	3	6	Learn the recognition criteria for the 3 areas.
FRS 19	16	16	17 (part a)	Learn the definition of a temporary difference and practice its application.
FRS 22	18	18	41	Learn the formula and apply to share issues.
Substance over form	14	14	7 8	This subject regularly features at qn 2 and sometimes as a qn 4 or 5 in its own right. Learn the definition and the 4 specific areas.
Non-group financial statements			31 32 35 36	You have to learn the accounting standards examinable first and then apply your knowledge to these recommended questions.

| Cash flow statements | 20 | 20 | 63 64 60 | A popular exam topic on a primary accounting statement. Learn the proforma. Start with question 63 and 64 which are basic warm up questions covering some key points. Build up to question 60 which is more demanding. |
| Ratio interpretation | 19 | 19 | 55 66 | Learn the ratio calculations and practice identifying where you pull the information for the formula out of the financial statements. |

Note that not all of the questions are referred to in the programme above. We have recommended an approach to build up from the basic to exam standard questions.

The remaining questions are available in the kit for extra practice for those who require more question on some areas.

Section 1

PRACTICE QUESTIONS

A CONCEPTUAL FRAMEWORK FOR FINANCIAL REPORTING

1 ASB STATEMENT

(a) The ASB's *Statement of principles for financial reporting* (Statement) sets out the concepts that underlie the preparation and presentation of financial statements that external users are likely to rely on when making economic decisions about an enterprise.

Required:

Explain the purpose and authoritative status of the Statement.   **(5 marks)**

(b) Of particular importance within the Statement are the definitions and recognition criteria for assets and liabilities.

Required:

Define assets and liabilities and explain the important aspects of their definitions. Explain why these definitions are of particular importance to the preparation of an entity's balance sheet and profit and loss account.   **(8 marks)**

(c) Peterlee is preparing its financial statements for the year ended 31 March 20X6. The following items have been brought to your attention:

(i) Peterlee acquired the entire share capital of Trantor during the year. The acquisition was achieved through a share exchange. The terms of the exchange were based on the relative values of the two companies obtained by capitalising the companies' estimated future cash flows. When the fair value of Trantor's identifiable net assets was deducted from the value of the company as a whole, its goodwill was calculated at £2.5 million. A similar exercise valued the goodwill of Peterlee at £4 million. The directors wish to incorporate both the goodwill values in the companies' consolidated financial statements.

(4 marks)

(ii) During the year Peterlee acquired an iron ore mine at a cost of £6 million. In addition, when all the ore has been extracted (estimated in 10 years time) the company will face estimated costs for landscaping the area affected by the mining that have a present value of £2 million. These costs would still have to be incurred even if no further ore was extracted. The directors have proposed that an accrual of £200,000 per year for the next ten years should be made for the landscaping.   **(4 marks)**

(iii) On 1 April 20X5 Peterlee issued an 8% £5 million convertible loan at par. The loan is convertible in three years time to ordinary shares or redeemable at par in cash. The directors decided to issue a convertible loan because a non-convertible loan would have required an interest rate of 10%. The directors intend to show the liability for the loan at £5 million. The following discount rates are available for £1 receivable at the end of the year:

	8%	10%
Year 1	0.93	0.91
Year 2	0.86	0.83
Year 3	0.79	0.75

(4 marks)

Required:

Describe (and quantify where possible) how Peterlee should treat the items in (i) to (iii) in its financial statements for the year ended 31 March 20X6 commenting on the directors' views where appropriate.

The mark allocation is shown against each of the three items above.

(Total: 25 marks)

2   ANGELINO

(a) Recording the substance of transactions, rather than their legal form, is an important principle in financial accounting. Abuse of this principle can lead to profit manipulation, non-recognition of assets and substantial debt not being recorded on the balance sheet.

Required:

Describe how the use of off balance sheet financing can mislead users of financial statements.

Note: Your answer should refer to specific user groups and include examples where recording the legal form of transactions may mislead them.   **(9 marks)**

(b) Angelino has entered into the following transactions during the year ended 30 September 20X6:

(i) In September 20X6 Angelino sold (factored) some of its trade debtors to Omar, a finance house. On selected account balances Omar paid Angelino 80% of their book value. The agreement was that Omar would administer the collection of the debtors and remit a residual amount to Angelino depending upon how quickly individual customers paid. Any balance uncollected by Omar after six months will be refunded to Omar by Angelino.   **(5 marks)**

(ii) On 1 October 20X5 Angelino owned a freehold building that had a carrying amount of £7.5 million and had an estimated remaining life of 20 years. On this date it sold the building to Finaid for a price of £12 million and entered into an agreement with Finaid to rent back the building for an annual rental of £1.3 million for a period of five years. The auditors of Angelino have commented that in their opinion the building had a market value of only £10 million at the date of its sale and to rent an equivalent building under similar terms to the agreement between Angelino and Finaid would only cost £800,000 per annum. Assume any finance costs are 10% per annum.   **(6 marks)**

(iii) Angelino is a motor car dealer selling vehicles to the public. Most of its new vehicles are supplied on consignment by two manufacturers, Monza and Capri, who trade on different terms.

Monza supplies cars on terms that allow Angelino to display the vehicles for a period of three months from the date of delivery or when Angelino sells the cars on to a retail customer if this is less than three months. Within this period Angelino can return the cars to Monza or can be asked by Monza to transfer the cars to another dealership (both at no cost to Angelino). Angelino pays the manufacturer's list price at the end of the three month period (or at the date of sale if sooner). In recent years Angelino has returned several cars to Monza that were not selling very well and has also been required to transfer cars to other dealerships at Monza's request.

Capri's terms of supply are that Angelino pays 10% of the manufacturer's price at the date of delivery and 1% of the outstanding balance per month as a display charge. After six months (or sooner if Angelino chooses), Angelino must pay the balance of the purchase price or return the cars to Capri. If the cars are returned to the manufacturer, Angelino has to pay for the transportation costs and forfeits the 10% deposit. Because of this Angelino has only returned vehicles to Capri once in the last three years. **(5 marks)**

Required:

Describe how the above transactions and events should be treated in the financial statements of Angelino for the year ended 30 September 20X6.Your answer should explain, where relevant, the difference between the legal form of the transactions and their substance.

Note: The mark allocation is shown against each of the three transactions above. **(Total: 25 marks)**

3 REVENUE RECOGNITION

Revenue recognition is the process by which companies decide when and how much income should be included in the profit and loss account. It is a topical area of great debate in the accounting profession. The ASB looks at revenue recognition from conceptual and substance points of view. There are occasions where a more traditional approach to revenue recognition does not entirely conform to the ASB guidance; indeed neither do some accounting standards.

Required:

(a) Explain the implications that the ASB's Statement of Principles and the application of substance over form have on the recognition of income. Give examples of how this may conflict with traditional practice and some accounting standards. **(6 marks)**

(b) Derringdo plc sells goods supplied by Gungho plc. The goods are classed as A grade (perfect quality) or B grade, having slight faults. Derringdo plc sells the A grade goods acting as an agent for Gungho plc at a fixed price calculated to yield a gross profit margin of 50%.Derringdo plc receives a commission of 12.5% of the sales it achieves for these goods. The arrangement for B grade goods is that they are sold by Gungho plc to Derringdo plc and Derringdo plc sells them at a gross profit margin of 25%.The following information has been obtained from Derringdo plc's financial records:

	£000
Stock held on premises 1 April 20X2	
– A grade	2,400
– B grade	1,000
Goods from Gungho plc year to 31 March 20X3	
– A grade	18,000
– B grade	8,800
Stock held on premises 31 March 20X3	
– A grade	2,000
– B grade	1,250

Required:

Prepare the profit and loss account extracts for Derringdo plc for the year to 31 March 20X3 reflecting the above information. **(5 marks)**

(c)   Derringdo plc acquired an item of plant at a gross cost of £800,000 on 1 October 20X2. The plant has an estimated life of 10 years with a residual value equal to 15% of its gross cost. Derringdo plc uses straight-line depreciation on a time apportioned basis. The company received a government grant of 30% of its cost price at the time of its purchase. The terms of the grant are that if the company retains the asset for four years or more, then no repayment liability will be incurred. If the plant is sold within four years a repayment on a sliding scale would be applicable. The repayment is 75% if sold within the first year of purchase and this amount decreases by 25% per annum. Derringdo plc has no intention to sell the plant within the first four years. Derringdo plc's accounting policy for capital based government grants is to treat them as deferred credits and release them to income over the life of the asset to which they relate.

Required:

(i)   Discuss whether the company's policy for the treatment of government grants meets the definition of a liability in the ASB's Statement of Principles.

(3 marks)

(ii)   Prepare extracts of Derringdo plc's financial statements for the year to 31 March 20X3 in respect of the plant and the related grant:

- applying the company's policy;
- in compliance with the definition of a liability in the Statement of Principles. Your answer should consider whether the sliding scale repayment should be used in determining the deferred credit for the grant. **(6 marks)**

(d)   Derringdo plc sells carpets from several retail outlets. In previous years the company has undertaken responsibility for fitting the carpets in customers' premises. Customers pay for the carpets at the time they are ordered. The average length of time from a customer ordering a carpet to its fitting is 14 days. In previous years, Derringdo plc had not recognised a sale in income until the carpet had been successfully fitted as the rectification costs of any fitting error would be expensive.

From 1 April 20X2 Derringdo plc changed its method of trading by sub-contracting the fitting to approved contractors. Under this policy the sub-contractors are paid by Derringdo plc and they (the sub-contractors) are liable for any errors made in the fitting. Because of this Derringdo plc is proposing to recognise sales when customers order and pay for the goods, rather than when they have been fitted. Details of the relevant sales figures are:

	£000
Sales made in retail outlets for the year to 31 March 20X3	23,000
Sales value of carpets fitted in the 14 days to 14 April 20X2	1,200
Sales value of carpets fitted in the 14 days to 14 April 20X3	1,600

Note: The sales value of carpets fitted in the 14 days to 14 April 20X2 are not included in the annual sales figure of £23 million, but those for the 14 days to 14 April 20X3 are included.

Required:

Discuss whether the above represents a change of accounting policy, and, based on your discussion, calculate the amount that you would include in sales revenue for carpets in the year to 31 March 20X3. **(5 marks)**

(Total: 25 marks)

4 HISTORIC COST

Over the years there have been many attempts by national and international standard setters to find an accepted method of dealing with the reporting of the effects of price changes.

There have been two main methods put forward by various accounting standard bodies for reporting the effects of price changes. One method is based on the movements in general price inflation and is referred to as a Current Purchasing Power (CPP) accounting, the other method is based on specific price changes of goods and assets and is generally referred to as a Current Cost accounting (CCA). Some bodies have also suggested an approach which combines features of each method.

Required:

(a) Explain the limitations of (pure) historic cost accounts when used as a basis for assessing the performance of an enterprise. You should give an example of how each of three different user groups may be misled by such information. **(8 marks)**

(b) Describe the advantages and criticisms of CPP and CCA. **(7 marks)**

(Total: 15 marks)

5 FINANCIAL STATEMENTS

(a) The ASB's *Statement of Principles for Financial Reporting* requires financial statements to be prepared on the basis that they comply with certain accounting concepts, underlying assumptions and (qualitative) characteristics. Five of these are:

Matching/accruals

Substance over form

Prudence

Comparability

Materiality

Required:

Briefly explain the meaning of each of the above principles/concepts. **(5 marks)**

(b) For most entities, applying the appropriate concepts/assumptions in accounting for stock is an important element in preparing their financial statements.

Required:

Illustrate with examples how each of the principles/concepts in (a) may be applied to accounting for stock. **(10 marks)**

(Total: 15 marks)

6   EMERALD

Product development costs are a material cost for many companies. They are either written off as an expense or capitalised as an asset.

Required:

(a)   Discuss the conceptual issues involved and the definition of an asset that may be applied in determining whether development expenditure should be treated as an expense or an asset. **(4 marks)**

(b)   Emerald has had a policy of writing off development expenditure to the profit and loss account as it was incurred. In preparing its financial statements for the year ended 30 September 2007 it has decided to change its accounting policy to one of capitalising qualifying development expenditure. Below is the qualifying development expenditure for Emerald:

	£000
Year ended 30 September 2004	300
Year ended 30 September 2005	240
Year ended 30 September 2006	800
Year ended 30 September 2007	400

All capitalised development expenditure is deemed to have a four year life. Assume amortisation commences at the beginning of the accounting period following capitalisation. Emerald had no development expenditure before that for the year ended 30 September 2004.

Required:

Calculate the amounts which should appear in the profit and loss account and balance sheet (including comparative figures), and statement of recognised gains and losses of Emerald in respect of the development expenditure for the year ended 30 September 2007. Note: ignore taxation.**(6 marks)**

(Total: 10 marks)

7   FLOW

On 1 April 20X7, Flow sold a freehold property to another company, River. Flow had purchased the property for £500,000 on 1 April 20W8 and had charged total depreciation of £60,000 for the period 1 April 20W8 to 31 March 20X7.

River paid £850,000 for the property on 1 April 20X7, at which date its true market value was £550,000.

From 1 April 20X7 the property was leased back by Flow on a ten-year operating lease for annual rentals (payable in arrears) of £100,000. A normal annual rental for such a property would have been £50,000.

Required:

Show the journal entries which Flow will make to record:

- its sale of the property to River on 1 April 20X8;
- the payment of the first rental to River on 31 March 20X9.

Justify your answer with reference to appropriate Accounting Standards.   **(10 marks)**

8   BLFB

You are the management accountant of BLFB. BLFB imports timber which it uses to manufacture and sell a large range of furniture products. BLFB makes up financial statements to 30 June each year.

On 1 June 20X9, BLFB purchased for £40 million a large quantity of timber from an overseas supplier. The timber was intended to be used in the manufacture of a large quantity of high-quality furniture. Before manufacturing such furniture, it is necessary to keep the new timber in controlled conditions for at least five years from the date of purchase.

On 1 July 20X9, BLFB sold the timber to Southland Bank for £45 million. The timber was physically retained by BLFB under the controlled conditions that were necessary to render the timber suitable for use. At the date of the sale on 1 July 20X9, BLFB signed an agreement to re-purchase the timber from Southland Bank on 30 June 20Y4 for a price of £66.12 million. Responsibility for the security and condition of the timber remained with BLFB.

Your assistant, who is responsible for preparing the draft financial statements for the year ended 30 June 20Y0, has shown the transaction as a sale of £45 million and recorded a profit of £5 million.

Required:

(a)   Write a memorandum to your assistant that:

    (i)   describes what is meant by the 'substance' of a transaction and how to determine 'substance'; and   **(6 marks)**

    (ii)   explains why transactions should be accounted for according to their substance.   **(6 marks)**

(b)   (i)   Prepare all the journal entries that should have been made in the financial statements of BLFB for the year ended 30 June 20Y0 in order to account correctly for the sale of timber to Southland Bank.   **(6 marks)**

(ii) Explain fully how the entries you have made comply with the requirement to account for the transaction according to its substance. You should also explain why the treatment suggested by your assistant is incorrect. **(7 marks)**

(Total: 25 marks)

9 LMN

(a) The ASB's Statement of Principles has a section on recognition in financial statements.

Required:

Explain the Statement's recognition criteria in general and in particular how assets, liabilities, gains and losses are to be recognised in financial statements. **(5 marks)**

(b) LMN trades in motor vehicles, which are manufactured and supplied by their manufacturer, IJK. Trading between the two entities is subject to a contractual agreement, the principal terms of which are as follows:

- LMN is entitled to hold on its premises at any one time up to 80 vehicles supplied by IJK. LMN is free to specify the ranges and models of vehicle supplied to it. IJK retains legal title to the vehicles until such time as they are sold to a third party by LMN.

- While the vehicles remain on its premises, LMN is required to insure them against loss or damage.

- The price at which vehicles are supplied is determined at the time of delivery; it is not subject to any subsequent alteration.

- When LMN sells a vehicle to a third party, it is required to inform IJK within three working days. IJK submits an invoice to LMN at the originally agreed price; the invoice is payable by LMN within 30 days.

- LMN is entitled to use any of the vehicles supplied to it for demonstration purposes and road testing. However, if more than a specified number of kilometres are driven in a vehicle, LMN is required to pay IJK a rental charge.

- LMN has the right to return any vehicle to IJK at any time without incurring a penalty, except for any rental charge incurred in respect of excess kilometres driven.

Required:

Discuss the economic substance of the contractual arrangement between the two entities in respect of the recognition of stock and of sales. **(10 marks)**

(Total: 15 marks)

10 FINO

(a) An important requirement of the ASB's Statement of Principles for Financial Reporting (Statement of principles) is that in order to be reliable, an entity's financial statements should represent faithfully the transactions and events that it has undertaken.

Required:

Explain what is meant by faithful representation and how it enhances reliability.

(5 marks)

(b) On 1 April 2007, Fino increased the operating capacity of its plant. Due to a lack of liquid funds it was unable to buy the required plant which had a cost of £350,000. On the recommendation of the finance director, Fino entered into an agreement to lease the plant from the manufacturer. The lease required four annual payments in advance of £100,000 each commencing on 1 April 2007. The plant would have a useful life of four years and would be scrapped at the end of this period. The finance director, believing the lease to be an operating lease, commented that the agreement would improve the company's return on capital employed (compared to outright purchase of the plant).

Required:

(i) Discuss the validity of the finance director's comment and describe how SSAP 21 *Accounting for Leases and Hire Purchase Contracts* ensures that leases such as the above are faithfully represented in an entity's financial statements.

(4 marks)

(ii) Prepare extracts of Fino's profit and loss account and balance sheet for the year ended 30 September 2007 in respect of the rental agreement assuming:

(1) It is an operating lease; **(2 marks)**

(2) It is a finance lease (use an implicit interest rate of 10% per annum) **(4 marks)**

(Total: 15 marks)

A REGULATORY FRAMEWORK FOR FINANCIAL REPORTING

11 UK REGULATORY FRAMEWORK

Financial reporting in the UK is regulated through a formal structure involving both statutory and institutional bodies.

The European Union and the International Accounting Standards Board also contribute to what is described as the UK Regulatory Framework.

Required:

(a) Describe the various bodies and institutions that make up the UK Regulatory Framework. **(10 marks)**

(b) Describe the UK standard setting process including how standards are produced, enforced and occasionally supplemented. **(10 marks)**

(c) Comment on whether you feel the structure in (a) and the processes in (b) above have been successful. **(5 marks)**

(Total: 25 marks)

PTUAL FRAMEWORK

the Accounting Standards Board issued its *Statement of Principles for financial* '. This document is part of the overall conceptual framework within which the ...ent ASB works.

Required:

(a) Describe what is meant by a conceptual framework. **(3 marks)**

(b) Explain the main reasons for having a conceptual framework **(8 marks)**

(c) Explain the purpose of the Statement of Principles for financial reporting. **(8 marks)**

(d) Discuss the extent to which accounting standards are relevant to not-for-profit entities. **(6 marks)**

(Total: 25 marks)

13   USERS AND QUALITIES

The *Statement of Principles for financial reporting* indicates the overall purpose of financial statements and considers the various users of these financial statements. It also gives much detail about the qualitative characteristics of financial statements which make them useful.

Required:

(a) Explain the overall objective of financial statements. **(2 marks)**

(b) Discuss the information needs of the different types of users of financial statements considered in the Statement of Principles. **(8 marks)**

(c) Discuss the qualitative characteristics which make information useful to users of the financial statements. **(12 marks)**

(d) Explain why in practice a balance is often required between the various characteristics. **(3 marks)**

(Total: 25 marks)

FINANCIAL STATEMENTS

14   ELITE LEISURE AND ADVENT

(a) Elite Leisure is a private limited company that operates a single cruise ship. The ship was acquired on 1 October 19W6. Details of the cost of the ship's components and their estimated useful lives are:

Component	Original cost (£million)	Depreciation basis
Ship's fabric (hull, decks etc)	300	25 years straight-line
Cabins and entertainment area fittings	150	12 years straight-line
Propulsion system	100	useful life of 40,000 hours

At 30 September 20X4 no further capital expenditure had been incurred on the ship.

In the year ended 30 September 20X4 the ship had experienced a high level of engine trouble which had cost the company considerable lost revenue and compensation costs. The measured expired life of the propulsion system at 30 September 20X4 was 30,000 hours. Due to the unreliability of the engines, a decision was taken in early October 20X4 to replace the whole of the propulsion system at a cost of £140 million. The expected life of the new propulsion system was 50,000 hours and in the year ended 30 September 20X5 the ship had used its engines for 5,000 hours.

At the same time as the propulsion system replacement, the company took the opportunity to do a limited upgrade to the cabin and entertainment facilities at a cost of £60 million and repaint the ship's fabric at a cost of £20 million. After the upgrade of the cabin and entertainment area fittings it was estimated that their remaining life was five years (from the date of the upgrade). For the purpose of calculating depreciation, all the work on the ship can be assumed to have been completed on 1 October 20X4. All residual values can be taken as nil.

Required:

Calculate the carrying value of Elite Leisure's cruise ship at 30 September 20X4 and prepare extracts in respect of it from Elite Leisure's profit and loss account for the year ended 30 September 20X5 and its balance sheet at that date. Your answer should explain the treatment of each item. **(12 marks)**

(b)   Advent is a publicly listed company.

Details of Advent's fixed assets at 1 October 20X3 were:

	Land and buildings £m	Plant £m	Telecommunications licence £m	Total £m
Cost/valuation	280	150	300	730
Accumulated depreciation/amortisation	(40)	(105)	(30)	(175)
Net book value	240	45.	270	555

The following information is relevant:

(i)   The land and building were revalued on 1 October 19W8 with £80 million attributable to the land and £200 million to the building. At that date the estimated remaining life of the building was 25 years. A further revaluation was not needed until 1 October 20X3 when the land and building were valued at £85 million and £180 million respectively. The remaining estimated life of the building at this date was 20 years.

(ii)   Plant is depreciated at 20% per annum on cost with time apportionment where appropriate. On 1 April 20X4 new plant costing £45 million was acquired. In addition, this plant cost £5 million to install and commission. No plant is more than four years old.

(iii)   The telecommunications licence was bought from the government on 1 October 20X2 and has a 10 year life. It is amortised on a straight line basis. In September 20X4, a review of the sales of the products related to the licence showed them to be very disappointing. As a result of this review the recoverable amount of the licence at 30 September 20X4 was estimated at only £100 million.

There were no disposals of fixed assets during the year to 30 September 20X4.

Required:

(i) Prepare balance sheet extracts of Advent's fixed assets as at 30 September 20X4 (including comparative figures), together with any disclosures (other than those of the accounting policies) required under current Accounting Standards and the Companies Acts as far as the information permits. **(9 marks)**

(ii) Explain the usefulness of the above disclosures to the users of the financial statements. **(4 marks)**

(Total: 25 marks)

15   WILDERNESS GROUP

(a) The main objective of FRS 11 *Impairment of fixed assets and goodwill* is to prescribe the procedures that should ensure that an entity's assets are included in its balance sheet at no more than their recoverable amounts. Where an asset is carried at an amount in excess of its recoverable amount, it is said to be impaired and FRS 11 requires an impairment loss to be recognised.

Required:

(i) Define an impairment loss explaining the relevance of net realisable value and value in use; and state how frequently assets should be tested for impairment. **(6 marks)**

Note: Your answer should NOT describe the possible indicators of an impairment.

(ii) Explain how an impairment loss is accounted for after it has been calculated. **(5 marks)**

(b) The assistant financial controller of the Wilderness group has identified the matters below which she believes may indicate an impairment to one or more assets:

(i) Wilderness owns and operates an item of plant that cost £640,000 and had accumulated depreciation of £400,000 at 1 October 20X4. It is being depreciated at $12\frac{1}{2}$% per annum on cost. On 1 April 20X5 (exactly half way through the year) the plant was damaged when a factory vehicle collided into it. Due to the unavailability of replacement parts, it is not possible to repair the plant, but it still operates, albeit at a reduced capacity. Also it is expected that as a result of the damage the remaining life of the plant from the date of the damage will be only two years. Based on its reduced capacity, the estimated present value of the plant in use is £150,000. The plant has a current disposal value of £20,000 (which will be nil in two years' time), but Wilderness has been offered a trade-in value of £180,000 against a replacement machine which has a cost of £1 million (there would be no disposal costs for the replaced plant). Wilderness is reluctant to replace the plant as it is worried about the long-term demand for the product produced by the plant. The trade-in value is only available if the plant is replaced.

Required:

Prepare extracts from the balance sheet and profit and loss account of Wilderness in respect of the plant for the year ended 30 September 20X5. Your answer should explain how you arrived at your figures. **(7 marks)**

(ii) On 1 April 20X4 Wilderness acquired 100% of the share capital of Mossel, whose only activity is the extraction and sale of spa water. Mossel had been profitable since its acquisition, but bad publicity resulting from several consumers becoming ill due to a contamination of the spa water supply in April 20X5 has led to unexpected losses in the last six months. The carrying amounts of Mossel's assets at 30 September 20X5 are:

	£000
Brand (Quencher – see below)	7,000
Land containing spa	12,000
Purifying and bottling plant	8,000
Stocks	5,000
	32,000

The source of the contamination was found and it has now ceased.

The company originally sold the bottled water under the brand name of 'Quencher', but because of the contamination it has rebranded its bottled water as 'Phoenix'. After a large advertising campaign, sales are now starting to recover and are approaching previous levels. The value of the brand in the balance sheet is the depreciated amount of the original brand name of 'Quencher'.

The directors have acknowledged that £1.5 million will have to be spent in the first three months of the next accounting period to upgrade the purifying and bottling plant.

The stocks contain some old 'Quencher' bottled water at a cost of £2 million; the remaining stock is labelled with the new brand 'Phoenix'. Samples of all the bottled water have been tested by the health authority and have been passed as fit to sell. The old bottled water will have to be relabelled at a cost of £250,000, but is then expected to be sold at the normal selling price of (normal) cost plus 50%.

Based on the estimated future cash flows, the directors have estimated that the value in use of Mossel at 30 September 20X5, calculated according to the guidance in FRS 11, is £20 million. There is no reliable estimate of the net realisable value of Mossel.

Required:

Applying UK GAAP, calculate the amounts at which the assets of Mossel should appear in the consolidated balance sheet of Wilderness at 30 September 20X5. Your answer should explain how you arrived at your figures. **(7 marks)**

(Total: 25 marks)

16   LINNET

(a)   (i)   Linnet is a large public listed company involved in the construction industry. Accounting standards normally require long-term contracts to be accounted for using the percentage (stage) of completion basis. However, under certain circumstances, they should be accounted for using the completed contracts basis.

Required:

Discuss the principles that underlie each of the two methods and describe the circumstances in which their use is appropriate.   **(6 marks)**

(ii)   Linnet is part way through a contract to build a new football stadium at a contracted price of £300 million. Details of the progress of this contract at 1 April 20X3 are shown below:

	£ million
Cumulative turnover invoiced	150
Cumulative cost of sales to date	112
Profit to date	38

The following information has been extracted from the accounting records at 31 March 20X4:

	£ million
Total progress payment received for work certified at 29 Feb 20X4	180
Total costs incurred to date (excluding rectification costs below)	195
Rectification costs	17

Linnet has received progress payments of 90% of the work certified at 29 February 20X4. Linnet's surveyor has estimated the sales value of the further work completed during March 20X4 was £20 million.

At 31 March 20X4 the estimated remaining costs to complete the contract were £45 million.

The rectification costs are the costs incurred in widening access roads to the stadium. This was the result of an error by Linnet's architect when he made his initial drawings.

Linnet calculates the percentage of completion of its contracts as the proportion of sales value earned to the date compared to the contract price.

All estimates can be taken as being reliable.

Required:

Prepare extracts of the financial statements for Linnet for the above contract for the year to 31 March 20X4.   **(11 marks)**

(b)   Linnet also manufactures and sells high quality printing paper. The auditor has drawn the company's attention to the sale of some packs of paper on 20 April 20X4 at a price of £45 each. These items were included in closing stock on 31 March 20X4 at their manufactured cost of £48 each. Further investigations revealed that during stocktaking on 31 March 20X4 a quantity of packs of A3 size paper had been damaged by a water leak. The following week the company removed the damage by cutting the paper down to A4 size (A4 size is smaller than A3). The paper was then repackaged and put back into stock. The cost of cutting and repackaging was £4 per pack. The normal selling price of the paper is £75 per pack for the A3 and £50 per pack for the A4, however on 12 April 20X4 the company reduced the selling prices of all its paper by 10% in response to similar price cuts by its competitors.

Securiprint plc, one of the customers that bought some of the 'damaged' paper, had used it to print some share certificates for a customer. Securiprint plc informed Linnet that these share certificates had been returned by the customer because they contained marks that were not part of the design. Securiprint plc believes the marks were part of a manufacturing flaw on the part of Linnet and is seeking appropriate compensation.

Required:

Discuss the impact the above information may have on the draft financial statements of Linnet for the year to 31 March 20X4. **(8 marks)**

(Total: 25 marks)

17   BOWTOCK

(a)   (i)   FRS 19 *Deferred Tax* details the requirements relating to the accounting treatment of deferred tax.

Required:

Explain why it is considered necessary to provide for deferred tax and briefly outline the principles of accounting for deferred tax contained in FRS 19 Deferred Tax. **(5 marks)**

(ii)   Bowtock purchased a fixed asset for £2,000,000 on 1 October 20X0. It had an estimated life of eight years and an estimated residual value of £400,000. The plant is depreciated on a straight-line basis. The Inland Revenue allow 40% of the cost of this type of asset to be claimed against corporation tax in the year of purchase and 20% per annum (on a reducing balance basis) of its tax written down value thereafter. The rate of corporation tax can be taken as 25%.

Required:

In respect of the above item of plant, calculate the deferred tax charge/credit in Bowtock's profit and loss account for the year to 30 September 20X3 and the deferred tax balance in the balance sheet at that date. **(6 marks)**

Note: Work to the nearest £000.

(b)   Bowtock has leased an item of plant under the following terms:

Commencement of the lease was 1 January 20X2.

Term of lease five years.

Annual payments in advance £12,000.

Cash price and fair value of the asset – £52,000 at 1 January 20X2.

Implicit interest rate within the lease (as supplied by the lessor) 8% per annum (to be apportioned on a time basis where relevant).

The company's depreciation policy for this type of plant is 20% per annum on cost (apportioned on a time basis where relevant).

Required:

Prepare extracts of the profit and loss account and balance sheet for Bowtock for the year to 30 September 20X3 for the above lease. **(5 marks)**

(c) (i) Explain why events occurring after the balance sheet date may be relevant to the financial statements of the previous period. **(4 marks)**

(ii) At 30 September 20X3 Bowtock had included in its draft balance sheet stock of £250,000 valued at cost. Up to 5 November 20X3, Bowtock had sold £100,000 of this stock for £150,000. On this date new government legislation (enacted after the year end) came into force which meant that the unsold stock could no longer be marketed and was worthless.

Bowtock is part way through the construction of a housing development. It has prepared its financial statements to 30 September 20X3 in accordance with SSAP 9 *Stocks and Long-term Contracts* and included a proportionate amount of the total estimated profit on this contract. The same legislation referred to above (in force from 5 November 20X3) now requires modifications to the way the houses within this development have to be built. The cost of these modifications will be £500,000 and will reduce the estimated total profit on the contract by that amount, although the contract is still expected to be profitable.

Required:

Assuming the amounts are material, state how the information above should be reflected in the financial statements of Bowtock for the year ended 30 September 20X3. **(5 marks)**

(Total: 25 marks)

18 MULTIPLEX PLC

The following transactions and events have arisen during the preparation of the draft financial statements of Multiplex plc for the year to 31 March 20X0:

(a) On 1 April 19W9 Multiplex issued £80 million 8% convertible loan stock at par. The stock is convertible into equity shares, or redeemable at par, on 31 March 20X4, at the option of the stockholders. The terms of conversion are that each £100 of loan stock will be convertible into 50 equity shares of Multiplex. A finance consultant has advised that if the option to convert to equity had not been included in the terms of the issue, then a coupon (interest) rate of 12% would have been required to attract subscribers for the stock. Interest is paid in arrears on 31 March each year.

The value of £1 receivable at the end of each year at a discount rate of 12% are:

Year	£
1	0.89
2	0.80
3	0.71
4	0.64
5	0.57

Required:

Calculate the profit and loss account finance charge for the year to 31 March 20X0 and the balance sheet extracts at 31 March 20X0 in respect of the issue of the loan stock. **(5 marks)**

(b)   On 1 January 20X0 Multiplex plc acquired Steamdays Ltd, a company that operates a scenic railway along the coast of a popular tourist area. The summarised balance sheet at fair values of Steamdays Ltd on 1 January 20X0, reflecting the terms of the acquisition was:

	£000
Goodwill	200
Operating licence	1,000
Property – train stations and land	250
Rail track and coaches	250
Two steam engines	1,000
Other net assets	300
	─────
Purchase consideration	3,000
	─────

The operating licence is for ten years. It was renewed on 1 January 20X0 by the transport authority and is stated at the cost of its renewal. The carrying values of the property and rail track and coaches are based on their value in use. The engines, and other net assets are valued at their net selling prices.

On 1 February 20X0 the boiler of one of the steam engines exploded, completely destroying the whole engine. Fortunately no one was injured, but the engine was beyond repair. Due to its age a replacement could not be obtained. Because of the reduced passenger capacity the estimated value in use of the whole of the business after the accident was assessed at £2 million.

Passenger numbers after the accident were below expectations even after allowing for the reduced capacity. A market research report concluded that tourists were not using the railway because of their fear of a similar accident occurring to the remaining engine. In the light of this the value in use of the business was re-assessed on 31 March 20X0 at £1.8 million. On this date Multiplex plc received an offer of £600,000 in respect of the operating licence (it is transferable). The realisable value of the other net assets has not changed significantly.

Required:

Calculate the carrying value of the assets of Steamdays Ltd (in Multiplex plc's consolidated balance sheet) at 1 February 20X0 and 31 March 20X0 after recognising the impairment losses. **(6 marks)**

(c)   On 1 January 20X0 the Board of Multiplex plc approved a resolution to close the whole of its loss-making engineering operation. A binding agreement to dispose of the assets was signed shortly afterwards. The sale will be completed on 10 July 20X0 at an agreed value of £30 million. The costs of the closure are estimated at:

•   £2 million for redundancy

•   £3 million in penalty costs for non-completion of contracted orders

•   £1.5 million for associated professional costs

- losses on the sale of the net assets whose book value at 31 March 20X0 was £46 million
- operating losses for the period from 1 April 20X0 to the date of sale are estimated at £4.5 million.

Multiplex plc accounts for its various operations on a divisional basis.

Required:

Advise the directors on the correct accounting treatment of the closure of the engineering division. **(5 marks)**

(d) Multiplex plc is in the intermediate stage of a long-term construction contract for the building of a new privately owned road bridge over a river estuary. The original details of the contract are:

Approximate duration of contract:	3 years
Date of commencement:	1 October 19W8
Total contract price:	£40 million
Estimated total cost:	£28 million

An independent surveyor certified the value of the work in progress as follows:

- on 31 March 19W9 £12 million
- on 31 March 20X0 £30 million (including the £12 million in 19W9).

Costs incurred at:

- 31 March 19W9 £9 million
- 31 March 20X0 £28.5 million (including the £9 million in 19W9).

Payments received on account by 31 March 20X0 were £25 million.

On 1 April 19W9 Multiplex plc agreed to a contract variation that would involve an additional fee of £5 million with associated additional estimated costs of £2 million.

The costs incurred during the year to 31 March 20X0 include £2.5 million relating to the replacement of some bolts which had been made from material that had been incorrectly specified by the firm of civil engineers who were contracted by Multiplex plc to design the bridge. These costs were not included in the original estimates, but Multiplex plc is hopeful that they can be recovered from the firm of civil engineers. The advice to Multiplex from its lawyers is that there is about a 60% chance of success.

Multiplex plc calculates profit on long-term contracts using the percentage of completion method. The percentage of completion of the contract is based on the value of the work certified to date compared with the total contract price.

Required:

Prepare the profit and loss account and balance sheet extracts in respect of the contract for the year to 31 March 20X0 only. **(9 marks)**

(Total: 25 marks)

19 TORRENT

(a) Torrent is a large publicly listed company whose main activity involves construction contracts. Details of three of its contracts for the year ended 31 March 20X6 are:

Contract	Alpha	Beta	Ceta
Date commenced	1 April 20X4	1 October 20X5	1 October 20X5
Estimated duration	3 years	18 months	2 years
	£m	£m	£m
Fixed contract price	20	6	12
Estimated costs at start of contract	15	7.5 (note (iii))	10
Costs to date:			
at 31 March 20X5	5	nil	nil
at 31 March 20X6	12.5 (note (ii))	2	4
Estimated costs at 31 March 20X6 to complete	3.5	5.5 (note (iii))	6
Progress payments received at 31 March 20X5 (note (i))	5.4	nil	nil
Progress payments received at 31 March 20X6 (note (I))	12.6	1.8	nil

Notes

(i) The company's normal policy for determining the percentage completion of contracts is based on the value of work invoiced to date compared to the contract price. Progress payments received represent 90% of the work invoiced. However, no progress payments will be invoiced or received from contract Ceta until it is completed, so the percentage completion of this contract is to be based on the cost to date compared to the estimated total contract costs.

(ii) The cost to date of £12.5 million at 31 March 20X6 for contract Alfa includes £1 million relating to unplanned rectification costs incurred during the current year (ended 31 March 20X6) due to subsidence occurring on site.

(iii) Since negotiating the price of contract Beta, Torrent has discovered the land that it purchased for the project is contaminated by toxic pollutants. The estimated cost at the start of the contract and the estimated costs to complete the contract include the unexpected costs of decontaminating the site before construction could commence.

Required:

Prepare extracts of the profit and loss account and balance sheet for Torrent in respect of the above construction contracts for the year ended 31 March 20X6

(12 marks)

(b) (i) The issued share capital of Savoir, a publicly listed company, at 31 March 20X3 was £10 million. Its shares are denominated at 25p each. Savoir's earnings attributable to its ordinary shareholders for the year ended 31 March 20X3 were also £10 million, giving an earnings per share of 25p.

Year ended 31 March 20X4

On 1 July 20X3 Savoir issued eight million ordinary shares at full market value. On 1 January 20X4 a bonus issue of one new ordinary share for every four ordinary shares held was made. Earnings attributable to ordinary shareholders for the year ended 31 March 20X4 were £13,800,000.

Year ended 31 March 20X5

On 1 October 20X4 Savoir made a rights issue of shares of two new ordinary shares at a price of £1.00 each for every five ordinary shares held. The offer was fully subscribed. The market price of Savoir's ordinary shares immediately prior to the offer was £2.40 each. Earnings attributable to ordinary shareholders for the year ended 31 March 20X5 were £19,500,000.

Required:

Calculate Savoir's earnings per share for the years ended 31 March 20X4 and 20X5 including comparative figures. **(9 marks)**

(ii)   On 1 April 20X5 Savoir issued £20 million 8% convertible loan stock at par. The terms of conversion (on 1 April 20X8) are that for every £100 of loan stock, 50 ordinary shares will be issued at the option of loan stockholders. Alternatively the loan stock will be redeemed at par for cash. Also on 1 April 20X5 the directors of Savoir were awarded share options on 12 million ordinary shares exercisable from 1 April 20X8 at £1.50 per share. The average market value of Savoir's ordinary shares for the year ended 31 March 20X6 was £2.50 each. The income tax rate is 25%. Earnings attributable to ordinary shareholders for the year ended 31 March 20X6 were £25,200,000. The share options have been correctly recorded in the profit and loss account.

Required:

Calculate Savoir's basic and diluted earnings per share for the years ended 31March 20X6 (comparative figures are NOT required).

You may assume that both the convertible loan stock and the directors' options are dilutive. **(4 marks)**

(Total: 25 marks)

20   QRS

The directors of QRS, a listed entity, have met to discuss the business's medium to long-term financing requirements. Several possibilities were discussed, including the issue of more shares using a rights issue. In many respects this would be the most desirable option because the entity is already quite highly geared. However, the directors are aware of several recent cases where rights issues have not been successful because share prices are currently quite low and many investors are averse to any kind of investment in shares.

Therefore, the directors have turned their attention to other options. The finance director is on sick leave, and so you, her assistant, have been given the task of responding to the following note from the Chief Executive:

'Now that we've had a chance to discuss possible financing arrangements, the directors are in agreement that we should structure our issue of financial instruments in order to be able to classify them as equity rather than debt. Any increase in the gearing ratio would be *unacceptable. Therefore, we have provisionally decided to make two issues of financial instruments as follows:*

1 *An issue of non-redeemable preferred shares to raise £4 million. These shares will carry a fixed interest rate of 6%, and because they are shares they can be classified as equity.*

2 *An issue of 6% convertible bonds, issued at par value, to raise £6 million. These bonds will carry a fixed date for conversion in four years' time. Each £100 of debt will be convertible at the holder's option into 120 £1 shares. In our opinion, these bonds can actually be classified as equity immediately, because they are convertible within five years on terms that are favourable to the holder.*

Please confirm that these instruments will not increase our gearing ratio should they be issued.'

Note: You determine that the market rate available for similar non-convertible bonds is currently 8%.

Required:

Explain to the directors the accounting treatment, in respect of debt/equity classification, required by FRS 25 *Financial Instruments:Presentation* for each of the proposed issues, advising them on the acceptability of classifying the instruments as equity.

Your explanation should be accompanied by calculations where appropriate.

Present value factors at 8% for each of the following four years are:

Year 1	0.926
Year 2	0.857
Year 3	0.794
Year 4	0.735

(10 marks)

21   PX

During its financial year ended 31 December 20X4, an entity, PX, entered into the transactions described below:

In November 20X4, having surplus cash available, PX made an investment in the securities of a listed entity. The directors intend to realise the investment in March or April 20X5, in order to fund the planned expansion of PX's principal warehouse.

PX lent one of its customers, DB, £3,000,000 at a variable interest rate pegged to average bank lending rates. The loan is scheduled for repayment in 20X9, and PX has provided an undertaking to DB that it will not assign the loan to a third party.

PX added to its portfolio of relatively small investments in the securities of listed entities. PX does not plan to dispose of these investments in the short term.

Required:

In accordance with FRS 26 *Financial Instruments: Recognition and Measurement:*

(i)   identify the appropriate classification of these three categories of financial asset and briefly explain the reason for each classification;   **(6 marks)**

(ii) explain how the financial assets should be measured in the financial statements of PX at 31 December 20X4. **(4 marks)**

(Total: 10 marks)

22 PINGWAY

Pingway issued a £10 million 3% convertible loan note at par on 1 April 2007 with interest payable annually in arrears. Three years later, on 31 March 2010, the loan note is convertible into equity shares on the basis of £100 of loan note for 25 equity shares or it may be redeemed in cash at par at the option of the loan note holder. One of the company's financial assistants observed that the use of a convertible loan note was preferable to a non-convertible loan note as the latter would have required an interest rate of 8% in order to make it attractive to investors. The assistant has also commented that the use of a convertible loan note will improve the profit as a result of lower interest costs and, as it is likely that the loan note holders will choose the equity option, the loan note can be classified as equity which will improve the company's high gearing position.

The present value of £1 receivable at the end of the year, based on discount rates of 3% and 8% can be taken as:

		3%	8%
		£	£
End of year	1	0·97	0·93
	2	0·94	0·86
	3	0·92	0·79

Required:

Comment on the financial assistant's observations and show how the convertible loan note should be accounted for in Pingway's profit and loss account for the year ended 31 March 2008 and balance sheet as at that date. **(10 marks)**

23 ERRSEA

(a) The following is an extract of Errsea's balances of plant and related government grants at 1 April 2006.

	Cost	Accumulated depreciation	Carrying amount
	£000	£000	£000
Plant	240	180	60
Creditors: amounts falling due within one year			
Government grants			10
Creditors: amounts falling due after more than one year			
Government grants			30

Details including purchases and disposals of plant and related government grants during the year are:

(i) Included in the above figures is an item of plant that was disposed of on 1 April 2006 for £12,000 which had cost £90,000 on 1 April 2003. The plant was being depreciated on a straight-line basis over four years assuming a residual value of £10,000. A government grant was received on its purchase and was being recognised in equal amounts in the profit and loss account over four years. In accordance with the terms of the grant, Errsea repaid £3,000 of the grant on the disposal of the related plant.

(ii) An item of plant was acquired on 1 July 2006 with the following costs:

	£
Base cost	192,000
Modifications specified by Errsea	12,000
Transport and installation	6,000

The plant qualified for a government grant of 25% of the base cost of the plant, but it had not been received by 31 March 2007. The plant Is to be depreciated on a straight-line basis over three years with a nil estimated residual value.

(iii) All other plant is depreciated by 15% per annum on cost.

(iv) £11,000 of the £30,000 creditor falling due after more than one year for government grants at 1 April 2006 should be reclassified as a creditor falling due within one year as at 31 March 2007.

(v) Depreciation is calculated on a time apportioned basis.

Required:

Prepare extracts of Errsea's profit and loss account and balance sheet in respect of the plant and government grants for the year ended 31 March 2007.

Note: Disclosure notes are not required. **(10 marks)**

24 PARTWAY

(a) (i) State the definition of discontinued operations and explain the usefulness of information for discontinued operations and why a robust definition of them is needed. (4 marks)

Partway is in the process of preparing its financial statements for the year ended 31 October 20X6. The company's main activity is in the travel industry mainly selling package holidays (flights and accommodation) to the general public through the Internet and retail travel agencies. During the current year the number of holidays sold by travel agencies has declined dramatically and the directors decided at a board meeting on 15 November 20X6 to close down its chain of travel agents. Immediately after the meeting the travel agencies' staff and suppliers were notified of the situation and an announcement was made in the press. The directors wish to show the travel agencies' results as a discontinued operation in the financial statements to 31 October 20X6. Due to the declining business of the travel agents, on 1 August 20X6 Partway expanded its Internet operations to offer car hire facilities to purchasers of its Internet holidays.

The following are Partway's summarised profit and loss account results – years ended:

	Internet	31 October 20X6 Travel agencies	Car hire	Total	31 October 20X5 Total
	£000	£000	£000	£000	£000
Turnover	23,000	14,000	2,000	39,000	40,000
Cost of sales	(18,000)	(16,500)	(1,500)	(36,000)	(32,000)
Gross profit/(loss)	5,000	(2,500)	500	3,000	8,000
Operating costs	(1,000)	(1,500)	(100)	(2,600)	(2,000)
Profit/(loss) before tax	4,000	(4,000)	400	400	6,000

The results for the travel agencies for the year ended 31 October 20X5 were: turnover £18 million, cost of sales £15 million and operating costs of £1.5 million.

Required:

(ii) Discuss whether the directors' wish to show the travel agencies' results as a discontinued operation is justifiable. **(4 marks)**

(iii) Assuming the closure of the travel agencies is a discontinued operation, prepare the (summarised) profit and loss account of Partway for the year ended 31 October 20X6 together with its comparatives. **(6 marks)**

(b) (i) Describe the circumstances in which an entity may change its accounting policies and how a change should be applied. **(5 marks)**

The terms under which Partway sells its holidays are that a 10% deposit is required on booking and the balance of the holiday must be paid six weeks before the travel date. In previous years Partway has recognised revenue (and profit) from the sale of its holidays at the date the holiday is actually taken. From the beginning of November 20X5, Partway has made it a condition of booking that all customers must have holiday cancellation insurance and as a result it is unlikely that the outstanding balance of any holidays will be unpaid due to cancellation. In preparing its financial statements to 31 October 20X6, the directors are proposing to change to recognising revenue (and related estimated costs) at the date when a booking is made. The directors also feel that this change will help to negate the adverse effect of comparison with last year's results (year ended 31 October 20X5) which were better than the current year's.

Required:

(ii) Comment on whether Partway's proposal to change the timing of its recognition of its revenue is acceptable and whether this would be a change of accounting policy. **(6 marks)**

(Total: 25 marks)

25 SITUATIONS

You have been asked to advise on a number of accounting problems which are each given separately below.

(a) XY recently acquired a new subsidiary, AB. Upon undertaking the fair value exercise in respect of AB the following issues arose:

    (i) At the date of acquisition a customer had brought a legal action against AB. The outcome of the case was uncertain at the date of acquisition, but it was considered possible that AB would be found liable to pay compensation to the customer. The individual financial statements of AB drawn up at the date of acquisition did not include any amount payable in respect of the legal case.

    (ii) The group will need to spend approximately £100 million in order to integrate the new subsidiary into the existing operation.

    Explain how each of the above issues will affect the net assets of AB to be included in the initial calculation of goodwill on consolidation? **(3 marks)**

(b) B issued new interest-bearing borrowings to finance a construction project on the following terms:

- The new borrowings had a nominal value of £50 million.
- The borrowings carried an annual interest rate of 4%.
- The costs of issuing the borrowings totalled £600,000. This comprised underwriting fees relating to the issue of £500,000 and fees of £100,000 payable for general advice on which of a number of sources of finance should be pursued.
- The borrowings were theoretically repayable at £60 million after five years. However, the borrowings contained an option to convert into ordinary shares after five years as an alternative to repayment. At the date of issue, the directors of B were reasonably certain that the investors would choose the conversion option.

    Calculate the total financing cost relating to these borrowings. **(3 marks)**

(c) At its year end, 31 March 20X5, entity JBK held 60,000 shares in a listed entity, X. The shares were purchased on 11 February 20X5 at a price of 85p per share. The market value of the shares on 31 March 20X5 was 87.5p. The investment is categorised as held-for-trading.

    Explain how this investment would be treated both at initial acquisition of the investment and when subsequently remeasured on 31 March 20X5. **(3 marks)**

(d) PQR holds several investments in subsidiaries. In December 20X5, it acquired 100% of the ordinary share capital of STU. PQR intends to exclude STU from consolidation in its group financial statements for the year ended 28 February 20X6, on the grounds that it does not intend to retain the investment in the longer term.

    Explain, with reference to the relevant Financial Reporting Standard, the conditions relating to exclusion of this type of investment from consolidation. **(3 marks)**

(e) On 1 January 20X6, EFG issued 10,000 5% convertible bonds at their par value of £50 each. The bonds will be redeemed on 1 January 2011. Each bond is convertible at the option of the holder at any time during the five-year period. Interest on the bond will be paid annually in arrears.

    The prevailing market interest rate for similar debt without conversion options at the date of issue was 6%

Explain how this financial instrument should be recognised in the financial statements of EFG at the date of issue and calculate any relevant amounts.

Discount factor at 6% for year 5 is 0.747 and the cumulative discount factor for years 1 to 5 is 4.212. **(3 marks)**

(Total: 15 marks)

26 PROMOIL

(a) The definition of a liability forms an important element of the Accounting Standards Board's *Statement of Principles for Financial Reporting* which, in turn, forms the basis for FRS 12 *Provisions, Contingent Liabilities and Contingent Assets*.

Required:

Define a liability and describe the circumstances under which provisions should be recognised. Give two examples of how the definition of liabilities enhances the reliability of financial statements. **(5 marks)**

(b) On 1 October 2007, Promoil acquired a newly constructed oil platform at a cost of £30 million together with the right to extract oil from an offshore oilfield under a government licence. The terms of the licence are that Promoil will have to remove the platform (which will then have no value) and restore the sea bed to an environmentally satisfactory condition in 10 years' time when the oil reserves have been exhausted. The estimated cost of this on 30 September 2017 will be £15 million. The present value of £1 receivable in 10 years at the appropriate discount rate for Promoil of 8% is £0.46.

Required:

(i) Explain and quantify how the oil platform should be treated in the financial statements of Promoil for the year ended 30 September 2008; **(7 marks)**

(ii) Describe how your answer to (b)(i) would change if the government licence did not require an environmental clean up. **(3 marks)**

(Total: 15 marks)

27 DEARING

On 1 October 2005 Dearing acquired a machine under the following terms:

	Hours	£
Manufacturer's base price		1,050,000
Trade discount (applying to base price only)		20%
Early settlement discount taken (on the payable amount of the base cost only)		5%
Freight charges		30,000
Electrical installation cost		28,000
Staff training in use of machine		40,000
Pre-production testing		22,000
Purchase of a three-year maintenance contract		60,000
Estimated residual value		20,000

	Hours
Estimated life in machine hours	6,000
Hours used – year ended 30 September 2006	1,200
– year ended 30 September 2007	1,800
– year ended 30 September 2008 (see below)	850

On 1 October 2007 Dearing decided to upgrade the machine by adding new components at a cost of £200,000. This upgrade led to a reduction in the production time per unit of the goods being manufactured using the machine. The upgrade also increased the estimated remaining life of the machine at 1 October 2007 to 4,500 machine hours and its estimated residual value was revised to £40,000.

Required:

Prepare extracts from the profit and loss account and balance sheet for the above machine for each of the three years to 30 September 2008. **(10 marks)**

Online question assistance

---

28 WAXWORK

(a) The objective of FRS 21 *Events after the Balance Sheet Date* is to prescribe the treatment of events that occur after an entity's balance sheet date.

Required:

Define the period to which FRS 21 relates and distinguish between adjusting and non-adjusting events. **(5 marks)**

(b) Waxwork's current year end is 31 March 2009. Its financial statements were authorised for issue by its directors on 6 May 2009 and the AGM (annual general meeting) will be held on 3 June 2009. The following matters have been brought to your attention:

(i) On 12 April 2009 a fire completely destroyed the company's largest warehouse and the stock it contained. The carrying amounts of the warehouse and the stock were £10 million and £6 million respectively. It appears that the company has not updated the value of its insurance cover and only expects to be able to recover a maximum of £9 million from its insurers. Waxwork's trading operations have been severely disrupted since the fire and it expects large trading losses for some time to come. **(4 marks)**

(ii) A single class of stock held at another warehouse was valued at its cost of £460,000 at 31 March 2009. In April 2009 70% of this stock was sold for £280,000 on which Waxworks' sales staff earned a commission of 15% of the selling price. **(3 marks)**

(iii) On 18 May 2009 the government announced tax changes which have the effect of increasing Waxwork's deferred tax liability by £650,000 as at 31 March 2009. **(3 marks)**

Required:

Explain the required treatment of items (i) to (iii) by Waxwork in its financial statements for the year ended 31 March 2009. (Note: assume all items are material and are independent of each other). **(10 marks as indicated)**

(Total: 15 marks)

29 FLIGHTLINE

> 🕐 *Timed question with Online tutor debrief*

Flightline is an airline operating company which treats its aircraft as complex fixed assets. The cost and other details of one of its aircraft are:

	£'000	estimated life
Exterior structure – purchase date 1 April 1995	120,000	20 years
Interior cabin fittings – replaced 1 April 2005	25,000	5 years
Engines (2 at £9 million each) – replaced 1 April 2005	18,000	36,000 flying hours

No residual values are attributed to any of the component parts.

At 1 April 2008 the aircraft log showed it had flown 10,800 hours since 1 April 2005. In the year ended 31 March 2009, the aircraft flew for 1,200 hours for the six months to 30 September 2008 and a further 1,000 hours in the six months to 31 March 2009.

On 1 October 2008 the aircraft suffered a 'bird strike' accident which damaged one of the engines beyond repair. This was replaced by a new engine with a life of 36,000 hours at cost of £10·8 million. The other engine was also damaged, but was repaired at a cost of £3 million; however, its remaining estimated life was shortened to 15,000 hours. The accident also caused cosmetic damage to the exterior of the aircraft which required repainting at a cost of £2 million. As the aircraft was out of service for some weeks due to the accident, Flightline took the opportunity to upgrade its cabin facilities at cost of £4·5 million. This did not increase the estimated remaining life of the cabin fittings, but the improved facilities enabled Flightline to substantially increase the air fares on this aircraft

Required:

Calculate the charges to the profit and loss account in respect of the aircraft for the year ended 31 March 2009 and its carrying amount in the balance sheet as at that date.

Note: the post accident changes are deemed effective from 1 October 2008.

(Total: 10 marks)

> 🕐 *Calculate your allowed time, allocate the time to the separate parts.....................*

30   WELLMAY

The summarised draft financial statements of Wellmay are shown below.

Profit and loss account year ended 31 March 2007

	£000
Turnover (note (i))	4,200
Cost of sales (note (ii))	(2,700)
Gross profit	1,500
Operating expenses	(470)
Investment property rental Income	20
Finance costs	(55)
Profit before tax	995
Taxation	(360)
Profit for the period	635

Balance sheet as at 31 March 2007:

	£000	£000
Fixed assets		
Tangible fixed assets (note (iii))		4,200
Investment property (note (iii))		400
		4,600
Current assets	1,400	
Creditors: amounts falling due within one year	(820)	
Net current assets		580
Creditors: amounts falling due after more than one year		
8% Convertible loan note (2010) (note (v))		(600)
Provisions for liabilities		
Deferred tax (note (vi))		(180)
		4,400
Capital and reserves		
Equity shares of 50 pence each (note (vii))		1,200
Reserves:		
Revaluation reserve – factory	300	
– investment property	50	
Profit and loss account (note (iv))	2,850	3,200
		4,400

The following information is relevant to the draft financial statements:

(i) Turnover includes £500,000 for the sale on 1 April 2006 of maturing goods to Westwood. The goods had a cost of £200,000 at the date of sale. Wellmay can repurchase the goods on 31 March 2008 for £605,000 (based on achieving a lender's return of 10% per annum) at which time the goods are estimated to have a value of £750,000.

(ii) Past experience shows that in the post balance sheet period the company often receives unrecorded invoices for materials relating to the previous year. As a result of this an accrued charge of £75,000 for contingent costs has been included in cost of sales and in creditors due within one year.

(iii) Tangible fixed assets:

Wellmay owns two properties. One is a factory (with office accommodation) used by Wellmay as a production facility and the other is an investment property that is leased to a third party under an operating lease. Relevant details of the fair values of the properties are:

	Factory	Investment property
	£000	£000
Valuation 31 March 2006	1,200	400
Valuation 31 March 2007	1,350	375

Although Wellmay has a policy of revaluing its properties, the valuations at 31 March 2007 have not yet been incorporated into the financial statements. Factory depreciation for the year ended 31 March 2007 of £40,000 was charged to cost of sales. As the factory includes some office accommodation, 20% of this depreciation should have been charged to operating expenses.

(iv) The balance of the profit and loss account reserve is made up of:

	£000
Balance b/f 1 April 2006	2,615
Profit for the period	635
Dividends paid during year ended 31 March 2007	(400)
	2,850

(v) 8% Convertible loan note (2010)

On 1 April 2006 an 8% convertible loan note with a nominal value of £600,000 was issued at par. It is redeemable on 31 March 2010 at par or it may be converted into equity shares of Wellmay on the basis of 100 new shares for each £200 of loan note. An equivalent loan note without the conversion option would have carried an interest rate of 10%. Interest of £48,000 has been paid on the loan and charged as a finance cost.

The present value of £1 receivable at the end of each year, based on discount rates of 8% and 10% are:

		8%	10%
End of year	1	0.93	0.91
	2	0.86	0.83
	3	0.79	0.75
	4	0.73	0.68

(vi) The company has timing differences (carrying amounts in excess of tax written down values) of £600,000 at 31 March 2007. The rate of corporation tax is 35%. The tax charge of £360,000 does not include the adjustment required to the deferred tax provision which should be assumed to go through the profit and loss account.

(vii) Bonus issue: On 15 March 2007, Wellmay made a bonus issue from the profit and loss account reserve of one share for every four held. The issue has not been recorded in the draft financial statements.

Required:

Redraft the financial statements of Wellmay, including a statement of the movement in share capital and reserves, for the year ended 31 March 2007 reflecting the adjustments required by notes (i) to (vii) above. **(Total: 25 marks)**

31   LLAMA

The following trial balance relates to Llama, a listed company, at 30 September 2007:

	£000	£000
Land and buildings – at valuation 1 October 2006 (note (i))	130,000	
Plant – at cost (note (i))	128,000	
Accumulated depreciation of plant at 1 October 2006		32,000
Investments – at fair value through profit and loss (note (i))	26,500	
Investment income		2,200
Cost of sales (note (i))	89,200	
Distribution costs	11,000	
Administrative expenses	12,500	
Loan interest paid	800	
Stock at 30 September 2007	37,900	
Corporation tax (note (ii))		400
Trade debtors	35,100	
Turnover		180,400
Equity shares of 50 pence each fully paid		60,000
Profit and loss account at 1 October 2006		25,500
2% loan note 2009 (note (iii))		80,000
Trade creditors		34,700
Revaluation reserve (arising from land and buildings)		14,000
Deferred tax		11,200
Suspense account (note (iv))		24,000
Bank		6,600
	471,000	471,000

The following notes are relevant:

(i)   Llama has a policy of revaluing its land and buildings at each year end. The valuation in the trial balance includes a land element of £30 million. The estimated remaining life of the buildings at that date (1 October 2006) was 20 years. On 30 September 2007, a professional valuer valued the buildings at £92 million with no change in the value of the land. Depreciation of buildings is charged 60% to cost of sales and 20% each to distribution costs and administrative expenses.

During the year Llama manufactured an item of plant that it is using as part of its own operating capacity. The details of its cost, which is included in cost of sales in the trial balance, are:

	£000
Materials cost	6,000
Direct labour cost	4,000
Machine time cost	8,000
Directly attributable overheads	6,000

The manufacture of the plant was completed on 31 March 2007 and the plant was brought into immediate use, but its cost has not yet been capitalised.

All plant is depreciated at 121/2% per annum (time apportioned where relevant) using the reducing balance method and charged to cost of sales. No fixed assets were sold during the year.

The fair value of the investments held at fair value through profit and loss at 30 September 2007 was £27.1 million.

(ii)   The balance of corporation tax in the trial balance represents the under/over provision of the previous year's estimate. The estimated corporation tax liability for the year ended 30 September 2007 is £18.7 million. At 30 September 2007 there were £40 million of net accelerated capital allowances. The corporation tax rate is 25%.

(iii)   The 2% loan note was issued on 1 April 2007 under terms that provide for a large premium on redemption in 2009. The finance department has calculated that the effect of this is that the loan note has an effective interest rate of 6% per annum.

(iv)   The suspense account contains the corresponding credit entry for the proceeds of a rights issue of shares made on 1 July 2007. The terms of the issue were one share for every four held at 80 pence per share. Llama's share price immediately before the issue was £1. The issue was fully subscribed.

Required:

Prepare for Llama:

(a)   A profit and loss account for the year ended 30 September 2007.   **(9 marks)**

(b)   A balance sheet as at 30 September 2007.   **(13 marks)**

(c)   A calculation of the earnings per share for the year ended 30 September 2007.

(3 marks)

Note: statements of total recognised gains and losses or movements on capital and reserves are not required.   **(Total: 25 marks)**

32   DEXON

Below is the summarised draft balance sheet of Dexon, a publicly listed company, as at 31 March 2008.

	£000	£000	£000
Fixed assets			
Property at valuation (land £20,000; buildings £165,000 (note (ii))			185,000
Plant (note (ii))			180,500
Investments at fair value through profit and loss at 1 April 2007 (note (iii))			12,500
			_____
			378,000
Current assets			
Stock		84,000	
Debtors (note (iv))		52,200	
Bank		3,800	
		_____	
		140,000	
Creditors: amounts falling due within one year		(81,800)	
		_____	
Net current assets			58,200
Provisions for liabilities			
Deferred tax – at 1 April 2007 (note (v))			(19,200)
			_____
Net assets			417,000
			_____
Share capital and reserves			
Ordinary shares of £1 each			250,000
Share premium		40,000	
Revaluation reserve		18,000	
Profit and loss account – at 1 April 2007	12,300		
– for the year ended 31 March 2008	96,700	109,000	167,000
	_____	_____	_____
			417,000
			_____

The following information is relevant:

(i)   Dexon's profit and loss account for the year includes £8 million in turnover from credit sales made on a 'sale or return' basis. At 31 March 2008, customers who had not paid for the goods, had the right to return £2·6 million of them. Dexon applied a mark up on cost of 30% on all these sales. In the past, Dexon's customers have sometimes returned goods under this type of agreement.

(ii)   The fixed assets have not been depreciated for the year ended 31 March 2008.

Dexon has a policy of revaluing its land and buildings at the end of each accounting year. The values in the above balance sheet are as at 1 April 2007 when the buildings had a remaining life of fifteen years. A qualified surveyor has valued the land and buildings at 31 March 2008 at £180 million.

Plant is depreciated at 20% on the reducing balance basis.

(iii)   The investments at fair value through profit and loss are held in a fund whose value changes directly in proportion to a specified market index. At 1 April 2007 the relevant index was 1,200 and at 31 March 2008 it was 1,296.

(iv)   In late March 2008 the directors of Dexon discovered a material fraud perpetrated by the company's credit controller that had been continuing for some time. Investigations revealed that a total of £4 million of the debtors as shown in the balance sheet at 31 March 2008 had in fact been paid and the money had been stolen by the credit controller. An analysis revealed that £1·5 million had been stolen in the year to 31 March 2007 with the rest being stolen in the current year. Dexon is not insured for this loss and it cannot be recovered from the credit controller, nor is it deductible for tax purposes.

(v)   During the year the company's timing differences increased by £10 million (capital allowances in excess of carrying values) of which £6 million related to the revaluation of the property. Dexon has a firm commitment to sell this property in the near future and has therefore been advised that a tax liability will arise on its sale. The applicable corporation tax rate is 20%.

(vi)   The above figures do not include the estimated provision for corporation tax on the profits for the year ended 31 March 2008. After allowing for any adjustments required in items (i) to (iv), the directors have estimated the provision at £11·4 million (this is in addition to the deferred tax effects of item (v)).

(vii)   On 1 September 2007 there was a fully subscribed rights issue of one new share for every four held at a price of £1·20 each. The proceeds of the issue have been received and the issue of the shares has been correctly accounted for in the above balance sheet.

(viii)   In May 2007 a dividend of 4 pence per share was paid. In November 2007 (after the rights issue in item (vii) above) a further dividend of 3 pence per share was paid. Both dividends have been correctly accounted for in the above balance sheet.

Required:

Taking into account any adjustments required by items (i) to (viii) above

(a)   Prepare a statement showing the recalculation of Dexon's profit for the year ended 31 March 2008.   **(8 marks)**

(b)   Prepare a statement of the movements in the share capital and reserves of Dexon for the year ended 31 March 2008.   **(8 marks)**

(c)   Redraft the balance sheet of Dexon as at 31 March 2008.   **(9 marks)**

Note: notes to the financial statements are NOT required.

(Total: 25 marks)

33 TOURMALET

The following extracted balances relate to Tourmalet at 30 September 20X3:

	£000	£000
Ordinary shares of 20p each		50,000
Profit and loss reserve 1 October 20X2		64,200
Revaluation reserves (including investment property revaluations)		2,100
6% Redeemable preference shares (redeemable 20X8)		30,000
Trade creditors		35,300
Corporation tax		2,100
Land and buildings – at valuation (note (iii))	150,000	
Plant and equipment – cost (note (v))	98,600	
Investment property – valuation at 1 October 20X2 (note (iv))	10,000	
Depreciation 1 October 20X2 – land and buildings		9,000
Depreciation 1 October 20X2 – plant and equipment		24,600
Trade debtors	31,200	
Stock – 1 October 20X2	26,550	
Bank	3,700	
Turnover (note (i))		313,000
Investment income (from properties)		1,200
Purchases	158,450	
Distribution expenses	26,400	
Administration expenses	23,200	
Interim preference dividend	900	
Interim ordinary dividend	2,500	
	531,500	531,500

The following notes are relevant:

(i) Turnover includes £50 million for an item of plant sold on 1 June 20X3. The plant had a book value of £40 million at the date of its sale, which was charged to cost of sales. On the same date, Tourmalet entered into an agreement to lease back the plant for the next five years (being the estimated remaining life of the plant) at a cost of £14 million per annum payable annually in arrears. An arrangement of this type is deemed to have a financing cost of 12% per annum. No depreciation has been charged on the item of plant in the current year.

(ii) The stock at 30 September 20X3 was valued at cost of £28.5 million. This includes £4.5 million of slow moving goods. Tourmalet is trying to sell these to another retailer but has not been successful in obtaining a reasonable offer. The best price it has been offered is £2 million.

(iii) On 1 October 19W9 Tourmalet had its land and buildings revalued by a firm of surveyors at £150 million, with £30 million of this attributed to the land. At that date the remaining life of the building was estimated to be 40 years. These figures were incorporated into the company's books. There has been no significant change in property values since the revaluation.

(iv)   Details of the investment property are:

Valuation – 1 October 20X2	£10 million
Valuation – 30 September 20X3	£9.8 million

The company policy is to revalue its investment property at the end of each financial year.

(v)   Plant and equipment (other than that referred to in note (i) above) is depreciated at 20% per annum on the reducing balance basis. All depreciation is to be charged to cost of sales.

(vi)   The above balances contain the results of Tourmalet's car retailing operations which ceased on 31 December 20X2 due to mounting losses. The results of the car retailing operation, which is to be treated as a discontinued operation, for the year to 30 September 20X3 are:

	£000
Sales	15,200
Cost of sales	16,000
Operating expenses	3,200

The operating expenses are included in the figure for administration expenses in the trial balance. Tourmalet is still paying rentals for the lease of its car showrooms. The rentals are included in operating expenses. Tourmalet is hoping to use the premises as an expansion of its administration offices. This is dependent on obtaining planning permission from the local authority for the change of use, however this is very difficult to obtain. Failing this, the best option would be early termination of the lease which will cost £1.5 million in penalties. This amount has not been provided for.

(vii)   The balance on the corporation tax account in the trial balance is the result of the settlement of the previous year's tax charge. The directors have estimated the provision for corporation tax for the year to 30 September 20X3 at £9.2 million.

Required:

(a)   Comment on the substance of the sale of the plant and the directors' treatment of it.

(5 marks)

(b)   Prepare the profit and loss account; and   **(18 marks)**

(c)   The statement of total recognised gains and losses of Tourmalet for the year to 30 September 20X3 in accordance with current accounting standards.   **(2 marks)**

Note: A balance sheet is NOT required. Disclosure notes are NOT required.

(Total: 25 marks)

34   HARRINGTON

Reproduced below are the draft financial statements of Harrington, a private limited company, for the year to 31 March 20X5:

Profit and loss account – Year to 31 March 20X5	£000
Turnover (note (i))	13,700
Cost of sales (note (ii))	(9,200)
	———
Gross profit	4,500
Operating expenses	(2,400)
	———

Profit on ordinary activities before interest		2,100
Loan note interest paid (refer to balance sheet)		(25)
		―――
Profit on ordinary activities before tax		2,075
Taxation (note (vi))		(55)
		―――
Profit on ordinary activities for the period		2,020
		―――

Balance sheet as at 31 March 20X5

	£000	£000
Tangible fixed assets (note (iii))		6,270
Investments (note (iv))		1,200
		―――
		7,470
Current assets		
Stock	1,750	
Trade debtors	2,450	
Bank	350	
	―――	
	4,550	
Creditors: amounts falling due within one year		
Trade creditors	(4,130)	
	―――	
Net current assets		420
Creditors: amounts falling due after more than one year		(500)
10% loan note (issued 20X2)		
Provisions for liabilities		
Deferred tax (note (vi))		(280)
		―――
Net assets		7,110
		―――
Capital and reserves:		
Ordinary shares of 25p each (note (v))		2,000
Reserves:		
Share premium		600
Profit and loss account – 1 April 20X4	2,990	
– Year to 31 March 20X5	1,520	4,510
	―――	
		―――
		7,110
		―――

The company policy for ALL depreciation is that it is charged to cost of sales and a full year's charge is made in the year of acquisition or completion and none in the year of disposal.

The following matters are relevant:

(i)   Included in turnover is £300,000 being the sale proceeds of an item of plant that was sold in January 20X5. The plant had originally cost £900,000 and had been depreciated by £630,000 at the date of its sale. Other than recording the proceeds in sales and cash, no other accounting entries for the disposal of the plant have been made. All plant is depreciated at 25% per annum on the reducing balance basis.

(ii) On 31 December 20X4 the company completed the construction of a new warehouse. The construction was achieved using the company's own resources as follows:

	£000
Purchased materials	150
Direct labour	800
Supervision	65
Design and planning costs	20

Included in the above figures are £10,000 for materials and £25,000 for labour costs that were effectively lost due to the foundations being too close to a neighbouring property. All the above costs are included in cost of sales. The building was brought into immediate use on completion and has an estimated life of 20 years (straight-line depreciation).

(iii) Details of the other tangible fixed assets at 31 March 20X5 are:

	£000	£000
Land at cost		1,000
Buildings at cost	4,000	
Less accumulated depreciation at 31 March 20X4	(800)	3,200
Plant at cost	5,200	
Less accumulated depreciation at 31 March 20X4	(3,130)	2,070
		6,270

At the beginning of the current year (1 April 20X4), Harrington commissioned an open market basis valuation of its properties (excluding the warehouse in note (ii) above). Land was valued at £1.2 million and the property at £4.8 million. The directors wish these values to be incorporated into the financial statements. The properties had an estimated remaining life of 20 years at the date of the valuation (straight-line depreciation is used). Harrington makes a transfer to realised profits in respect of the excess depreciation on revalued assets.

Note: Depreciation for the year to 31 March 20X5 has **not** yet been accounted for in the draft financial statements.

(iv) The investments are in quoted companies that are carried at their stock market values and are classified as at fair value through profit and loss. The value shown in the balance sheet is that at 31 March 20X4 and during the year to 31 March 20X5 the investments have risen in value by an average of 10%. Harrington has not reflected this increase in its financial statements.

(v) On 1 October 20X4 there had been a fully subscribed rights issue of 1 for 4 at 60p. This has been recorded in the above balance sheet. Dividends of £500,000 were paid during the year.

(vi) Corporation tax on the profits for the year to 31 March 20X5 is estimated at £260,000. The figure in the profit and loss account is the underprovision for the year to 31 March 20X4. There are net accelerated timing differences of £1.4 million at 31 March 20X5. The corporation tax rate is 25%.

Required:

(a) Prepare a restated profit and loss account for the year to 31 March 20X5 reflecting the information in notes (i) to (vi) above. **(9 marks)**

(b) Prepare a statement showing the movement of share capital and reserves for the year to 31 March 20X5. **(6 marks)**

(c) Prepare a restated balance sheet at 31 March 20X5 reflecting the information in notes (i) to (vi) above. **(10 marks)**

(Total: 25 marks)

35 CHAMBERLAIN

The following trial balance relates to Chamberlain, a publicly listed company, at 30 September 20X4:

	£000	£000
Ordinary share capital		200,000
Profit and loss reserve 1 October 20X3		162,000
6% Loan note (issued in 20X2)		50,000
Deferred tax (note (iv))		17,500
Land and buildings at cost (land element £163 million (note (i)))	403,000	
Plant and equipment at cost (note (i))	180,000	
Accumulated depreciation 1 October 20X3 – buildings		60,000
Accumulated depreciation 1 October 20X3 – plant and equipment		60,000
Trade debtors	48,000	
Stock – 1 October 20X3	35,500	
Bank	12,500	
Trade creditors		45,000
Turnover		246,500
Purchases	78,500	
Long-term contract balance (note (ii))	5,000	
Operating expenses	29,000	
Loan interest paid	1,500	
Interim dividend	8,000	
Research and development expenditure (note (iii))	40,000	
	———	———
	841,000	841,000
	———	———

The following notes are relevant:

(i) The building had an estimated life of 40 years when it was acquired and is being depreciated on a straight-line basis. Plant and equipment, other than the leased plant, is depreciated at $12\frac{1}{2}\%$ per annum using the reducing balance basis. Depreciation of buildings and plant and equipment is charged to cost of sales.

(ii) The long-term contract balance represents costs incurred to date of £35 million less progress payments received of £30 million on a two year construction contract that commenced on 1 October 20X3. The total contract price has been agreed at £125 million and Chamberlain expects the total contract cost to be £75 million. The company policy is to accrue for profit on uncompleted contracts by applying the percentage of completion to the total estimated profit. The percentage of completion is determined by the proportion of the contract costs to date compared to the total estimated contract costs. At 30 September 20X4, £5 million of the £35 million costs incurred to date related to unused stocks of materials on site.

Other stock at 30 September 20X4 amounted to £38.5 million at cost.

(iii)   The research and development expenditure is made up of £25 million of research, the remainder being development expenditure. The directors are confident of the success of this project which is likely to be completed in March 20X5 and wish to capitalise the maximum amount permitted under current accounting standards.

(iv)   The directors have estimated the provision for corporation tax for the year to 30 September 20X4 at £22 million. The deferred tax provision at 30 September 20X4 is to be adjusted to a credit balance of £14 million.

Required:

Prepare for Chamberlain:

(a)   a profit and loss account for the year to 30 September 20X4; and   **(12 marks)**

(b)   a balance sheet as at 30 September 20X4 in accordance with the Companies Acts and current Accounting Standards as far as the information permits.   **(13 marks)**

Note: A statement of total recognised gains and losses is NOT required.

(Total: 25 marks)

36   TINTAGEL

Reproduced below is the draft balance sheet of Tintagel, a public listed company, as at 31 March 20X4.

	£000	£000
Tangible fixed assets (note (i))		
Freehold property		126,000
Plant		110,000
Investment property (note (ii))		15,000
		———
		251,000
Current assets		
Stock (note (iii))	60,400	
Trade debtors and prepayments	31,200	
Bank	13,800	
	———	
	105,400	
	———	
Creditors: amounts falling due within one year		
Trade creditors (note (iii))	47,400	
Provision for plant overhaul (note (iv))	12,000	
Taxation	4,200	
	———	
	(63,600)	
	———	

Net current assets		41,800
Provisions for liabilities		
Deferred tax – at 1 April 20X3 (note (v))		(18,700)
Suspense account (note (vi))		(14,100)
		_____
Net assets		260,000
		_____
Share capital and reserves:		
Ordinary shares of 25p each		150,000
Reserves:		
Share premium	10,000	
Investment property revaluation reserve (note (ii))	3,400	
Profit and loss account – 1 April 20X3	48,100	
– Year to 31 March 20X4	48,500	110,000
	_____	_____
		260,000
		_____

(i) The profit and loss account has been charged with £3.2 million being the first of four equal annual rental payments for an item of excavating plant. This first payment was made on 1 April 20X3. Tintagel has been advised that this is a finance lease. The plant had a cash price of £11.2 million at the inception of the lease, which has an implicit interest rate of 10% per annum.

None of the fixed assets have been depreciated for the current year. The freehold property should be depreciated at 2% on its cost of £130 million. Plant, other than the lease plant, is depreciated at 20% on a reducing balance basis. The leased plant is depreciated on a straight-line basis over the four year life of the lease.

(ii) The investment property is a freehold property carried at its valuation on 31 March 20X3. Its value at 31 March 20X4 has been assessed by a qualified surveyor at £12.4 million.

(iii) During a stock count on 31 March 20X4 items that had cost £6 million were identified as being either damaged or slow moving. It is estimated that they will only realise £4 million in total, on which sales commission of 10% will be payable. An invoice for materials delivered on 12 March 20X4 for £500,000 has been discovered. It has not been recorded in Tintagel's bookkeeping system, although the materials were included in the stock count.

(iv) Tintagel operates some heavy excavating plant which requires a major overhaul every three years. The overhaul is estimated to cost £18 million and is due to be carried out in April 20X5. The provision of £12 million represents two annual amounts of £6 million made in the years to 31 March 20X3 and 20X4.

(v) The deferred tax provision required at 31 March 20X4 has been calculated at £22.5 million.

(vi)   The suspense account contains the credit entry relating to the issue on 1 October 20X3 of a £15 million 8% loan note. It was issued at a discount of 5% and incurred direct issue costs of £150,000. It is redeemable after four years at a premium of 10%. Interest is payable six months in arrears. The first payment of interest has not been accrued and is due on 1 April 20X4. The effective interest rate on the loan note is 6% per half year.

Required:

(a)   Commencing with the profit and loss account reserve figures in the above balance sheet (£48.1 million and £48.5 million), prepare a schedule of adjustments required to these figures taking into account any adjustments required by notes (i) to (vi) above.   **(10 marks)**

(b)   Redraft the balance sheet of Tintagel as at 31 March 20X4 taking into account the adjustments required in notes (i) to (vi) above.   **(15 marks)**

Notes to the financial statements are **not** required.   **(Total: 25 marks)**

Online question assistance

37   DARIUS

The following trial balance relates to Darius at 31 March 20X6:

	£000	£000
Turnover		213,800
Cost of sales	143,800	
Closing stock – 31 March 20X6 (note (i))	10,500	
Operating expenses	22,400	
Rental income form investment property		1,200
Finance costs (note (ii))	5,000	
Land and building – at valuation (note (iii))	63,000	
Plant and equipment – cost (note (iii))	36,000	
Investment property – valuation 1 April 20X5 (note (iii))	16,000	
Accumulated depreciation 1 April 20X5 – plant and equipment		16,800
Plant due to be sold (note (iv))	8,000	
Trade debtors	13,500	
Bank		900
Trade creditors		11,800
Ordinary shares of 25p each		20,000
10% Redeemable preference shares of £1 each		10,000
Deferred tax (note (v))		5,200
Revaluation reserve (note (iii))		21,000
Investment property revaluation reserve		1,800
Retained earnings 1 April 20X5		15,700
	———	———
	318,200	318,200
	———	———

The following notes are relevant:

(i)   A stock take at 31 March 20X6 listed goods with a cost of £10.5 million. This includes some damaged goods that had cost £800,000. These would require remedial work costing £450,000 before they could be sold for an estimated £950,000.

(ii)   Finance costs include overdraft charges, the full year's preference dividend and an ordinary dividend of 4p per share that was paid in September 20X5.

(iii) **Fixed assets:**

Land and building

The land and building were revalued at £15 million and £48 million respectively on 1 April 20X5 creating a £21 million revaluation reserve. At this date the building had a remaining life of 15 years.

Depreciation is on a straight-line basis. Darius does not make a transfer to realised profits in respect of excess depreciation.

Plant

All plant is depreciated at 12.5% on the reducing balance basis.

Depreciation on both the building and the plant should be charged to cost of sales.

Investment property

On 31 March 20X6 a qualified surveyor valued the investment property at £13.5 million. The property was acquired in January 20X4 at a cost of £14.2 million.

(iv) In April some plant with a cost of £12 million and accumulated depreciation of £4 million at 31 March 20X6 was sold for £6 million out of which a fee of 5% of the sales proceeds is payable. This plant is shown separately in the trial balance.

(v) The directors have estimated the provision for corporation tax for the year ended 31 March 20X6 at £8 million. The deferred tax provision at 31 March 20X6 is to be adjusted (through the profit and loss account) to reflect accumulated net accelerated capital allowances of £12 million. The rate of income tax is 30%.

Required:

(a) Prepare the profit and loss account for Darius for the year ended 31 March 20X6.

(10 marks)

(b) Prepare the statement of total recognised gains and losses for Darius for the year ended 31 March 20X6.　　　　　　　　　　　　　　　**(2 marks)**

(c) Prepare the balance sheet for Darius as at 31 March 20X6.　　　**(13 marks)**

Notes to the financial statements are NOT required.　　　　　　**(Total: 25 marks)**

38　TADEON

The following trial balance relates to Tadeon, a publicly listed company, at 30 September 20X6:

	£000	£000
Turnover		277,800
Cost of sales	118,000	
Operating expenses	40,000	
Loan interest paid (note (i))	1,000	
Rental of vehicles (note (ii))	6,200	
Investment income		2,000
25 year leasehold property at cost (note (iii))	225,000	
Plant and equipment at cost	181,000	
Investments at amortised cost	42,000	

Accumulated depreciation at 1 October 20X5		
– leasehold property		36,000
– plant and equipment		85,000
Equity shares of 20 pence each fully paid		150,000
Profit and loss account at 1 October 20X5		18,600
2% Loan note (note (i))		50,000
Deferred tax 1 October 20X5 (note (iv))		12,000
Trade debtors	53,500	
Stock at 30 September 20X6	33,300	
Bank		1,900
Trade creditors		18,700
Suspense account (note (v))		48,000
	———	———
	700,000	700,000
	———	———

The following notes are relevant:

(i) The loan note was issued on 1 October 20X5. It is redeemable on 30 September 2010 at a large premium (in order to compensate for the low nominal interest rate). The finance department has calculated that the effective interest rate on the loan is 5.5% per annum.

(ii) The rental of the vehicles relates to two separate contracts. These have been scrutinised by the finance department and they have come to the conclusion that £5 million of the rentals relate to a finance lease. The finance lease was entered into on 1 October 20X5 (the date the £5 million was paid) for a four year period. The vehicles had a fair value of £20 million (straight-line depreciation should be used) at 1 October 20X5 and the lease agreement requires three further annual payments of £6 million each on the anniversary of the lease. The interest rate implicit in the lease is to be taken as 10% per annum. The other contract is an operating lease and should be charged to operating expenses.

Other plant and equipment is depreciated at $12\frac{1}{2}$% per annum on the reducing balance basis.

All depreciation of property, plant and equipment is charged to cost of sales.

(iii) On 30 September 20X6 the leasehold property was revalued to £200 million. The directors wish to incorporate this valuation into the financial statements as the sale of the property is likely to take place in the near future and it will be replaced by a rented property. Tadeon has been advised that a tax charge will arise on the sale of the leasehold (see (iv) below).

(iv) The directors have estimated the provision for corporation tax for the year ended 30 September 20X6 at £38 million. At 30 September 20X6 there were £74 million of timing differences which would lead to a deferred tax liability. £20 million of the timing differences related to the revaluation of the leasehold property (see (iii) above). The corporation tax rate is 20%.

(v)   The suspense account balance can be reconciled from the following transactions:

The payment of a dividend in October 20X5. This was calculated to give a 5% yield on the company's share price of 80 pence as at 30 September 20X5.

The net receipt in March 20X6 of a fully subscribed rights issue of one new share for every three held at a price of 32 pence each. The expenses of the share issue were £2 million and should be charged to share premium.

Note: The cash entries for these transactions have been correctly accounted for.

Required:

Prepare for Tadeon:

(a)   A profit and loss account for the year ended 30 September 20X6; and   **(8 marks)**

(b)   A balance sheet as at 30 September 20X6.   **(17 marks)**

Note: A statement of total recognised gains and losses is not required. Disclosure notes are not required.   **(Total: 25 marks)**

39   CANDEL

The following trial balance relates to Candel at 30 September 2008:

	£000	£000
Leasehold property – at valuation 1 October 2007 (note (i))	50,000	
Plant and equipment – at cost (note (i))	76,600	
Plant and equipment – accumulated depreciation at 1 October 2007		24,600
Capitalised development expenditure – at 1 October 2007 (note (ii))	20,000	
Development expenditure – accumulated amortisation at 1 October 2007		6,000
Closing stock at 30 September 2008	20,000	
Trade debtors	43,100	
Bank		1,300
Trade creditors and provisions (note (iii))		23,800
Turnover (note (i))		300,000
Cost of sales	204,000	
Distribution costs	14,500	
Administrative expenses (note (iii))	22,200	
Preference dividend paid	800	
Interest on bank borrowings	200	
Equity dividend paid	6,000	
Research and development costs (note (ii))	8,600	
Equity shares of 25 pence each		50,000
8% redeemable preference shares of £1 each (note (iv))		20,000
Profit and loss account at 1 October 2007		24,500
Deferred tax (note (v))		5,800
Leasehold property revaluation reserve		10,000
	466,000	466,000

The following notes are relevant:

(i)   Fixed assets – tangible:

The leasehold property had a remaining life of 20 years at 1 October 2007. The company's policy is to revalue its property at each year end and at 30 September 2008 it was valued at £43 million.

On 1 October 2007 an item of plant was disposed of for £2.5 million cash. The proceeds have been included in turnover by Candel. The plant is still included in the above trial balance figures at its cost of £8 million and depreciation of £4 million (to the date of disposal).

All plant is depreciated at 20% per annum using the reducing balance method.

Depreciation and amortisation of all fixed assets is charged to cost of sales.

(ii)   Fixed assets – intangible:

In addition to the capitalised development expenditure (of £20 million), further research and development costs were incurred on a new project which commenced on 1 October 2007. The research period of the new project lasted until 31 December 2007 and incurred £1·4 million of costs. From that date the project incurred development costs of £800,000 per month. On 1 April 2008 the directors became confident that the project would be successful and yield a profit well in excess of its costs. The project is still in development at 30 September 2008.

Candel has a policy of capitalising development expenditure where permitted by accounting standards. Capitalised development expenditure is amortised at 20% per annum using the straight-line method. All expensed research and development is charged to cost of sales.

(iii) Candel is being sued by a customer for £2 million for breach of contract over a cancelled order. Candel has obtained legal opinion that there is a 20% chance that Candel will lose the case. Accordingly Candel has provided £400,000 (£2 million × 20%) included in administrative expenses in respect of the claim. The unrecoverable legal costs of defending the action are estimated at £100,000. These have not been provided for as the legal action will not go to court until next year.

(iv)   The preference shares were issued on 1 April 2008 at par. They are redeemable at a large premium which gives them an effective finance cost of 12% per annum.

(v)   The directors have estimated the provision for corporation tax for the year ended 30 September 2008 at £11.4 million. The required deferred tax provision at 30 September 2008 is £6 million.

Required:

(a)   Prepare the profit and loss account for the year ended 30 September 2008.

(11 marks)

(b)   Prepare the statement of the movements in share capital and reserves for the year ended 30 September 2008.   **(4 marks)**

(c)   Prepare the balance sheet as at 30 September 2008.   **(10 marks)**

Note: notes to the financial statements are not required.

(Total: 25 marks)

40   PRICEWELL

> **Timed question with Online tutor debrief**

The following trial balance relates to Pricewell at 31 March 2009:

	£'000	£'000
Leasehold property – at valuation 31 March 2008 (note (i))	25,200	
Plant and equipment (owned) – at cost (note (i))	46,800	
Plant and equipment (leased) – at cost (note (i))	20,000	
Accumulated depreciation at 31 March 2008		
Owned plant and equipment		12,800
Leased plant and equipment		5,000
Finance lease payment (paid on 31 March 2009) (note (i))	6,000	
Obligations under finance lease at 1 April 2008 (note (i))		15,600
Long-term contract (note (ii))	14,300	
Stock at 31 March 2009	28,200	
Debtors	33,100	
Bank	5,500	
Trade creditors		33,400
Turnover (note (iii))		310,000
Cost of sales (note (iii))	234,500	
Distribution costs	19,500	
Administrative expenses	27,500	
Preference dividend paid (note (iv))	2,400	
Equity dividend paid	8,000	
Equity shares of 50 pence each		40,000
6% redeemable preference shares at 31 March 2008 (note (iv))		41,600
Profit and loss account reserve at 31 March 2008		4,900
Current tax (note (v))	700	
Deferred tax (note (v))		8,400
	471,700	471,700

The following notes are relevant:

(i)   Fixed assets:

The 15 year leasehold property was acquired on 1 April 2007 at a cost of £30 million. The company's policy is to revalue the property at market value at each year end. The valuation in the trial balance of £25·2 million as at 31 March 2008 led to an impairment charge of £2·8 million which was reported in the profit and loss account of the previous year (i.e. year ended 31 March 2008). At 31 March 2009 the property was valued at £24·9 million.

Owned plant is depreciated at 25% per annum using the reducing balance method.

The leased plant was acquired on 1 April 2007. The rentals are £6 million per annum for four years payable in arrears on 31 March each year. The interest rate implicit in the lease is 8% per annum. Leased plant is depreciated at 25% per annum using the straight-line method.

No depreciation has yet been charged on any fixed assets for the year ended 31 March 2009. All depreciation is charged to cost of sales.

(ii)　On 1 October 2008 Pricewell entered into a contract to construct a bridge over a river. The agreed price of the bridge is £50 million and construction was expected to be completed on 30 September 2010. The £14·3 million in the trial balance is:

	£000
materials, labour and overheads	12,000
specialist plant (acquired 1 October 2008)	8,000
payment from customer	(5,700)
	14,300

The sales value of the work done at 31 March 2009 has been agreed at £22 million and the estimated cost to complete (excluding plant depreciation) is £10 million. The specialist plant will have no residual value at the end of the contract and should be depreciated on a monthly basis. Pricewell recognises profits on uncompleted contracts on the percentage of completion basis as determined by the agreed work to date compared to the total contract price.

(iii)　Pricewell's turnover includes £8 million for goods it sold acting as an agent for Trilby. Pricewell earned a commission of 20% on these sales and remitted the difference of £6·4 million (included in cost of sales) to Trilby.

(iv)　The 6% preference shares were issued on 1 April 2007 at par for £40 million. They have an effective finance cost of 10% per annum due to a premium payable on their redemption.

(v)　The directors have estimated the provision for corporation tax for the year ended 31 March 2009 at £4·5 million. The required deferred tax provision at 31 March 2009 is £5·6 million. The balance on the current tax in the trial balance represents the under/over provision of the corporation tax liability for the year ended 31 March 2008.

Required:

(a)　Prepare the profit and loss account for the year ended 31 March 2009.

(12 marks)

(b)　Prepare the balance sheet as at 31 March 2009.　**(13 marks)**

Note: notes to the financial statements are not required.　**(Total: 25 marks)**

Calculate your allowed time, allocate the time to the separate parts.....................

41   UPDATE PLC

Extracts of Update plc's consolidated profit and loss account for the year to 31 March 20X3 are:

	£000
Sales	36,000
Cost of sales	(21,000)
Gross profit	15,000
Other operating expenses	(6,200)
Operating profit	8,800
Income from associated companies	1,500
Interest payable	(800)
Profit before exceptional item	9,500
Exceptional item – fixed asset impairment	(4,000)
Profit before tax	5,500
Taxation	(2,800)
Profit after tax	2,700
Minority interest	(115)
Profit for financial year	2,585

The exceptional item attracted tax relief of £1 million which has been included in the tax charge.

Update plc paid an interim ordinary dividend of 3p per share in June 20X2 and declared a final dividend at the year end of 6p per share.

The issued share capital of Update plc on 1 April 20X2 was:

Ordinary shares of 25p each	£3 million
8% Irredeemable preference shares	£1 million

The company also had in issue £2 million 7% convertible loan stock dated 20X5. The loan stock will be redeemed at par in 20X5 or converted to ordinary shares on the basis of 40 new shares for each £100 of loan stock at the option of the stockholders. Update plc's corporation tax rate is 30%.

There are also in existence directors' share warrants (issued in 20X1) which entitle the directors to receive 750,000 new shares in total in 20X5 at no cost to the directors.

The following share issues took place during the year to 31 March 20X3:

–   1 July 20X2; a rights issue of 1 new share at £1.50 for every 5 shares held. The market price of Update plc's shares the day before the rights was £2.40.

–   1 October 20X2; an issue of £1 million 6% irredeemable preference shares at par.

Both issues were fully subscribed.

Update plc's basic earnings per share in the year to 31 March 20X2 was correctly disclosed as 24p.

Required:

Calculate for Update plc for the year to 31 March 20X3:

(i)   the dividend cover and explain its significance;   **(3 marks)**

(ii)   the basic earnings per share including the comparative;   **(5 marks)**

(iii)   the fully diluted earnings per share (ignore comparative); and advise a prospective investor of the significance of the diluted earnings per share figure.   **(7 marks)**

(Total: 15 marks)

42   JKL

JKL is a listed entity preparing financial statements to 31 August. At 1 September 20X3, JKL had 6,000,000 50p shares in issue. On 1 February 20X4, the entity made a rights issue of 1 for 4 at 125p per share; the issue was successful and all rights were taken up. The market price of one share immediately prior to the issue was 145p per share. Earnings after tax for the year ended 31 August 20X4 were £2,763,000.

Several years ago, JKL issued a convertible loan of £2,000,000. The loan carries an effective interest rate of 7% and its terms of conversion (which are at the option of the stockholder) are as follows:

For each £100 of loan stock:

Conversion at 31 August 20X8	105 shares
Conversion at 31 August 20X9	103 shares

JKL is subject to a tax rate of 32%.

Required:

(a)   Calculate basic earnings per share and diluted earnings per share for the year ended 31 August 20X4.   **(7 marks)**

(b)   The ASB Statement of Principles states that the objective of financial statements is to provide information that is:

'useful to a wide range of users in making economic decisions'.

Explain to a holder of ordinary shares in JKL both the usefulness and limitations of the diluted earnings per share figure.   **(3 marks)**

(Total: 10 marks)

BUSINESS COMBINATIONS

43   HIGHMOOR

Highmoor, a public listed company, acquired 80% of Slowmoor's ordinary shares on 1 October 20X2. Highmoor paid an immediate £2 per share in cash and agreed to pay a further £1.20 per share if Slowmoor made a profit within two years of its acquisition. Highmoor has not recorded the contingent consideration.

The balance sheets of the two companies at 30 September 20X3 are shown below:

	Highmoor		Slowmoor	
	£ million	£ million	£ million	£ million
Tangible fixed assets		585		172
Investments (note (ii))		225		13
Software (note (iii))		nil		40
		810		225
Current assets				
Stock	85		42	
Debtors	95		36	
Tax asset	nil		80	
Bank	20		nil	
	200		158	
Creditors: amounts falling due within one year				
Creditors	210		71	
Taxation	70		nil	
Overdraft	nil		17	
	(280)		(88)	
Net current (liabilities)/assets		(80)		70
Creditors: amounts falling due after more than one year				
12% loan note	nil		35	
16% inter company loan (note (ii))	nil	nil	45	(80)
Net assets		730		215
Share capital and reserves:				
Ordinary shares of £1 each		400		100
Reserves:				
Profit and loss account				
– 1 October 20X2	230		150	
Profit and loss account				
– profit /(loss) for year	100	330	(35)	115
		730		215

The following information is relevant:

(i)   At the date of acquisition the fair values of Slowmoor's net assets approximated to their book values.

(ii)   Included in Highmoor's investments is a loan of £50 million made to Slowmoor on 1 April 20X3. On 28 September 20X3, Slowmoor paid £9 million to Highmoor. This represented interest of £4 million for the year and the balance was a capital repayment. Highmoor had not received nor accounted for the payment, but it had accrued for the loan interest receivable as part of its debtors figure. There are no other intra group balances.

(iii) The software was developed by Highmoor during 20X2 at a total cost of £30 million. It was sold to Slowmoor for £50 million immediately after its acquisition. The software had an estimated life of five years and is being amortised by Slowmoor on a straight-line basis.

(iv) Due to the losses of Slowmoor since its acquisition, the directors of Highmoor are not confident it will return to profitability in the short term.

(v) For the purposes of crediting any negative goodwill to realised profits, £4 million of it relates to the stock at the date of acquisition, £8 million relates to land and the balance relates to the other non-monetary assets. All of the stock at the date of acquisition was sold before the year end and the average remaining life at the date of acquisition of the depreciable non-monetary assets can be taken as four years. The group accounting policy for any positive goodwill is to write it off on a straight-line basis over a period of four years.

Required:

(a) Prepare the consolidated balance sheet of Highmoor as at 30 September 20X3, explaining your treatment of the contingent consideration. **(20 marks)**

(b) Describe the circumstances in which negative goodwill may arise. Your answer should refer to the particular issues of the above acquisition. **(5 marks)**

(Total: 25 marks)

44 HIGHVELDT

Highveldt, a private company, acquired 75% of Samson's ordinary shares on 1 April 20X4. Highveldt paid an immediate £3.50 per share in cash and agreed to pay a further amount of £108 million on 1 April 20X5. Highveldt's cost of capital is 8% per annum. Highveldt has only recorded the cash consideration of £3.50 per share.

The summarised balance sheets of the two companies at 31 March 20X5 are shown below:

	Highveldt		Samson	
	£ million	£ million	£ million	£ million
Tangible fixed assets (note (i))		420		320
Investments (note (ii))		300		20
Development costs (note (iv))		Nil		40
		720		380
Current assets	133		91	
Creditors: amounts falling due within one year	(108)		(81)	
Net current assets		25		10
Creditors: amounts falling due after more than one year				
10% inter company loan (note (ii))		Nil		(60)
Net assets		745		330

Share capital and reserves:				
Ordinary shares of £1 each		270		80
Reserves:				
Share premium		80		40
Revaluation reserve		45		Nil
Profit and loss account at 1 April 20X4	160		134	
Profit for year to 31 March 20X5	190	350	76	210
		745		330

The following information is relevant:

(i)   Highveldt has a policy of revaluing land and buildings to fair value. At the date of acquisition Samson's land and buildings had a fair value £20 million higher than their book value and at 31 March 20X5 this had increased by a further £4 million (ignore any additional depreciation).

(ii)   Included in Highveldt's investments is a loan of £60 million made to Samson at the date of acquisition. Interest is payable annually in arrears. Samson paid the interest due for the year on 31 March 20X5, but Highveldt did not receive this until after the year end. Highveldt has not accounted for the accrued interest from Samson.

(iii)   Samson had established a line of products under the brand name of Titanware. Acting on behalf of Highveldt, a firm of specialists, had valued the brand name at a value of £40 million with an estimated life of 10 years as at 1 April 20X4. The brand is not included in Samson's balance sheet.

(iv)   Samson's development project was completed on 30 September 20X4 at a cost of £50 million. £10 million of this had been amortised by 31 March 20X5. Development costs capitalised by Samson at the date of acquisition were £18 million. Highveldt's policy for development costs is that they should be written off as incurred.

(v)   Samson sold goods to Highveldt during the year at a profit of £6 million, one third of these goods were still in the stock of Highveldt at 31 March 20X5.

(vi)   Goodwill is amortised over a four-year life.

Required:

(a)   Calculate the following figures as they would appear using UK GAAP in the consolidated balance sheet of Highveldt at 31 March 20X5:

   (i)   goodwill;   **(8 marks)**

   (ii)   minority interest;   **(4 marks)**

   (iii) the following consolidated reserves:

          share premium, revaluation reserve and the profit and loss reserve.   **(8 marks)**

   Note: Show your workings.

(b)   Explain why consolidated financial statements are useful to the users of financial statements (as opposed to just the parent company's separate (entity) financial statements).   **(5 marks)**

                                                                              (Total: 25 marks)

45   HILLUSION PLC

In recent years Hillusion plc has acquired a reputation for buying modestly performing businesses and selling them at a substantial profit within a period of two to three years of their acquisition. On 1 July 20X2 Hillusion plc acquired 80% of the ordinary share capital of Skeptik plc at a cost of £10,280,000. On the same date it also acquired 50% of Skeptik plc's 10% loan notes at par. The summarised draft financial statements of both companies are:

Profit and loss accounts: Year to 31 March 20X3

	Hillusion plc		Skeptik plc	
	£000	£000	£000	£000
Turnover		60,000		24,000
Cost of sales		(42,000)		(20,000)
Gross profit		18,000		4,000
Operating expenses		(6,000)		(200)
Loan interest received (paid)		75		(200)
Operating profit		12,075		3,600
Taxation		(3,000)		(600)
Profit for the year		9,075		3,000

Balance sheets: as at 31 March 20X3

	Hillusion plc		Skeptik plc	
Tangible fixed assets		19,320		8,000
Investments		11,280		nil
		30,600		8,000
Current assets	15,000		8,000	
Creditors: amounts falling due within one year	(10,000)		(3,600)	
Net current assets		5,000		4,400
		35,600		12,400
Creditors: amounts falling due after more than one year				
10% Loan notes		nil		(2,000)
Net assets		35,600		10,400

Capital and reserves		
Ordinary shares of £1 each	10,000	2,000
Profit and loss account	25,600	8,400
	35,600	10,400

The following information is relevant:

(i) The fair values of Skeptik plc's assets were equal to their book values with the exception of its plant, which had a fair value of £3.2 million in excess of its book value at the date of acquisition. The remaining life of all of Skeptik plc's plant at the date of its acquisition was four years and this period has not changed as a result of the acquisition. Depreciation of plant is on a straight-line basis and charged to cost of sales. Skeptik plc has not adjusted the value of its plant as a result of the fair value exercise.

(ii) In the post acquisition period Hillusion plc sold goods to Skeptik plc at a price of £12 million. These goods had cost Hillusion plc £9 million. During the year Skeptik plc had sold £10 million (at cost to Skeptik plc) of these goods for £15 million.

(iii) Hillusion plc bears almost all of the administration costs incurred on behalf of the group (invoicing, credit control, etc). It does not charge Skeptik plc for this service as to do so would not have a material effect on the group profit.

(iv) Revenues and profits should be deemed to accrue evenly throughout the year.

(v) The current accounts of the two companies were reconciled at the year-end with Skeptik plc owing Hillusion plc £750,000.

(vi) Goodwill is to be written off as an operating expense over a three-year life. Time apportionment should be used in the year of acquisition.

Required:

(a) Prepare a consolidated profit and loss account and balance sheet for Hillusion plc for the year to 31 March 20X3. **(20 marks)**

(b) Explain why it is necessary to eliminate unrealised profits when preparing group financial statements; and how reliance on the entity financial statements of Skeptik plc may mislead a potential purchaser of the company. **(5 marks)**

(Total: 25 marks)

Note: Your answer should refer to the circumstances described in the question.

46 HAPSBURG

(a) Hapsburg, a public listed company, acquired the following investments:

– On 1 April 20X3, 24 million shares in Sundial. This was by way of an immediate share exchange of 2 shares in Hapsburg for every 3 shares in Sundial plus a cash payment of £1 per Sundial share payable on 1 April 20X6. The market price of Hapsburg's shares on 1 April 20X3 was £2 each.

– On 1 October 20X3, 6 million shares in Aspen paying an immediate £2.50 in cash for each share.

Based on Hapsburg's cost of capital (taken as 10% per annum), £1 receivable in the three years' time can be taken to have a present value of £0.75. Hapsburg has not yet recorded the acquisition of Sundial but it has recorded the investment in Aspen.

The summarised balance sheets at 31 March 20X4 are:

	Hapsburg		Sundial		Aspen	
	£000	£000	£000	£000	£000	£000
Fixed assets						
Land and buildings		16,600		9,700		17,500
Plant		24,400		25,100		20,200
Investments		15,000		3,000		nil
		——		——		——
		56,000		37,800		37,700
Current assets						
Stock	9,900		4,800		7,900	
Debtors	13,600		8,600		14,400	
Cash	1,200		3,800		nil	
	——		——		——	
	24,700		17,200		22,300	
	——		——		——	
Creditors: amounts falling due within one year						
Trade creditors	16,500		6,900		13,600	
Bank overdraft	nil		nil		4,500	
Taxation	9,600		3,400		1,900	
	——		——		——	
	(26,100)		(10,300)		(20,000)	
	——		——		——	
Net current (liabilities)/assets		(1,400)		6,900		2,300
Creditors: amounts falling due after more than one year						
10% loan note		(16,000)		(4,200)		(12,000)
		——		——		——
Net assets		38,600		40,500		28,000
		——		——		——
Share capital and reserves						
Ordinary shares £1 each		20,000		30,000		20,000
Reserves:						
Share premium	8,000		2,000		nil	
Profit and loss reserve	10,600	18,600	8,500	10,500	8,000	8,000
		——		——		——
		38,600		40,500		28,000
		——		——		——

The following information is relevant:

(i) Below is a summary of the results of a fair value exercise for Sundial carried out at the date of acquisition:

Asset	Carrying value at acquisition	Fair value at acquisition	Notes
	£000	£000	
Plant	10,000	15,000	remaining life at acquisition four years
Investments	3,000	4,500	no change in value since acquisition

The book values of the net assets of Aspen at the date of acquisition approximated to their fair values.

(ii) The profits of Sundial and Aspen for the year to 31 March 20X4, as reported in their entity financial statements, were £4.5 million and £6 million respectively. No dividends have been paid by any of the companies during the year. All profits are deemed to accrue evenly throughout the year.

(iii) In January 20X4 Aspen sold goods to Hapsburg at a selling price of £4 million. These goods had cost Aspen £2.4 million. Hapsburg had £2.5 million (at cost to Hapsburg) of these goods still in stock at 31 March 20X4.

(iv) Goodwill is to be written off over a five-year life with a proportionate charge in the year of acquisition.

(v) All depreciation/amortisation is charged on a straight-line basis.

Required:

Prepare the consolidated balance sheet of Hapsburg as at 31 March 20X4.

(20 marks)

Note: The additional disclosures relating to material associates are not required.

(b) Some commentators have criticised the use of equity accounting on the basis that it can be used as a form of off balance sheet financing

Required:

Explain the reasoning behind the use of equity accounting and discuss the above comment. **(5 marks)**

(Total: 25 marks)

Online question assistance

47 HEDRA

Hedra, a public listed company, acquired the following investments:

(i) On 1 October 20X4, 72 million shares in Salvador for an immediate cash payment of £195 million. Hedra agreed to pay further consideration on 30 September 20X5 of £49 million if the post acquisition profits of Salvador exceeded an agreed figure at that date. Hedra has not accounted for this deferred payment as it did not believe it would be payable, however Salvador's profits have now exceeded the agreed amount (ignore discounting).

Salvador also received a £50 million 8% loan from Hedra at the date of its acquisition.

(ii) On 1 April 20X5, 40 million shares in Aragon by way of a share exchange of two shares in Hedra for each acquired share in Aragon. The stock market value of Hedra's shares at the date of this share exchange was £2.50. Hedra has not yet recorded the acquisition of the investment in Aragon.

The summarised balance sheets of the three companies as at 30 September 20X5 are:

	Hedra		Salvador		Aragon	
	£m	£m	£m	£m	£m	£m
Fixed assets						
Land and buildings		208		105		100
Plant		150		135		170
Investments – in Salvador		245		nil		nil
– other		45		nil		nil
		648		240		270
Current assets						
Stocks	130		80		110	
Debtors	142		97		70	
Cash	nil		4		20	
	272		181		200	
Creditors: amounts falling due within one year						
Trade creditors	118		141		40	
Overdraft	12		nil		nil	
Taxation	50		nil		30	
	(180)		(141)		(70)	
Net current assets		92		40		130
Creditors: amounts falling due after more than one year						
8% loan note		nil		(50)		nil
Provisions for liabilities						
Deferred tax		(45)		nil		nil
		695		230		400
Capital and reserves						
Ordinary shares (£1 each)		400		120		100
Reserves:						
Share premium	40		50		nil	
Revaluation	15		nil		nil	
Profit and loss reserve	240	295	60	110	300	300
		695		230		400

The following information is relevant:

(a) Fair value adjustments and revaluations:

(i) Hedra's accounting policy for land and buildings is that they should be carried at their fair values. The fair value of Salvador's land at the date of acquisition was £20 million in excess of its carrying value. By 30 September 20X5 this excess had increased by a further £5 million. Salvador's buildings did not require any fair value adjustments. The fair value of Hedra's own land and buildings at 30 September 20X5 was £12 million in excess of its carrying value in the above balance sheet.

(ii)   The fair value of some of Salvador's plant at the date of acquisition was £20 million in excess of its carrying value and had a remaining life of four years (straight-line depreciation is used).

(iii)   At the date of acquisition Salvador had unrelieved tax losses of £40 million from previous years. Salvador had not accounted for these as a deferred tax asset as its directors did not believe the company would be sufficiently profitable in the near future. However, the directors of Hedra were confident that these losses would be utilised and accordingly they should be recognised as a deferred tax asset. By 30 September 20X5 the group had not yet utilised any of these losses. The corporation tax rate is 25%.

(b)   The profit and loss reserves of Salvador and Aragon at 1 October 20X4, as reported in their separate financial statements, were £20 million and £200 million respectively. All profits are deemed to accrue evenly throughout the year.

(c)   All goodwill is amortised over a five year life with a proportionate charge in the year of acquisition where appropriate.

Required:

Prepare, under UK GAAP, the consolidated balance sheet of Hedra as at 30 September 20X5.

(25 marks)

48   HOLDRITE, STAYBRITE AND ALLBRITE

Holdrite purchased 75% of the issued share capital of Staybrite and 40% of the issued share capital of Allbrite on 1 April 20X4.

Details of the purchase consideration given at the date of purchase are:

Staybrite: A share exchange of 2 shares in Holdrite for every 3 shares in Staybrite plus an issue to the shareholders of Staybrite of 8% loan notes redeemable at par on 30 June 20X6 on the basis of £100 loan note for every 250 shares held in Staybrite.

Allbrite: A share exchange of 3 shares in Holdrite for every 4 shares in Allbrite plus £1 per share acquired in cash.

The market price of Holdrite's shares at 1 April 20X4 was £6 per share.

The summarised profit and loss accounts for the three companies for the year to 30 September 20X4 are:

	Holdrite	Staybrite	Allbrite
	£000	£000	£000
Turnover	75,000	40,700	31,000
Cost of sales	(47,400)	(19,700)	(15,300)
Gross profit	27,600	21,000	15,700
Operating expenses	(10,480)	(9,000)	(9,700)
Operating profit	17,120	12,000	6,000

Interest expense	(170)	–	–
Profit before tax	16,950	12,000	6,000
Taxation	(4,800)	(3,000)	(2,000)
Profit after tax	12,150	9,000	4,000

The following information is relevant:

(i)   A fair value exercise was carried out for Staybrite at the date of its acquisition with the following results:

	Book value	Fair value
	£000	£000
Land	20,000	23,000
Plant	25,000	30,000

The fair values have not been reflected in Staybrite's financial statements. The increase in the fair value of the plant would create additional depreciation of £500,000 in the post acquisition period in the consolidated financial statements to 30 September 20X4.

Depreciation of plant is charged to cost of sales.

(ii)   The details of each company's share capital and reserves at 1 October 20X3 are:

	Holdrite	Staybrite	Allbrite
	£000	£000	£000
Equity shares of £1 each	20,000	10,000	5,000
Share premium	5,000	4,000	2,000
Profit and loss reserve	18,000	7,500	6,000

(iii) In the post-acquisition period Holdrite sold goods to Staybrite for £10 million. Holdrite made a profit of £4 million on these sales. One-quarter of these goods were still in the stock of Staybrite at 30 September 20X4.

(iv)   Goodwill is to be amortised over a five-year life, time apportioned where appropriate.

(v)   Holdrite paid a dividend of £5 million on 20 September 20X4.

Required:

(a)   Calculate the goodwill arising on the purchase of the shares in both Staybrite and Allbrite at 1 April 20X4.
(8 marks)

(b)   Prepare a consolidated profit and loss account for the Holdrite Group for the year to 30 September 20X4.
(15 marks)

(c)   Show the movement on the consolidated profit and loss reserve for the year to 30 September 20X4.
(2 marks)

(Total: 25 marks)

49 HOSTERLING

Hosterling purchased the following equity investments:

On 1 October 20X5: 80% of the issued share capital of Sunlee. The acquisition was through a share exchange of three shares in Hosterling for every five shares in Sunlee. The market price of Hosterling's shares at 1 October 20X5 was £5 per share.

On 1 July 20X6: 6 million shares in Amber paying £4 per share in cash. The summarised profit and loss accounts for the three companies for the year ended 30 September 20X6 are:

	Hosterling	Sunlee	Amber
	£000	£000	£000
Turnover	105,000	62,000	50,000
Cost of sales	(68,000)	(36,500)	(61,000)
Gross profit/(loss)	37,000	25,500	(11,000)
Distribution costs	(4,000)	(2,000)	(4,500)
Administrative expenses	(7,500)	(7,000)	(8,500)
Other income (note (i))	400	nil	nil
Finance costs	(1,200)	(900)	nil
Profit/(loss) before tax	24,700	15,000	(24,000)
Tax (charge)/credit	(8,700)	(2,600)	4,000
Profit/(loss) for the financial year	16,000	13,000	(20,000)

The following information is relevant:

(i)   The other income is a dividend received from Sunlee on 31 March 20X6.

(ii)   The details of Sunlee's and Amber's share capital and reserves at 1 October 20X5 were:

	Sunlee	Amber
	£000	£000
Equity shares of £1 each	20,000	15,000
Profit and loss account	18,000	35,000

(iii)   A fair value exercise was carried out at the date of acquisition of Sunlee with the following results:

	Carrying amount	Fair value	Remaining life (straight line)
	£000	£000	
Intellectual property	18,000	22,000	still in development
Land	17,000	20,000	not applicable
Plant	30,000	35,000	five years

The fair values have not been reflected in Sunlee's financial statements.

Plant depreciation is included in cost of sales.

No fair value adjustments were required on the acquisition of shares in Amber.

(iv) In the year ended 30 September 20X6 Hosterling sold goods to Sunlee at a selling price of £18 million. Hosterling made a profit of cost plus 25% on these sales. £7.5 million (at cost to Sunlee) of these goods were still in the stock of Sunlee at 30 September 20X6.

(v) All goodwill is amortised on a straight-line basis with time apportionment where appropriate. The estimated life of all goodwill is five years.

(vi) All trading profits and losses are deemed to accrue evenly throughout the year.

Required:

(a) Calculate the goodwill arising on the acquisition of Sunlee at 1 October 20X5.

(5 marks)

(b) Calculate the carrying amount of the investment in Amber at 30 September 20X6 under the equity method.
(4 marks)

(c) Prepare the consolidated profit and loss account for the Hosterling Group for the year ended 30 September 20X6.
(16 marks)

(Total: 25 marks)

50 PARENTIS

Parentis, a public listed company, acquired 600 million equity shares in Offspring on 1 April 2006. The purchase consideration was made up of:

* a share exchange of one share in Parentis for two shares in Offspring

* the issue of £100 10% loan note for every 500 shares acquired and

* a deferred cash payment of 11 pence per share acquired payable on 1 April 2007.

Parentis has only recorded the issue of the loan notes. The value of each Parentis share at the date of acquisition was 75 pence and Parentis has a cost of capital of 10% per annum.

The balance sheets of the two companies at 31 March 2007 are shown below:

	Parentis		Offspring	
	£ million	£ million	£ million	£ million
Tangible fixed assets (note (i))		640		340
Investments		120		Nil
Intellectual property (note (ii))		Nil		30
		760		370
Current assets				
Stock (note (iii))	76		22	
Trade debtors (note (iii))	84		44	
Bank	Nil		4	
	160		70	

Creditors: amounts falling due within one year			
Trade creditors (note (iii))	130	57	
Taxation	45	23	
Overdraft	25	Nil	
	____	____	
	200	80	
	____	____	
Net current liabilities		(40)	(10)
Creditors: amounts falling due after more than one year			
10% loan notes		(120)	(20)
		____	____
		600	340
		____	____
Capital and reserves:			
Equity shares of 25 pence each		300	200
Profit and loss account			
– 1 April 2006	210	120	
– year ended 31 March 2007	90	300	20	140
	____	____	____	____
		600	340
		____	____

The following information is relevant:

(i)   At the date of acquisition the fair values of Offspring's net assets were approximately equal to their carrying amounts with the exception of its properties. These properties had a fair value of £40 million in excess of their carrying amounts which would create additional depreciation of £2 million in the post acquisition period to 31 March 2007. The fair values have not been reflected in Offspring's balance sheet.

(ii)   The intellectual property is a system of encryption designed for internet use. Offspring has been advised that government legislation (passed since acquisition) has now made this type of encryption illegal. Offspring will receive £10 million in compensation from the government.

(iii) Offspring sold Parentis goods for £15 million in the post acquisition period. £5 million of these goods are included in the stock of Parentis at 31 March 2007. The profit made by Offspring on these sales was £6 million. Offspring's trade creditor account (in the records of Parentis) of £7 million does not agree with Parentis's trade debtor account (in the records of Offspring) due to cash in transit of £4 million paid by Parentis.

(iv)   Goodwill is amortised on a straight-line basis over a five year life.

Required:

Prepare the consolidated balance sheet of Parentis as at 31 March 2007.

(Total: 25 marks)

51 PLATEAU

On 1 October 2006 Plateau acquired the following investments:

-   3 million equity shares in Savannah by an exchange of one share in Plateau for every two shares in Savannah plus £1 per acquired Savannah share in cash. The market price of each Plateau share at the date of acquisition was £6.

-   30% of the equity shares of Axle at a cost of £7.50 per share in cash.

Only the cash consideration of the above investments has been recorded by Plateau.

The summarised draft balance sheets of the three companies at 30 September 2007 are:

	Plateau	Savannah	Axle
	£000	£000	£000
Tangible fixed assets	18,400	10,400	18,000
Investments in Savannah and Axle	12,000	Nil	Nil
Available-for-sale investments	6,500	Nil	Nil
	36,900	10,400	18,000
Current assets			
Stock	6,900	6,200	3,600
Debtors	3,200	1,500	2,400
	10,100	7,700	6,000
Creditors: amounts falling due within one year	(8,000)	(4,200)	(3,000)
Creditors: amounts falling due after more than one year 7% Loan notes	(5,000)	(1,000)	(1,000)
	34,000	12,900	20,000
Capital and reserves			
Equity shares of £1 each	10,000	4,000	4,000
Profit and loss account – at 30 September 2006	16,000	6,500	11,000
– for year ended 30 September 2007	8,000	2,400	5,000
	34,000	12,900	20,000

The following information is relevant:

(i)   At the date of acquisition the fair values of Savannah's assets were equal to their carrying amounts with the exception of Savannah's land which had a fair value of £500,000 below its carrying amount; it was written down by this amount shortly after acquisition and has not changed in value since then.

(ii) On 1 October 2006, Plateau sold an item of plant to Savannah at its agreed fair value of £2.5 million. Its carrying amount prior to the sale was £2 million. The estimated remaining life of the plant at the date of sale was five years (straight-line depreciation).

(iii) During the year ended 30 September 2007 Savannah sold goods to Plateau for £2.7 million. Savannah had marked up these goods by 50% on cost. Plateau had a third of the goods still in its stock at 30 September 2007. There were no intra-group debtors/creditors at 30 September 2007.

(iv) The goodwill of Savannah is amortised over a five year life. The goodwill of Axle is deemed to have an indefinite life and was not impaired at 30 September 2007.

(v) The available-for-sale investments are included in Plateau's balance sheet (above) at their fair value on 1 October 2006, but they have a fair value of £9 million at 30 September 2007.

(vi) No dividends were paid during the year by any of the companies.

Required:

(a) Prepare the consolidated balance sheet for Plateau as at 30 September 2007.

(20 marks)

(b) A financial assistant has observed that the fair value exercise means that a subsidiary's net assets are included at acquisition at their fair (current) values in the consolidated balance sheet. The assistant believes that it is inconsistent to aggregate the subsidiary's net assets with those of the parent because most of the parent's assets are carried at historical cost.

Required:

Comment on the assistant's observation and explain why the net assets of acquired subsidiaries are consolidated at acquisition at their fair values. **(5 marks)**

(Total: 25 marks)

52 PATRONIC

On 1 August 2007 Patronic purchased 18 million of a total of 24 million equity shares in Sardonic. The acquisition was through a share exchange of two shares in Patronic for every three shares in Sardonic. Both companies have shares with a par value of £1 each. The market price of Patronic's shares at 1 August 2007 was £5·75 per share. Patronic will also pay in cash on 31 July 2009 (two years after acquisition) £2·42 per acquired share of Sardonic. Patronic's cost of capital is 10% per annum. The reserves of Sardonic on 1 April 2007 were £69 million.

Patronic has held an investment of 30% of the equity shares in Acerbic for many years.

The summarised profit and loss accounts for the three companies for the year ended 31 March 2008 are:

	Patronic	Sardonic	Acerbic
	£000	£000	£000
Turnover	150,000	78,000	80,000
Cost of sales	(94,000)	(51,000)	(60,000)
Gross profit	56,000	27,000	20,000

Distribution costs	(7,400)	(3,000)	(3,500)
Administrative expenses	(12,500)	(6,000)	(6,500)
Operating profit	36,100	18,000	10,000
Finance costs (note (ii))	(2,000)	(900)	nil
Profit before tax	34,100	17,100	10,000
Tax	(10,400)	(3,600)	(4,000)
Profit for the year	23,700	13,500	6,000

The following information is relevant:

(i)   The fair values of the net assets of Sardonic at the date of acquisition were equal to their carrying amounts with the exception of property and plant. Property and plant had fair values of £4·1 million and £2·4 million respectively in excess of their carrying amounts. The increase in the fair value of the property would create additional depreciation of £200,000 in the consolidated financial statements in the post acquisition period to 31 March 2008 and the plant had a remaining life of four years (straight-line depreciation) at the date of acquisition of Sardonic. All depreciation is treated as part of cost of sales.

The fair values have not been reflected in Sardonic's financial statements.

No fair value adjustments were required on the acquisition of Acerbic.

(ii) The finance costs of Patronic do not include the finance cost on the deferred consideration.

(iii) Prior to its acquisition, Sardonic had been a good customer of Patronic. In the year to 31 March 2008, Patronic sold goods at a selling price of £1·25 million per month to Sardonic both before and after its acquisition. Patronic made a profit of 20% on the cost of these sales. At 31 March 2008 Sardonic still held stock of £3 million (at cost to Sardonic) of goods purchased in the post acquisition period from Patronic.

(iv) The goodwill of Sardonic should be amortised over a nine-year life with time apportionment in the year of acquisition. The goodwill in Acerbic was deemed to have an indefinite life and was not impaired at 31 March 2008.

(v)   All items in the above profit and loss accounts are deemed to accrue evenly over the year.

(vi) Ignore deferred tax.

Required:

(a)   Calculate the goodwill arising on the acquisition of Sardonic at 1 August 2007.

(6 marks)

(b)   Prepare the consolidated profit and loss account for the Patronic Group for the year ended 31 March 2008.

Note: assume that the investment in Acerbic has been accounted for using the equity method since its acquisition.   **(15 marks)**

(c) At 31 March 2008 the other equity shares (70%) in Acerbic were owned by many separate investors. Shortly after this date Spekulate (a company unrelated to Patronic) accumulated a 60% interest in Acerbic by buying shares from the other shareholders. In May 2008 a meeting of the board of directors of Acerbic was held at which Patronic lost its seat on Acerbic's board.

Required:

Explain, with reasons, the accounting treatment Patronic should adopt for its investment in Acerbic when it prepares its financial statements for the year ending 31 March 2009. **(4 marks)**

(Total: 25 marks)

53 PEDANTIC

On 1 April 2008, Pedantic acquired 60% of the equity share capital of Sophistic in a share exchange of two shares in Pedantic for three shares in Sophistic. The issue of shares has not yet been recorded by Pedantic. At the date of acquisition shares in Pedantic had a market value of £6 each. Pedantic also incurred directly related acquisition costs of £300,000 which are included in administrative expenses. Below are the summarised draft financial statements of both companies.

Profit and loss accounts for the year ended 30 September 2008

	Pedantic	Sophistic
	£000	£000
Turnover	85,000	42,000
Cost of sales	(63,000)	(32,000)
Gross profit	22,000	10,000
Distribution costs	(2,000)	(2,000)
Administrative expenses	(6,000)	(3,200)
Operating profit	14,000	4,800
Finance costs	(300)	(400)
Profit before tax	13,700	4,400
Taxation	(4,700)	(1,400)
Profit for the year	9,000	3,000

Balance sheets as at 30 September 2008

Fixed assets		
Tangible assets	40,600	12,600
Current assets	16,000	6,600
Creditors: amounts falling due within one year	(8,200)	(4,700)
Creditors: amounts falling due after more than one year		
10% loan notes	(3,000)	(4,000)
	————	————
	45,400	10,500
	————	————
Capital and reserves		
Equity shares of £1 each	10,000	4,000
Profit and loss account	35,400	6,500
	————	————
	45,400	10,500
	————	————

The following information is relevant:

(i)   At the date of acquisition, the fair values of Sophistic's assets were equal to their carrying amounts with the exception of an item of plant, which had a fair value of £2 million in excess of its carrying amount. It had a remaining life of five years at that date [straight-line depreciation is used]. Sophistic has not adjusted the carrying amount of its plant as a result of the fair value exercise.

(ii)   Sales from Sophistic to Pedantic in the post acquisition period were £8 million. Sophistic made a mark-up on cost of 40% on these sales. Pedantic had sold £5.2 million (at cost to Pedantic) of these goods by 30 September 2008.

(iii) Other than where indicated, profit and loss account items are deemed to accrue evenly on a time basis.

(iv)   Sophistic's trade debtors at 30 September 2008 include £600,000 due from Pedantic which did not agree with Pedantic's corresponding trade creditor. This was due to cash in transit of £200,000 from Pedantic to Sophistic. Both companies have positive bank balances.

(v)   Consolidated goodwill has an indefinite life and has not been impaired at 30 September 2008.

Required:

(a)   Prepare the consolidated profit and loss account for Pedantic for the year ended 30 September 2008.   **(9 marks)**

(b)   Prepare the consolidated balance sheet for Pedantic as at 30 September 2008.

(16 marks)

(Total: 25 marks)

54   PACEMAKER

> 🕐 *Timed question with Online tutor debrief*

Below are the summarised balance sheets for three companies as at 31 March 2009:

	Pacemaker		Syclop		Vardine	
Fixed assets	$ million	$ million	$ million	$ million	$ million	$ million
Tangible		520		280		240
Investments		345		40		nil
		———		———		———
		865		320		240
Current assets						
Stock	142		160		120	
Debtors	95		88		50	
Cash and bank	8		22		10	
	———		———		———	
	245		270		180	
Creditors: amounts falling due within one year	(200)		(165)		(80)	
	———		———		———	
Net current assets		45		105		100
Creditors: amounts falling due after more than one year						
10% loan notes		(180)		(20)		(nil)
		———		———		———
Net assets		730		405		340
		———		———		———
Capital and reserves						
Equity shares of £1 each		500		145		100
Share premium	100		nil		nil	
Profit and loss account	130	230	260	260	240	240
	———	———	———	———	———	———
		730		405		340
		———		———		———

Notes:

Pacemaker is a public listed company that acquired the following investments:

(i)   Investment in Syclop

On 1 April 2007 Pacemaker acquired 116 million shares in Syclop for an immediate cash payment of £210 million and issued at par one 10% £100 loan note for every 200 shares acquired. Syclop's profit and loss account reserve at the date of acquisition was £120 million.

(ii)   Investment in Vardine

On 1 October 2008 Pacemaker acquired 30 million shares in Vardine in exchange for 75 million of its own shares. The market value of Pacemaker's shares at the date of this share exchange was £1·60 each. Pacemaker has not yet recorded the investment in Vardine.

(iii)   Pacemaker's other investments, and those of Syclop, are available-for-sale investments which are carried at their fair values as at 31 March 2008. The fair values of these investments at 31 March 2009 are £82 million and £37 million respectively.

Other relevant information:

(vi)   At the date of acquisition of Syclop owned a recently built property that was carried at its (depreciated) construction cost of £62 million. The fair value of this property at the date of acquisition was £82 million and it had an estimated remaining life of 20 years.

For many years Syclop has been selling some of its products under the brand name of 'Kyklop'. At the date of acquisition the directors of Pacemaker valued this brand at £25 million with a remaining life of 10 years. The brand is not included in Syclop's balance sheet.

The fair values of all other identifiable assets and liabilities of Syclop were equal to their carrying values at the date of acquisition.

(v)   The stock of Syclop at 31 March 2009 includes goods supplied by Pacemaker for £56 million (at selling price from Pacemaker). Pacemaker adds a mark-up of 40% on cost when selling goods to Syclop. There are no intra-group debtors or creditors at 31 March 2009.

(vii)   Vardine's profit is subject to seasonal variation. Its profit for the year ended 31 March 2009 was £100 million. £20 million of this profit was made from 1 April 2008 to 30 September 2008.

(viii) None of the companies have paid any dividends for many years.

(ix)   The goodwill of Syclop has an estimated life of five years. The goodwill of Vardine has an indefinite life and it has not been impaired.

Required:

Prepare the consolidated balance sheet of Pacemaker as at 31 March 2009.

(Total: 25 marks)

Calculate your allowed time, allocate the time to the separate parts....................

ANALYSING AND INTERPRETING FINANCIAL STATEMENTS

55   COMPARATOR

Comparator assembles computer equipment from bought in components and distributes them to various wholesalers and retailers. It has recently subscribed to an interfirm comparison service. Members submit accounting ratios as specified by the operator of the service, and in return, members receive the average figures for each of the specified ratios taken from all of the companies in the same sector that subscribe to the service. The specified ratios and the average figures for Comparator's sector are shown below.

Ratios of companies reporting a full year's results for periods ending between 1 July 20X3 and 30 September 20X3

Return on capital employed	22.1%
Net assets turnover	1.8 times
Gross profit margin	30%
Net profit (before tax) margin	12.5%
Current ratio	1.6:1
Quick ratio	0.9:1
Stock holding period	46 days
Debtors' collection period	45 days
Creditors' payment period	55 days
Debt to equity	40%
Dividend yield	6%
Dividend cover	3 times

Comparator's financial statements for the year to 30 September 20X3 are set out below:

Profit and loss account	£000
Turnover	2,425
Cost of sales	(1,870)
Gross profit	555
Other operating expenses	(215)
Operating profit	340
Interest payable	(34)
Exceptional item (note (ii))	(120)
Profit before taxation	186
Taxation	(90)
Profit for the year	96

Movement on profit and loss account reserve

Retained profit b/f	179
Profit for the year	96
Dividends (interim 60, final 30)	(90)
Retained profit c/f	185

Balance sheet	£000	£000
Fixed assets (note (i))		540
Current Assets		
Stock	275	
Debtors	320	
Bank	nil	
	595	
Creditors: amounts falling due within one year		
Bank overdraft	65	
Trade creditors	350	
Taxation	85	
	(500)	95
Creditors: amounts falling due after more than one year		
8% loan notes		(300)
		335
Share capital and reserves		
Ordinary shares (25p each)		150
Profit and loss account reserve		185
		335

Notes

(i)   The details of the fixed assets are:

	Cost	Accumulated depreciation	Net book value
	£000	£000	£000
At 30 September 20X3	3,600	3,060	540

(ii)   The exceptional item relates to losses on the sale of a batch of computers that had become worthless due to improvements in microchip design.

(iii) The market price of Comparator's shares throughout the year averaged £6.00 each.

Required:

(a) Explain the problems that are inherent when ratios are used to assess a company's financial performance.

Your answer should consider any additional problems that may be encountered when using interfirm comparison services such as that used by Comparator.

(7 marks)

(b) Calculate the ratios for Comparator equivalent to those provided by the interfirm comparison service. **(6 marks)**

(c) Write a report analysing the financial performance of Comparator based on a comparison with the sector averages. **(12 marks)**

(Total: 25 marks)

56   RYTETREND PLC

Rytetrend plc is a retailer of electrical goods. Extracts from the company's financial statements are set out below:

Profit and loss account for the year ended 31 March:

	20X3		20X2	
	£000	£000	£000	£000
Turnover		31,800		23,500
Cost of sales		(22,500)		(16,000)
Gross profit		9,300		7,500
Other operating expenses		(5,440)		(4,600)
Operating profit		3,860		2,900
Interest payable – loan notes	(260)		(500)	
overdraft	(200)	(460)	nil	(500)
Profit before taxation		3,400		2,400
Taxation		(1,000)		(800)
Profit for the year		2,400		1,600
Movement on profit and loss account reserve				
Opening balance		5,880		4,680
Profit for the year		2,400		1,600
Dividends		(600)		(400)
Closing balance		7,680		5,880

Balance sheets as at 31 March:

	20X3		20X2	
	£000	£000	£000	£000
Fixed assets (note (i))		24,500		17,300
Current assets				
Stock	2,650		3,270	
Debtors	1,100		1,950	
Bank	nil		400	
	3,750		5,620	
Creditors: amounts falling due within one year				
Bank overdraft	1,050		nil	
Trade creditors	3,300		2,260	
Taxation	720		630	
Warranty provision (note (ii))	500		150	
	(5,570)	(1,820)	(3,040)	2,580
Creditors: amounts falling due after more than one year				
10% loan notes		(nil)		(4,000)
6% loan notes		(2,000)		(nil)
		20,680		15,880
Share capital and reserves				
Ordinary capital (£1 shares)		11,500		10,000
Share premium		1,500		nil
Profit and loss reserve		7,680		5,880
		20,680		15,880

Notes

(i)   The details of the fixed assets are:

	Cost	Accumulated depreciation	Net book value
	£000	£000	£000
At 31 March 20X2	27,500	10,200	17,300
At 31 March 20X3	37,250	12,750	24,500

During the year there was a major refurbishment of display equipment. Old equipment that had cost £6 million in September 19W8 was replaced with new equipment at a gross cost of £8 million. The equipment manufacturer had allowed Rytetrend plc a trade in allowance of £500,000 on the old display equipment. In addition to this Rytetrend plc used its own staff to install the new equipment. The value of staff time spent on the installation has been costed at £300,000, but this has not been included in the cost of the asset. All staff costs have been included in operating expenses. All display equipment held at the end of the financial year is depreciated at 20% on its cost. No equipment is more than five years old.

(ii)   Operating expenses contain a charge of £580,000 for the cost of warranties on the goods sold by Rytetrend plc. The company makes a warranty provision when it sells its products and cash payments for warranty claims are deducted from the provision as they are settled.

Required:

(a)   Prepare a cash flow statement for Rytetrend plc for the year ended 31 March 20X3.

(12 marks)

(b)   Write a report briefly analysing the operating performance and financial position of Rytetrend plc for the years ended 31 March 20X2 and 20X3.   **(13 marks)**

Your report should be supported by appropriate ratios.   **(Total: 25 marks)**

57   BIGWOOD

Bigwood, a public company, is a high street retailer that sells clothing and food. The managing director is very disappointed with the current year's results. The company expanded its operations and commissioned a famous designer to restyle its clothing products. This has led to increased turnover in both retail lines, yet overall profits are down.

Details of the financial statements for the two years to 30 September 20X4 are shown below.

Profit and loss account.	Year to 30 September 20X4		Year to 30 September 20X3	
	£000	£000	£000	£000
Turnover – clothing	16,000		15,600	
– food	7,000	23,000	4,000	19,600
Cost of sales– clothing	14,500		12,700	
– food	4,750	(19,250)	3,000	(15,700)
Gross profit		3,750		3,900
Other operating expenses		(2,750)		(1,900)
Operating profit		1,000		2,000
Interest expense		(300)		(80)
Profit before taxation		700		1,920
Taxation		(250)		(520)
Profit for the year		450		1,400

Balance sheets as at:	Year to 30 September 20X4		Year to 30 September 20X3	
	£000	£000	£000	£000
Fixed assets at cost		17,000		9,500
Accumulated depreciation		(5,000)		(3,000)
		12,000		6,500
Current assets				
Stock – clothing	2,700		1,360	
– food	200		140	
Debtors	100		50	
Bank	Nil		450	
	3,000		2,000	
Creditors: amounts falling due within one year				
Bank overdraft	930		nil	
Trade creditors	3,100		2,150	
Taxation	220		450	
	(4,250)	(1,250)	(2,600)	(600)
Creditors: amounts falling due after more than one year				
Long-term loans		(3,000)		(1,000)
		7,750		4,900
Share capital and reserves				
Issued ordinary capital (£1 shares)		5,000		3,000
Share premium		1,000		Nil
Profit and loss account		1,750		1,900
		7,750		4,900

The following information is relevant:

(i)   The increase in fixed assets was due to the acquisition of five new stores and the refurbishment of some existing stores. The carrying value of fixtures scrapped at the refurbished stores was £1.2 million; they had originally cost £3 million. Bigwood did not receive any scrap proceeds for the fixtures, but did incur costs of £50,000 to remove and dispose of them. The losses on the refurbishment have been charged to operating expenses. Depreciation is charged to cost of sales apportioned in relation to floor area (see below).

(ii) The floor sales areas (in square metres) were:

	30 September 20X4	30 September 20X3
Clothing	48,000	35,000
Food	6,000	5,000
	54,000	40,000

(iii) The share price of Bigwood averaged £6.00 during the year to 30 September 20X3, but was only £3.00 at 30 September 20X4. The company only pays an interim dividend which was £600,000 for both years.

(iv) The following ratios have been calculated:

	20X4	20X3
Return on capital employed	9.3%	33.9%
Net assets turnover	2.1 times	3.3 times
Gross profit margin		
– clothing	9.4%	18.6%
– food	32.1%	25%
Net profit (after tax) margin	2.0%	7.1%
Current ratio	0.71:1	0.77:1
Stock holding period		
– clothing	68 days	39 days
– food	15 days	17 days
Creditor payment period	59 days	50 days
Gearing	28%	17%
Interest cover	3.3 times	25 times

Required:

(a) Prepare, using the indirect method, a cash flow statement for Bigwood for the year to 30 September 20X4 **(12 marks)**

Note: The analysis and movement of net debt are not required.

(b) Write a report analysing the financial performance and financial position of Bigwood for the two years ended 30 September 20X4. **(13 marks)**

Your report should utilise the above ratios and the information in your cash flow statement. It should refer to the relative performance of the clothing and food sales and be supported by any further ratios you consider appropriate.

(Total: 25 marks)

58 MINSTER

Minster is a publicly listed company. Details of its financial statements for the year ended 30 September 20X6, together with a comparative balance sheet, are:

Balance sheet at	30 September 20X6		30 September 20X5	
	£000	£000	£000	£000
Fixed assets (note(i))				
Tangible		1,280		940
Software		135		Nil
Investments at fair value through profit and loss		150		125
		1,565		1,065

Current assets				
Stock	480		510	
Trade debtors	270		380	
Amounts due from long-term contracts	80		55	
Bank	Nil		35	
	830		980	
Creditors: amounts falling due within one year				
Bank overdraft	25		40	
Trade creditors	350		555	
Taxation	60		50	
	(435)		(645)	
Net current assets		395		335
Creditors: amounts falling due after more than one year				
9% loan note		(120)		Nil
Provisions for liabilities				
Environmental provision	162		Nil	
Deferred tax	18	(180)	25	(25)
Net assets		1,660		1,375
Share capital and reserves				
Equity shares of 25 pence each		500		300
Reserves				
Share premium (note (ii))	150		85	
Revaluation reserve	60		25	
Profit and loss account	950	1,160	965	1,075
		1,660		1,375

Profit and loss account for the year ended 30 September 20X6

Turnover	1,397
Cost of sales	(1,110)
Gross profit	287
Operating expenses	(125)
	162
Investment income and gain on investments	20
Finance costs (note (i))	(40)
Profit before tax	142
Tax	(57)
Profit for the year	85

The following supporting information is available:

(i) Included in tangible fixed assets is a coal mine and related plant that Minster purchased on 1 October 20X5. Legislation requires that in ten years' time (the estimated life of the mine) Minster will have to landscape the area affected by the mining. The future cost of this has been estimated and discounted at a rate of 8% to a present value of £150,000. This cost has been included in the carrying amount of the mine and, together with the unwinding of the discount, has also been treated as a provision. The unwinding of the discount is included within finance costs in the profit and loss account.

Other land was revalued (upward) by £35,000 during the year.

Depreciation of tangible fixed assets for the year was £255,000.

There were no disposals of tangible fixed assets during the year.

The software was purchased on 1 April 20X6 for £180,000.

The market value of the investments had increased during the year by £15,000. There have been no sales of these investments during the year.

(ii) On 1 April 20X6 there was a bonus (scrip) issue of ordinary shares of one for every four held utilising the share premium reserve. A further cash share issue was made on 1 June 20X6. No shares were redeemed during the year.

(iii) A dividend of 5 pence per share was paid on 1 July 20X6.

Required:

(a) Prepare a cash flow statement for Minster for the year to 30 September 20X6 in accordance with FRS 1 *Cash flow statements.*

Note: You are not required to prepare a reconciliation of net cash flow to movement in net debt or an analysis of changes in net debt. **(15 marks)**

(b) Comment on the financial performance and position of Minster as revealed by the above financial statements and your cash flow statement. **(10 marks)**

(Total: 25 marks)

Online question assistance

59 PENDANT LTD

Pendant Ltd is a small family owned business. A client of yours has been asked to provide a line of credit for Pendant Ltd. The client has provided you with the balance sheets and some supporting information for Pendant Ltd for the years to 31 March 20X0 and 20X1. The client wants an opinion on Pendant Ltd's financial position.

Pendant Ltd – Balance sheet as at	31 March 20X1		31 March 20X0	
Fixed assets	£000	£000	£000	£000
Intangible				
Software (in development)		300		100
Tangible assets		1,290		1,120
		———		———
		1,590		1,220
Current assets				
Stock	490		540	
Debtors	787		584	
Investments – Government securities	30		180	
Bank	nil		125	
	———		———	
	1,307		1,429	

	31 March 20X1		31 March 20X0	
	£000	£000	£000	£000
Creditors: amounts falling due within one year				
Creditors	663		602	
Bank overdraft	45		nil	
Taxation	83		213	
Finance lease obligations	70		30	
	——		——	
	(861)		(845)	
	——		——	
Net current assets		446		584
Creditors: amounts falling due after more than one year				
Finance lease obligations		(290)		(60)
Provisions for liabilities				
Deferred tax		(12)		(172)
		——		——
Net assets		1,734		1,572
		——		——
Share capital and reserves				
Ordinary shares of £1 each		500		400
Reserves				
Share premium	150		80	
Profit and loss account	1,084	1,234	1,092	1,172
	——	——	——	——
		1,734		1,572
		——		——

The following supporting information is available:

(i) Details relating to the tangible fixed assets are (in £000s):

	31 March 20X1			31 March 20X0		
	Cost	Depreciation	NBV	Cost	Depreciation	NBV
Freehold land and buildings	Nil	Nil	Nil	700	120	580
Leasehold land and buildings	500	20	480	Nil	Nil	Nil
Purchased plant	550	250	300	620	200	420
Plant on finance lease	650	140	510	150	30	120
			——			——
			1,290			1,120
			——			——

On 1 April 20X0 Pendant Ltd sold its freehold property for £800,000. Pendant then acquired another property on a 25-year lease at a capital cost of £500,000.

The total amount of payments made in the year to 31 March 20X1 in respect of finance leases was £265,000, of which £35,000 was interest costs. Interest costs for the bank overdraft were £10,000.

During the same period 'purchased' plant which had originally cost £200,000 was sold for £75,000 giving a profit of £18,000.

(ii)   The total tax charge (including deferred tax) in the profit and loss account for the year to 31 March 20X1 was £31,000.

(iii) During the year some Government securities, which are shown at cost in the balance sheet, were sold at a profit of £27,000. This profit was credited to the profit and loss account, as was £15,000 of income received from the securities. No other Government securities were traded during the year.

(iv)   Pendant Ltd paid an interim dividend during the year to 31 March 20X1 of £150,000.

Required:

(a)   As far as the information permits, prepare a cash flow statement for Pendant Ltd for the year to 31 March 20X1 in accordance with FRS 1 *Cash Flow Statements)*

(20 marks)

Note: You are not required to prepare a reconciliation of net cash flow to movement in net debt or an analysis of changes in net debt.

(b)   Identify the important areas that you would draw your client's attention to based on the information in the question and the cash flow statement prepared in (a). You are not required to calculate ratios.   **(5 marks)**

(Total: 25 marks)

60   CHARMER

The summarised financial statements of Charmer plc for the year to 30 September 20X1, together with a comparative balance sheet, are:

Profit and loss account	£000
Turnover	7,482
Cost of sales	(4,284)
Gross profit	3,198
Operating expenses	(1,479)
Interest payable	(260)
Investment income	120
Profit before tax	1,579
Taxation	(520)
Profit for the year	1,059

Movement on profit and loss account reserve

	£000
Opening balance	92
Profit for the year	1,059
Dividends	(180)
Closing balance	971

Balance sheet as at	30 September 20X1			30 September 20X0		
Fixed assets:	Cost/ valuation	Deprecia-tion	NBV	Cost/ valuation	Deprecia-tion	NBV
	£000	£000	£000	£000	£000	£000
Tangible:						
Land and buildings	2,000	760	1,240	1,800	680	1,120
Plant	1,568	464	1,104	1,220	432	788
	3,568	1,224	2,344	3,020	1,112	1,908
Investment			690			nil
			3,034			1,908
Current assets:						
Stock		1,046			785	
Trade debtors		935			824	
Short-term treasury bills		120			50	
Bank		Nil			122	
		2,101			1,781	
Creditors: amounts falling due within one year:						
Trade creditors		644			760	
Accrued interest		40			25	
Provision for negligence claim		Nil			120	
Taxation		480			367	
Government grants		100			125	
Overdraft		136			Nil	
		(1,400)			(1,397)	
Net current assets			701			384

Creditors: amounts falling due after more than one year:

Deferred tax	439		400	
Government grants	275		200	
10% Convertible loan stock	nil		400	
		(714)		(1,000)
		3,021		1,292

Share capital and reserves:

Ordinary shares of £1 each		1,400		1,000
Reserves:				
Share premium	460		160	
Revaluation reserve	190		40	
Profit and loss account	971		92	
		1,621		292
		3,021		1,292

The following information is relevant:

(i) **Fixed assets**

On 1 October 20X0 Charmer plc recorded an increase in the value of its land of £150,000.

During the year an item of plant that had cost £500,000 and had accumulated depreciation of £244,000 was sold at a loss (included in cost of sales) of £86,000 on its carrying value.

(ii) **Government grant**

A credit of £125,000 for the current year's amortisation of government grants has been included in cost of sales.

(iii) **Share capital and loan stocks**

The increase in the share capital during the year was due to the following events:

– On 1 January 20X1 there was a bonus issue (out of the share premium account) of one bonus share for every 10 shares held;

– On 1 April 20X1 the 10% convertible loan stock holders exercised their right to convert to ordinary shares. The terms of conversion were 25 ordinary shares of £1 each for each £100 of 10% convertible loan stock; and

– The remaining increase in the ordinary shares was due to a stock market placement of shares for cash on 12 August 20X1.

(iv) **Provision for negligence claim:**

In June 20X1 Charmer plc made an out of court settlement of a negligence claim brought about by a former employee. The dispute had been in progress for two years and Charmer plc had made provisions for the potential liability in each of the two previous years. The unprovided amount of the claim at the time of settlement was £30,000 and this was charged to operating expenses.

Required:

Prepare a cash flow statement for Charmer plc for the year to 30 September 20X1 in accordance with FRS 1 *Cash Flow Statements.*

Note: You are NOT required to prepare an analysis of, or reconciliation of the movement in, net debt.

(25 marks)

61   PLANTER

The following information relates to Planter, a small private company. It consists of an opening balance sheet as at 1 April 20X3 and a listing of the company's ledger accounts at 31 March 20X4 after the draft operating profit (of £15,600) has been calculated.

Planter – Balance sheet as at 1 April 20X3

Fixed assets	£	£
Land and buildings (at valuation of £49,200 less accumulated depreciation of £5,000)		44,200
Plant (at cost of £70,000 less accumulated depreciation of £22,500)		47,500
Investments at cost		16,900
		108,600
Current assets		
Stock	57,400	
Debtors	28,600	
Bank	1,200	
	87,200	
Creditors: amounts falling due within one year		
Trade creditors	31,400	
Taxation	8,900	
	(40,300)	
Net current assets		46,900
Creditors: amounts falling due after more than one year		
8% Loan notes		(43,200)
		112,300

Share capital and reserves		
Ordinary shares of £1 each		25,000
Reserves		
Share premium	5,000	
Revaluation reserve	12,000	
Profit and loss account	70,300	87,300
		112,300

Ledger account listings at 31 March 20X4

	Dr	Cr
	£	£
Ordinary shares of £1 each		50,000
Share premium		8,000
Profit and loss reserve – 1 April 20X3		70,300
Operating profit – year to 31 March 20X4		15,600
Revaluation reserve		18,000
8% Loan notes		39,800
Trade creditors		26,700
Accrued loan interest		300
Taxation	1,100	
Land and buildings at valuation	62,300	
Plant at cost	84,600	
Buildings – accumulated depreciation 31 March 20X4		6,800
Plant – accumulated depreciation 31 March 20X4		37,600
Investments at cost	8,200	
Trade debtors	50,400	
Stock – 31 March 20X4	43,300	
Bank		1,900
Investment income		400
Profit on sale of investments		2,300
Loan interest	1,700	
Ordinary dividend	26,100	
	277,700	277,700

Notes

(i) There were no disposals of land and buildings during the year. The increase in the revaluation reserve was entirely due to the revaluation of the company's land.

(ii) Plant with a net book value of £12,000 (cost £23,500) was sold during the year for £7,800. The loss on sale has been included in the profit before interest and tax.

(iii) Investments with a cost of £8,700 were sold during the year for £11,000. There were no further purchases of investments. These investments are all in unquoted companies and therefore their fair value cannot be reliably estimated.

(iv) On 10 October 20X3 a bonus issue of 1 for 10 ordinary shares was made utilising the share premium account. The remainder of the increase in ordinary shares was due to an issue for cash on 30 October 20X3.

(v) The balance on the taxation account is after settlement of the provision made for the year to 31 March 20X3. A provision for the current year has not yet been made.

Required:

From the above information, prepare a cash flow statement using the indirect method for Planter in accordance – with FRS 1 *Cash Flow Statements* for the year to 31 March 20X4.

(25 marks)

Note: The reconciliation of cash flows to the movement in net debt and analysis thereof is not required.

62 CASINO

(a) Casino is a private company. Details of its balance sheets as at 31 March 20X5 and 20X4 are shown below together with other relevant information:

Balance sheet as at	31 March 20X5		31 March 20X4	
Fixed assets (note (i))	£m	£m	£m	£m
Intangible assets		400		510
Tangible assets		880		760
		1,280		1,270
Current assets				
Stock	350		420	
Debtors	808		372	
Interest receivable	5		3	
Short-term deposits	32		120	
Bank	15		75	
	1,210		990	
Creditors: amounts falling due within one year				
Creditors	530		515	
Bank overdraft	125		Nil	
Taxation	15		110	
	(670)		(625)	
Net current assets		540		365

Creditors: amounts falling due after more than one year		
12% fixed interest loan note	Nil	(150)
8% variable rate loan note	(160)	Nil
Provisions for liabilities		
Deferred tax	(90)	(75)
Net assets	1,570	1,410

Capital and reserves				
Ordinary shares of £1 each		300		200
Reserves				
Share premium	60		Nil	
Revaluation reserve	112		45	
Profit and loss account	1,098	1,270	1,165	1,210
		1,570		1,410

The following supporting information is available:

(i) Details relating to the fixed assets are:

Tangible	31 March 20X5			31 March 20X4		
	Cost/ Valuation	Depreci- ation	Carrying value	Cost/ Valuation	Depreci- ation	Carrying value
	£m	£m	£m	£m	£m	£m
Land and buildings	600	12	588	500	80	420
Plant	440	148	292	445	105	340
			880			760

Casino revalued the carrying value of its land and buildings by an increase of £70 million on 1 April 20X4. On 31 March 20X5 Casino transferred £3 million from the revaluation reserve to the profit and loss account reserve representing the realisation of the revaluation reserve due to the depreciation of buildings. During the year Casino acquired new plant at a cost of £60 million and sold some old plant for £15 million at a loss of £12 million.

There were no acquisitions or disposals of intangible assets.

(ii) The following extract is from the draft profit and loss account for the year to 31 March 20X5:

	£m	£m
Operating loss		(32)
Interest receivable		12
Finance costs		(24)
Loss before tax		(44)
Corporation tax repayment claim	14	
Deferred tax charge	(15)	(1)
Loss for the period		(45)
The finance costs are made up of:		
Interest expense		(18)
Penalty costs of variable rate loan		(6)

(iii)   Dividends of £25 million were paid during the year.

Required:

As far as the information permits, prepare a cash flow statement for Casino for the year to 31 March 20X5 in accordance with FRS 1 *Cash Flow Statements*.

Note: You are not required to prepare a reconciliation of net cash flow to movement in net debt or an analysis of changes in net debt.   **(20 marks)**

(b)   In recent years many analysts have commented on a growing disillusionment with the usefulness and reliability of the information contained in some companies' profit and loss accounts.

Required:

Discuss the extent to which a company's cash flow statement may be more useful and reliable than its profit and loss account.   **(5 marks)**

(Total: 25 marks)

63   TABBA

The following draft financial statements relate to Tabba, a private company.

Balance sheets as at:	30 September 20X5		30 September 20X4	
	£000	£000	£000	£000
Tangible fixed assets (note (ii))		10,600		15,800
Current assets				
Stocks	2,550		1,850	
Debtors	3,100		2,600	
Insurance claim (note (iii))	1,500		1,200	
Bank	850		nil	
	_____		_____	
	8,000		5,650	
Creditors: amounts falling due within one year				
Bank overdraft	nil		550	
Trade creditors	4,050		2,950	
Government grants (note (ii))	600		400	
Finance lease obligations (note (ii))	900		800	
Taxation	100		1,200	
	_____		_____	
	(5,650)		(5,900)	
	_____		_____	
Net current assets/(liabilities)		2,350		(250)
Creditors: amounts falling due after more than one year				
Government grants (note (ii))	1,400		900	
Finance lease obligations (note (ii))	2,000		1,700	
6% loan notes	800		nil	
10% loan notes	nil	(4,200)	4,000	(6,600)
	_____		_____	
Provisions for liabilities				
Deferred tax		(200)		(500)
		_____		_____

Balance sheets as at:	*30 September 20X5*		*30 September 20X4*	
	£000	£000	£000	£000
		8,550		8,450
		———		———
Capital and reserves				
Ordinary shares (£1 each)		6,000		6,000
Reserves				
Revaluation (note (ii))	nil		1,600	
Profit and loss reserve	2,550	2,550	850	2,450
	———	———	———	———
		8,550		8,450
		———		———

The following information is relevant:

(i)   Profit and loss account extract for the year ended 30 September 20X5:

	£000
Operating profit before interest and tax	270
Interest expense	(260)
Interest receivable	40
	———
Profit before tax	50
Net tax credit	50
	———
Profit after tax	100
	———

Note: The interest expense includes finance lease interest.

(II)   The details of the tangible fixed assets are:

	Cost	Accumulated depreciation	Carrying value
	£000	£000	£000
At 30 September 20X4	20,200	4,400	15,800
At 30 September 20X5	16,000	5,400	10,600

During the year Tabba sold its factory for its fair value £12 million and agreed to rent it back, under an operating lease, for a period of five years at £1 million per annum. At the date of sale it had a carrying value of £7.4 million based on a previous revaluation of £8.6 million less depreciation of £1.2 million since the revaluation. The profit on the sale of the factory has been included in operating profit. The surplus on the revaluation reserve related entirely to the factory. No other disposals of fixed assets were made during the year.

Plant acquired under finance leases during the year was £1.5 million. Other purchases of plant during the year qualified for government grants of £950,000 received in the year.

Amortisation of government grants has been credited to cost of sales.

(iii)   The insurance claim relates to flood damage to the company's stocks which occurred in September 20X4. The original estimate has been revised during the year after negotiations with the insurance company. The claim is expected to be settled in the near future.

Required:

(a) Prepare a cash flow statement using the indirect method for Tabba in accordance with FRS 1 *Cash flow statements* for the year ended 30 September 20X5. **(17 marks)**

Note: The reconciliation of cash flows to the movement in net debt and analysis thereof is not required.

(b) Using the information in the question and your cash flow statement, comment on the change in the financial position of Tabba during the year ended 30 September 20X5.Note: You are not required to calculate any ratios. **(8 marks)**

(Total: 25 marks)

64 PINTO

Pinto is a publicly listed company. The following financial statements of Pinto are available:

Profit and loss account for the year ended 31 March 2008	**£000**
Turnover	5,740
Cost of sales	(4,840)
Gross profit	900
Distribution costs	(120)
Administrative expenses (note (ii))	(350)
Operating profit	430
Income from and gains on investment property	60
Finance costs	(50)
Profit before tax	440
Tax	(160)
Profit for the year	280

Balance sheets as at	**31 March 2008**		**31 March 2007**	
	£000	**£000**	**£000**	**£000**
Fixed assets				
Tangible assets (note (i))		2,880		1,860
Investment property		420		400
		3,300		2,260
Current assets				
Stock	1,210		810	
Debtors	480		540	
Tax asset	nil		50	
Bank	10		nil	
	1,700		1,400	

Creditors: amounts falling due within one year				
Bank overdraft		nil		120
Creditors		1,410		1,050
Warranty provision (note (iv))		200		100
Taxation		150		nil
		(1,760)		(1,270)
Net current assets (liabilities)		(60)		130
Creditors: amounts falling due after more than one year				
6% loan notes (note (ii))		nil		(400)
Provisions for liabilities				
Deferred tax		(50)		(30)
		3,190		1,960
Capital and reserves				
Equity shares of 20 pence each (note (iii))		1,000		600
Share premium	600		nil	
Revaluation reserve (note (i))	150		50	
Profit and loss account	1,440	2,190	1,310	1,360
		3,190		1,960

The following supporting information is available:

(i)   The increase in the revaluation reserve is attributable to a revaluation of Pinto's property during the year.

An item of plant with a carrying amount of £240,000 was sold at a loss of £90,000 during the year. Depreciation of £280,000 was charged (to cost of sales) for tangible fixed assets the year ended 31 March 2008.

There were no purchases or sales of investment property during the year.

(ii)   The 6% loan notes were redeemed early incurring a penalty payment of £20 thousand which has been charged as an administrative expense in the profit and loss account.

(iii)   There was an issue of shares for cash on 1 October 2007. There were no bonus issues of shares during the year.

(iv)   Pinto gives a 12 month warranty on some of the products it sells. The amounts shown as warranty provision are an accurate assessment, based on past experience, of the amount of claims likely to be made in respect of warranties outstanding at each year end. Warranty costs are included in cost of sales.

(v)   A dividend of 3 pence per share was paid on 1 January 2008.

Required:

(a)   Prepare a cash flow statement for Pinto for the year to 31 March 2008 in accordance with FRS 1 *Cash Flow Statements.*   **(15 marks)**

(b)   Comment on the cash flow management of Pinto as revealed by the cash flow statement and the information provided by the above financial statements.

Note: ratio analysis is not required, and will not be awarded any marks.   **(10 marks)**

(Total: 25 marks)

65   HARBIN

Shown below are the recently issued (summarised) financial statements of Harbin, a listed company, for the year ended 30 September 2007, together with comparatives for 2006 and extracts from the Chief Executive's report that accompanied their issue.

Profit and loss account

	2007	2006
	£000	£000
Turnover	250,000	180,000
Cost of sales	(200,000)	(150,000)
Gross profit	50,000	30,000
Operating expenses	(26,000)	(22,000)
Finance costs	(8,000)	(Nil)
Profit before tax	16,000	8,000
Corporation tax (at 25%)	(4,000)	(2,000)
Profit for the period	12,000	6,000

Balance sheet

	2007	2006
Fixed assets		
Goodwill	10,000	Nil
Tangible fixed assets	210,000	90,000
	220,000	90,000
Current assets		
Stock	25,000	15,000
Debtors	13,000	8,000
Bank	Nil	14,000
	38,000	37,000

Creditors: amounts falling due within one year		
Bank overdraft	17,000	Nil
Trade creditors	23,000	13,000
Corporation tax payable	4,000	2,000
	(44,000)	(15,000)

Creditors: amounts falling due after more than one year		
8% loan notes	(100,000)	(Nil)
	114,000	112,000

Capital and reserves		
Equity shares of £1 each	100,000	100,000
Profit and loss account	14,000	12,000
	114,000	112,000

Extracts from the Chief Executive's report:

'Highlights of Harbin's performance for the year ended 30 September 2007:

an increase in turnover of 39%

gross profit margin up from 16.7% to 20%

a doubling of the profit for the period.

In response to the improved position the Board paid a dividend of 10 pence per share in September 2007 an increase of 25% on the previous year.'

You have also been provided with the following further information.

On 1 October 2006 Harbin purchased the whole of the net assets of Fatima (previously a privately owned entity) for £100 million. The contribution of the purchase to Harbin's results for the year ended 30 September 2007 was:

	£000
Turnover	70,000
Cost of sales	(40,000)
Gross profit	30,000
Operating expenses	(8,000)
Profit before tax	22,000

There were no disposals of fixed assets during the year.

The following ratios have been calculated for Harbin for the year ended 30 September 2006:

Return on year-end capital employed	7.1%
(profit before interest and tax over total assets less current liabilities)	
Net asset (equal to capital employed) turnover	1.6
Net profit (before tax) margin	4.4%
Current ratio	2.5
Closing stock holding period (in days)	37
Debtors' collection period (in days)	16
Creditors' payment period (based on cost of sales) (in days)	32
Gearing (debt over debt plus equity)	Nil

Required:

(a) Calculate ratios for Harbin for the year ended 30 September 2007 equivalent to those calculated for the year ended 30 September 2006 (showing your workings). **(8 marks)**

(b) Assess the financial performance and position of Harbin for the year ended 30 September 2007 compared to the previous year. Your answer should refer to the information in the Chief Executive's report and the impact of the purchase of the net assets of Fatima. **(17 marks)**

(Total: 25 marks)

66   GREENWOOD

Greenwood is a public listed company. During the year ended 31 March 2007 the directors decided to cease operations of one of its activities and put the assets of the operation up for sale (the discontinued activity has no associated liabilities). The directors have been advised that the cessation qualifies as a discontinued operation. In order to facilitate an assessment of the effects of the discontinuation, its operating results are shown separately and its operating assets have been revalued to their fair values and shown separately as current assets in the balance sheet at 31 March 2007.

Note: the profit and loss account figures down to the profit for the period from continuing operations are those of the continuing operations only.

Profit and loss accounts for the year ended 31 March:

	2007	2006
	£000	£000
Turnover	27,500	21,200
Cost of sales	(19,500)	(15,000)
Gross profit	8,000	6,200
Operating expenses	(2,900)	(2,450)
	5,100	3,750
Finance costs	(600)	(250)
Profit before taxation	4,500	3,500
Corporation tax	(1,000)	(800)
Profit for the period from continuing operations	3,500	2,700

Profit/(Loss) from discontinued operations	(1,500)	320
Profit for the period	2,000	3,020

	2007	2006
	£000	£000
Analysis of discontinued operations:		
Turnover	7,500	9,000
Cost of sales	(8,500)	(8,000)
Gross profit/(loss)	(1,000)	1,000
Operating expenses	(400)	(550)
Profit/(loss) before tax	(1,400)	450
Tax (expense)/relief	300	(130)
	(1,100)	320
Loss on measurement to fair value of discontinued assets	(500)	–
Tax relief on discontinued assets	100	–
Profit/(Loss) from discontinued operations	(1,500)	320

Balance sheets as at 31 March

	2007		2006	
	£000	£000	£000	£000
Fixed assets		17,500		17,600
Current assets				
Stock	1,500		1,350	
Trade debtors	2,000		2,300	
Bank	Nil		50	
Assets of discontinued operation	6,000		Nil	
	9,500		3,700	
Creditors: amounts falling due within one year				
Bank overdraft	1,150		Nil	
Trade creditors	2,400		2,800	
Taxation	950		1,000	
	(4,500)		(3,800)	
Net current assets/(liabilities)		5,000		(100)

Creditors: amounts falling due after more than one year			
5% loan notes	(8,000)		(5,000)
	14,500		12,500
Capital and reserves			
Equity shares of £1 each	10,000		10,000
Profit and loss account reserve	4,500		2,500
	14,500		12,500

Note: the carrying amount of the assets of the discontinued operation at 31 March 2006 was £6.3 million.

Required:

Analyse the financial performance and position of Greenwood for the two years ended 31 March 2007.

Note: Your analysis should be supported by appropriate ratios (up to 10 marks available) and refer to the effects of the discontinued operation.

(Total: 25 marks)

67 VICTULAR

Victular is a public company that would like to acquire (100% of) a suitable private company. It has obtained the following draft financial statements for two companies, Grappa and Merlot. They operate in the same industry and their managements have indicated that they would be receptive to a takeover.

Profit and loss accounts for the year ended 30 September 2008

		Grappa		Merlot
	£000	£000	£000	£000
Turnover		12,000		20,500
Cost of sales		(10,500)		(18,000)
Gross profit		1,500		2,500
Operating expenses		(240)		(500)
Operating profit		1,260		2,000
Finance costs – loan		(210)		(300)
– overdraft		Nil		(10)
– lease		Nil		(290)
Profit before tax		1,050		1,400
Taxation		(150)		(400)
Profit for the year		900		1,000
Note: dividends paid during the year		250		700

Balance sheets as at 30 September 2008

Fixed assets

Freehold factory (note (i))		4,400		Nil
Owned plant (note (ii))		5,000		2,200
Leased plant (note (ii))		Nil		5,300
		9,400		7,500

Current assets

Stock	2,000			3,600	
Trade debtors	2,400			3,700	
Bank	600			Nil	
	5,000			7,300	

Creditors: amounts falling due within one year

Bank overdraft	Nil			1,200	
Trade creditors	3,100			3,800	
Government grants	400			Nil	
Finance lease obligations (note (iii))	Nil			500	
Taxation	600			200	
	(4,100)			(5,700)	

Net current assets		900		1,600
Total assets less current liabilities		10,300		9,100

Creditors: amounts falling due after more than one year

Finance lease obligations (note (iii))	Nil			3,200	
7% loan notes	3,000			Nil	
10% loan notes	Nil			3,000	
Deferred tax	600			100	
Government grants	1,200	(4,800)		Nil	(6,300)
		5,500			2,800

Capital and reserves

Equity shares of £1 each		2,000			2,000
Property revaluation reserve	900			Nil	
Profit and loss account	2,600	3,500		800	800
		5,500			2,800

Notes

(i) Both companies operate from similar premises.

(ii)   Additional details of the two companies' plant are:

	Grappa £000	Merlot £000
Owned plant – cost	8,000	10,000
Leased plant – original fair value	Nil	7,500

There were no disposals of plant during the year by either company.

(iii)   The interest rate implicit within Merlot's finance leases is 7.5% per annum. For the purpose of calculating ROCE and gearing, **all** finance lease obligations are treated as long-term interest bearing borrowings.

(iv)   The following ratios have been calculated for Grappa and can be taken to be correct:

Return on year end capital employed (ROCE)	14.8%
(capital employed taken as shareholders' funds plus long-term interest bearing borrowings – see note (iii) above)	
Pre-tax return on equity (ROE)	19.1%
Net asset (total assets less current liabilities) turnover	1.2 times
Gross profit margin	12.5%
Operating profit margin	10.5%
Current ratio	1.2:1
Closing stock holding period	70 days
Trade debtors' collection period	73 days
Trade creditors' payment period (using cost of sales)	108 days
Gearing (see note (iii) above)	35·3%
Interest cover	6 times
Dividend cover	3.6 times

Required:

(a)   Calculate for Merlot the ratios equivalent to all those given for Grappa above.

(8 marks)

(b)   Assess the relative performance and financial position of Grappa and Merlot for the year ended 30 September 2008 to inform the directors of Victular in their acquisition decision.   **(12 marks)**

(c)   Explain the limitations of ratio analysis and any further information that may be useful to the directors of Victular when making an acquisition decision.   **(5 marks)**

(Total: 25 marks)

68   COALTOWN

> *Timed question with Online tutor debrief*

Coaltown is a wholesaler and retailer of office furniture. Extracts from the company's financial statements are set out below:

Profit and loss account for the year ended

	31 March 2009		31 March 2008	
	$'000	$'000	$'000	$'000
Turnover – cash	12,800		26,500	
– credit	53,000	65,800	28,500	55,000
Cost of sales		(43,800)		(33,000)
Gross profit		22,000		22,000
Operating expenses		(11,200)		(6,920)
Finance costs – loan notes	(380)		(180)	
– overdraft	(220)	(600)	nil	(180)
Profit before tax		10,200		14,900
Tax		(3,200)		(4,400)
Profit for the year		7,000		10,500

Statement of movements in share capital and reserves for the year ended 31 March 2009:

	$'000	$'000	$'000	$'000	$'000
	Equity shares	Share premium	Revaluation reserve	Profit and loss account	Total
Balances b/f	8,000	500	2,500	15,800	26,800
Share issue	8,600	4,300			12,900
Revaluation of property			5,000		5,000
Profit for period				7,000	7,000
Dividends paid				(4,000)	(4,000)
Balances c/f	16,600	4,800	7,500	18,800	47,700

Balance sheets as at 31 March:

	2009		2009	
	$'000	$'000	$'000	$'000
Fixed assets (see note)				
Cost		93,500		80,000
Accumulated depreciation		(43,000)		(48,000)
		50,500		32,000
Current assets				
Stock	5,200		4,400	
Debtors	7,800		2,800	
Bank	nil		700	
Total assets	13,000		7,900	
Creditors: amounts falling due within one year				
Bank overdraft	3,600		nil	
Trade creditors	4,200		4,500	
Taxation	3,000		5,300	
Warranty provision	1,000		300	
	(11,800)		(10,100)	
Net current assets (liabilities)		1,200		(2,200)
		51,700		29,800
Creditors: amounts falling due after more than one year				
10% loan notes		(4,000)		(3,000)
		47,700		26,800
Capital and reserves				
Equity shares of £1 each		16,600		8,000
Share premium		4,800		500
Revaluation reserve		7,500		2,500
Profit and loss account		18,800		15,800
		47,700		26,800

Note: Fixed assets

During the year the company redesigned its display areas in all of its outlets. The previous displays had cost £10 million and had been written down by £9 million. There was an unexpected cost of £500,000 for the removal and disposal of the old display areas.

Also during the year the company revalued the carrying amount of its property upwards by £5 million, the accumulated depreciation on these properties of £2 million was reset to zero.

All depreciation is charged to operating expenses.

Required:

(a)   Prepare a cash flow statement for Coaltown for the year ended 31 March 2009 in accordance with FRS 1 *Cash flow statements* using the indirect method.   (15 marks)

(b)   The directors of Coaltown are concerned at the deterioration in the company's bank balance and are surprised that the amount of gross profit has not increased for the year ended 31 March 2009. At the beginning of the current accounting period (i.e. on 1 April 2008), the company changed to importing its purchases from a foreign supplier because the trade prices quoted by the new supplier were consistently 10% below those of its previous supplier. However, the new supplier offered a shorter period of credit than the previous supplier (all purchases are on credit). In order to encourage higher sales, Coaltown increased its credit period to its customers, and some of the cost savings (on trade purchases) were passed on to customers by reducing selling prices on both cash and credit sales by 5% across all products.

Required:

(i)   Calculate the gross profit margin that you would have expected Coaltown to achieve for the year ended 31 March 2009 based on the selling and purchase price changes described by the directors;   **(2 marks)**

(ii)   Comment on the directors' surprise at the unchanged gross profit and suggest what other factors may have affected gross profit for the year ended 31 March 2009;

(4 marks)

(iii)   Applying the debtor collection and creditor payment periods for the year ended 31 March 2008 to the credit sales and purchases of the year ended 31 March 2009, calculate the effect this would have had on the company's bank balance at 31 March 2009 assuming sales and purchases would have remained unchanged.

(4 marks)

Note: the stock at 31 March 2008 was unchanged from that at 1 March 2007; assume 365 trading days.   **(Total: 25 marks)**

Calculate your allowed time, allocate the time to the separate parts.......................

Section 2

ANSWERS TO PRACTICE QUESTIONS

A CONCEPTUAL FRAMEWORK FOR FINANCIAL REPORTING

1   ASB STATEMENT *Walk in the footsteps of a top tutor*

> **Key answer tips**
>
> Parts (a) and (b) are very straightforward if you have done your work properly. The three adjustments required in part (c) focus on controversial areas. Remember that with compound financial instruments such as a convertible loan, the liability amount is calculated by discounting the cash flows at the rate applicable to a non-convertible loan; this rate will be higher than the rate on the convertible, because it does not include the 'equity sweetener'. The highlighted words are key phrases that markers are looking for.

(a)   The purpose of the Statement is to assist the various bodies and users that may be interested in the financial statements of an entity. It is there to assist the ASB itself, preparers, auditors and users of financial statements and any other party interested in the work of the Board. More specifically:

- the primary purpose is to assist the Board by providing a coherent frame of reference to be used in the development of new and the review of existing standards

- this should ensure standards (and other pronouncements) are developed consistently by reducing the need to debate fundamental issues (such as whether an item is an asset or a liability) each time a standard is produced

- the Statement will help preparers to understand the Board's approach and thus enable them to apply accounting standards more effectively. Additionally the Statement should help preparers in dealing with new or emerging issues which are, as yet, not covered by an accounting standard

- the above is also true of the work of the auditor; in particular the Statement can assist the auditor in determining whether the financial statements conform to accounting standards. The Statement contributes to the development of the true and fair concept which is of prime importance to the auditor.

It is important to realise that the Statement is not itself an accounting standard and thus cannot override the requirements of a specific standard. Because of this the Statement does not contain requirements on how financial statements should be prepared. Indeed, the Board recognises that there may be occasions where a particular accounting standard is in conflict with the Statement. In these cases the requirements of the standard should prevail. The Board believes that such conflicts will diminish over time as the development of new and the revision of existing standards will be guided by the Statement and the Statement itself may be revised based on the experience of working with it.

(b) **Definition of assets:**

The Statement defines assets as 'rights or other access to future economic benefits controlled by an entity as a result of past transactions or events'. The definition puts the emphasis on control rather than ownership. This is done so that the balance sheet reflects the substance of transactions rather than their legal form. This means that assets that are not legally owned by an entity, but over which the entity has the rights that are normally conveyed by ownership, are recognised as assets of the entity. Common examples of this would be finance leased assets and other contractual rights such as aircraft landing rights. An important aspect of control of assets is that it allows the entity to restrict the access of others to them. The reference to past events prevents assets that may arise in future from being recognised early.

Definition of liabilities:

The Statement defines liabilities as 'obligations of an entity to transfer economic benefits as a result of past transactions or events'. Many aspects of this definition are complementary (as a mirror image) to the definition of assets. However, the Statement stresses that the essential characteristic of a liability is that the entity has an obligation, which is interpreted as being unable to avoid the future outflow of resources to settle it. Such obligations are usually legally enforceable (by a binding contract or by statute), but obligations also arise where there is an expectation (by a third party) of an entity to assume responsibility for costs where there is no legal requirement to do so. Such obligations are referred to as constructive obligations (by FRS 12 *Provisions, contingent liabilities and contingent assets*). An example of this would be repairing or replacing faulty goods (beyond any warranty period) or incurring environmental costs (e.g. landscaping the site of a previous quarry) where there is no legal obligation to do so. Where entities do incur constructive obligations it is usually to maintain the goodwill and reputation of the entity. One area of difficulty is where entities cannot be sure whether an obligation exists or not, as it may depend upon a future uncertain event. These are more generally known as contingent liabilities.

Importance of the definitions of assets and liabilities:

The definitions of assets and liabilities are fundamental to the Statement. Apart from forming the obvious basis for the preparation of a balance sheet, they are also the two elements of the financial statements that are used to derive the other elements. Equity (ownership) interest is the residue of assets less liabilities. Gains and losses are changes in ownership interests, other than contributions from, and distributions to, the owners. In effect, a gain is an increase in an asset or a reduction of a liability whereas a loss is the reverse of this. Transactions with owners are excluded from the definitions of gains and losses. Gains and losses should be recognised when there is sufficient evidence of a new asset or liability (or an increase in an existing asset or liability) and they can be measured at a monetary amount with sufficient reliability.

Currently there is a great deal of concern over 'off balance sheet finance'. This is an aspect of what is commonly referred to as creative accounting. Many recent company failure scandals have been in part due to companies having often massive liabilities that have not been included on the balance sheet. Robust definitions, based on substance, of assets and liabilities in particular should ensure that only real assets are included on the balance sheet and all liabilities are also included. In contradiction to the above point, there have also been occasions where companies have included liabilities on their balance sheets where they do not meet the definition of liabilities in the Statement. Common examples of this are general provisions and accounting for future costs and losses (usually as part of the acquisition of a subsidiary). Companies have used these general provisions to smooth profits i.e. creating a provision when the company has a good year (in terms of profit) and releasing it to boost profits in a bad year. Providing for future costs and losses during an acquisition may effectively allow them to bypass the profit and loss account as they would become part of the goodwill figure.

(c)   (i)   Whilst it is acceptable to value the goodwill of £2.5 million of Trantor (the subsidiary) on the basis described in the question and include it in the consolidated balance sheet, the same treatment cannot be afforded to Peterlee's own goodwill. The calculation may indeed give a realistic value of £4 million for Peterlee's goodwill, and there may be no difference in nature between the goodwill of the two companies, but it must be realised that the goodwill of Peterlee is internal goodwill and accounting standards prohibit such goodwill appearing in the financial statements. The main basis of this conclusion is one of reliable measurement. The value of acquired (purchased) goodwill can be evidenced by the method described in the question (there are also other acceptable methods), but this method of valuation is not acceptable as a basis for recognising internal goodwill.

       (ii)   Accruing for future costs such as this landscaping on an annual basis may seem appropriate and used to be common practice, but is no longer acceptable. FRS 12 *Provisions, contingent liabilities and contingent assets* requires such costs to be accounted for in full as soon as they become unavoidable. The Standard says that the estimate of the future cost should be discounted to a present value (as in this example at £2 million). The accounting treatment is rather controversial; the cost should be included in the balance sheet as a provision (a credit entry/balance), but the debit is to the cost of the asset to give an initial carrying amount of £8 million. This has the effect of 'grossing up' the balance sheet by including the landscaping costs as both an asset and a liability. As the asset is depreciated on a systematic basis (£800,000 per annum assuming straight-line depreciation), the landscaping costs are charged to the profit and loss account over the life of the asset. As the discount is 'unwound' (and charged as a finance cost) this is added to the balance sheet provision such that, at the date when the liability is due to be settled, the provision is equal to the amount due (assuming estimates prove to be accurate).

       (iii) The directors' suggestion that the convertible loan should be recorded as a liability of the full £5 million is incorrect. The reason why a similar loan without the option to convert to equity shares (such that it must be redeemed by cash only) carries a higher interest rate is because of the value of the equity option that is contained within the issue proceeds of the £5 million. If the company performs well over the period of the loan, the value of its equity shares should rise and thus it would (probably) be beneficial for the loan note holders to opt for the equity share alternative. FRS 25 *Financial instruments: presentation* and FRS 26 *Financial instruments: measurement* require that the value of the option is to be treated as equity rather than debt. The calculation of value of the equity is as follows:

	£000
Year 1 400 × 0.91	364
Year 2 400 × 0.83	332
Year 3 (5,000 + 400) × 0.75	4,050
Present value of the cash flows at 10% = initial liability	4,746
Proceeds of issue	5,000
Equity (β)	254

	£000
The 20X6 finance charge in the P&L account is 10% × 4,746	475
The end-20X6 liability is 4,746 + 475 – interest paid (8% × 5,000)	4,821

2   ANGELINO

> **Key answer tips**
>
> Part (a) is a fairly standard discussion but in part (b) you must apply your knowledge to debt factoring, sale and leaseback and consignment stock. These are likely to be popular areas of the syllabus with the examiner.

(a)   Most forms of off balance sheet financing have the effect of what is, in substance, debt finance either not appearing on the balance sheet at all or being netted off against related assets such that it is not classified as debt. Common examples would be structuring a lease such that it fell to be treated as an operating lease when it has the characteristics of a finance lease, complex financial instruments classified as equity when they may have, at least in part, the substance of debt and 'controlled' entities having large borrowings (used to benefit the group as a whole), that are not consolidated because the financial structure avoids the entities meeting the definition of a subsidiary.

The main problem of off balance sheet finance is that it results in financial statements that do not faithfully represent the transactions and events that have taken place. This may mean that they show a 'true' view (in a legal sense), but not a 'fair' view. Reflecting the substance of transactions is an important qualitative characteristic of useful information (as described in the *Statement of principles for financial reporting* and FRS 5 *Reporting the substance of transactions*). Failure to reflect the commercial substance of transactions will mean that the financial statements lack reliability. A lack of reliability may mean that any decisions made on the basis of the information contained in financial statements are likely to be incorrect or, at best, sub-optimal.

The level of debt on a balance sheet is a direct contributor to the calculation of an entity's balance sheet gearing, which is considered as one of the most important financial ratios. It should be understood that, to a point, the use of debt financing is perfectly acceptable. Where balance sheet gearing is considered low, borrowing is relatively inexpensive, often tax efficient and can lead to higher returns to shareholders. However, when the level of borrowings becomes high, it increases risk in many ways. Off balance sheet financing may lead to a breach of loan covenants (a serious situation) if such debt were to be recognised on the balance sheet in accordance with its substance.

High gearing is a particular issue to equity investors. Equity (ordinary shares) is sometimes described as residual return capital. This description identifies the dangers (to equity holders) when an entity has high gearing. The dividend that the equity shareholders might expect is often based on the level of reported profits. The finance cost of debt acts as a reduction of the profits available for dividends. As the level of debt increases, higher interest rates are also usually payable to reflect the additional risk borne by the lender, thus the higher the debt the greater the finance charges and the lower the profit. Many off balance sheet finance schemes also disguise or hide the true finance cost which makes it difficult for equity investors to assess the amount of profits that will be needed to finance the debt and consequently how much profit will be available to equity investors. Furthermore, if the market believes or suspects an entity is involved in 'creative accounting' (and off balance sheet finance is a common example of this) it may adversely affect the entity's share price.

An entity's level of gearing will also influence any decision to provide further debt finance (loans) to the entity. Lenders will consider the nature and value of the assets that an entity owns which may be provided as security for the borrowings. The presence of existing debt will generally increase the risk of default of interest and capital repayments (on further borrowings) and existing lenders may have a prior charge on assets available as security. In simple terms if an entity has high borrowings, additional borrowing is more risky and consequently more expensive. A prospective lender to an entity that already has high borrowings, but which do not appear on the balance sheet, is likely to make the wrong decision. If the correct level of borrowings were apparent, either the lender would not make the loan at all (too high a lending risk) or, if it did make the loan, it would be on substantially different terms (e.g. charge a higher interest rate) so as to reflect the real risk of the loan.

Some forms of off balance sheet financing may specifically mislead suppliers that offer credit. It is a natural precaution that a prospective supplier will consider the balance sheet strength and liquidity ratios of the prospective customer. The existence of consignment stock may be particularly relevant to trade suppliers. Sometimes consignment stock, and its related current liabilities, are not recorded on the balance sheet as the wording of the purchase agreement may be such that the legal ownership of the goods remains with the supplier until specified events occur (often the onward sale of the goods). This means that other suppliers cannot accurately assess an entity's trade creditors and consequently the average creditor payment period, both of which are important determinants in deciding whether to grant credit.

(b) (i) Debt factoring is a common method of companies releasing the liquidity of their trade debtors. The accounting issue that needs to be decided is whether the trade debtors have been sold, or whether the income from the finance house for their 'sale' should be treated as a short-term loan. The main substance issue with this type of transaction is to identify which party bears the risks (i.e. of slow and non-payment by the customer) relating to the asset.

If the risk lies with the finance house (Omar), the trade debtors should be removed from the balance sheet (derecognised in accordance with FRS 5 and FRS 26). In this case it is clear that Angelino still bears the risk relating to slow and non-payment. The residual payment by Omar depends on how quickly the debtors are collected; the longer it takes, the less the residual payment (this imputes a finance cost). Any balance uncollected by Omar after six months will be refunded by Angelino which reflects the non-payment risk.

Thus the correct accounting treatment for this transaction is that the cash received from Omar (80% of the selected debtors) should be treated as a current liability (a short-term loan). A 'linked' presentation is not appropriate as Omar may be repaid from Angelino's other assets (say if the level of bad debts were very high). The difference between the gross trade debtors and the amount ultimately received from Omar (plus any amounts directly from the trade debtors themselves) should be charged to the profit and loss account. The classification of the charge is likely to be a mixture of administrative expenses (for Omar collecting debtors), finance expenses (reflecting the time taken to collect the debtors) and bad debt charges.

(ii) This is an example of a sale and leaseback of a property. Such transactions are part of normal commercial activity, often being used as a way to improve cash flow and liquidity. However, if an asset is sold at an amount that is different to its fair value there is likely to be an underlying reason for this. In this case it appears (based on the opinion of the auditor) that Finaid has paid Angelino £2 million more than the building is worth. No (unconnected) company would do this knowingly without there being some form of 'compensating' transaction. This sale is 'linked' to the five year rental agreement. The question indicates the rent too is not at a fair value, being £500,000 per annum (£1,300,000 − £800,000) above what a commercial rent for a similar building would be.

It now becomes clear that the excess purchase consideration of £2 million is an 'in substance' loan (rather than sales proceeds − the legal form) which is being repaid through the excess (£500,000 per annum) of the rentals. Although this is a sale and leaseback transaction, as the building is freehold and has an estimated remaining life (20 years) that is much longer than the 5 year leaseback period, the lease is not a finance lease and the building should be treated as sold and thus derecognised.

The correct treatment for this item is that the sale of the building should be recorded at its fair value of £10 million, thus the profit on disposal would be £2.5 million (£10 million − £7.5 million). The 'excess' of £2 million (£12 million − £10 million) should be treated as a loan (long-term liability). The rental payment of £1.3 million should be split into three elements; £800,000 building rental cost, £200,000 finance cost (10% of £2 million) and the remaining £300,000 is a capital repayment of the loan.

(iii) The treatment of consignment stock depends on the substance of the arrangements between the manufacturer and the dealer (Angelino). The main issue is to determine if and at what point in time the cars are 'sold'. The substance is determined by analysing which parties bear the risks (e.g. slow moving/obsolete stock, finance costs) and receive the benefits (e.g. use of stock, potential for higher sales, protection from price increases) associated with the transaction.

Supplies from Monza

Angelino has, and has actually exercised, the right to return the cars without penalty (or been required by Monza to transfer them to another dealer), which would indicate that it has not 'bought' the cars. There are no finance costs incurred by Angelino, however Angelino would suffer from any price increases that occurred during the three month holding/display period. These factors seem to indicate that the substance of this arrangement is the same as its legal form i.e. Monza should include the cars in its balance sheet as stock and therefore Angelino will not record a purchase transaction until it becomes obliged to pay for the cars (three months after delivery or until sold to customers if sooner).

Supplies from Capri

Although this arrangement seems similar to the above, there are several important differences. Angelino is bearing the finance costs of 1% per month (calling it a display charge is a distraction). The option to return the cars should be ignored because it is not likely to be exercised due to commercial penalties (payment of transport costs and loss of deposit). Finally the purchase price is fixed at the date of delivery rather than at the end of six months. These factors strongly indicate that Angelino bears the risks and rewards associated with ownership and should recognise the stock and the associated liability in its financial statements at the date of delivery.

3 REVENUE RECOGNITION

🔑

Key answer tips

The introductory paragraph is there to set the scene and to lead you in the general direction that the Examiner intends you to go. Therefore in part (a) it is not enough to discuss general examples of the differences between substance and form without relating this to revenue recognition issues.

Be prepared to consider other issues in the rest of your answer, for example part (c) tests your knowledge of SSAP 4 and FRS 12 and part (d) also tests your knowledge of FRS 18.

(a)   The Statement of Principles advocates that revenue recognition issues are resolved within the definition of gains. Gains include all forms of Income and revenue as well as gains on non-revenue items. Gains and losses are defined as increases or decreases in net assets other than those resulting from transactions with owners. Thus the ASB takes a balance sheet approach to defining revenue. In effect a recognisable increase in an asset results in a gain. The more traditional view is that (net) revenue recognition is part of a transactions based accruals or matching process with the balance sheet recording any residual assets or liabilities such as debtors and creditors. The issue of revenue recognition arises out of the need to report company performance for specific periods. The Statement of Principles identifies three stages in the recognition of assets (and liabilities): initial recognition, when an item first meets the definition of an asset; subsequent remeasurement, which may involve changing the value (with a corresponding effect on income) of a recognised item; and possible derecognition, where an item no longer meets the definition of an asset. For many simple transactions both the ASB's approach and the traditional approach will result in the same profit (net income). If an item of stock is bought for £100 and sold for £150, net assets have increased by £50 and the increase would be reported as a profit. The same figure would be reported under the traditional transactions based reporting (sales of £150 less cost of sales of £100).

However, in more complex areas the two approaches can produce different results. A good example of this would be deferred income. If a company received a fee for a 12 month tuition course in advance, traditionally this income would be deferred and released to income as the tuition is provided and matched with the cost of providing the tuition. Thus the profit would be spread (accrued) over the period of the course. If an asset/liability approach were taken, then the only liability the company would have after the receipt of the fee would be for the cost of providing the course. If only this liability is recognised in the balance sheet, the whole of the profit on the course would be recognised on receipt of the income. This is not a prudent approach and has led to criticism of the ASB for this very reason.

Arguably the treatment of government grants under SSAP 4 (as deferred income) does not comply with the Statement of Principles as deferred income does not meet the definition of a liability. Other standards that may be in conflict with the Statement of Principles are the use of the accretion approach in SSAP 9 for long-term contracts and a deferred tax liability in FRS 19 may not fully meet the ASB's definition of a liability.

The principle of substance over form should also be applied to revenue recognition. An example of where this can impact on reporting practice is on sale and repurchase agreements. Companies sometimes 'sell' assets to another company with the right to buy them back on predetermined terms that will almost certainly mean that they will be repurchased in the future. In substance this type of arrangement is a secured loan and the 'sale' should not be treated as revenue. A less controversial area of the application of substance in relation to revenue recognition is with agency sales. Where a company sells goods acting as an agent, those sales should not be treated as sales of the agent, instead only the commission from the sales is income of the agent. Recently several internet companies have been accused of boosting their revenue figures by treating agency sales as their own.

(b)   Sales made by Derringdo plc of goods from Gungho plc must be treated under two separate categories. Sales of the A grade goods are made by Derringdo plc acting as an agent of Gungho plc. For these sales Derringdo plc must only record in income the amount of commission (12.5%) it is entitled to under the sales agreement. There may also be a debtor or creditor for Gungho plc in the balance sheet. Sales of the B grade goods are made by Derringdo plc acting as a principal, not an agent. Thus they will be included in turnover with their cost included in cost of sales.

	£000
Sales (4,600 (W1) + 11,400 (W2))	16,000
Cost of sales (W2)	(8,550)
	———
Gross profit	7,450
	———

Workings *(all figures in £000)*	*A grade*
(W1) **Opening stock**	2,400
Transfers/purchases	18,000
	————
	20,400
Closing stock	(2,000)
	————
Cost of sales	18,400
Selling price (to give 50% gross profit)	36,800
	————
Gross profit	18,400
	————
Commission (12.5% × 36,800)	4,600
	————
	B grade
(W2) **Opening stock**	1,000
Transfers/purchases	8,800
	————
	9,800
Closing stock	(1,250)
	————
Cost of sales	8,550
	————
Selling price (8,550 × 4 /3 see below)	11,400
	————

A gross profit margin of 25% is equivalent to a mark up on cost of 1 /3. Thus if cost of sale is multiplied by 4 /3 this will give the relevant selling price.

(c)   (i)   The Statement of Principles defines liabilities as obligations to transfer economic benefits as a result of past transactions. Such transfers of economic benefits are to third parties and normally as cash payments. Traditionally and in compliance with SSAP 4, capital based government grants are treated as deferred credits and spread over the life of the related assets. This is the application of the matching concept. A strict interpretation of the Statement of Principles would not normally allow deferred credits to be treated as liabilities as there is usually no obligation to transfer economic benefits.

In this particular example the only liability that may occur in respect of the grant would be if Derringdo plc were to sell the related asset within four years of its purchase. A possible argument would be that the grant should be treated as a reducing liability (in relation to a potential repayment) over the four-year claw back period. On closer consideration this would not be appropriate. The repayment would only occur if the asset were sold, thus it is potentially a contingent liability. As Derringdo plc has no intention to sell the asset there is no reason to believe that the repayment will occur, thus it is not a reportable contingent liability.

The implication of this is that the company's policy for the government grant does not comply with the definition of a liability in the Statement of Principles.

Applying the guidance in the Statement of Principles would require the whole of the grant to be included in income as it is 'earned' i.e. in the year of receipt.

(ii) **Treatment under the company's policy**

Profit and loss account extract year to 31 March 20X3

	£
Depreciation – plant ((800,000 – 120,000 estimated residual value)/10 years × $^6/_{12}$)	Dr 34,000
Government grant ((800,000 × 30%)/10 years × $^6/_{12}$)	Cr 12,000

Balance sheet extracts as at 31 March 20X3	£
Fixed assets:	
Plant at cost	800,000
Accumulated depreciation	(34,000)
	766,000

Creditors: amounts falling due within one year:	
Government grant (240,000/10 years)	24,000
Creditor: amounts falling due after more than one year:	
Government grant (240,000 – 12,000 – 24,000)	204,000

Treatment under the Statement of Principles

Profit and loss account extract year to 31 March 20X3

	£
Depreciation – plant ((800,000 – 120,000 estimated residual value) /10 years × $^6/_{12}$)	Dr 34,000
Government grant (whole amount)	Cr 240,000

Balance sheet extracts as at 31 March 20X3	£
Fixed assets:	
Plant at cost	800,000
Accumulated depreciation	(34,000)
	766,000

(d) On first impression, it appears that the company has changed its accounting policy from recognising carpet sales at the point of fitting to recognising them at the point when they are ordered and paid for. If this were the case then the new accounting policy should be applied as if it had always been in place and the income recognised in the year to 31 March 20X3 would be £23 million. Without the change in policy, sales would have been £22.6 million (23m + 1.2m – 1.6m). Sales made from the retail premises during the current year, but not yet fitted (£1.6 million) will not be recognised until the following period. A corresponding adjustment is made recognising the equivalent figure (£1.2 million) from the previous year. The difference between the £23 million and £22.6 million would be a prior year adjustment (less the cost of sales relating to this amount). This analysis assumes that the figures are material.

Despite first impressions, the above is not a change of accounting policy. This is because a change of accounting policy only occurs where the same circumstances are treated differently. In this case there are different circumstances. Derringdo plc has changed its method of trading; it is no longer responsible for any errors that may occur during the fitting of the carpets. An accounting policy that is applied to circumstances that differ from previous circumstances is not a change of accounting policy. Thus the amount to be recognised in income for the year to 31 March 20X3 would be £24.2 million (23m + 1.2m). Whilst this appears to boost the current year's income it would be mitigated by the payments to the sub-contractors for the carpet fitting.

4 HISTORIC COST

> **Key answer tips**
>
> In part (a), simply describing the limitations of historical cost accounting will not earn maximum marks. The requirement is to discuss the limitations of historic cost accounting when used as a basis for assessing the performance of an enterprise from the perspective of three different user groups. Note the reference to 'pure' historic cost in the question; you are not required to discuss modified historical cost accounting.
>
> In part (b), make sure that you address all four parts of the requirement: advantages of CPP; criticisms of CPP; advantages of CCA; criticisms of CCA. You are not required to discuss the 'real terms' system of accounting (despite the reference to it at the end of the introduction to the question).

(a)   The main drawback of the use of historic cost accounts for assessing the performance of a business is that they do not take into account the current values of assets and, to a lesser extent, liabilities. This can become a serious problem and give misleading information when either specific or general price inflation levels are considered to be high. The effect is that many of the values of the assets on the balance sheet are understated, and, partly because of the related depreciation, profits tend to be overstated. More detailed criticisms of historic cost accounts during a period of rising prices are:

Effects on the balance sheet

(i)   Most fixed assets can be considerably understated in terms of their current worth. The most affected assets tend to be land and buildings, investments and some plant.

(ii)   In general, net current assets tend not to be affected by inflation mainly because they are monetary in nature. The possible exception is trading stock which is non-monetary.

(iii) Traditionally liabilities are ignored when current values are discussed because they are monetary in nature. This may be an error because, for example, a long-term loan carrying a fixed rate of interest, may have a current value that is considerably different to when it was taken out (ignoring the possibility of any repayments). This is because current interest rates may have changed, often as a reaction to levels of inflation since the loan was originally taken out.

Although not dealing specifically with the problems of inflation, this is the view taken by FRS 7 *Fair Values in Acquisition Accounting*.

(iv)   The balance sheet equation dictates that if the net assets are understated, then so too are shareholders' funds.

Effects on the profit and loss account

Some expenses tend to be understated in terms of their current value and this causes the profit to be overstated. Many commentators argue that pure historical cost profits are made up of a current operating profit (see below) plus inflationary gains relating to costs that have been consumed. The main items of cost affected tend to be:

–   costs of goods sold (both purchased and manufactured). This can be mitigated by the use of LIFO, but this is not common practice and virtually banned by SSAP 9 *Stocks and Long-term Contracts*.

–   depreciation charges on fixed assets. In historic cost accounts these are based on historical values rather than current values, and therefore understate the values of the assets that have been used (consumed) during the period.

–   some methods of accounting for inflation include monetary working capital and/or 'gearing' adjustments to historic cost profits. These are intended to reflect the inflation effects of holding net monetary working capital and debt.

The above combined effects lead to the following criticisms and limitations of the use of historic cost accounts to assess a business's performance:

Lack of comparability

It may be invalid to compare the results of two companies. One company may have assets that are relatively old (and of lower cost) whereas another company may have similar, but more recently purchased (and of higher cost) assets. In effect such companies would have a similar operating capacity, but it would be recorded at different values. This situation can also be found within a single company that has operating divisions with similar characteristics to the above scenario. Management may assess their relative performance using historical costs (which would be an invalid basis) to make decisions relating to future investment or even closure. There is also a lack of comparability between a company's current year's results and those of previous years i.e. trend analysis may be distorted.

Conceptual inconsistency

Accounting theorists sometimes argue that historic cost accounts are not internally consistent because they are in fact 'mixed value' accounts. This means that some historical costs are at current values, whereas other historical costs are at out-of-date values. Thus current values of, say sales figures, are being matched with out-of-date values such as depreciation relating to older assets.

Many important ratios which are calculated as a basis for interpreting and assessing company performance can be distorted by inflation. Important examples are: return on capital employed, profit margins, many asset turnover ratios, gearing levels and earnings per share.

The misleading effects of the above on different users may be:

Investors may find it is difficult to compare the results of different companies as a basis for investment decisions. A shareholder may be tempted to accept a low bid for his/her shares if weight is given to the asset backing (based on book values) of the shares. Dividends may seem low in relation to reported profits, because management is recommending dividends based on a current operating profit.

Employees may make high wage demands based on reported profit rather than current operating profits.

The Government taxes adjusted (but not for inflation) historical cost profits which means companies pay tax based on higher, inflation boosted, profits.

(b) The advantages and criticisms of Current Purchasing Power and Current Cost Accounting are set out below:

Current Purchasing Power (CPP) Accounts

It is claimed that CPP accounts retain many of the advantages of historic cost accounts and overcome some of their deficiencies. Like historic cost accounts CPP accounts are transactions based and are therefore objective and verifiable. This is because they are a restatement of historic cost accounts (which possess the above qualities) adjusted for the movement in the Government published Retail Price Index (RPI).

Because the profit and loss account and the balance sheet are adjusted for price movements over time, CPP accounts are said to be comparable between companies and over time. This overcomes many of the difficulties of historic cost accounts.

As the index used to adjust the historical cost accounts is a consumer based index (the RPI), then CPP accounts are more relevant to shareholders because this index is well understood by them and more appropriate to their spending patterns. The figure for shareholders funds is said to be a measure of the spending power (or consumption) that is being forgone in making (or holding) the investment in the company, and can be judged in those terms.

Opponents or critics of CPP accounting argue that many of the claimed advantages may not be true. CPP accounts suffer from some practical as well as theoretical problems:

(i) CPP values are not real values, current or otherwise: they are the result of statistical calculations. For many companies the CPP values of their fixed assets will only be similar to their real (current) values if the movement of the specific price indexes relating to those assets is similar to that of the RPI. An extreme case of this problem would occur where there was retail price inflation but the company trades in an activity where the prices of the goods they manufacture and supply are falling. Hi-fi, video and computer equipment may be examples of this. Average measures of inflation, particularly if they are measures of consumer inflation, are not usually appropriate to account for specific price inflation experienced by companies, which differs from company to company.

(ii) Most items in the profit and loss account are adjusted by the average inflation factor for the period. During periods of inflation this is greater than one and can give the general effect of increased profits. Although this effect is mitigated by higher depreciation charges, CPP profits for profitable companies can be higher than their historic cost profits. A major criticism of historic cost accounts is that they overstate operating profits. CPP accounts can worsen this problem rather than solve it. Highly geared companies tend to show even greater CPP profits (due to gains on net monetary items) and such companies are more vulnerable when inflation is high. This is because interest rates are often increased by Governments in an attempt to control inflation. This has a detrimental effect on companies with high variable rate borrowings.

Current Cost Accounting

Current cost accounting principles, from a conceptual point of view, are more soundly based and therefore more difficult to criticise than CPP accounts. They correct most of the limitations (due to increased price changes) of historic cost accounts. They reflect the current values [which is not necessarily the current costs] of a company's specific assets. The reported current operating profit is considered to be more relevant to many decisions such as dividend distribution, employee wage claims and even as a basis for taxation.

The problems of CCA lie in their preparation and understanding. In practical terms it can be very difficult to determine the current value of assets, and many alternative forms of current value exist e.g., replacement cost, realisable value and value in use. Methods of determining current costs include the use of manufacturers' price lists for plant and stock, professional revaluation of assets (e.g., land and buildings), and the use of specific price indexes published by government agencies (the Office for National Statistics – ONS). Whatever method is used it is often subjective and sometimes complex. This makes the cost of the preparation and audit of current cost accounts expensive.

An interesting point arising from the past use of CCA in the UK in the 1980's is that when the current cost results of companies were published there was no significant change (relating to the publication) in share prices. The Efficient Market Hypothesis would suggest that if CCA provided new information market prices would react. An interpretation of the above observation is that the information revealed by CCA was already 'known' by the market makers and imputed into share prices. Thus many accountants felt that the expensive production of CCA gave no benefit to users. This perhaps explains why historic cost accounts are still dominant in financial reporting.

5 FINANCIAL STATEMENTS *Walk in the footsteps of a top tutor*

Key answer tips

Part (a) was extremely straightforward requiring the definitions of assumed knowledge accounting concepts. To score full marks here a candidate would need to support their definitions with an example. Part (b) required candidates to relate the accounting concepts specifically to stock, again an example would be required to add depth to your answer – simply restating what has already been written in part (a) would not score any marks. The highlighted words are key phrases that markers are looking for.

(a)   The accruals basis requires transactions (or events) to be recognised when they occur (rather than on a cash flow basis). Revenue is recognised when it is earned (rather than when it is received) and expenses are recognised when they are incurred (i.e. when the entity has received the benefit from them), rather than when they are paid.

Recording the substance of transactions (and other events) requires them to be treated in accordance with economic reality or their commercial intent rather than in accordance with the way they may be legally constructed. This is an important element of faithful representation.

Prudence is used where there are elements of uncertainty surrounding transactions or events. Prudence requires the exercise of a degree of caution when making judgements or estimates under conditions of uncertainty. Thus when estimating the expected life of a newly acquired asset, if we have past experience of the use of similar assets and they had had lives of (say) between five and eight years, it would be prudent to use an estimated life of five years for the new asset.

Comparability is fundamental to assessing the performance of an entity by using its financial statements. Assessing the performance of an entity over time (trend analysis) requires that the financial statements used have been prepared on a comparable (consistent) basis. Generally this can be interpreted as using consistent accounting policies (unless a change is required to show a fairer presentation). A similar principle is relevant to comparing one entity with another; however it is more difficult to achieve consistent accounting policies across entities.

Information is material if its omission or misstatement could influence (economic) decisions of users based on the reported financial statements. Clearly an important aspect of materiality is the (monetary) size of a transaction, but in addition the nature of the item can also determine that it is material. For example the monetary results of a new activity may be small, but reporting them could be material to any assessment of what it may achieve in the future. Materiality is considered to be a threshold quality, meaning that information should only be reported if it is considered material. Too much detailed (and implicitly immaterial) reporting of (small) items may confuse or distract users.

(b) Accounting for stock, by adjusting purchases for opening and closing stocks is a classic example of the application of the accruals principle whereby revenues earned are matched with costs incurred. Closing stock is by definition an example of goods that have been purchased, but not yet consumed. In other words the entity has not yet had the 'benefit' (i.e. the sales revenue they will generate) from the closing stock; therefore the cost of the closing stock should not be charged to the current year's profit and loss account.

Consignment stock is where goods are supplied (usually by a manufacturer) to a retailer under terms which mean the legal title to the goods remains with the supplier until a specified event (say payment in three months time). Once the goods have been transferred to the retailer, normally the risks and rewards relating to those goods then lie with the retailer. Where this is the case then (in substance) the consignment stock meets the definition of an asset and the goods should appear as such (stock) on the retailer's balance sheet (along with the associated liability to pay for them) rather than on the balance sheet of the manufacturer.

At the year end, the value of an entity's closing stock is, by its nature, uncertain. In the next accounting period it may be sold at a profit or a loss. Accounting standards require stock to be valued at the lower of cost and net realisable value. This is the application of prudence. If the stock is expected to sell at a profit, the profit is deferred (by valuing stock at cost) until it is actually sold. However, if the goods are expected to sell for a (net) loss, then that loss must be recognised immediately by valuing the stock at its net realisable value.

There are many acceptable ways of valuing stock (e.g. average cost or FIFO). In order to meet the requirement of comparability, an entity should decide on the most appropriate valuation method for its stock and then be consistent in the use of that method. Any change in the method of valuing (or accounting for) stock would break the principle of comparability.

For most businesses stock is a material item. An error (omission or misstatement) in the value or treatment of stock has the potential to affect decisions users may make in relation to financial statements. Therefore (correctly) accounting for stock is a material event. Conversely there are occasions where, on the grounds of immateriality, certain 'stocks' are not (strictly) accounted for correctly. For example, at the year end a company may have an unused supply of stationery. Technically this is stock, but in most cases companies would charge this 'stock' of stationery to the profit and loss account of the year in which it was purchased rather than show it as an asset.

Note: other suitable examples would be acceptable.

Examiners Report

Part (a) asked candidates to explain the meaning of five common accounting concepts/assumptions followed by a section requiring candidates to illustrate how these could be applied to a specific item, namely inventory. The first part of this question really bordered on the level of the lower paper F3 Financial Accounting. Not surprisingly many candidates did very well on this section, but there were a significant number of candidates that showed a very poor and deeply worrying lack of knowledge of basic concepts. There was also evidence of further poor examination; the question asked candidates to explain the concepts whereas many answer gave unsupported examples of the concepts. For example an answer that says providing for bad debts is an example of prudence is quite true, but it is not an explanation of prudence. Other weak answers said things like income and expenditure should be matched or accountants use substance over form; again these are not explanations of the concepts. A few candidates got carried away with this section not realising that there was only 1 mark for each explanation.

Part (b), requiring the application of the concepts to inventory, was very mixed. Well-prepared candidates often gained full marks and weaker candidates scored very little. Many markers reported that candidates were repeating their answers to part (a) and made no attempt to relate the concepts to inventory. Some candidates related the concepts to other accounting items, for example leasing was often cited as an example of substance over form; it is, but this is nothing to with inventory.

Other candidates wrote all they new about the rules for inventory without relating it to which concepts the rules were applying. Neither of the above examples would gain any marks because they are not answering the question asked.

A few candidates seemed to think it was an auditing paper and described the audit work they would do in relation to inventory.

ACCA marking scheme		
		Marks
(a)	explanations 1 mark each	5
(b)	examples 2 marks each	10
		—
Total		15
		—

6 EMERALD *Walk in the footsteps of a top tutor*

(a)   The Statement of Principles defines assets as 'rights or other access to future economic benefits controlled by an entity as a result of past transactions or events'. However assets can only be recognised (on the balance sheet) when those expected benefits are probable and can be measured reliably. The Statement of Principles recognises that there is a close relationship between incurring expenditure and generating assets, but they do not necessarily coincide. Development expenditure, perhaps more than any other form of expenditure, is a classic example of the relationship between expenditure and creating an asset. Clearly entities commit to expenditure on both research and development in the hope that it will lead to a profitable product, process or service, but at the time that the expenditure is being incurred, entities cannot be certain (or it may not even be probable) that the project will be successful. Relating this to accounting concepts would mean that if there is doubt that a project will be successful the application of prudence would dictate that the expenditure is charged (expensed) to the profit and loss account. At the stage where management becomes confident that the project will be successful, it meets the definition of an asset and the accruals/matching concept would mean that it should be capitalised (treated as an asset) and amortised over the period of the expected benefits. Accounting Standards (SSAP 13 Accounting for Research and Development) interpret this as writing off all research expenditure and having the choice to capitalise development costs from the point in time where they meet strict conditions which effectively mean the expenditure meets the definition of an asset.

(b)

	30 September 2007 £000		30 September 2006 £000	
Emerald Profit and loss account:				
Amortisation of development expenditure	335	(w (ii))	135	(w (i))
Balance sheet				
Development expenditure	1,195	(w (iv))	1,130	(w (iii))
Statement of total recognised gains and losses Prior period adjustment (credit)	1,130			

Workings

(All figures in £000. Note: references to 2004, 2005 etc should be taken as for the year ended 30 September 2004 and 2005 etc.)

Year	2004	2005	2006	Cumulative 2006	2007	Cumulative 2007
Expenditure	300	240	800	1,340	400	1,740
Amortisation (25%)	Nil	(75)	(75)	(150)	(75)	(225)
	Nil	Nil	(60)	(60)	(60)	(120)
	Nil	Nil	Nil	Nil	(200)	(200)
Total amortisation	Nil	(75) (w (i))	(135)	(210) (w (ii))	(335)	(545)
Carrying amount	300	165	665 (w (iii))	1,130	65 (w (iv))	1,195

Examiners Report

This question required candidates to apply the definition of an asset to the issue of research and development expenditure, followed by a calculation of the effect of changing from writing off development costs to capitalising them.

This was often the last question attempted and answers were generally quite poor.

In part (a) many candidates recited the definition of an asset then listed the criteria to be applied to determine whether development expenditure should be written off or deferred as two quite separate and unrelated issues. In other words, they did not attempt to apply the definition of an asset to the point at issue.

Some candidates who attempted part (b) assumed that amortisation commenced in the year of capitalisation rather than in the year following. Generally candidates found the approach to this question difficult, the answers were often confused and very rarely mentioned the prior period adjustment.

ACCA marking scheme

		Marks
(a)	One mark per valid point to maximum	4
(b)	Profit and loss account amortisation	1½
	Cost in balance sheets	1
	Accumulated amortisation	1½
	Prior year adjustment in STRGL	2
		6
Total		15

7 FLOW

> ### Key answer tips
>
> By asking for journal entries this question does make you really think about what is going on.

Journal entries

Sale of the property to River on 1 April 20X7

	£	£
Dr Bank	850,000	
Cr Deferred income (balance sheet)		300,000
Cr Property disposal		550,000
Dr Property disposal	500,000	
Cr Property: Cost		500,000
Dr Property: Accumulated depreciation	60,000	
Cr Property disposal		60,000
Dr Property disposal	110,000	
Cr Profit and loss account		110,000

Being the sale and leaseback of property

Comments:

S has entered into a sale and leaseback agreement with River which must be accounted for in accordance with the requirements of SSAP 21 and the guidance notes in FRS 5. Because the leaseback is an operating lease, rather than a finance lease, the substance of the agreement is that S has sold the property to River and no longer has the risks and rewards of ownership. Therefore the property is removed from the balance sheet.

The profit on disposal of the property should be calculated as the difference between the fair value of the property and its net book value at the date of sale (550,000 – 440,000).

Payment of the first rental to River on 31 March 20X8

	£	£
Dr Operating lease rental	100,000	
Cr Bank		100,000
Being the first rental payment to River		
Dr Deferred income	30,000	
Cr Operating lease rental		30,000

Being the amortisation of the excess of the sale proceeds of the property over its fair value (300,000 ÷ 10).

Comments:

The property was sold for an amount in excess of its fair value and so the difference of £300,000 between the sale proceeds and the fair value of the property (850,000 – 550,000) is deferred and credited to income over the period for which the asset is expected to be used, in this case ten years. This has the effect of reducing the annual rental to £70,000.

Tutorial note: It would be possible to argue that the lease should be treated in accordance with its commercial substance, which is that of an operating lease for the continued use of the property, plus an interest bearing loan. The journal entries for the sale of the property would be as before, except that the £300,000 excess of the sales proceeds over fair value would be credited to a loan account, rather than to deferred income. The loan repayment would be divided into three parts:

- Normal annual operating lease rental of £50,000. This is accounted for on a straight line basis over the term of the lease.

- Interest on the loan of £300,000, charged at the rate which River normally applies to similar fixed rate loans.

- Repayment of the capital portion of the loan.

The journal entry would be as follows:

	£	£
Dr Operating lease rental	50,000	
Dr Interest charge (balancing figure)	20,000	
Dr Loan (300,000 ÷ 10)	30,000	
Cr Bank		100,000

8   BLFB

Key answer tips

The examiner has been kind to you in asking for journal entries to show how the transactions should have been shown. Working these out actually makes the situation much clearer. Even at this stage of your studies, you will often find that sketching out journals is a useful tool.

(a) MEMORANDUM

To:	Assistant
From:	Management Accountant
Subject:	Reorting the substance of transactions
Date:	22 November 20Y0

(i)   **Determining the substance of a transaction**

The substance of a transaction is its true commercial effect, which may be different from its legal form. Financial statements do not provide a true and fair view (or fair presentation) of an entity's performance and position unless they report the economic substance of transactions.

For most transactions there is no difference between economic substance and legal form. However, some transactions are very complex and the effect of these is not always apparent. For example, a transaction may be linked with others so that the effect can only be understood when all the transactions are considered together. In determining the substance of a transaction, all aspects of it should be considered, including any future transactions that are likely to arise as a result.

In order to determine the substance of a transaction, it is necessary to decide whether the transaction has given rise to new assets or liabilities or changed existing assets or liabilities. An entity has an asset if it experiences the benefits and risks associated with ownership of an asset, regardless of whether it legally owns the asset. An entity has a liability if it cannot avoid an outflow of economic benefits (money or services) as a result of a past transaction or event. Assets and liabilities (and changes in them) are recognised if it is probable that any future economic benefit associated with them will flow to or from the entity and they are capable of being measured reliably at a monetary amount.

(ii) **Why transactions should be accounted for according to their substance**

Some transactions used to be deliberately structured so that their commercial substance was different from their strict legal form. For example, an entity might sell an asset to another party. Under the terms of the sale agreement, it would be able to repurchase the asset at a specified future date and in the meantime the entity would continue to use it. This transaction is legally a sale, but has the commercial effect of a secured loan.

By recording the strict legal form of this type of transaction, entities could avoid recognising assets and liabilities in their financial statements. This distorted performance measures such as return on capital employed and gearing so that users of the financial statements were given misleading information.

Users of the financial statements need information that is relevant and reliable. Financial statements cannot provide relevant or reliable information unless they report the true effect of transactions. The comparability and understandability of financial statements is also enhanced by reporting economic substance rather than legal form.

(b) (i) **Journal entries to record the correct treatment of the timber**

	£m	£m
1 July 20X9		
Dr Sales revenue	45.0	
Cr Creditors (Southland Bank)		45.0
Dr Stock	40.0	
Cr Cost of sales		40.0

Being the reversal of the sale of the timber and recognition of the profit, the reinstatement of the timber and the recognition of a secured loan from Southland Bank.

30 June 20Y0		
Dr Interest payable (Profit and loss account)	3.6	
Cr Creditors (Southland Bank)		3.6

Being the accrual of interest payable on the secured loan from Southland Bank for the year (45 × 8% (W)).

(ii) **Explanation of journal entries**

Although this transaction appears to be a sale, it is actually a means of raising finance. BLFB continues to hold the timber during the five year period, and therefore it experiences the risks associated with holding this type of stock; it must keep the timber secure and maintain controlled conditions. It will also eventually be able to repurchase the timber and use it to generate income (economic benefits).

The commercial substance of the transaction is that Southland Bank has made a loan to the company, using the timber as security. Therefore the transaction cannot be treated as a sale and the journal entries recording the sale for £45 million and the profit of £5 million must be reversed. The loan of £45 million must also be recognised.

The difference between the 'selling price' of £45 million and the 'repurchase price' of £66.12 million represents loan interest and this should be accrued over the term of the loan at a constant rate on the carrying amount. The interest is charged as an expense in the profit and loss account and added to the carrying value of the loan. The rate of interest implicit in the loan is 8% (W) and therefore interest payable for the year ended 30 June 20Y0 is £3.6 million and the carrying value of the loan at 30 June 20Y0 is £48.6 million.

Working

The interest rate implicit in the loan is calculated as:

$$\frac{\text{Amount borrowed}}{\text{Amount repayable}} = \frac{45}{66.12} = 0.681.$$

From discount tables this is 8% over five years.

9   LMN

(a)   Recognition is the depiction of an element of the financial statements in words and by a monetary amount and the inclusion of that amount in the financial statement totals.

If a transaction or other event has created a new asset or liability or added to an existing asset or liability, that effect is recognised if:

- sufficient evidence exists that the new asset or liability has been created, or that there has been an addition to an existing asset or liability; and

- the new asset or liability, or the addition to the existing asset or liability, can be measured as a monetary amount with sufficient reliability.

An asset or liability is wholly or partly **derecognised** if:

- sufficient evidence exists that a transaction or other past event has eliminated all or part of a previously recognised asset or liability; or

- although an item continues to be an asset or liability, the criteria for recognition are no longer met.

Whether there is sufficient evidence is a matter of judgement in the particular circumstances of each case. The main source of evidence is experience, including:

- evidence provided by the event that has given rise to the item

- past experience with similar items

- current information directly relating to the item

- evidence provided by transactions of other entities in similar items.

Items that are recognised must be capable of being measured at a monetary amount. This involves two steps: selecting a suitable measurement basis (e.g. historical cost or current value) for the item, and then determining an appropriate monetary amount on the basis chosen.

An asset will only be recognised if it gives rights or other access to future economic benefits controlled by an entity as a result of past transactions or events, and it can be measured with sufficient reliability

A liability will only be recognised if there is an obligation to transfer economic benefits as a result of past transactions or events, and it can be measured with sufficient reliability.

Gains are recognised in the profit and loss account when an increase in future economic benefits arises from an increase in an asset (or a reduction in a liability), and it can be measured reliably.

Evidence is needed to ascertain whether the gain has been 'earned', i.e. an increase in equity interest/net assets had occurred before the end of the reporting period. Income reflected in the profit and loss account is seen as particularly important since the income statement is used as a primary measure of performance. Hence a gain included here must be earned and realised.

Realisation is concerned with restricting recognition to those items whose existence and amount is particularly well evidenced. This will usually mean that conversion into cash has occurred or is reasonably assured.

If a gain fails to meet the tests of being earned and realised, it may still meet the general recognition criteria. In this case, such a gain should be included in the statement of recognised gains and losses, e.g. unrealised holding gain on the revaluation of a property held for consumption in the business (rather than for its investment potential).

Losses or expenses are recognised in the profit and loss account when a decrease in future economic benefits arises from a decrease in an asset or an increase in a liability, and it can be measured reliably.

Evidence is needed to ascertain whether a decrease in equity interest/net assets had occurred before the end of the reporting period. Where a loss is not to be recognised, i.e. the expenditure is carried forward to the next period as an asset under the matching concept, sufficient evidence must exist.

(b)   The key issue here is whether the motor vehicles are actually assets of LMN in substance, or whether IJK continues to hold them. The fact that IJK continues to have legal title to the vehicles may be irrelevant.

Revenue from the sale of goods should be recognised when the seller transfers the significant risks and rewards of ownership to the buyer. The vehicles have been sold to LMN if the significant risks and rewards of ownership have also been transferred.

LMN appears to bear some of the risks of ownership:

- It is required to incur the costs of insuring the vehicles against loss or damage.

- Because the price of the vehicles is fixed at the time of their delivery, it bears the risk of loss if the price is reduced between the date of delivery and the date of sale.

However, LMN does not appear to bear the risk of loss due to obsolescence, because it can return the vehicles to IJK without incurring a penalty. In addition, LMN does not have to pay for the vehicles until they are sold to a third party.

LMN has some of the benefits of ownership:

- It can hold whichever ranges and models it wishes, subject to an upper limit of 80 vehicles.

- The price of the vehicles is fixed at the time of delivery, so LMN is protected from price rises between the date of delivery and the date of sale to a third party.

- It can use any of the vehicles for demonstration purposes or road testing.

However, LMN does have to pay a rental charge to IJK if it drives the vehicles for more than a specified number of kilometres. This suggests that LMN does not have all the benefits of ownership.

From the analysis above it is not clear which of the parties has the significant risks and rewards of ownership. It may be necessary to look at what actually happens in practice. For example, how often are vehicles actually returned to IJK? If the answer is 'never', this suggests that the vehicles are assets of LMN. However, on the basis of the information above, IJK appears to have the more significant risks and rewards, including the risk of obsolescence and the risk of slow payment, as it does not receive payment until the vehicles are sold to a third party.

This suggests that IJK should recognise the unsold vehicles as inventory and should not recognise revenue until the goods are sold to a third party.

10 FINO ☙☙ *Walk in the footsteps of a top tutor*

> 🔑
>
> **Key answer tip**
>
> Part (a) simply requires the discussion of faithful representation - to add depth to your answer make sure you include examples. Part (b) required you to criticise the finance director's current accounting treatment/demonstrate how SSAP 21 enables a faithful representation and to show how the lease would be accounted for both as an operating and a finance lease. The highlighted words are key phrases that markers are looking for.

(a)   Faithful representation

The *Statement of Principles for Financial Reporting* (Statement) states that in order to be useful, information must be reliable and the two main components of reliability are freedom from material error and faithful representation. The Statement describes faithful representation as where the financial statements (or other information) have the characteristic that they faithfully represent the transactions and other events that have occurred. Thus a balance sheet should faithfully represent transactions that result in assets, liabilities and equity of an entity. This is a component part of showing a true and fair view. An essential element of faithful representation is the application of the concept of substance over form. There are many examples where recording the legal form of a transaction does not convey its real substance or commercial reality. For example an entity may sell some stock to a finance house and later buy it back at a price based on the original selling price plus a finance cost. Such a transaction is really a secured loan attracting interest costs. To portray it as a sale and subsequent repurchase of stock would not be a faithful representation of the transaction. The 'sale' would probably create a 'profit', there would be no finance cost in the profit and loss account and the balance sheet would not show the asset of stock or the liability to the finance house – all of which would not be representative of the economic reality. A further example is that an entity may issue loan notes that are (optionally) convertible to equity. In the past, sometimes management has argued that as they expect the loan note holders to take the equity option, the loan notes should be treated as equity (which of course would flatter the entity's gearing). In some cases transactions similar to the above, particularly off balance sheet finance schemes, have been deliberately entered into to manipulate the balance sheet and profit and loss account (so called creative accounting). Ratios such as return on capital employed (ROCE), asset turnover, interest cover and gearing are often used to assess the performance of an entity. If these ratios were calculated from financial statements that have been manipulated, they would be distorted (usually favourably) from the underlying substance. Clearly users cannot rely on such financial statements or any ratios calculated from them.

(b) (i) The finance director's comment that the ROCE would improve, based on the agreement being classified as an operating lease is correct (but see below). Over the life of the lease the reported profit is not affected by the lease being designated as an operating or finance lease, but the balance sheet is. This is because the depreciation and finance costs charged on a finance lease would equal (over the full life of the lease) what would be charged as lease rentals if it were classed as an operating lease instead. However, classed as an operating lease, there would not be a leased asset or lease obligation recorded in the balance sheet; whereas there would be if it were a finance lease or an outright purchase. Thus capital employed under an operating lease would be lower leading to a higher (more favourable) ROCE. SSAP 21 *Accounting for Leases and Hire Purchase Contracts* defines a finance lease as one which transfers to the lessee substantially all the risks and rewards incidental to ownership (an application of the principle of substance over form). In this case, as the asset will be used by Fino for four years (its entire useful life) and then be scrapped, it is almost certain to require classification as a finance lease. Thus the finance director's comments are unlikely to be valid.

Fino

(ii) (1) | | Operating lease |
|---|---|
| | £ |
| Profit and loss account – cost of sales (machine rental) (100,000 × 6/12) | 50,000 |
| Balance sheet Current assets Prepayment (100,000 × 6/12) | 50,000 |

(2) Finance lease

Profit and loss account – cost of sales (depreciation) (350,000/4 × 6/12)	43,750

– finance costs (see working)	12,500
Balance sheet	
Fixed assets	
Leased plant at cost	350,000
Depreciation (from above)	(43,750)
	————
	306,250
	————

Creditors: amounts falling due within one year	
Accrued interest (see working)	12,500
Lease obligation (100,000 – 25,000 see below)	75,000
	————
	87,500
Creditors: amounts falling due after more than one year	
Lease obligation (250,000 – 75,000)	175,000

Working:

Cost	350,000
Deposit	(100,000)
	————
	250,000
Interest to 30 September 2007 (6 months at 10%)	12,500
	————
Total obligation at 30 September 2007	262,500
	————

The payment of £100,000 on 1 April 2008 will contain £25,000 of interest (£250,000 × 10%) and a capital repayment of £75,000.

Examiners Report

Part (a) asked candidates to explain how faithful representation related to reliability followed by an example designed to illustrate (amongst other things) how the use of the principle of substance over form gives a more faithful representation of a lease transaction. Answers to this question were very mixed and covered the whole range of marks. Good answers to part (a) recognised the important issues; however weaker candidates could not adequately identify that faithful representation necessitated reflecting the commercial substance of transactions rather than their legal form. Many answers dealt with the qualitative characteristics of financial information discussing relevance, completeness of information, comparability, accuracy and freedom from bias. These seemed more a regurgitation of what had been taught/learned rather than answering the question asked.

Part (b)(i) required candidates to assess the differential effect of treating a lease as an operating lease compared to a finance lease and relating this to the director's comments in relation to ROCE.

There were a number of good answers to this section, most recognising that the lease was in fact a finance lease along with the effect that this would have on the financial statements and the ROCE. Weaker answers spent too much time defining a finance lease (this was not required) and not addressing the issue of the effect on ROCE. In a few very poor answers the point was missed altogether with candidates discussing leasing as a means of purchasing assets when cash was unavailable.

ACCA marking scheme				
				Marks
(a)		One mark per valid point to maximum		5
(b)	(i)	One mark per valid point to maximum		4
	(ii)	(1)	Operating lease	
			– profit and loss account charge	1
			– prepayment	1
		(2)	Finance lease	
			– profit and loss account: depreciation and finance costs	1
			– balance sheet: fixed asset	1
			Current liabilities interest and capital	1
			Long-term liabilities	1
				6
Total				15

A REGULATORY FRAMEWORK FOR FINANCIAL REPORTING

11   UK REGULATORY FRAMEWORK

Key answer tips

Parts (a) and (b) are standard bookwork. Make sure that you answer all the requirements that are listed. Part (c) invites you to give your opinion. Don't be dogmatic, but state both successes and weaknesses in the structure and the processes of developing UK accounting standards.

(a)   **The UK Regulatory Framework**

The UK is a member country of the European Union. One of the objectives of the European Union is that member states will eventually become a single economic entity. To achieve this objective, businesses within Europe must operate and report under comparable legal and accounting requirements. This process is sometimes referred to as European harmonisation. The European Union issues EC directives. These require member states to enact legislation and/or other forms of regulation such that companies within the European Union present their financial statements in a prescribed format. The UK government issues Companies Acts to comply with the EC directives. For example the provisions of the EC Fourth Directive are contained in schedule A of the Companies Act 1985 and the provisions of the EC Seventh Directive are contained in Companies Act 1989. Major requirements of EC Directives include a prescribed format (profit and loss account and balance sheet) for reporting financial performance, the requirement for financial statements to show a true and fair view, and detailed requirements relating to groups including the definition of subsidiaries and exemptions from preparing group accounts.

As referred to above, legislation in the form of Companies Acts is the primary influence on UK company reporting. Despite this, it has long been recognised that Companies Acts alone are not detailed enough to achieve a high standard of reporting and the government has charged institutional bodies with developing accounting standards that complement legislation. The current bodies involved in this process are the Financial Reporting Council (FRC), the Accounting Standards Board (ASB), the Financial Reporting Review Panel (FRRP) and the Urgent Issues Task Force (UITF). The FRC is the parent body with ultimate responsibility for the standard setting and enforcement process.

In recent years the work and influence of the International Accounting Standards Board (IASB) has come to prominence. The original standard setting body was the International Accounting Standards Committee (IASC). In April 2001 it changed its constitution and name to the IASB. As part of its harmonisation process the European Union requires listed companies in all member states to prepare their consolidated financial statements using international accounting standards (IFRSs and IASs). Even before this requirement the UK, who was a founder member of the IASC, has sought to achieve consistency with international accounting standards within its domestic standards. The prominence of the IASB has been enhanced even further by its relationship with the International Organisation of Securities Commissions (IOSCO). In 1995 the IASC agreed to develop a core set of standards which, when endorsed by IOSCO, would be used as an acceptable basis for cross-border listings. In May 2000 this was achieved. Thus it can be said that international accounting standards may be the first tentative steps towards global accounting harmonisation.

In addition to the above influences, listed companies in the UK have to comply with the Listing Rules of the Financial Services Authority (FSA). The main purposes of the Listing Rules are to determine the requirements for admission to the Official List; the manner in which securities are marketed; and the continuing obligations of the issuers. Although the Listing Rules require additional disclosures for listed companies, their main objective is that of investor protection, in particular the prevention of insider dealing.

(b) **The standard setting process**

As referred to above the Financial Reporting Council is ultimately responsible for setting and enforcing accounting standards in the UK. The FRC liaises with the government and other interested parties. It has around 25 members drawn from many groups including users and preparers of accounts and auditors. Its two subsidiary bodies of relevance here are the Accounting Standards Board and the Financial Reporting Review Panel. It finances the Accounting Standards Board and sets its agenda.

It is the Accounting Standards Board that oversees the standard setting process. Although the production of a specific standard may vary slightly, the process normally begins with the issue of a Discussion Paper. A Discussion Paper describes and analyses the problem of a particular topic and sets out possible ways of dealing with it. At that stage the ASB may not necessarily have decided upon a preferred option. The Paper often sets out a list of questions that respondents are invited to address and comment on. The next stage in the process is the issue of a Financial

Reporting Exposure Draft (FRED) which sets out firm proposals. In the past, if an accounting topic is considered non-controversial, a FRED has been issued without a Discussion Paper. A FRED is an Accounting Standard in draft form. Interested parties such as preparers of financial statements, users and auditors have the exposure period (normally three months) to comment on the exposure draft. At the end of the exposure period a Financial Reporting Standard is usually issued. The feedback to the exposure draft may lead to modifications prior to the final issue as a standard. In addition, throughout this process the ASB will meet and discuss its proposals with interested parties, including representative organisations, companies and others.

Once issued, a Financial Reporting Standard is enforced by another subsidiary body of the FRC, the Financial Reporting Review Panel (FRRP). The FRRP is concerned with departures from Accounting Standards by large (public interest) companies. In consultation with the Financial Services Authority (the regulator of listed companies) it selects industry sectors which are likely to give rise to difficult accounting issues and then selects from each of them a number of accounts for review; it also investigates matters that are brought to its attention. If the FRRP concludes that there has been a breach of an accounting requirement or an Accounting Standard has been incorrectly applied, the action required by the FRRP will depend on the seriousness of the breach. For relatively minor faults the FRRP will simply seek assurances that the company will in future comply with the relevant requirement. For more serious breaches the FRRP may consider the financial statements to be defective and require that they are redrafted and reissued. Company directors do have the right to disagree with the FRRP views and if the matter cannot be concluded by mutual agreement, the FRRP may take the matter to the courts. This would not be a desirable course of action, and, as yet, it has not been necessary to go down this route. Another interesting aspect of the FRRP investigations is that where a breach has occurred, the FRRP may publicly censure the company's auditors. Although some companies feel the FRRP has at times been relatively heavy-handed, the general consensus is that enforcement of Accounting Standards is now much more effective and has been an overall success to date.

The Urgent Issues Task Force (UITF) is a subsidiary body of the ASB. Its work can be broken down into two main areas. In areas of accounting where there is no definitive accounting standard or Companies Acts requirement, the UITF will seek a consensus on how a particular issue should be treated. In these circumstances it will be guided by the declared aims and principles of the ASB (contained in the Statement of Principles). Its second task is to assist the ASB in areas where an Accounting Standard or a Companies Act provision exists, but it has been unsatisfactorily interpreted. The results of the UITF's deliberations are the issue of UITF Abstracts. The FRRP consider compliance with UITF Abstracts to be a part of showing a true and fair view. It should be noted that the UITF only deals with serious divergences of practice or with important developing areas. It does not have the power, nor the intention, to amend or override an Accounting Standard or Companies Act requirement.

(c)   **The success of the process**

Any measure of success is really a matter of opinion. Compared with the previous system of producing and enforcing Accounting Standards there has been much improvement. In the past many Accounting Standards were contravened, often without serious repercussions. Also past accounting standards (SSAPs) were not based on a recognised conceptual framework. They were often ill thought out, subjected to undue influence and sometimes dominated by certain parties. The present process is a considerable improvement.

Standards are based on the Statement of Principles (a form of conceptual framework), properly financed, prepared in consultation with users and other supra-national bodies, issued on the ASB's own authority, and adequately enforced. There is no doubt that many companies do not always agree with the requirements of all accounting standards, but this is to be expected and should not be used as an excuse for non-compliance.

However, not everyone has given overwhelming support; the Statement of Principles has come in for much criticism particularly in its balance sheet approach to determining income. Indeed many accounting practices and even some Accounting Standards conflict with this approach. Critics have also commented that many Accounting Standards are overly long, complex and can be difficult to apply in practice and may not pass a cost benefit test. It can also be noted that despite the improvement in accounting standards, infamous corporate failures have continued. Whether rigorous accounting standards coupled with improvement in corporate governance requirements could ever prevent corporate failure is a debatable issue.

In spite of the above criticisms there is general agreement that the ASB has been more successful and effective than its predecessor. Its future success will undoubtedly be closely linked to that of the International Accounting Standards Board.

12   CONCEPTUAL FRAMEWORK

Key answer tips

Parts (a), (b) and (c) are standard bookwork from the Framework but it is essential background knowledge. Part d) introduces not-for-profit entities which are a new element of the F7 syllabus.

(a)   A conceptual framework could be defined as a coherent system of interrelated objectives and fundamental principles. It is a framework which prescribes the nature, function and limits of financial accounting and financial statements. In the US there is a more specific definition which is that it is 'a constitution, a coherent system of interrelated objectives and fundamentals that can lead to consistent standards and that prescribes the nature, function and limits of financial accounting and financial statements'.

(b)   There are a variety of arguments for having a conceptual framework. Firstly it enables accounting standards and GAAP to be developed in accordance with agreed principles and underlying assumptions and concepts. It therefore avoids 'fire fighting', whereby accounting standards are developed in a piecemeal way in response to specific problems or abuses. Such an approach can lead to inconsistencies between different accounting standards and also between accounting standards and relevant local legislation.

The lack of a conceptual framework may mean that certain critical issues are not addressed.

For example, until the Statement of Principles was published there was no definition of basic terms such as 'asset' or 'liability' in any accounting standard which is obviously fundamental to a consistent treatment of accounting transactions and events.

In a world where transactions have become more complex and businesses more sophisticated an overall conceptual framework can help preparers of financial statement and their auditors deal with complex transactions and particularly those which are not the subject of an accounting standard.

The alternative to a principles based conceptual framework as we have under the ASB and indeed the IASB is a rules based framework which some would argue is what is seen in the US. However it can be argued that a principles based framework means that accounting standards based upon such principles are harder to circumvent. It also means that the standard setting process is less likely to be influenced by those with vested interests such as large companies or particular business sectors.

(c) The intended role of the Statement of Principles is:

- to assist the ASB in its development of future accounting standards and in its review of existing accounting standards;

- to assist the ASB by providing a basis for reducing the number of alternative accounting treatments permitted by law and accounting standards;

- to assist preparers of financial statements in applying accounting standards and in dealing with topics that do not form the subject of an accounting standard;

- to assist auditors in forming an opinion as to whether financial statements conform with accounting standards;

- to help users of financial statements to interpret the information contained in financial statements prepared in conformity with accounting standards;

- to provide those who are interested in the work of the ASB with information about its approach to the formulation of accounting standards.

(d) The main aim of not-for-profit entities is to provide value for money rather than making a profit. Value for money is achieved by a combination of effectiveness, efficiency and economy.

Effectiveness means achieving the objectives (usually non-monetary) of the organisation. The objectives of not-for-profit and public sector entities will differ depending upon the type of entity. For example, a school may have the objectives of teaching a certain number of children and achieving certain academic standards. A hospital may have the objectives of treating out-patients within a particular time scale or minimising the number of empty beds. Effectiveness is therefore measured by identifiable measures of achievement in reaching those goals or objectives.

Efficiency means using the resources available well. It is effectively the quantity of output obtained for a given measure of input. Efficiency means getting more out of fewer inputs and thereby reducing the cost of output. In a school it might be measured by the pupil to teacher ratio and in a hospital by the number of patients seen by a consultant during a surgery.

Economy means keeping the cost of input resources as low as possible. This is achieved by paying less for the inputs that are required to meet the objectives or provide the service. In a school giving more teaching time to classroom assistants rather than higher paid teachers would be a form of economy or in a hospital scheduling duties to a nurse rather than a doctor.

In general accounting standards are designed to measure financial performance accurately and consistently, to report the financial position accurately and consistently and to account for the stewardship of the directors of the resources and assets.

Not-for-profit and public sector organisations do not aim to achieve a profit but will have to account for their income and costs. Such entities will have to account for their effectiveness, economy and efficiency even if they do not have to produce financial statements for the public (although in many cases may do so).

Therefore some measurement accounting standards will be relevant such as those relating to stock, fixed assets, leasing, etc. However, others relating purely to reporting such as earnings per share will not be so relevant.

13   USERS AND QUALITIES

Key answer tips

All of the topics covered in this question are essential background knowledge which you may have to use or apply in other questions.

(a)   The objective of financial statements is to provide information about the financial position, performance and changes in financial position of an enterprise that is useful to a wide range of users in making economic decisions. Financial statements also show the results of the stewardship of management, that is the accountability of management for the resources entrusted to it.

(b)   Financial statements meet the common needs of most users. However, financial statements do not provide all the information that users may need to make economic decisions, since they largely portray the financial effects of past events and do not necessarily provide non-financial information.

Arguably the most important group of users are investors or shareholders who are the providers of risk capital.

They are interested in information that helps them to assess how effectively management has fulfilled its stewardship role which is the safekeeping of the entity's resources and their proper, efficient and profitable use. They also require information that is useful in taking decisions about their investment or potential investment in the entity. As a result, they are concerned with the risk inherent in, and return provided by, their investments. They need information on the entity's financial performance and financial position that helps them to assess its cash generation abilities and its financial adaptability.

Other users of financial statements, and their information needs, include the following:

• 	Lenders who will be interested in information that enables them to determine whether their loans will be repaid, and whether the interest attaching to them will be paid, when due. Potential lenders are interested in information that helps them to decide whether to lend to the entity and on what terms.

- Suppliers and other trade payables who will be interested in information that enables them to decide whether to sell to the entity and to assess the likelihood that amounts owing to them will be paid when due.

- Employees who will be interested in information about the stability and profitability of their employer and their long-term employment prospects. They will also be interested in information that helps them to assess the ability of their employer to provide remuneration, employment opportunities and retirement benefits.

- Customers will be interested in information about the entity's continued existence. This is especially so when they are dependent on the entity for example if product warranties are involved or if specialised replacement parts may be needed.

- Governments and their agencies will be interested in the allocation of resources and, therefore, the activities of entities. They also require information in order to regulate the activities of entities, assess taxation and provide a basis for national statistics.

- The public will be interested in information about the trends and recent developments in the entity's prosperity and the range of its activities. For example, an entity may make a substantial contribution to a local economy by providing employment and using local suppliers.

(c) Qualitative characteristics are the attributes that make information provided in financial statements useful to others. The Statement of Principles identifies four qualitative characteristics – relevance, reliability, comparability and understandability – which are subject to a threshold quality of materiality

Information has the quality of **relevance** when it influences the economic decisions of users by helping them evaluate past, present or future events or by confirming, or correcting, their past evaluations. Information about financial position and past performance is frequently used as the basis for predicting future financial position and performance and other matters in which users are directly interested, such as dividend and wage payments. To have predictive value, information need not be in the form of an explicit forecast.

The ability to make predictions from financial statements is enhanced, however, by the manner in which information concerning past transactions and events is displayed. For example, the predictive value of the profit and loss account is enhanced if unusual, abnormal and infrequent items of income or expense are separately disclosed.

The predictive and confirmatory roles of information are interrelated. For example, information about the current level and structure of asset holdings has value to users when they endeavour to predict the ability of the enterprise to take advantage of opportunities and its ability to react to adverse situations.

There are several monetary attributes that could be used in financial statements, e.g. historical cost, current cost or net realisable value. The choice of attribute to be reported should be based on its relevance to the economic decisions of users.

Reliable information can be depended upon to present a faithful representation and is neutral, error free, complete and prudent.

If information is to represent faithfully the transactions and other events that it purports to represent, they must be accounted for and presented in accordance with their substance and economic reality and not merely their legal form. Information must also be neutral to be reliable, that is, free from bias. Financial statements are not neutral if, by the selection or presentation of information, they influence the making of a decision or judgement in order to achieve a predetermined result or outcome.

Information must be complete and free from error within the bounds of materiality. A material error or an omission can cause the financial statements to be false or misleading and thus unreliable and deficient in terms of their relevance.

Uncertainty surrounds many of the events and circumstances that are reported on in financial statements. It is dealt with in those statements by disclosing the nature and extent of the uncertainty involved and by exercising prudence. Prudence means exercising a degree of caution in making judgements about estimates required under conditions of uncertainty, such that gains and assets are not overstated and losses and liabilities are not understated. The existence of assets and gains requires more confirmatory evidence and greater reliability of measurement than are required for liabilities and losses.

It is not necessary to exercise prudence where there is no uncertainty. Nor is it appropriate to use prudence as a reason for, for example, creating hidden reserves or excessive provisions, deliberately understating assets or gains, or deliberately overstating liabilities or losses. That would mean that the financial statements are not neutral and, therefore, are not reliable.

Comparability is also a required attribute of financial information. Users must be able to compare the financial statements of an entity over time to identify trends in its financial position and performance and also be able to compare the financial statements of different entities to evaluate their relative financial performance and financial position.

For this to be the case there must be consistency of accounting treatment and adequate disclosure. An important implication of comparability is that users are informed of the accounting policies employed in preparation of the financial statements, any changes in those policies and the effects of such changes. Compliance with accounting standards, including the disclosure of the accounting policies used by the enterprise, helps to achieve comparability.

Because users wish to compare the financial position, performance and changes in financial position of an enterprise over time, it is important that the financial statements show corresponding information for the preceding periods.

Finally, information must be understandable. **Understandability** depends on the way in which information is presented and the capabilities of users. It is assumed that users have a reasonable knowledge of business and economic activities and are willing to study the information provided with reasonable diligence.

For information to be understandable users need to be able to perceive its significance. However, information that is relevant and reliable should not be excluded from the financial statements simply because it is difficult for some users to understand.

(d) In practice, a balancing, or trade-off, between qualitative characteristics is often necessary. Generally the aim is to achieve an appropriate balance among the characteristics in order to meet the objective of financial statements.

Relevance and reliability

Where there is a conflict between qualitative characteristics, use the information that is the most relevant of whichever information is available.

Conflicts may arise over timeliness. A delay in providing information can make it out of date and less relevant, but reporting on transactions and other events before all the uncertainties are resolved may make information less reliable. Financial information should not be provided until it is sufficiently reliable.

Neutrality and prudence

Neutrality involves freedom from bias. Prudence is potentially biased because it seeks to ensure that gains or assets are not overstated and losses or liabilities are not understated in conditions of uncertainty. It is necessary to find a balance that ensures that deliberate understatement of assets or gains and overstatement of liabilities or losses does not occur.

Cost and benefit

It is also important to balance the benefit and the cost of providing information and this is a pervasive constraint rather than a qualitative characteristic. The benefits derived from information should exceed the cost of providing it.

FINANCIAL STATEMENTS

14   ELITE LEISURE AND ADVENT

🔑

Key answer tips

Both parts of this question are fairly straightforward fixed asset questions.

(a)   The cruise ship is an example of what can be called a complex asset. This is a single asset that should be treated as if it was a collection of separate assets, each of which may require a different depreciation method/life. In this case the question identifies three components to the cruise ship. The carrying amount of the asset at 30 September 20X4 (eight years after acquisition) would be:

Component	Cost	Depreciation		Carrying value
	£m	£m		£m
Ship's fabric	300	96	(300/25 × 8)	204
Cabins and entertainment area fittings	150	100	(150/12 × 8)	50
Propulsion system	100	75	(100/40,000 × 30,000)	25
	550	271		279

Ship's fabric

This is the most straightforward component. It is being depreciated over a 25 year life and depreciation of £12 million (300/25 years) would be required in the year ended 30 September 20X5. The repainting of the ship's fabric does not meet the recognition criteria of an asset and should be treated as repairs and maintenance.

Cabins and entertainment area fittings

During the year these have had a limited upgrade at a cost of £60 million. This has extended the remaining useful life from four to five years. The costs of the upgrade meet the criteria for recognition as an asset. The original fittings have not been replaced thus the additional £60 million would be added to the cost of the fittings and the new carrying amount of £110 million will be depreciated over the remaining life of five years to give a charge for the year of £22 million.

Propulsion system

This has been replaced by a new system so the carrying value of the system (£25 million) must be written off and depreciation of the new system for the year ended 30 September 20X5 (based on use) would be £14 million (140 million/50,000 × 5,000).

Elite Leisure – profit and loss account extract – year ended 30 September 20X5:

		£m
Depreciation	– ship's fabric	12
	– cabin and entertainment fittings	22
	– propulsion system	14
Disposal loss	– propulsion system	25
Repainting ship's fabric		20
		——
		93
		——

Elite Leisure – balance sheet extract – as at 30 September 20X5

Fixed assets

Cruise ship (see working)   406

Workings (in £ million):

Component	Cost £m	Depreciation £m		Carrying value £m
Ship's fabric	300	108	(300/25 × 9)	192
Cabins and entertainment area fittings	210	122	(100 + 22)	88
Propulsion system	140	14		126
	——	——		——
	650	244		406
	——	——		——

(b) (i) Fixed assets

	30 September 20X4 £million	30 September 20X3 £million
Tangible fixed assets (note 1)	316	285
Intangible fixed assets (note 2)	100	270

Note 1 Tangible fixed assets	Land and buildings £million	Plant £million	Total £million
Cost or valuation:			
At 1 October 20X3	280	150	430
Additions	Nil	50	50
Revaluation (see tutorial note)	(15) 1	Nil	(15)
At 30 September 20X4	265	200	465
Accumulated depreciation:			
At 1 October 20X3	40	105	145
Charge for year (see tutorial note)	9 1	35	44
Revaluation (see tutorial note)	(40) 1	Nil	(40)
At 30 September 20X4	19	140	149
Carrying value 30 September 20X4	256 1	60	316

The land and buildings were revalued by [   ] on an existing use basis on 1 October 20X3. They are being depreciated on a straight-line basis over a 25 year life. Plant is depreciated at 20% per annum on cost.

Tutorial note: These amounts can be calculated as:

	Land £million	Buildings £million
Cost	80	200
Depreciation (5/25)	Nil	(40)
Carrying value at 30.9.X3	80	160
Revaluation surplus	5	20
Revalued amount at 1.10.X3	85	180

The £40 million buildings depreciation accumulated at 30.9.X3 must be written back. As the total revaluation surplus is only £25 million, the £15 million difference must write down the valuation amount, to £265 million (85 + 180).

Deprecation on the buildings in 20X4 is £9 million (180/20 remaining useful life).

	£million
Plant depreciation	
Re b/f: 150 × 20%	30
Re acquisition: 50 × 20% × ½	5
	35

Note 2 Intangible fixed assets

	Telecommunication licence £million	Total £million
Cost at 1 October 20X3	300	300
And at 30 September 20X4	300	300
Accumulated amortisation 1 October 20X3	130	130
Amortisation charge for year	30	130
Impairment charge for year	140	140
At 30 September 20X4	200	200
Carrying value 30 September 20X4	100	100

After the impairment charge the licence will be amortised over its remaining life of eight years on a straight-line basis.

(ii) The usefulness of the above disclosures is:

- Users can determine which type of fixed assets a business owns. There is a great deal of difference between owning say land and buildings compared with intangibles. The above figures give an illustration of this; the property has increased in value whereas the licence has fallen dramatically. Another factor relevant to this distinction is that it is usually easier to raise finance using property as security, whereas it can be difficult to raise finance on intangibles due to the volatility of their values.

- It is useful to know whether fixed assets are carried at historical cost or at revalued amount. If a company is using historical cost, it may be that balance sheet values are seriously understated with a consequential effect on depreciation charges.

- Information on accumulated depreciation gives a broad indication of the age of the relevant assets. In the case of Advent above, other than the plant acquired during the year, plant is almost fully depreciated. The implication of this, assuming the depreciation policy is appropriate, is that further acquisitions will be required in the near future. This in turn has future cash flow implications.

- It can also be noted that no disposals of plant have occurred, thus the acquisition of plant represents an increase in capacity. This may be an indication of growth.

- The disclosure of the impairment charge as part of the accumulated depreciation disclosures is self-evident. Users can determine that the acquisition of the licence appears to have been a financial disaster. Where a fixed asset is carried at historical cost, as in this case, the impairment is included as part of the depreciation rather than as a write down (revaluation) of the cost of the asset.

15 WILDERNESS GROUP

Key answer tips

In part (a), remember to discuss income generating units as well as individual assets. Part (b) requires application of this knowledge but part (ii) also requires you to consider FRS 10 and brands.

(a) (i) An Impairment loss arises where the carrying amount of an asset is higher than its recoverable amount. The recoverable amount of an asset is defined In FRS 11 as the higher of its net realisable value and its value in use. Thus an Impairment loss is simply the difference between the carrying amount of an asset and the higher of its net realisable value and its value in use.

Net realisable value:

The net realisable value is the amount at which an asset could be disposed of less any direct costs of selling. The net realisable value of an asset that is traded on an active market is based on the market price. A problem with this is that many (used) assets do not have active markets. Where this is the case, the net realisable value could be based on the amount of a binding sale agreement or on the best estimate for an arm's length transaction. It would not normally be based on the value of a forced sale.

Value in use:

The value in use of an asset is the estimated future net cash flows expected to be derived from the asset discounted to a present value. The estimates should allow for variations in the amount, timing and inherent risk of the cash flows. A major problem with this approach in practice is that most assets do not produce independent cash flows, i.e. they usually produce cash flows in conjunction with other assets. For this reason FRS 11 introduces the concept of an income-generating unit (IGU) which is the smallest identifiable group of assets, which may include goodwill, that generates (largely) independent cash flows.

Frequency of testing for impairment:

Goodwill and any intangible asset that is deemed to have an indefinite useful life, or an estimated life of over 20 years, should be tested for impairment at least annually. A similar requirement applies to tangible fixed assets that are not depreciated on the grounds of immateriality or where their remaining estimated useful life exceeds 50 years. In addition, at each balance sheet date an entity must consider if there has been any indication that other assets may have become impaired and, if so, an impairment test should be done. If there are no indications of impairment, testing is not required.

(ii) Once an impairment loss for an individual asset has been identified and calculated it is applied to reduce the carrying amount of the asset, which will then be the base for future depreciation charges. The impairment loss should be charged to the profit and loss account immediately. However, if the asset has previously been revalued upwards, the impairment loss should first be charged to the revaluation surplus. The application of impairment losses to an IGU is more complex.

It should first be applied to eliminate any goodwill and then to any other intangible asset and then finally to the tangible assets of the unit on a pro rata basis to their carrying amounts. However, an entity should not reduce the carrying amount of an asset (other than goodwill) to below the higher of its net realisable and value its value in use if these are determinable.

(b) (i) The plant had a carrying amount of £240,000 on 1 October 20X4. The accident that may have caused an impairment occurred on 1 April 20X5 and an impairment test would be done at this date. The depreciation on the plant from 1 October 20X4 to 1 April 20X5 would be £40,000 (640,000 × 12$\frac{1}{2}$% × 6/12) giving a carrying amount of £200,000 at the date of impairment. An impairment test requires the plant's carrying amount to be compared with its recoverable amount. The recoverable amount of the plant is the higher of its value in use of £150,000 or its net realisable value. If Wilderness trades in the plant it would receive £180,000 by way of a part exchange, but this is conditional on buying new plant, which Wilderness is reluctant to do. A more realistic amount of the net realisable value of the plant is its current disposal value of only £20,000. Thus the recoverable amount would be its value in use of £150,000 giving an impairment loss of £50,000 (£200,000 − £150,000). The remaining effect on the profit and loss account would be that a depreciation charge for the last six months of the year would be required. As the damage has reduced the remaining life to only two years (from the date of the impairment) the remaining depreciation would be £37,500 (£150,000/2 years × 6/12).Thus extracts from the financial statements for the year ended 30 September 20X5 would be:

Balance sheet

	£
Fixed assets (tangible)	
Plant (150,000 − 37,500)	112,500
Profit and loss account	
Plant depreciation (40,000 + 37,500)	77,500
Plant impairment loss	50,000

(ii) There are a number of issues relating to the carrying amount of the assets of Mossel that have to be considered before an impairment test is done. It appears the value of the brand is based on the original purchase of the 'Quencher' brand.

The company no longer uses this brand name; it has been renamed 'Phoenix'. Thus it would appear the purchased brand of 'Quencher' is now worthless. Mossel cannot transfer the value of the old brand to the new brand, because this would be the recognition of an internally developed intangible asset and the brand of 'Phoenix' does not appear to meet the recognition criteria in FRS 10 'Goodwill and Intangible Assets'. Thus prior to the allocation of the impairment loss the value of the brand should be written off as it no longer exists. The stock is valued at cost and contains £2 million worth of old bottled water (Quencher) that can be sold, but will have to be relabelled at a cost of £250,000. However, as the expected selling price of these bottles will be £3 million (£2 million × 150%), their net realisable value is £2,750,000. Thus it is correct to carry them at cost, i.e. they are not impaired. The future expenditure on the plant is a matter for the following year's financial statements.

Applying this, the revised carrying amount of the net assets of Mossel's income-generating unit (IGU) would be £25 million (£32 million – £7 million re the brand). The IGU has a recoverable amount of £20 million, thus there is an impairment loss of £5 million. This would be applied first to goodwill (of which there is none) then to any other intangible asset (the brand has already been written off) then to the remaining tangible assets pro rata. However the stock should not be reduced as its net realisable value is in excess of its carrying amount. This would give revised carrying amounts at 30 September 20X5 of:

	£000
Brand	nil
Land containing spa (12,000 – (12,000/20,000 × 5,000))	9,000
Purifying and bottling plant (8,000 – (8,000/20,000 × 5,000))	6,000
Stocks	5,000
	20,000

16   LINNET

Key answer tips

Part (a) is a routine question on long-term contracts which should not present you with too many problems.

Your answer to part (b) should do more than calculate the stock write down and state that the company should recognise a provision or a contingent liability. It is not clear how much of the loss in value of the stock is due to the water leak or whether Myriad is liable to pay compensation to Securiprint and you should cover all the possibilities (meeting the requirement to discuss).

(a)   (i)   Long-term construction contracts span more than one accounting year-end. This leads to the problem of determining how the uncompleted transactions should be dealt with over the life of the contract. Normal sales are not recognised until the production and sales cycle is complete. Prudence is the most obvious concept that is being applied in these circumstances, and this is the principle that underlies the complete contract basis. Where the outcome of a long-term contract cannot be reasonably foreseen due to inherent uncertainty, the completed contract basis should be applied. The effect of this is that sales revenue earned to date is matched to the cost of sales and no profit is taken.

The problem with the above is that for say a three-year contract it can lead to a situation where no profits are recognised, possibly for two years, and in the year of completion the whole of the profit is recognised (assuming the contract is profitable). This seems consistent with the principle that only realised profits should be recognised in the profit and loss account. The problem is that the overriding requirement is for financial statements to show a true and fair view which implies that financial statements should reflect economic reality. In the above case it can be argued that the company has been involved in a profitable contract for a three-year period, but its financial statements over the three years show a profit for only one period. This also leads to volatility of profits which many companies feel is undesirable and not favoured by analysts.

An alternative approach is to apply the matching/accruals concept which underlies the percentage of completion method. This approach requires the percentage of completion of a contract to be assessed (there are several methods of doing this) and then recognising in the profit and loss account that percentage of the total estimated profit on the contract. This method has the advantage of more stable profit recognition and can be argued to show a more true and fair view than the completed contract method. A contrary view is that this method can be criticised as being a form of profit smoothing which, in other circumstances, is considered to be an (undesirable) example of creative accounting.

Accounting standards require the use of the percentage of completion method where the outcome of the contract is reasonably foreseeable. It should also be noted that where a contract is expected to produce a loss, the whole of the loss must be recognised as soon as it is anticipated.

(ii) **Linnet – profit and loss account extract – year to 31 March 20X4** (see working below):

	£ million
Sales	70
Cost of sales (64 + 17)	(81)
Loss for period	(11)

Linnet – balance sheet extracts – as at 31 March 20X4

Current assets

Long-term contract balances (195 – 176)	19
Amounts recoverable on contracts (220 – 180)	40

Workings

	Cumulative 1 April 20X3 £ million		Cumulative 31 March 20X4 £ million	Amounts for year £ million
Sales	150	(W1)	220	70
Cost of sales	(112)	(W2)	(176)	(64)
Rectification costs	nil		(17)	(17)
Profit (loss)	38	(W2)	27	(11)

(W1) Progress payments received are £180 million. This is 90% of the work certified (at 29 February 20X4), therefore the work certified at the date was £200 million. The value of the further work completed in March 20X4 is given as £20 million, giving a total value of contract sales at 31 March 20X4 of £220 million.

(W2) The total estimated profit (excluding rectification costs) is £60 million:

	£ million
Contract price	300
Cost to date	(195)
Estimated cost to complete	(45)
Estimated total profit	60

The degree of completion (by the method given in the question) is 220/300.

Therefore the profit to date (before rectification costs) is £44 million (£60 million × 220/300). Rectification costs must be charged to the period they were incurred and not spread over the remainder of the contract life. Therefore after rectification costs £17 million the total reported contract profit to 31 March 20X4 would be £27 million. With turnover of £220 million and profit to date of £44 million, this means cost of sales (excluding rectification costs) would be £176 million.

(b) This is a complex situation. The selling prices of some items of stock after the balance sheet date appear to be below their cost and this indicates that part of the closing stock (at 31 March 20X4) may require writing down to net realisable value with the resultant loss recognised in the current year. This is an adjusting event after the balance sheet date if the losses are due to circumstances that occurred before the year-end. However, if the losses are due to circumstances that developed in the post balance sheet period, they should be included in the following year's financial statements (to 31 March 20X5). If these losses (in 20X5) are material they should be brought to the attention of shareholders in the notes to the financial statements for the year to 31 March 20X4 as a non-adjusting event. Applying the above to the circumstances of the question would give the following analysis.

	£
Cost	48
Net realisable value (NRV)	41
	————
Apparent loss	7 per pack
	————

The NRV of £41 is the reduced selling price for A4 paper of £45 less the cost of getting the goods into a saleable condition of £4.

From the question it would appear that this loss is partly attributable to the remedial cost of the water leak. This is an adjusting event requiring a write down of £2 per pack of the relevant items. The net realisable value at the year-end would have been £46 (the original selling price of £50 less £4 remedial costs), which is £2 below the cost of £48. The remainder of the loss, £5 (£50 – £45), is caused by the price reduction in response to competitive pressure in the post balance period. This is a non-adjusting event requiring appropriate disclosure if material.

The above ignores the effect of the information concerning the sale to Securiprint plc. If the 'marks' are due to the water leak or other flaw in manufacture, Myriad plc will probably be liable to pay compensation to Securiprint plc. This would be an actual liability requiring provision to be made in the current year unless the amount cannot be determined reliably (the ASB says this should be rare). The provision would be for a refund of the cost of the goods sold and compensation for consequential losses caused by the faulty goods. If the marks were not due to the actions of Myriad plc then there would be no liability. It may be that at this early stage there is insufficient information to come to a conclusion as to who is at fault, but this represents at least a contingent liability on the part of Myriad plc and should be disclosed appropriately in the notes to the financial statements. The information may also indicate that other customers could have similar claims against Myriad plc.

A final point to consider is that if the above fault is not due to Securiprint plc, it may mean that all of the stock affected by the water leak is still damaged (despite the remedial work). If so, this would be evidence that the value of the stock is impaired and a further provision would be required to write down the stock (probably to nil) in the current year. Clearly no more of this stock should be sold until the problem is resolved.

17 BOWTOCK

Key answer tips

This is a fairly simple question combining knowledge of FRS 19, SSAP 21 and FRS 21. Questions involving several standards are usually easier than 25-mark questions that examine a single standard, so you must ensure that you have a broad knowledge of the whole syllabus, rather than a specialised knowledge of just a few topics.

The lease in part (b) is clearly a finance lease since the lease term is five years, which is also the useful life of the asset.

(a) (i) Accounting profit (as reported in a company's financial statements) differs from the profit figure used by the Inland Revenue to calculate a company's tax liability for a given period. If deferred tax were ignored (flow through system), then a company's tax charge for a particular period may bear very little resemblance to the reported profit. For example, if a company makes a large profit in a particular period, but, perhaps because of high levels of capital expenditure, it is entitled to claim large capital allowances for that period, this would reduce the amount of tax it had to pay. The result of this would be that the company reported a large profit, but very little, if any, tax charge. This situation is usually 'reversed' in subsequent periods such that tax charges appear to be much higher than the reported profit would suggest that they should be. Many commentators feel that such a reporting system is misleading in that the profit after tax, which is used for calculating the company's earnings per share, may bear very little resemblance to the pre tax profit. In effect this can mean that government fiscal policy may distort a company's profit trends. Providing for deferred tax goes some way towards relieving this anomaly, but it can never be entirely corrected due to permanent differences (i.e. where items may be included in the profit and loss account, but will never be allowed for tax purposes). Where capital allowances are higher than the related depreciation charges (these differences are called timing differences) a provision for deferred tax is made. This brings the total tax charge (i.e. the provision for corporation tax plus the deferred tax) in proportion to the profit reported to shareholders. This situation is usually reversed in later years and the deferred tax provision is released (credited) to the profit and loss account.

The main area of debate when providing for deferred tax is whether the provision meets the definition of a liability in the ASB's Statement of Principles. If the provision is likely to crystallise, then it is a liability, however if it will not crystallise in the foreseeable future, then arguably, it is not a liability and should not be provided for. This leads to the position in FRS 19 *Deferred Tax* which requires deferred tax to be provided on all timing differences that are expected to be reversed, accelerated capital allowances, tax losses and short-term timing differences, but does not require a provision where timing differences are not expected to reverse. The most common example of the latter is a revaluation gain on an asset where it is not expected to be sold.

(ii) FRS 19 requires deferred tax to be calculated using the basis of the incremental liability approach. For accelerated capital allowances this amounts to the current rate of corporation tax applied to the difference between the accumulated depreciation charged to the profit and loss account and the accumulated capital allowances.

	£000	£000
Accumulated depreciation at 30 September 20X3		600
(£2 million – £0.4 million)/8 years for 3 years)		
Accumulated capital allowance at 30 September 20X3		
Year to 30 September 20X1 (£2 million × 40%)	800	
Year to 30 September 20X2 (£1.2 million × 20%)	240	
Year to 30 September 20X3 (£960,000 × 20%)	192	1,232
Total timing differences at 30 September 20X3		632

Deferred tax liability at 30 September 20X3 (£632,000 at 25%)	158
Profit and loss account credit year to 30 September 20X3 ((£200,000 depn − £192,000 capital allow) × 25%)	2

(b)

	£
Profit and loss account extracts year to 30 September 20X3	
Depreciation of leased asset (W1)	10,400
Lease interest expense (W2)	2,672
Balance sheet extracts as at 30 September 20X3	
Leased fixed asset at cost	52,000
Accumulated depreciation (W1)	18,200
	———
Net book value	33,800
	———
Creditors: amounts falling due within one year	
Accrued lease interest (W2)	1,872
Obligations under finance leases (W2)	9,504
Creditors: amounts falling due after more than one year	
Obligations under finance leases (W2)	21,696

Workings

(W1) Depreciation for the year ended 30 September 20X2 would be £7,800 (£52,000 × 20% × 9/12). Depreciation for the year ended 30 September 20X3 would be £10,400 (£52,000 × 20%)

(W2) The lease obligations are calculated as follows:

	£
Cash price/fair value	52,000
Rental 1 January 20X2	(12,000)
	———
	40,000
Interest to 30 September 20X2 (40,000 × 8% × 9/12)	2,400
Interest to 1 January 20X3 (40,000 × 8% × 3/12)	800
	———
	43,200
Rental 1 January 20X3	(12,000)
	———
Capital outstanding 1 January 20X3	31,200
Interest to 30 September 20X3 (31,200 × 8% × 9/12)	1,872
Interest to 1 January 20X4 (31,200 × 8% × 3/12)	624
	———
	33,696
	———

Interest expense for the year to 30 September 20X3 is £2,672 (800 + 1,872 from above), of which £1,872 is a current liability. The total capital amount outstanding at 30 September 20X3 is £31,200 (the same as at 1 January 20X3 as no further payments have been made). This must be split between current and non-current liabilities. Next year's payment will be £12,000 of which £2,496 (1,872 + 624) is interest. Therefore capital repaid in the next year will be £9,504 (12,000 – 2,496). This leaves capital of £21,696 (31,200 – 9,504) as a non-current liability.

(c) (i) Most events occurring after the balance sheet date should be properly reflected in the following year's financial statements. There are two circumstances where post balance sheet events are relevant to the current year's financial statements. The first category, known as adjusting events, provides additional evidence of conditions that existed at the balance sheet date. This usually means they help to determine the value of an item that may have been uncertain at the year-end. Common examples of this are post balance sheet receipts from debtors and sales of stock. These receipts help to confirm the bad debt and stock write down provisions.

The second category is non-adjusting events. As the name suggests these do not affect the amounts contained in the financial statements, but are considered of such importance that unless they are disclosed, users of financial statements would not be properly able to assess the financial position of the company. Common examples of these would be the loss of a major asset (say due to a fire) after the balance sheet date or the sale of an investment (often a subsidiary) after the balance sheet date.

(ii) **Stock**

Sales of goods after the balance sheet date are normally a reflection of circumstances that existed prior to the year end. They are usually interpreted as a confirmation of the value of stock as it existed at the year end, and are thus adjusting events. In this case the sale of the goods after the year-end confirmed that the value of the stock was correctly stated as it was sold at a profit. Goods remaining unsold at the date the new legislation was enacted are worthless. While this may imply that they should be written off in preparing the financial statements to 30 September 20X3, this is not the case. What it is important to realise is that the event that caused the stock to become worthless did not exist at the year end and its consequent losses should be reflected in the following accounting period. Thus there should be no adjustment to the value of stock in the draft financial statements, but given that it is material, it should be disclosed as a non-adjusting event.

Long-term contract

On first appearance this new legislation appears similar to the previous example, but there is a major difference. Profits on an uncompleted long-term construction contract are based on assessment of the overall eventual profit that the contract is expected to make. This new legislation will mean the overall profit is £500,000 less than originally thought. This information must be taken into account when calculating the attributable profit at 30 September 20X3. This is an adjusting event.

18 MULTIPLEX PLC

> 🔑
>
> **Key answer tips**
>
> Notice the key requirement word in each of the four parts of the question. In parts (a) and (b) it is *calculate* and in part (d) it is *prepare*. Part (c) is the odd one out as you are asked to *advise*.

(a) **Profit and loss account extracts:**

	£000	£000
Loan stock interest paid (£80 million × 8%)		6,400
Required accrual of finance cost		1,844
		———
Total finance cost for loan stock (£68,704,000 × 12%)		8,244
		———

Balance sheet extracts:

Non-current liabilities		
8% loan stock 20X4	68,704	
Accrual of finance costs	1,844	70,548
	———	———
Equity and liabilities		
Share options		11,296

Workings

FRS 25 and 26, dealing with financial instruments, require compound or hybrid financial instruments such as convertible loan stock to be treated under the substance of the contractual agreement. For this type of instrument this means that its equity element and liability (debt) element must be separately identified and presented as such on the balance sheet. There are several methods of calculating the split between the two elements. For example, there are several option pricing models. However, given the limited information in the question, the split can only be calculated by a 'residual value of equity' approach. This involves calculating the present value of the cash flows attributable to a 'pure' debt instrument and treating the difference between this and the issue proceeds (the residue) as the equity component.

	Cash flow	Factor	Discounted cash flow
	£m	12%	£000
Year 1 interest	6.4	× 0.89	5,696
Year 2 interest	6.4	× 0.80	5,120
Year 3 interest	6.4	× 0.71	4,544
Year 4 interest	6.4	× 0.64	4,096
Year 5 interest and capital	86.4	× 0.57	49,248
			68,704
Residual equity element (share options)			11,296
Proceeds of issue			80,000

(b)

	Assets 1 Jan 20X0	First impair ment	Revised assets: 1 Feb 20X0	Second impair ment	Revised assets: 31 Mar 20X0
	£000	£000	£000	£000	£000
Goodwill	200	(200)	Nil		Nil
Operating licence	1,000	(300)	700	(100)	600
Property – train stations and land	250		250	(50)	200
Rail track and coaches	250		250	(50)	200
Steam engines	1,000	(500)	500		500
Other assets	300		300		300
Purchase consideration	3,000	(1,000)	2,000	(200)	1,800

Notes:

The first impairment loss of £1 million:

– £500,000 must be written off the engines as one of them no longer exists and its recoverable amount (nil) can be assessed individually

– the goodwill of £200,000 must be eliminated

– the balance of £300,000 is allocated to the intangible asset of the licence.

The second impairment loss of £200,000:

– the first £100,000 is applied to the licence to write it down to its net selling price

– the balance is applied pro rata to assets other than those carried at their net selling prices i.e. £50,000 to both the property and the rail track and coaches.

(c)   As a binding decision to close the engineering division and sell its assets was made during the current year the expected losses of the closure must be provided for in the current year. As the amounts involved are material the losses must be classified as an exceptional item. Losses on the closure of an operation is one of the three exceptional items in FRS 3 *Reporting Financial Performance* that require separate disclosure on the face of the profit and loss account. The closure of the engineering division appears to satisfy only three of the four criteria needed for it to be treated as a discontinued operation:

– the activities will have ceased permanently

– the closure has a material effect on the nature and focus of Multiplex plc's operations

– its results are separately distinguishable.

However, as the closure is not completed within three months of the year end it cannot be classified as a discontinued operation. Therefore a provision for the cost of the closure should be made (described as an exceptional item) as part of the results of continuing operations. The provision will be made up of the following amounts:

	£ million	£ million
Losses on the sale of net assets (46 – 30)		16.0
Associated costs – redundancies	2.0	
– professional costs	1.5	
– penalty costs	3.0	6.5
		———
		22.5

The operating losses of £4.5 million in the period from 1 April 20X0 until the date of closure cannot be provided for at the date the closure is announced. FRS 12 *Provisions, Contingent Liabilities and Contingent Assets* prohibits this type of provision unless it relates to losses on onerous contracts. There is no indication in the question that these future losses relate to onerous contracts.

Tutorial note: There is a potential conflict between FRS 3 and FRS 12. FRS 3 requires a provision to be recognised for the direct costs of the sale or termination, plus any operating losses up to the date of sale or termination. FRS 12 prohibits provisions for future losses. The official answer takes the view that FRS 12 prevails, but it would be possible to argue that FRS 3 applies and that a provision should be made. FRS 12 does not cover specific types of provision dealt with by other standards. In addition, although a minor amendment was made to FRS 3 when FRS 12 was issued, the requirement to recognise a provision for operating losses still stands.

(d)   **Profit and loss account year to 31 March 20X0**

	£ million
Turnover (W2)	18.0
Cost of sales (balancing figure)	(14.1)
	———
Profit (W3)	3.9
	———

Balance sheet extracts as at 31 March 20X0   £ million

Current assets

Long-term contract balances (28.5 costs to date – 8.4 W9 COS – 14.1 X0   6.0
COS)

Debtors – Amounts recoverable on long-term contracts (30 turnover – 25   5.0
payments on account)

Note to the financial statements: Contingent asset

The company is in the process of attempting to recover £2.5 million from a firm of civil engineers. The engineers were contracted to design the structure of a road bridge to be built by Multiplex plc. The engineers incorrectly specified certain materials to be used on the contract, which had to be replaced at a later date. The company's lawyers have advised that there is a good prospect of a successful recovery of these costs.

Workings

(W1) The percentage of completion is calculated as:

	at 31 March 19W9	*at 31 March 20X0*
$\dfrac{\text{Work certified}}{\text{contract price}}$	$\dfrac{£12\,\text{million}}{£40\,\text{million}} = 30\%$	$\dfrac{£30\,\text{million}}{£45\,\text{million}} = 66.7\%\,(\text{or } \tfrac{2}{3})$

The figure for 20X0 includes the variation to the contract.

(W2) The accumulated turnover at 31 March 20X0 would be £30 million ($\tfrac{2}{3}$ × £45 million)

The turnover to be reported in 20X0 would be £18 million i.e. accumulated turnover of £30 million less the turnover of £12 million reported in the previous year.

(W3) The accumulated profit at 31 March 20X0 would have been 2/3 of the revised estimated total profit of £15 million (£45 million sales less £30 million costs) = £10 million. The cost of the rectification work of £2.5 million must be charged to the year in which it occurs (i.e. the year to 31 March 20X0).

This gives a reported profit for the year of £3.9 million (£10 million – £3.6 million in 19W9 – £2.5 million rectification work).

(W4) The profit and loss account for the year to 31 March 19W9 would be:

Turnover	12.0
Cost of sales (balancing figure)	(8.4)
	————
Profit ((40 – 28) × 30%)	3.6
	————

19 TORRENT

> ### Key answer tips
>
> The best way is to deal with the accounting for construction contracts is to work through one contract at a time, establishing whether over its life the contract is expected to generate profits (recognise only by the stage of completion method) or incur losses (recognise in full immediately). The requirement that unplanned rectification costs should be recognised in full in the year in which they are incurred (rather than being a normal cost which is spread over the life of the contract) is quite tricky.

(a)   **Profit and loss account for the year ended 31 March 20X6**

	Alpha £m	Beta £m	Ceta £m	Total £m
Turnover (W1 – W3)	8	2.0	4.8	14.8
Cost of sales (W1 – W3)	(7)	(3.5)	(4.0)	(14.5)
Profit/(loss)	1	(1.5)	0.8	0.3

Balance sheet at 31 March 20X6

Current assets				
Long-term contract balance (12.5 – 11.5)	1.0			1.0
Amounts recoverable on contracts ((14 – 12.6) and (2 – 1.8))	1.4	0.2	4.8	6.4
Current liabilities				
Provision for losses charged to cost of sales		(1.5)		(1.5)

Workings (£m)

(W1) **Alpha**

	At 31.3.05	At 31.3.06	Year to 31.3.06
Work invoiced	6.0 (5.4/90%)	14.0 (12.6/90%)	8
Cost of sales (β)	(4.5)	(11.5)	(7)
Profit	1.5	2.5	1

Profit is calculated as:

% complete	30% (6/20 ×100)	70% (14/20 × 100)
Attributable profit	1.5 ((20 – 15) ×30%)	2.5 ((20 – 15) ×70%) – 1 rectification)

Rectification costs must be charged in the year in which they are incurred.

The balance sheet figure for long-term contract balances for Alpha is the total costs incurred to date of £12.5m less the costs charged to cost of sales to date of £11.5m.

(W2) **Beta**

Due to the increase in the estimated cost, Beta is a loss-making contract and the whole of the loss must be provided for as soon as it is can be anticipated. The loss is expected to be £1.5 million (£7.5m – £6m). The sales value of the contract at 31 March 20X6 is £2 million (£1.8/90%), thus the cost of sales must be recorded as £3.5 million. As costs to date are £2 million, this means a provision of £1.5 million is required.

(W3) **Ceta**

Based on the costs to date at 31 March 20X6 of £4 million and the total estimated costs of £10 million, this contract is 40% complete. The estimated profit is £2 million (£12m – £10m); therefore the profit at 31 March 20X6 is £0.8 million (£2m × 40%). This gives an imputed sales (and debtor) value of £4.8 million.

(b) (i) Savoir – EPS year ended 31 March 20X4:

The issue on 1 July 20X3 at full market value needs to be weighted:

Old shares (10/25p)	40m	3/12 =	10m
New shares	8m		
	48m	× 9/12 =	36m
			46m

Without the bonus issue this would give an EPS of 30p (£13.8m/46m × 100).

The bonus issue of one for four would result in 12 million new shares giving a total number of ordinary shares of 60 million. The dilutive effect of the bonus issue would reduce the EPS to 24p (30p × 48m/60m). The comparative EPS (for 20X3) would be restated at 20p (25p × 48m/60m).

EPS year ended 31 March 20X5:

The rights issue of two for five on 1 October 20X4 is half way through the year. The theoretical ex rights value can be calculated as:

Holder of	100 shares worth £2.40 =	£240	
Subscribes for	40 shares at £1 each =	£40	
Now holds	140 worth (in theory)	£280	i.e. £2 each.

Weighting:

	60m × 6/12 × 2.40/2.00 =	36 million
Rights issue (2 for 5)	24m	
New total	84m × 6/12 =	42 million
Weighted average		78 million

EPS is therefore 25p (£19.5m/78m × 100).

The comparative (for 20X4) would be restated at 20p (24p × 2.00/2.40).

(ii) The basic EPS for the year ended 31 March 20X6 is 30p (£25.2m/84m × 100).

Dilution

Convertible loan stock

On conversion loan interest of £1.2 million after tax would be saved (£20 million × 8% × (100% − 25%)) and a further 10 million shares would be issued (£20m/£100 × 50).

Directors' options

Options for 12 million shares at £1.50 each would yield proceeds of £18 million. At the average market price of £2.50 per share this would purchase 7.2 million shares (£18m/£2.50). Therefore the 'bonus' element of the options is 4.8 million shares (12m − 7.2m).

Using the above figures the diluted EPS for the year ended 31 March 20X6 is 26.7p (£25.2m + £1.2m)/(84m + 10m + 4.8m)).

20 QRS

Key answer tips

The two types of instruments in part (a) are the most important for this syllabus so you must know how to classify them.

In general, under the requirements of FRS 25 *Financial Instruments: Presentation,* financial instruments that fulfil the characteristics of a liability should be classified as such. Although preferred shares carry the description of 'shares' this does not mean that they can necessarily be classified as equity. In cases where the payment of the 'dividend' is a fixed sum that is normally paid in respect of each accounting period, the instrument is really a long-term liability and must be classified as such.

The convertible bonds would be classified as a compound, or hybrid, instrument by FRS 25; that is, they have characteristics of both debt and equity, and would therefore be presented partly as debt and partly as equity in the balance sheet. Valuation of the equity element is often difficult. One method permitted by FRS 25 involves valuation of the liability element using an equivalent market rate of interest for non-convertible bonds, with equity as a residual figure.

Applying this approach to the proposed instrument, the following debt/equity split results:

	£
Present value of the capital element of the bond issue:	
£6 million × 0.735	4,410,000
Interest at present value:	
(£6,000,000 × 6%) × (0.926 + 0.857 + 0.794 + 0.735)	
= £360,000 × 3.312	1,192,320
Value of liability element	5,602,320
Equity element (balancing figure)	397,680
Total value of instrument	6,000,000

Apart from the relatively small element of the hybrid instrument that can be classified as equity, the two proposed issues will be classified as debt under the provisions of FRS 25. If the directors wish to obtain finance through an issue of financial instruments that can be properly classified as equity, they should reconsider the rights issue proposal.

21 PX

> **Key answer tips**
>
> Think carefully about the types of investment being made.

(i) **Appropriate classification**

Securities of a listed entity

This investment has been acquired in order to be sold in the near future and so it meets the FRS 26 definition of an instrument 'held for trading'. Therefore it should be classified as a financial asset at fair value through profit or loss, as required by FRS 26.

Variable interest rate loan

This is a financial asset and PX intends to hold the loan until it is due for repayment (it has guaranteed not to assign the loan to a third party). The payments are also fixed and determinable and the repayment date is fixed. Therefore the loan should be classified as a held to maturity investment.

Portfolio of investments

These investments are not held for trading because there is no intention to sell them in the near future. They are not derivatives, nor do they fall into the other categories. Therefore they must be classified as available for sale financial assets.

(ii) **How the financial assets should be measured**

The following requirements apply:

- The listed securities are 'at fair value through profit or loss' and therefore are measured at fair value.

- The variable interest rate loan is measured at amortised cost (as a held to maturity investment).

- The investment portfolio is measured at fair value (as an available for sale financial asset).

22   PINGWAY *Walk in the footsteps of a top tutor*

Key answer tip

This question requires you to demonstrate your knowledge of FRS 25/26 relating to a convertible loan and how it should be accounted for in the financial statements. Ensure you do not simply calculate the effect of the convertible loan as you must discuss the accounting implication to be eligible for all the marks available in the question. The highlighted words are key phrases that markers are looking for.

Accounting correctly for the convertible loan note in accordance with FRS 25 *Financial Instruments: Disclosure and Presentation* and FRS 26 *Financial Instruments: Recognition and Measurement* would mean that virtually all the financial assistant's observations are incorrect. The convertible loan note is a compound financial instrument containing a (largely) debt component and an equity component – the value of the option to receive equity shares. These components must be calculated using the residual equity method and appropriately classified (as debt and equity) on the balance sheet. As some of the proceeds of the instrument will be equity, the gearing will not be quite as high as if a non-convertible loan was issued, but gearing will be increased. However, if the loan note is converted to equity in March 2010, gearing will be reduced. The interest rate that would be applicable to a non-convertible loan (8%) is representative of the true finance cost and should be applied to the carrying amount of the debt to calculate the finance cost to be charged to the profit and loss account thus giving a much higher charge than the assistant believes.

Accounting treatment: financial statements year ended 31 March 2008

Profit and loss account:

Finance costs (see working)	£693,920

Balance sheet:
Creditors: amount falling due after more than one year

3% convertible loan note (8,674 + 393·92)	£9,067,920

Capital and reserves

Option to convert	£1,326,000

Working (figures in brackets in £000)

	cash flows	factor at 8%	present value
			£000
year 1 interest	300	0·93	279
year 2 interest	300	0·86	258
year 3 interest and capital	10,300	0·79	8,137
total value of debt component			8,674
proceeds of the issue			10,000
equity component (residual amount)			1,326

The interest cost in the profit and loss account should be £693,920 (8,674 × 8%), requiring an accrual of £393,920 (693·92 − 300 i.e. 10,000 × 3%). This accrual should be added to the carrying value of the debt.

Examiners Report

This question proved to be the most difficult question for the majority of candidates with a significant percentage not even attempting it. A few answers were very good, although the majority were very poor.

The question required candidates to account for the issue of a $10 million convertible loan and comment on some misguided views expressed by a financial assistant in relation to its issue.

The convertible loan note had a coupon (nominal) interest rate of 3%, but an effective rate of 8%. The proceeds of the loan had to be split between debt and equity by discounting the future cash flows at 8% to give the debt element with the balance being the value of the equity option. Common mistakes were to project the cash flows with an interest rate of 8% (rather then 3%), to discount them at 3% (rather than 8%) and to calculate the interest charge to the income statement as 3% of $10 million (rather than 8% of the debt element).

The financial assistant suggested that the profit would be higher (implying he/she assumed the interest cost would be only 3%) and the loan note could be included as equity because most loan note holders would be expected to choose the equity option. Both of these comments are wrong, but many weaker candidates found themselves agreeing with them, thus showing a complete lack of understanding of this type of financial instrument.

Taken as a whole this was by far the worst answered question, which is surprising as this topic has been asked on many occasions, often as part of a larger question.

ACCA marking scheme	
	Marks
1 mark per valid comment up to	4
use of 8%	1
initial carrying amount of debt and equity	2
finance cost	2
carrying amount of debt at 31 March 2008	1
	—
Total	10

23 ERRSEA

(a) **Errsea – profit and loss account extracts year ended 31 March 2007**

	£
Loss on disposal of plant – see note below ((90,000 − 60,000) − 12,000)	18,000
Depreciation for year (wkg (i))	75,000
Government grants (a credit item) – see note below and (wkg (iv))	(19,000)

Note: the repayment of government grant of £3,000 may instead have been included as an increase of the loss on disposal of the plant.

Errsea – balance sheet extracts as at 31 March 2007

	Cost	Accumulated depreciation	Carrying amount
	£	£	£
Plant (wkg (v))	360,000	195,000	165,000

Creditors: amounts falling due within one year

	£
Government grants (wkg (iv))	27,000

Creditors: amounts falling due after more than one year

	£
Government grants (wkg (iv))	39,000

Workings

(i)   Depreciation for year ended 31 March 2007

	£
On acquired plant (wkg (ii))	52,500
Other plant (wkg (iii))	22,500
	75,000

(ii)   The cost of the acquired plant is recorded at £210,000 being its base cost plus the costs of modification and transport and installation. Annual depreciation over three years will be £70,000. Time apportioned for year ended 31 March 2007 by 9/12 = £52,500.

(iii)   The other remaining plant is depreciated at 15% on cost

	£
(b/f 240,000 – 90,000 (disposed of) × 15%)	22,500

(iv)   **Government grants**

	£
Transferred to income for the year ended 31 March 2007:	
From current liability in 2006 (10,000 – 3,000 (repaid))	7,000
From acquired plant (see below):	12,000
	19,000
Current liability	
Transferred from long-term (per question)	11,000
On acquired plant (see below)	16,000
	27,000

Long-term liability

B/f	30,000
Transferred to current	(11,000)
On acquired plant (see below)	20,000
	39,000

Grant on acquired plant is 25% of base cost only = £48,000

This will be treated as:

To income in year ended 31 March 2007 (48,000/3 × 9/12)	12,000
Classified as current liability (48,000/3)	16,000
Classified as a long-term liability (balance)	20,000
	48,000

Note: government grants are accounted for from the date they are receivable (i.e. when the qualifying conditions for the grant have been met).

(v)

	Cost	Accumulated depreciation	Carrying amount
	£	£	£
Balances b/f	240,000	180,000	60,000
Disposal	(90,000)	(60,000)	(30,000)
Addition (w (ii))	210,000	52,500	157,500
Other plant depreciation for year (wkg (iii))		22,500	(22,500)
Balances at 31 March 2007	360,000	195,000	165,000

(b) (i) This is an example of an adjusting event within FRS 21 *Events after the balance sheet date*. This means that an impairment of trade debtors of £23,000 must be recognised (and charged to the profit and loss account). The increase in the debtor after the year end should be written off in the following year's financial statements.

(ii) Sales of the year-end stock in the following accounting period may provide evidence that the stock's net realisable value has fallen below its cost. This appears to be the case for product W32 and is another example of an adjusting event. With a selling price of £5.40 and after paying a 15% commission, the net realisable value of W32 is £4.59 each. Assuming that the fall in selling price is not due to circumstances that occurred after the year end and that the selling price is typical of what the remainder of the product will sell for, stock should be written down (via a charge to the profit and loss account) by £16,920 ((6.00 − 4.59) × 12,000 units).

(iii) Tentacle has correctly treated the outstanding litigation as a contingent liability and estimated its financial effect. The settlement of a court case after the balance sheet date may confirm (or otherwise) the existence of an obligation at the year end and would be an example of an adjusting event. This would then require that either the disclosure note of the contingency is removed or the obligation should be provided for dependent on the outcome of the litigation. However, this is not quite the case in Tentacle's example. The circumstances of the claim against Tentacle are different from those of the recently settled case. So this settlement does not appear to have any effect on the likelihood of Tentacle losing the case. What it does (potentially) affect is the estimated financial effect of the liability. Thus, the only required change to the financial statements would be to update the disclosure note on the contingent liability to reflect that the potential liability has increased from £500,000 to £750,000.

(iv) Normally the effect of price increases of materials after the balance sheet date would be a matter for the following year's financial statements as such increases do not affect the costs as they existed at the balance sheet date (i.e. they would not be an adjusting event). However, Tentacle's method of recognising profit (using a cost basis to determine the percentage of completion) requires an estimate (at 31 March 2007) of the future costs of the contract. This estimate directly determines the amount of profit recognised at 31 March 2007. Therefore the information indicating that the total estimated costs of the contract have increased should be taken as providing additional evidence of conditions that existed at the year end. Thus this is an adjusting event which requires the recognised profit to be recalculated. The original estimate of the recognised profit at 31 March 2007 of £1.2 million would be half of the estimated total profit of £2.4 million (percentage of completion is 50% i.e. £3 million/£6 million). The increase in the costs of £1.5 million means the revised estimated total profit is only £900,000 (2.4m – 1.5m). The revised total costs are £7.5 million (6m + 1.5m). Thus the recognised profit on the contract should be recalculated as £360,000 (900,000 × 3m/7.5m) with appropriate amendments to the profit and loss account and balance sheet figures.

24 PARTWAY

(a) (i) FRS 3 Reporting financial performance defines discontinued operations as those that are sold or terminated and satisfy all of the following conditions:

- the sale or termination is completed within the year or up to a maximum of three months after the year end

- the activities have ceased permanently

- the discontinuation has a material effect on the nature and focus of the operations and represents a material reduction in operating facilities either by withdrawing from a particular market (whether class of business or geographical) or from continuing operations

- the assets, liabilities, operating results and activities are clearly distinguishable, physically, operationally and for financial reporting purposes.

The intention of this requirement is to improve the usefulness of the financial statements by improving the predictive value of the (historical) profit and loss account. Clearly the results from discontinued operations should have little impact on future operating results. Thus users would focus on the continuing activities in any assessment of future income and profit. Part of FRS 3's requirements in this area is that new business should be separately disclosed as a sub analysis of continuing operations. Possibly the reason for this is that the comparative figures would not include any amounts for these new activities (this would enable more reliable trend analysis).

The above definition is, at first appearance, rather rigorous and perhaps complex. It is suggested that a precise definition of a discontinued operation is required to avoid 'misleading' reporting. The presumption that analysts and other users will focus on continuing operations, and therefore tend to disregard the results of discontinuing operations may lead some directors to wish to classify loss making operations as discontinued (where they would attract less attention) when they are not. Conversely directors may prefer operations that have been profitable, but are about to be sold, to be included in continuing operations. Taking this to an extreme, all profit making operations would be shown in continuing operations and loss making operations would be shown as discontinuing regardless of which were continuing or discontinuing. The ASB regards such practice as unacceptable, hence the rigorous definition. It should be noted that some company directors have complained that operations that have genuinely been sold or terminated do not meet all the requirements of the definition of a discontinued operation in FRS 3 (in particular relating to part (iv) of the definition above). Consequently they have to be reported in continuing operations which they believe is misleading and contravenes the purpose of the Standard.

(ii) The timing of the board meeting and consequent notifications is within the post balance sheet three month period allowed by FRS 3. The notification to staff, suppliers and the press seems to indicate that the directors are 'demonstrably committed to the termination' and, although the business had not yet been closed down, once it has it will clearly have 'ceased permanently'. From the financial and other information given in the question it appears that the travel agencies are 'clearly distinguishable'. Probably the main issue is with part (iii) of the above definition. The company is still operating in the holiday business; therefore there is no material reduction in a class of business or geographical location. However, there does appear to be a change in the 'nature and focus of the business'. The selling of holidays through the Internet compared with through high-street travel agencies requires very different assets, staff knowledge and training and has a different cost structure. Therefore it would seem the announced closure of the travel agencies would appear to meet the definition of a discontinued operation.

Tutorial note: There is no information as to whether the closure of the chain of travel agents was completed within 3 months of the year; announcement within that time period is not enough – see (i) above. It could be argued that in the absence of such information, this part of the business should not be presented as discontinued.

(iii) Partway Profit and loss account for the year ended:

	31 October 20X6		31 October 20X5	
	£000	£000	£000	£000
Turnover				
Continuing operations	23,000		22,000	
Acquisitions	2,000		nil	
	25,000		22,000	
Discontinued operations	14,000	39,000	18,000	40,000
Cost of sales		(36,000)		(32,000)
Gross profit		3,000		8,000
Net operating expenses		(2,600)		(2,000)
Operating profit/(loss)				
Continuing operations	4,000		4,500	
Acquisitions	400		nil	
	4,400		4,500	
Discontinued operations	(4,000)		1,500	
Profit before tax		400		6,000

Note: Other presentations are acceptable.

Tutorial note: It only an assumption that the car hire business was acquired during the year.

(b) (i) Comparability is one of the principal qualitative characteristics of useful financial information. It is a vital attribute when assessing the performance of an entity over time (trend analysis) and to some extent with other similar entities. For information to be comparable it should be based on the consistent treatment of transactions and events. In effect a change in an accounting policy breaks the principle of consistency and should generally be avoided. That said, FRS 18 *Accounting polices* says that consistency is not an end in itself and there are circumstances where it becomes necessary to change an accounting policy. These are mainly where it is required by a new or revised accounting standard, UITF Abstract or applicable legislation or where the change would result in financial statements giving a fairer presentation (true and fair view) of the entity's results and financial position.

It is important to note that the application of a different accounting policy to transactions or events that are substantially different to existing transactions or events or to transactions or events that an entity had not previously experienced does NOT represent a change in an accounting policy. It is also necessary to distinguish between a change in an accounting policy and a change in an estimation technique.

In an attempt to limit the problem of reduced comparability caused by a change in an accounting policy, FRS 18 (and FRS 3 *Reporting financial performance*) say the general principle is that the financial statements should be prepared as if the new accounting policy had always been in place. This is known as retrospective application. The main effect of this is that both current and comparative financial statements should be restated by applying the new policy to them and adjusting the opening balance of equity in the comparative statements. Any change in accounting policy required by a specific Standard or UITF Abstract should be dealt with under the transitional provisions (if any) of that Standard or Abstract (normally these apply the general rule of retrospective application).

(ii) This issue is one of the timing of when revenue should be recognised in the profit and loss account. This can be a complex issue which involves identifying the transfer of significant risks, reliable measurement, the probability of receiving economic benefits, relevant accounting standards and legislation and generally accepted practice. Applying the general guidance in FRS 5 *Reporting the substance of transactions* (including application note G), the previous policy, applied before cancellation insurance was made a condition of booking, seemed appropriate. At the time the holiday is taken it can no longer be cancelled, all monies would have been received and the flights and accommodation have been provided. There may be some compensation costs involved if there are problems with the holiday, but this is akin to product warranties on normal sales of goods which may be immaterial or provided for based on previous experience of such costs. Payments in advance of the 'delivery' of goods would not normally be a trigger to recognise a sale of goods, they are simply a prepayment. Interpreting this for Partway's transaction would seem to confirm the appropriateness of its previous policy.

The directors of Partway wish to change the timing of recognition of sales because of the change in circumstances relating to the compulsory cancellation insurance. The directors are apparently arguing that the new 'transactions and events' are substantially different to previous transactions therefore the old policy should not apply. Even if this does justify revising the timing of the recognition of sales, it is not a change of accounting policy because of the reasons outlined in (i) above.

An issue to consider is whether compulsory cancellation insurance represents a substantial change to the risks that Partway experiences. An analysis of past experience of losses caused by uninsured cancellations may help to assess this, but even if the past losses were material (and in future they will not be), it is unlikely that this would override the general guidance and accepted accounting policy relating to payments made in advance of delivery. It seems the main motivation for the proposed change is to improve the profit for the year ended 31 October 20X6 so that it compares more favourably with that of the previous year.

To summarise, it is unlikely that the imposition of compulsory cancellation insurance justifies recognising sales at the date of booking when a deposit is received, and, even if it did, it would not be a change in accounting policy. This means that comparatives would not be restated (which is something that would actually suit the suspected objectives of the directors).

25 SITUATIONS

(a) (i) This is an example of a contingent liability. As it was only considered possible that AB would have to pay damages there has been no provision made for this liability. However under FRS 7 XY must recognise the fair value of this contingent liability within net assets acquired for the purpose of the goodwill calculation.

(ii) At the acquisition date there was no obligation to incur the integration costs and no liability should be recognised within net assets acquired (FRS 7 and FRS 12).

(b) Finance cost = Total payments payable in respect of an instrument *minus* Net proceeds on issue of the instrument

			£m
Total payments	=	Interest (5 × 4% × £50m)	10
		+ Repayment amount	60
			——
			70
			——

Assuming that the borrowings were issued at par:

			£m
Net proceeds on issue	=	Gross proceeds	50
		minus Direct costs of the issue	(0.5)
			——
			49.5
			——

∴ Total finance cost = 70 − 49.5 = £20.5m

(c) At the time of the initial acquisition of the investment it would have been designated as held-for-trading and included in the balance sheet as such at a value of £51,000 (60,000 × 85p).

At 31 March 20X5 the investment would be remeasured to fair value of £52,500 (60,000 × 87.5p) and would appear in the balance sheet at this value. The gain on the remeasurement of £1,500 would be taken to the profit and loss account.

(d) A subsidiary that is held exclusively with a view to resale is not consolidated provided that it has not previously been consolidated according to FRS 2. As this subsidiary was acquired during the year and is being held exclusively for resale, it should not be consolidated.

(e) As this is a hybrid financial instrument it should be recognised in the balance sheet as partly debt and partly capital. The measurement of the equity element is the residual value once the present value of the liability element has been computed using the 6% interest rate for such debt without conversion terms.

	£
Present value of principal (10,000 × 50 × 0.747)	373,500
Present value of interest payments (500,000 × 5% × 4.212)	105,300
	———
Debt element	478,800
Equity element (balance)	21,200
	———
	500,000
	———

26   PROMOIL   WALK IN THE FOOTSTEPS OF A TOP TUTOR

Key answer tips

This question covers FRS 16 provisions, contingent assets and contingent liabilities. Part (a) requires the definition of liabilities and provisions and how the definitions enhance reliability of financial statements. Part (b) requires both the discussion and accounting for a long-term environmental provision – don't miss the discussion element as you will be restricted on the marks that can be achieved.

(a)   Liabilities are probable future sacrifices of economic benefits arising from present obligations of a particular entity to transfer assets or provide services to other entities in the future as a result of past transactions or events. Provisions are liabilities of uncertain timing or amounts, i.e. they are normally estimates. In essence provisions should be recognised if they meet the definition of a liability. Equally they should not be recognised if they do not meet the definition. A balance sheet would not give a 'fair representation' if it did not include all of a company's liabilities (or if it did include, as liabilities, items that were not liabilities). These definitions benefit the reliability of financial statements by preventing profits from being 'smoothed' by making a provision to reduce profit in years when they are high and releasing those provisions to increase profit in years when they are low. It also means that the balance sheet cannot avoid the immediate recognition of long-term liabilities (such as environmental provisions) on the basis that those liabilities have not matured.

(b)   (i)   Future costs associated with the acquisition/construction and use of fixed assets, such as the environmental costs in this case, should be treated as a liability as soon as they become unavoidable. For Promoil this would be at the same time as the platform is acquired and brought into use. The provision is for the present value of the expected costs and this same amount is treated as part of the cost of the asset. The provision is 'unwound' by charging a finance cost to the profit and loss account each year and increasing the provision by the finance cost. Annual depreciation of the asset effectively allocates the (discounted) environmental costs over the life of the asset.

Profit and loss account for the year ended 30 September 2008 £000

Depreciation (see below)	3,690
Finance costs (£6.9 million × 8%)	552

Balance sheet as at 30 September 2008

Fixed assets

Cost (£30 million + £6.9 million (£15 million × 0.46))	36,900
Depreciation (over 10 years)	(3,690)
	———
	33,210
	———

Creditors due after more than one year

Environmental provision (£6.9 million × 1·08)   7,452

(ii)   If there was no legal requirement to incur the environmental costs, then Promoil should not provide for them as they do not meet the definition of a liability. Thus the oil platform would be recorded at £30 million with £3 million depreciation and there would be no finance costs.

However, if Promoil has a published policy that it will voluntarily incur environmental clean up costs of this type (or if this may be implied by its past practice), then this would be evidence of a 'constructive obligation' under FRS 12 and the required treatment of the costs would be the same as in part (i) above.

27   DEARING [footprints icon] WALK IN THE FOOTSTEPS OF A TOP TUTOR

[key icon]

Key answer tips

To achieve the marks in this question you must have a knowledge of the difference between capital and revenue expenditure. Once the cost of the asset has been determined you are required to apply your knowledge of FRS 15 property, plant and equipment. The question complications include calculating depreciation and the treatment of subsequent expenditure.

Year ended/as at	30 September 2006	30 September 2007	30 September 2008
Profit and loss account	£	£	£
Depreciation (see workings)	180,000	270,000	119,000
Maintenance (60,000/3 years)	20,000	20,000	20,000
Discount received (840,000 × 5%)	(42,000)		
Staff training	40,000		
	198,000	290,000	139,000
Balance sheet (see below)			
Plant and equipment			
Cost	670,000	920,000	920,000
Accumulated depreciation	(180,000)	(450,000)	(119,000)
Carrying amount	740,000	470,000	551,000

Workings	£
Manufacturer's base price	1,050,000
Less trade discount (20%)	(210,000)
	────────
Base cost	840,000
Freight charges	30,000
Electrical installation cost	28,000
Pre-production testing	22,000
	────────
Initial capitalised cost	920,000
	────────

This question requires depreciation to be calculated on a machine hours basis rather than the standard straight-line or reducing balance basis. Make sure you read the information in the question carefully.

The depreciable amount is £900,000 (920,000 – 20,000 residual value) and, based on an estimated machine life of 6,000 hours, this gives depreciation of £150 per machine hour. Therefore depreciation for the year ended 30 September 2006 is £180,000 (£150 × 1,200 hours) and for the year ended 30 September 2007 is £270,000 (£150 × 1,800 hours).

Note: early settlement discount, staff training in use of machine and maintenance are all revenue items and cannot be part of capitalised costs.

Carrying amount at 1 October 2007	470,000
Subsequent expenditure	200,000
	────────
Revised 'cost'	670,000
	────────

The revised depreciable amount is £630,000 (670,000 – 40,000 residual value) and with a revised remaining life of 4,500 hours, this gives a depreciation charge of £140 per machine hour. Therefore depreciation for the year ended 30 September 2008 is £119,000 (£140 × 850 hours).

28 WAXWORK

(a) Events after the balance sheet date are defined by FRS 21 *Events after the Balance Sheet Date* as those events, both favourable and unfavourable, that occur between the balance sheet date and the date that the financial statements are authorised for issue (normally by the Board of directors).

An adjusting event is one that provides further evidence of conditions that existed at the balance sheet date, including an event that indicates that the going concern assumption in relation to the whole or part of the entity is not appropriate. Normally trading results occurring after the balance sheet date are a matter for the next accounting period. However, if there is an event which would normally be treated as non-adjusting that causes a dramatic downturn in trading (and profitability) such that it is likely that the entity will no longer be a going concern, this should be treated as an adjusting event.

A non-adjusting event is an event after the balance sheet date that is indicative of a condition that arose after the balance sheet date and, subject to the exception noted above, the financial statements would not be adjusted to reflect such events.

The outcome (and values) of many items in the financial statements have a degree of uncertainty at the balance sheet date. FRS 21 effectively says that, where events occurring after the balance sheet date help to determine what those values were at the balance sheet date, they should be taken in account (i.e. adjusted for) in preparing the financial statements.

If non-adjusting events, whilst not affecting the financial statements of the current year, are of such importance (i.e. material) that without disclosure of their nature and estimated financial effect, users' ability to make proper evaluations and decisions about the future of the entity would be affected, then they should be disclosed in the notes to the financial statements.

(b)   (i)   At first sight this is a non-adjusting event as there was no reason to doubt that the value of warehouse and the stock it contained was worth less than its carrying amount at 31 March 2009 (the balance sheet date). The total loss suffered as a result of the fire is £16 million. The company expects that £9 million of this loss will be recovered from an insurance policy. Recoveries from third parties should be assessed separately from the related loss. As this event has caused serious disruption to trading, FRS 21 would require the details of this non-adjusting event to be disclosed in the financial statements for the year ended 31 March 2009 as a total loss of £16 million and the effect of the insurance recovery to be disclosed separately.

The severe disruption in Waxwork's trading operations since the fire, together with the expectation of large trading losses for some time to come, may call in to question the going concern status of the company. If it is judged that Waxwork is no longer a going concern, then the fire and its consequences become an adjusting event requiring the financial statements for the year ended 31 March 2009 to be redrafted on the basis that the company is no longer a going concern (i.e. they would be prepared on a liquidation basis).

(ii)   70% of the stock amounts to £322,000 (460,000 × 70%) and this was sold for a net amount of £238,000 (280,000 × 85%). Thus a large proportion of a class of stock was sold at a loss after the reporting period. This would appear to give evidence of conditions that existed at 31 March 2009 (i.e. that the net realisable value of that class of stock was below its cost). Stock is required to be valued at the lower of cost and net realisable value, thus this is an adjusting event. If it is assumed that the remaining stock will be sold at similar prices and terms as that already sold, the net realisable value of the whole of the class of stock would be calculated as:

£280,000/70% = £400,000, less commission of 15% = £340,000.

Thus the carrying amount of the stock of £460,000 should be written down by £120,000 to its net realisable value of £340,000.

In the unlikely event that the fall in the value of the stock could be attributed to a specific event that occurred after the balance sheet date then this would be a non-adjusting event.

(iii) The date of the government announcement of the tax change is beyond the period of consideration in FRS 21. Thus this would be neither an adjusting nor a non-adjusting event. The increase in the deferred tax liability will be provided for in the year to 31 March 2010. Had the announcement been before 6 May 2009, it would have been treated as a non-adjusting event requiring disclosure of the nature of the event and an estimate of its financial effect in the notes to the financial statements.

ACCA marking scheme			Marks
(a)	definition		1
	discussion of adjusting events		2
	reference to going concern		1
	discussion of non-adjusting events		1
	Maximum		5
(b)	(i) to (iv) 1 mark per valid point as indicated	Maximum	10
	Total for question		15

Examiner's comments

I was particularly disappointed with candidates' performance on this question. Part (a) was straightforward for anyone who had read FRS 21 Events after the Reporting Period (or variant equivalents) and the three illustrative examples are well documented in the Standard and text books. In part (a) many candidates attempted to distinguish between adjusting and non-adjusting events through the use of examples rather than by description. Examples were not asked for in Part (a) and therefore did not earn marks.

In part (a) there was a lot of confusion over the period covered by the Standard, many candidates thought there is a set time (e.g. 3 or 6 months) or that the period extends to the AGM. To state that an adjusting event requires adjustment - and a non-adjusting event doesn't - did not earn any marks as it says nothing and certainly does not relate to the issues raised by FRS 21. Many candidates also thought that the determining factor regarding whether to adjust or not lies with whether the item is material or not. Several candidates suggested that examples (ii) and (iii) were not material, despite the note to the question providing clear guidance on this point. Weaker candidates confused the topic with prior period adjustments and the use of provisions and contingent items.

Unsurprisingly, if candidates were not able to correctly answer part (a), they did not gain many marks in the examples in part (b), however many candidates who did know the definitions in (a) still could not apply the circumstances to the part (b) scenarios. There were a lot of comments in (b) that contradicted definitions given in part (a).

(b)(i) This example dealt with the consequences a fire after the reporting period. The common errors were to say this was an adjusting event (it was non-adjusting), most candidates netted off potential insurance proceeds from the losses and did not appreciate that the losses and the related insurance claim required different considerations. Hardly anyone realised that the subsequent disruption of trading may have brought into question the going concern of the company (which would then make it an adjusting event). Even those candidates who correctly stated this was a non-adjusting event proceeded, often at great length, to itemise the journal entries needed as if it was an adjusting event (without any mention of the going concern aspects). (ii) This was an example of sale of inventory at a loss after the reporting period. Most candidates focused on the sale itself and said it should be dealt with in the following year therefore no adjustment was required. Some correctly appreciated that the relevant issue was that the inventory's value should be adjusted because its net realisable value was below cost. However two further errors were common; either they did not extend the lower of NRV or cost principle to the whole of the inventory (instead just the 70% that had been sold) or they wanted to put the sale through the current year's accounts rather than just write the inventory down. Weaker candidates stated the transaction was a non-adjusting event, as it took place after the reporting date, but, in contradiction, then proceeded to explain at great length the adjustments that the sale and commission would create. (iii) This concerned a change in taxation legislation after the financial statements had been authorised. The main point of this example was the timing of the event, specifically after the financial statements had been authorised by the board and was thus neither an adjusting nor non-adjusting event (it was outside the scope of the Standard). Most candidates did not appreciate the timing of the event and even those that did still wanted to adjust for it and proceeded to explain the nature and purpose of deferred tax.

29 FLIGHTLINE

Flightline – Profit and loss account for the year ended 31 March 2009

	£000
Depreciation (w (i))	13,800
Loss on write off of engine (w (iii))	6,000
Repairs – engine	3,000
– Exterior painting	2,000

Balance sheet as at 31 March 2009

Fixed asset – Aircraft

	Cost	Accumulated depreciation	Carrying amount
	£000	£000	£000
Exterior (w (i))	120,000	84,000	36,000
Cabin fittings (w (ii))	29,500	21,500	8,000
Engines (w (iii))	19,800	3,700	16,100
	169,300	109,200	60,100

Workings (figures in brackets in £000)

(i) The exterior of the aircraft is depreciated at £6 million per annum (120,000/20 years). The cabin is depreciated at £5 million per annum (25,000/5 years). The engines would be depreciated by £500 (£18 million/36,000 hours) i.e. £250 each, per flying hour.

The carrying amount of the aircraft at 1 April 2008 is:

	Cost	Accumulated depreciation	Carrying amount
	£000	£000	£000
Exterior (13 years old)	120,000	78,000	42,000
Cabin (3 years old)	25,000	15,000	10,000
Engines (used 10,800 hours)	18,000	5,400	12600
	163,000	98,400	64,600

Depreciation for year to 31 March 2009:	£000
Exterior (no change)	6,000
Cabin fittings – six months to 30 September 2008 (5,000 × 6/12)	2,500
– six months to 31 March 2009 (w (ii))	4,000
Engines – six months to 30 September 2008 (500 × 1,200 hours)	600
– six months to 31 March 2009 ((400 + 300) w (iii))	700
	13,800

(ii) Cabin fittings – at 1 October 2008 the carrying amount of the cabin fittings is £7·5 million (10,000 – 2,500). The cost of improving the cabin facilities of £4.5 million should be capitalised as it led to enhanced future economic benefits in the form of substantially higher fares. The cabin fittings would then have a carrying amount of £12 million (7,500 + 4,500) and an unchanged remaining life of 18 months. Thus depreciation for the six months to 31 March 2009 is £4 million (12,000 × 6/18).

(iii) Engines – before the accident the engines (in combination) were being depreciated at a rate of £500 per flying hour. At the date of the accident each engine had a carrying amount of £6 million ((12,600 – 600)/2). This represents the loss on disposal of the written off engine. The repaired engine's remaining life was reduced to 15,000 hours. Thus future depreciation on the repaired engine will be £400 per flying hour, resulting in a depreciation charge of £400,000 for the six months to 31 March 2009. The new engine, with a cost of £10.8 million and a life of 36,000 hours, will be depreciated by £300 per flying hour, resulting in a depreciation charge of £300,000 for the six months to 31 March 2009. Summarising both engines:

	Cost	Accumulated depreciation	Carrying amount
	£000	£000	£000
Old engine	9,000	3,400	5,600
New engine	10,800	300	10,500
	19,800	3,700	16,100

ACCA marking scheme			Marks
Profit and loss account depreciation	– exterior		1
	– cabin fittings		2
	– engines		2
loss on write off of engine repairs			1
repairs			1
Balance sheet			
carrying amount at 31 March 2009			3
			–––
Total			10
			–––

Examiner's comments

This question required candidates to depreciate the separate components of a 'complex' asset (an aircraft) dealing with different methods of depreciation and distinguishing between capital and revenue expenditures.

A significant number of candidates did not start this question and many more that did appeared to run out of time. There were no general issues here with candidates not understanding what they were meant to do or not reading the requirements properly, however many answers lacked a methodical approach meaning they got hopelessly lost in the detail. Generally the exterior structure of the aircraft was dealt with correctly although many capitalised the repainting costs (which is revenue expenditure). For the cabin fittings, the upgrade was often correctly capitalised but then the depreciation was calculated on (total) cost, not the new carrying amount and also over the wrong period. The engines caused the most problems. Candidates often tried to perform the calculations of them together, instead of separating them, and then became confused in what they were doing.

30 WELLMAY

Wellmay Profit and loss account year ended 31 March 2007

	£000
Turnover (4,200 – 500 (w (i)))	3,700
Cost of sales (w (ii))	(2,417)
	–––––
Gross profit	1,283
Operating expenses (470 + 8 depreciation)	(478)
Investment property income – rental	20
Finance costs (w (iii))	(113)
	–––––
Profit before tax	712
Taxation (360 + 30 (w (v)))	(390)
	–––––
Profit for the period	322
	–––––

Movement in share capital and reserves – year ended 31 March 2007

	Equity shares	Equity option	Factory revn reserve	Investment property revn	Profit and loss reserve	Total
	£000	£000	£000	£000	£000	£000
Balances at 1 April 2006	1,200		300	50	2,615	4,165
Equity conversion option (w (iv))		40				40
Bonus issue (1 for 4)	300				(300)	
Revaluation of factory (w (vi))			190			190
Revaluation of investment property (w (vi))				(25)		(25)
Profit for the period					322	322
Dividends					(400)	(400)
Balances at 31 March 2007	1,500	40	490	25	2,237	4,292

Balance sheet as at 31 March 2007

	£000	£000
Tangible fixed assets (w (vi))		4,390
Investment property (w (vi))		375
		4,765
Current assets (1,400 + 200 stock (w (i)))	1,600	
Creditors: amounts falling due within one year (820 – 75 (w (ii)))	(745)	
Loan from Westwood (500 + 50 accrued interest) (w (i))	(550)	
Net current assets		305
Creditors: amounts falling due after more than one year		
8% Convertible loan note ((560 + 8) (w (iv)))		(568)
Provisions for liabilities		
Deferred tax (w (v))		(210)
		4,292
Share capital and reserves (see movement in share capital and reserves above)		
Equity shares of 50 pence each		1,500
Equity option (w (iv))		40
		1,540

Reserves:			
Revaluation reserve	– factory	490	
	– investment property	25	
	– profit and loss account	2,237	2,752
			4,292

Workings (note: all figures in £000)

(i)   The 'sale' to Westwood is, in substance, a secured loan. The repurchase price is the cost of sale plus compound interest at 10% for two years. The correct accounting treatment is to reverse the sale with the goods going back into stock and the 'proceeds' treated as a loan with accrued interest of 10% (£50,000) for the current year.

(ii)   **Cost of sales**

From draft financial statements	2,700
Sale of goods added back to stock (see above)	(200)
Reversal of contingency provision (see below)	(75)
Depreciation transferred to operating costs (40 × 20%)	(8)
	2,417

General or non-specific provisions do not meet the definition of a liability in FRS 12 *Provisions, contingent liabilities and contingent assets* and must therefore be reversed.

(iii) **Finance costs**

From draft financial statements	55
Additional accrued interest on convertible loan (w (iv))	8
Finance cost on in-substance loan (500 × 10%)	50
	113

(iv)   **Convertible Loan**

This is a compound financial instrument that contains an element of debt and an element of equity (the option to convert). FRS 25 *Financial instruments: disclosure and presentation* requires that the substance of such instruments should be applied to the reporting of them. The value of the debt element is calculated by discounting the future cash flows (at 10%). The residue of the issue proceeds is recorded as the value of the equity option:

	Cash flows	Factor at 10%	Present value £000
Year 1 interest	48	0.91	43.6
Year 2 interest	48	0.83	39.8
Year 3 interest	48	0.75	36.0
Year 4 interest, redemption premium and capital	648	0.68	440.6
Total value of debt component			560.0
Proceeds of the issue			600.0
Equity component (residual amount)			40.0

For the year ended 31 March 2007, the interest cost for the convertible loan in the profit and loss account should be increased from £48,000 to £56,000 (10% × 560) by accruing £8,000, which should be added to the carrying value of the debt.

(v) **Taxation**

The required deferred tax balance is £210,000 (600 × 35%), the current balance is £180,000, and thus a further transfer of £30,000 (via the profit and loss account) is required.

(vi) **Properties**

Factory

After depreciation of £40,000 for the year ended 31 March 2007, the factory (used by Wellmay) would have a carrying amount of £1,160,000 (1,200 – 40). The valuation of £1,350,000 at 31 March 2007 would give a further revaluation surplus of £190,000 (1,350 – 1,160) and a carrying amount of tangible fixed assets of £4,390,000 (4,200 + 190) at that date.

Investment property

SSAP 19 *Accounting for investment properties* requires the fall in the fair value of the investment property during the year ended 31 March 2007 of £25,000 to be reported in equity (investment property revaluation reserve).

31 LLAMA

Key answer tip

This published accounts question has a heavy FRS 15 focus so there are many easy marks available. For parts (a) and (b) you need to ensure that you set your answer up in advance outlining the proforma's. Once these have been set up keep moving through the question building up the answer as you go. Part (c) required the calculation of FPS following a rights issue of shares. Ensure that you use the profit figure calculated in part (a) to do this.

(a) Llama – Profit and loss account – Year ended 30 September 2007

	£000	£000
Turnover		180,400
Cost of sales (w (i))		(81,700)
		———
Gross profit		98,700
Distribution costs (11,000 + 1,000 depreciation)	(12,000)	
Administrative expenses (12,500 + 1,000 depreciation)	(13,500)	(25,500)
	———	
Investment income	2,200	
Gain on fair value of investments (27,100 – 26,500)	600	2,800
	———	
Finance costs (w (ii))		(2,400)
		———
Profit before tax		73,600

Corporation tax expense
(18,700 − 400 − (11,200 − 10,000) deferred tax)   (17,100)

Profit for the period   56,500

(b)   Llama – Balance sheet as at 30 September 2007

	£000	£000
Fixed assets		
Land and buildings (w (iv))		122,000
Plant and equipment (w (iv))		106,500
Investments at fair value through profit and loss		27,100
		255,600
Current assets		
Stock	37,900	
Trade debtors	35,100	
	73,000	
Creditors: amounts falling due within one year		
Bank overdraft	6,600	
Trade creditors	34,700	
Corporation tax	18,700	
	(60,000)	
Net current assets		13,000
Creditors: amounts falling due after more than one year		
2% loan note (80,000 + 1,600 (w (ii)))		(81,600)
Provisions for liabilities		
Deferred tax (40,000 × 25%)		(10,000)
		177,000
Capital and reserves		
Equity shares of 50 pence each ((60,000 + 15,000) w (iii))		75,000
Reserves:		
Share premium (w (iii))	9,000	
Revaluation (14,000 − 3,000 (w (iv)))	11,000	
Profit and loss account (56,500 + 25,500)	82,000	102,000
		177,000

Workings (monetary figures in brackets are in £000)

(i)   **Cost of sales:**

		£000
Per question		89,200
Plant capitalised (w (iv))		(24,000)
Depreciation (w (iv))	– buildings	3,000
	– plant	13,500
		81,700

(ii)   The loan has been in issue for six months. The total finance charge should be based on the effective interest rate of 6%. This gives a charge of £2.4 million (80,000 × 6% × 6/12). As the actual interest paid is £800,000 an accrual (added to the carrying amount of the loan) of £1.6 million is required.

(iii) The rights issue was 30 million shares (60 million/50 pence is 120 million shares at 1 for 4) at a price of 80 pence this would increase share capital by £15 million (30 million × 50 pence) and share premium by £9 million (30 million × 30 pence).

(iv)   Fixed assets/depreciation:

Land and buildings:

On 1 October 2006 the value of the buildings was £100 million (130,000 – 30,000 land). The remaining life at this date was 20 years, thus the annual depreciation charge will be £5 million (3,000 to cost of sales and 1,000 each to distribution and administration). Prior to the revaluation at 30 September 2007 the carrying amount of the building was £95 million (100,000 – 5,000). With a revalued amount of £92 million, this gives a revaluation deficit of £3 million which should be debited to the revaluation reserve. The carrying amount of land and buildings at 30 September 2007 will be £122 million (92,000 buildings + 30,000 land (unchanged)).

Plant

The existing plant will be depreciated by £12 million ((128,000 – 32,000) × 12 1/2%) and have a carrying amount of £84 million at 30 September 2007.

The plant manufactured for internal use should be capitalised at £24 million (6,000 + 4,000 + 8,000 + 6,000).

Depreciation on this will be £1.5 million (24,000 × 12 1/2% × 6/12). This will give a carrying amount of £22.5 million at 30 September 2007. Thus total depreciation for plant is £13.5 million with a carrying amount of £106.5 million (84,000 + 22,500)

(c)   Earnings per share (eps) for the year ended 30 September 2007

Theoretical ex rights value			£
Holding (say)	100	at £1	100
Issue (1 for 4)	25	at 80 pence	20
New holding	125	ex rights price is 96 pence	120

Weighted average number of shares

120,000,000	× 9/12 × 100/96	93,750,000
150,000,000 (120 × 5/4)	× 3/12	37,500,000
		131,250,000

Earnings per share (£56,500,000/131,250,000) 43 pence

Examiners Report

This question asked candidates to prepare an income statement and balance sheet from a trial balance after dealing with several notes. A calculation of earnings per share (eps) was also required.

Most candidates did well on this question scoring good marks even if they did not fully understand all the issues or were not able to complete all the parts. The main adjustments contained in the question were generally well understood and correctly accounted for. Again, in order to assist future studies, the common errors were:

- confusion over the timing of the revaluation of the land and buildings. The question clearly stated that the revaluation was at the end of the year. This meant that the annual deprecation charge for the buildings should be based on the value at the beginning of the year (i.e. the value included in the trial balance) and the revaluation (giving a impairment/deficit in this example) should be based on the carrying amount of the asset after the year's depreciation had been deducted. It was common to see candidates performing the revaluation at the beginning of the year. Another surprisingly common error was calculating depreciation of the plant based on cost rather than the reducing balance. Most candidates did correctly identify the capitalisation of the internally manufactured plant, although many did not realise that this occurred half way through the year necessitating time-apportioned depreciation.

- another common error was to reduce cost of sales by the closing inventory; by definition cost of sales has already been adjusted for closing inventory.

- the gain in the fair value of the investments was often treated as part of the revaluation reserve, rather than as income in the period.

- a number of candidates did not appreciate that the loan interest paid was for only six months and that the year's finance costs should be based on the effective interest rate of 6% rather than the nominal rate of 2%. Those that did correctly account for the accrued finance costs in the income statement often forgot to add it to the carrying amount of the loan in the balance sheet.

- the tax calculation was often confused. The opening credit balance of $400,000 was often treated as charge (debit) and the adjustment for deferred tax was often taken as $40 million rather than 25% of $40 million.

- similar to question 1, many candidates could not correctly account for the share capital and share premium of a rights issue, often showing a combined figure or showing it as a suspense account in the balance sheet.

- the revaluation reserve was often left at its opening balance without taking account of the revaluation of the land and buildings.

- a very common and basic error was to include the bank overdraft in current assets.

– answers to the calculation of the eps were very mixed. A significant number of candidates did not attempt it and those that did often struggled with effect of the rights issue on the ex-rights price and the weighting exercise.

ACCA marking scheme		
		Marks
(a)	Profit and loss account	
	Turnover	½
	Cost of sales	3½
	Distribution costs and administrative expenses	1
	Investment income and gain on investment	1½
	Finance costs	1
	Tax	1½
		9
(b)	Balance sheet	
	Land and buildings	1½
	Plant and equipment	1½
	Investments	1
	Current assets	1
	Overdraft and trade creditors	1
	Corporation tax provision	½
	2% loan notes	1½
	Deferred tax	1
	Equity shares	1
	Share premium	1
	Revaluation reserve	1
	Profit and loss account	1
		13
(c)	Earnings per share	
	Calculation of theoretical ex rights value	1
	Weighted average number of shares	1
	Earnings and calculation of eps	1
		3
Total		**25**

32   DEXON

> **Key answer tip**
>
> Part (a) required a recalculation of profit – you were expected to consider how the further information would therefore affect profit.   Remember a credit entry to the P&L will increase profit whereas a debit entry will reduce profit. Part (b) required you to prepare a Statement of the movement of share capital and reserves, many easy marks could be gained here – you need to recognise that the share issue had already been recorded so you are required to work backwards to find the opening balances. Part (c) required you to restate the balance sheet. An added complication in this question exists with deferred tax. You are required to calculate the deferred tax relating to the revaluation reserve as well the P&L movement.

(a)		£000	£000
Profit for period per question			96,700
Dividends paid (w (i))			15,500
			———
Draft profit for year ended 31 March 2008			112,200
Discovery of fraud (w (ii))			(2,500)
Goods on sale or return (w (iii))			(600)
Depreciation (w (iv)) – buildings (165,000/15 years)		11,000	
– plant (180,500 × 20%)		36,100	(47,100)
		———	
Increase in investments ((12,500 × 1,296/1,200) – 12,500)			1,000
Provision for corporation tax			(11,400)
Increase in deferred tax (w (v))			(800)
			———
Recalculated profit for year ended 31 March 2008			50,800
			———

(b)   **Dexon – statement of the movement in share capital and reserves – Year ended 31 March 2008**

	Ordinary shares	Share premium	Revaluation reserve	P & L £000	Total £000
At 1 April 2007	200,000	30,000	18,000	12,300	260,300
Prior period adjustment (w (ii))				(1,500)	(1,500)
				———	———
Restated earnings at 1 April 2007				10,800	
Revaluation of property (w (iv))			4,800		4,800
Rights issue (see below)	50,000	10,000			60,000
Profit for period (from (a))				50,800	50,800
Dividends paid (w (i))				(15,500)	(15,500)
	———	———	———	———	———
At 31 March 2008	250,000	40,000	22,800	46,100	358,900

Rights issue: 250 million shares in issue after a rights issue of one for four would mean that 50 million shares were issued (250,000 × 1/5). As the issue price was £1·20, this would create £50 million of share capital and £10 million of share premium.

(c) **Dexon – Balance sheet as at 31 March 2008:**

	£000	£000
Fixed assets		
Property (w (iv))		180,000
Plant (180,500 – 36,100 depreciation see (a))		144,400
Investments at fair value through profit and loss (12,500 + 1,000 see (a))		13,500
		———
		337,900
Current assets		
Stock (84,000 + 2,000 (w (iii)))	86,000	
Debtors (52,200 – 4,000 – 2,600 (w (ii) and (iii)))	45,600	
Bank	3,800	
	———	
	135,400	
Creditors: amounts falling due within one year		
(81,800 + 11,400 tax)	(93,200)	
	———	
Net current assets		42,200
Provision for liabilities		
Deferred tax (19,200 + 2,000 (w (v)))		(21,200)
		———
		358,900
		———
Share capital and reserves (from (b))		
Ordinary shares of £1each		250,000
Share premium	40,000	
Revaluation reserve	22,800	
Profit and loss account	46,100	108,900
	———	———
		358,900
		———

Workings (figures in brackets in £'000)

(i) Dividends paid

The dividend in May 2007 would be £8 million (200 million shares at 4 pence) and in November 2007 would be £7·5 million (250 million shares × 3 pence). Total dividends would therefore have been £15·5 million.

(ii) The discovery of the fraud means that £4 million should be written off debtors. £1·5 million is debited to the profit and loss account reserve as a prior period adjustment (in the statement of recognised gains and losses and shown here in the statement of the movements in share capital and reserves above) and £2·5 is written off in the profit and loss account for the year ended 31 March 2008.

(iii)   Goods on sale or return

The sales over which customers still have the right of return should not be included in Dexon's turnover. The reversing effect is to reduce the relevant debtors by £2·6 million, increase stock by £2 million (the cost of the goods (2,600 × 100/130)) and reduce the profit and loss account for the year by the profit of £600,000.

(iv)   Property

The carrying amount of the property (after the year's depreciation) is £174 million (185,000 – 11,000). A valuation of £180 million would create a revaluation surplus of £6 million of which £1·2 million (6,000 × 20%) would be transferred to deferred tax as the liability is likely to arise in the near future.

(v)   Deferred tax

An increase in the timing differences of £10 million would create a transfer (credit) to deferred tax of £2 million (10,000 × 20%). Of this £1·2 million relates to the revaluation of the property and is debited to the revaluation reserve. The balance, £800,000, is charged to the profit and loss account.

ACCA marking scheme		Marks
(a)	Adjustments:	
	add back dividends	1
	balance of fraud loss	1
	goods on sale or return	1
	depreciation charges	2
	investment gain	1
	taxation provision	1
	deferred tax	1
	Maximum	8
(b)	Statement of movement in share capital and reserves	
	balances b/f	1
	restated earnings b/f	1
	gain on revaluation of property	2
	rights issue	2
	profit for period	1
	dividends paid	1
	Maximum	8
(c)	Balance sheet	
	property	1
	plant	1
	investment	1
	stock	1
	debtors	2
	current liabilities	1
	deferred tax	1
	capital and reserves from (b)	1
	Maximum	9
Total		25

Examiners Report

This question asked candidates to recalculate the annual profit, prepare a statement of changes in equity (SOCIE) and redraft a given statement of financial position (balance sheet) after accounting for a series of adjustments. The adjustments required were for: reversing a sale or return transaction, depreciation (after a revaluation), an increase in the value of investments, correcting for a discovered fraud, tax and deferred tax and dealing with the effects of a share issue and dividend payments. For those that knew how to tackle this type of question, the recalculation/restatement of the annual profit was done quite well with many candidates gaining 5 or 6 out of the 8 marks available. The most common errors were:

- failing to add back the dividends to the retained earnings for the year to give a starting point for the profit for the year

- adjusting for the sales revenue rather than the profit made on goods subject to an outstanding sale and return agreement (some adjusted for both the sales revenue and the cost of sales which was marked as correct)

- taking the revaluation of the land and buildings as if it were at the beginning of the year (the question clearly stated it was at the end of the year)

- deducting the whole of the cost of a fraud from the current year's profit (part of it related to the previous year and should have been treated as a prior period adjustment in the SOCIE)

- taking the whole of the increase in deferred tax to the income statement (part of it related to the property revaluation and should also have been included in the SOCIE)

Many of the errors made in the recalculation of the profit for the year were carried on to the SOCIE or/and the statement of financial position. Additionally in the SOCIE many candidates did not realise that the share issue had already been accounted for (the question made this quite clear) thus they treated the figures in the statement of financial position as if they were at the beginning of the year rather than at the end of the year and consequently calculated the wrong share capital and share premium movements. Very few included the deferred tax effect of the revaluation and an incorrect calculation of the dividends was also common (or omitted completely).

The statement of financial position was generally well done and most of the errors that were made generally related to the following through of earlier (previously mentioned) errors. For example it was common not to eliminate the sale and return receivable and not to include the related inventory in current assets. Strangely a few candidates spent time trying to calculate an ex-rights price for the share issue. This was not asked for.

---

33 TOURMALET

🔑

Key answer tips

The requirement in part (a) to comment on the directors' treatment of the plant is a strong hint that they have got it wrong. Note that a balance sheet is not required in your answer. It would waste time and earn no marks if you decided to prepare one.

(a) The sale of the plant has been incorrectly treated on two counts. Firstly even if it were a genuine sale it should not have been included in sales and cost of sales, rather it should have been treated as the disposal of a fixed asset. Only the profit or loss on the disposal would be included in the profit and loss account (requiring separate disclosure as an exceptional item if material). However, even this treatment would be incorrect. As Tourmalet will continue to use the plant for the remainder of its useful life, the substance of this transaction is a secured loan. Thus the receipt of £50 million for the 'sale' of the plant should be treated as a loan. The rentals, when they are eventually paid, will be applied partly as interest (at 12% per annum) and the remainder will be a capital repayment of the loan. In the profit and loss account an accrual for loan interest of 12% per annum on £50 million for four months (£2 million) is required.

(b) **Tourmalet profit and loss account – Year to 30 September 20X3**

	Continuing operations	Discontinuing operations	Total
	£000	£000	£000
Turnover (313,000 – 50,000 (see (a) above))	247,800	15,200	263,000
Cost of sales (W1)	(128,800)	(16,000)	(144,800)
Gross profit (loss)	119,000	(800)	118,200
Distribution expenses	(26,400)	nil	(26,400)
Administration expenses (W3)	(20,000)	(4,700)	(24,700)
Profit (loss) on ordinary activities before interest	72,600	(5,500)	67,100
Financing cost (see (a) + 1,800 (W4))			(3,800)
Investment income			(1,200)
Profit before tax			64,500
Taxation (9,200 – 2,100)			(7,100)
Profit for the period			57,400

(c) **Statement of total recognised gains and losses – Year to 30 September 20X3**

	£000
Profit for the financial year	57,400
Unrealised deficit on investment properties (W5)	(200)
Total gains and losses recognised since last annual report	57,200

Workings

(W1) **Cost of sales:**

	£000
Opening stock	26,550
Purchases	158,450
Transfer to plant (see (a))	(40,000)
Depreciation (W2)	25,800
Closing stock (28,500 – (4,500 – 2,000) see below)	(26,000)
	144,800

The slow moving stock should be written down to its estimated realisable value. Despite the optimism of the Directors, it would seem prudent to base the realisable value on the best offer so far received (i.e. £2 million).

(W2) **Fixed assets depreciation**

	£000
Buildings £120/40 years	3,000
Plant – per trial balance ((98,600 – 24,600) × 20%)	14,800
Plant – plant treated as sold (40,000/5 years)	8,000
	25,800

For information only:

In the balance sheet	Cost/valuation	Accumulated Depreciation	Net book Value
	£000	£000	£000
Land and buildings	150,000	12,000	138,000
Plant – per trial balance	98,600	39,400	59,200
Plant incorrectly treated as sold	40,000	8,000	32,000
			229,200

(W3) It would seem prudent to accrue for the penalty on the lease as it is uncertain that the permission for a change of use will be granted. In these circumstances, the payment of the penalty will be the lowest liability. This gives total administration expenses of £24,700 (23,200 + 1,500), of which £4,700 (3,200 + 1,500) is classed as discontinued

(W4) The second half of the preference dividend (£900,000) must be accrued. The preference shares are redeemable and therefore in the balance sheet would be treated as liabilities. Therefore in line with FRS 25 *Financial Instruments: Presentation* the preference dividend is shown as a finance cost along with the finance cost of other liabilities.

(W5) Revaluation reserve

	£000
Per trial balance	2,100
Loss on investment property (10,000 – 9,800)	(200)
Balance at 30 September 20X3	1,900

Note: This balance sheet is provided for information only. It does not form part of the answer or marking scheme.

Tourmalet – Balance sheet as at 30 September 20X3

	£000	£000
Tangible fixed assets (W2)		229,200
Investment properties		9,800
		239,000
Current assets		
Stocks (W1)	26,000	
Trade debtors	31,200	
Bank	3,700	
	60,900	
Creditors: amounts falling due within one year		
Trade creditors	35,300	
Accrued penalty cost (W3)	1,500	
Accrued finance costs (2,000 per (a) above + 900 (W4))	2,900	
Taxation	9,200	
	48,900	
Net current assets		12,000
Creditors: amounts falling due after more than one year		
In-substance loan (see (a))		(50,000)
6% Redeemable preference shares		(30,000)
Net assets		171,000
Share capital and reserves		
Ordinary shares of 20p each		50,000
Reserves:		
Profit and loss account (57,400 + 64,200 – 2,500 interim div)	119,100	
Revaluation reserve (W5)	1,900	121,000
		171,000

34 HARRINGTON

> **Key answer tips**
>
> In the profit and loss account most of the adjustments are reflected in cost of sales but there are other adjustments for investment income, loan interest and taxation as well. In part (b) take care with the share capital and share premium as the rights issue has already been recorded, therefore you will need to work backwards to find the opening balances.

(a)   **Restated profit and loss account – Year to 31 March 20X5**

	£000
Turnover (13,700 – 300 plant sale proceeds)	13,400
Cost of sales (W1)	(8,910)
	———
Gross profit	4,490
Operating expenses	(2,400)
	———
Profit on ordinary activities before interest	2,090
Investment income (1,320 – 1,200)	120
Loan interest (25 + 25 per (c) below)	(50)
	———
Profit on ordinary activities before tax	2,160
Taxation (55 + 260 + (350 – 280 deferred tax))	(385)
	———
Profit for the period	1,775
	———

(b)   **Movement of share capital and reserves – Year to 31 March 20X5**

	Ordinary shares	Share premium	Revaluation reserve	Profit and loss account	Total
	£000	£000	£000	£000	£000
At 1 April 20X4	1,600	40	Nil	2,990	4,630
Rights issue (see below)	400	560			960
Profit for period (see (a))				1,775	1,775
Revaluation of property (W2)			1,800		1,800
Transfer to realised profit (W2)			(80)	80	Nil
Ordinary dividends paid				(500)	(500)
	———	———	———	———	———
At 31 March 20X5	2,000	600	1,720	4,345	8,665
	———	———	———	———	———

The number of 25p ordinary shares at the year end is 8 million (£2 million × 4). This is after a rights issue of 1 for 4. Thus the number of shares prior to the issue would be 6.4 million (8 million × 4/5) and the rights issue would have been for 1.6 million shares. The rights issue price is 60p each which would be recorded as an increase in share capital of £400,000 (1.6 million × 25p) and an increase in share premium of £560,000 (1.6 million × 35p).

(c)   Balance Sheet as at 31 March 20X5

	£000	£000
Land and buildings (W2)		6,710
Plant (W3)		1,350
Investments (1,200 × 110%)		1,320
		9,380
Current assets		
Stock	1,750	
Trade debtors	2,450	
Bank	350	
	4,550	
Creditors: amounts falling due within one year		
Trade creditors	4,130	
Accrued loan interest ((500 × 10%) − 25 paid)	25	
Taxation	260	
	(4,415)	
Net current assets		135
Creditors: amounts falling due after more than one year		
10% loan note (issued 20X2)		(500)
Provisions for liabilities		
Deferred tax (1,400 × 25%)		(350)
Net assets		8,665
Capital and reserves (per part (b)):		
Ordinary shares of 25p each		2,000
Reserves		
Share premium	600	
Revaluation reserve	1,720	
Profit and loss account	4,345	6,665
		8,665

Workings (all figures in £000)

(W1) **Cost of sales:**

Per question	9,200
Profit on sale of plant ((900 – 630 (W3)) – 300 proceeds)	(30)
Depreciation – plant (W3)	450
– buildings (W2)	290
Capitalised expenses net of error (W2)	(1,000)
	8,910

(W2) **Land and buildings: cost/revaluation depreciation**

	Cost/revaluation	Depreciation
Self-constructed (see below)	1,000	50 (20-year life)
Revalued	6,000	240 (see below)
	7,000	290, so 6,710 net

Depreciation on the building element will be £240 (4,800/20 years). The revaluation will create a revaluation reserve initially of £1,800 (6,000 – (1,000 + 3,200)), however a transfer of £80 ((4,800 – 3,200/20 building element of the revaluation) to realised profit is required.

Self-constructed asset:

Purchased materials	150
Direct labour	800
Supervision	65
Design and planning costs	20
Error in construction (10 + 25)	(35)
	1,000

Note the cost of the error cannot be capitalised; it must therefore be written off.

(W3) **Plant**

	Cost	Depreciation 31 March 20X4	Carrying value
Per balance sheet	5,200	3,130	
Disposal	(900)	(630)	
	4,300	2,500	1,800

Depreciation for the year will be £450,000 (25% reducing balance), giving a net book value at 31 March 20X5 of £1,350,000.

35   CHAMBERLAIN

> **Key answer tips**
>
> The main complications are for the long-term contract. It started at the beginning of the current year, so there are no balances b/f.

(a)   **Chamberlain – Profit and loss account – Year to 30 September 20X4**

	£000
Turnover (246,500 + 50,000 (W1))	296,500
Cost of sales (W2)	(151,500)
Gross profit	145,000
Operating expenses	(29,000)
Profit on ordinary activities before interest	116,000
Interest expense (1,500 + 1,500 accrued)	(3,000)
Profit on ordinary activities before tax	113,000
Taxation (22,000 – (17,500 – 14,000))	(18,500)
Profit on ordinary activities for the period	94,500

(b)   **Chamberlain – Balance sheet as at 30 September 20X4**

	£000	£000
Intangible fixed assets		
Development costs (40,000 – 25,000)		15,000
Tangible fixed assets		
Land and buildings (W3)	337,000	
Plant and equipment (W3)	105,000	442,000
		457,000
Current assets		
Long-term contract balance (W1)	5,000	
Other stock	38,500	
Amounts recoverable on contracts (W1)	20,000	
Trade debtors	48,000	
Bank	12,500	
	124,000	

Creditors: amounts falling due within one year		
Trade creditor	45,000	
Accrued finance costs	1,500	
Taxation	22,000	
	————	
	(68,500)	
	————	
Net current assets		55,500
Creditors: amounts falling due after more than one year		
6% loan note		(50,000)
Provisions for liabilities		
Deferred tax		(14,000)
		————
Net assets		448,500
		————

	£000	£000
Share capital and reserves:		
Ordinary share capital		200,000
Reserves:		
Profit and loss account		
– 1 October 20X3	162,000	
– Year to 30 September 20X4 (94,500 – 8,000)	86,500	248,500
	————	————
		448,500
		————

Workings (all figures in £000)

(W1) Contract:

Contract price	125,000
Estimated cost	(75,000)
	————
Estimated total profit	50,000
	————
Contract cost for year (35,000 – 5,000 stock on site)	30,000
Estimated cost	75,000
Percentage complete (30,000/75,000)	40%
Year to 30 September 20X4	
Contract revenue – included in turnover (125,000 × 40%)	50,000
Contract costs – included in cost of sales (35,000 – 5,000)	(30,000)
Amounts recoverable on contracts (50,000 – 30,000 progress payment)	20,000
Long-term contract balance (stock)	5,000

(W2) **Cost of sales:**

Opening stock	35,500
Purchases	78,500
Contract costs (W1)	30,000
Research costs	25,000
Depreciation (W3) – buildings	6,000
– plant	15,000
Closing stock	(38,500)
	151,500

(W3) **Fixed assets/depreciation:**

Buildings:

A cost of £240 million (403m – 163m for the land) over a 40-year life gives annual depreciation of £6 million per annum.

This gives accumulated depreciation at 30 September 20X4 of £66 million (60m + 6m) and a net book value of £337 million (403m – 66m).

Plant:

The carrying value prior to the current year's depreciation is £120 million (180m – 60m). Depreciation at 12.5% on the reducing balance basis gives an annual charge of £15 million. This gives a carrying value at 30 September 20X4 of £105 million (120m – 15m).

36 TINTAGEL

🔑

Key answer tips

Part (a) requires adjustments to the figure for retained profits brought forward and retained profits for the year. The method of accounting for the overhaul costs of the excavating plant must be corrected, necessitating an adjustment to be made against the opening retained profits. In part (b), use the proforma balance sheet provided in the question, and slot in the revised figures, referenced to workings were necessary.

(a)   **Tintagel**

	£000	£000	£000
Profit and loss reserve at 1 April 20X3			48,100
Reversal of provision for plant overhaul (W4)			6,000
			54,100
Profit for the year to 31 March 20X4		48,500	
Lease rental charge added back (W1)		3,200	
Lease interest (W1)		(800)	
Depreciation (W2) – building	2,600		
– owned plant	22,000		
– leased plant	2,800	(27,400)	

Write down of stock (W3)	(2,400)	
Unrecorded creditor (W3)	(500)	
Reversal of provision for plant overhaul (W4)	6,000	
Increase in deferred tax (22.5 – 18.7)	(3,800)	
Loan note interest	(846)	21,954
Profit and loss reserve at 31 March 20X4		76,054

(b) **Tintagel – Balance sheet as at 31 March 20X4**

	£000	£000
Tangible fixed assets		
Freehold property (126,000 – 2,600 (W2))		123,400
Plant – owned (110,000 – 22,000 (W2))		88,000
– leased (11,200 – 2,800 (W2))		8,400
Investment property		12,400
		232,200
Current assets		
Stock (60,400 – 2,400 (W3))	58,000	
Trade debtors and prepayments	31,200	
Bank	13,800	
	103,000	
Creditors: amounts falling due within one year		
Trade creditors (47,400 + 500)	47,900	
Accrued loan interest (W5)	600	
Finance lease obligation (W1)	3,200	
Taxation	4,200	
	(55,900)	
Net current assets		47,100
Creditors: amounts falling due after more than one year		
Finance lease obligations (W1)	(5,600)	
8% Loan note	(14,346)	
		(19,946)
Provisions for liabilities		
Deferred tax		(22,500)
Net assets		236,854

Share capital and reserves

Ordinary shares of 25p each		150,000
Reserves:		
Share premium	10,000	
Investment property revaluation reserve (3,400 – (15,000 – 12,400)	800	
Profit and loss account – 31 March 20X4 (part (a))	76,054	86,854
		236,854

Workings

(W1) **Finance lease:**

The lease has been incorrectly treated as an operating lease. Treating it as a finance lease gives the following figures:

	£000
Cash price/recorded cost	11,200
First instalment (reversed in profit and loss account)	(3,200)
Capital outstanding at 1 April 20X3	8,000
Interest at 10% p.a. to 31 March 20X4 (current liability)	800

The capital outstanding of £8 million must be split between current and long-term liabilities. The second instalment payable on 1 April 20X4 will contain £800,000 of interest (8,000 × 10%), therefore the capital element in this payment will be £2.4 million and this is current liability. The leaves £5.6 million (8,000 – 2,400) as a long-term liability.

(W2) **Fixed assets depreciation:**

	£000
Buildings (130,000 × 2%)	2,600
Owned plant (110,000 × 20%)	22,000
Leased plant (11,200 × 25%)	2,800

(W3) The damaged and slow moving stock should be written down to its estimated realisable value. This is £3.6 million (£4 million less sales commission at 10%). Therefore the required write down is £2.4 million (£6 million – £3.6 million).

The unrecorded invoice would be an addition to purchases, so a reduction in profit.

(W4) A provision for future cyclic repairs does not meet the definition of a liability in FRS 12 *Provisions, Contingent Liabilities and Contingent Assets* and must be reversed; this will increase the current year's profit and the previous year's profit by £6 million each.

(W5) FRS 26 *Financial Instruments: Measurement* requires this type of loan instrument to be valued at amortised cost with issue costs, discounts on issues and premiums on redemptions of loan instruments to be included as part of the finance costs. The net proceeds are £14.1 million ((£15 million × 95%) less £0.15 million issue costs) per the suspense account. The finance cost and liability amounts are computed as:

	£000
Initial carrying value	14,100
Interest at 6% for first 6 months	846
	14,946

Of this £600,000 is represented by the cash payment to be made on 1 April 20X4 (current liability) and the £14.346 million remainder is a long-term liability.

37   DARIUS

> **Key answer tips**
>
> Remember that redeemable shares are classified as liabilities, so the dividend on them is presented within finance costs, rather than as a deduction from profit and loss reserve. Under SSAP 19 investment properties must be accounted for at open market value, and the basic rule is that surpluses and deficits are taken to the statement of total recognised gains and losses, not recognised in profit or loss. But changes which are expected to be permanent must be recognised in profit or loss.

(a)   **Darius profit and loss account for the year ended 31 March 20X6**

	£000
Turnover	213,800
Cost of sales (W1)	(152,000)
Gross profit	61,800
Operating expenses	(22,400)
Investment income	1,200
Loss on investment property (W2)	(700)
Profit on ordinary activities before finance costs	39,900
Finance costs (5,000 − (20,000 × 4 × 4p ord div)	(1,800)
Profit before tax	38,100
Taxation (W3)	(6,400)
Profit for the financial year	31,700

(b)   **Darius statement of total recognised gains and losses for the year ended 31 March 20X6**

	£000
Profit for the financial year	31,700
Revaluation surplus on land and buildings	21,000
Revaluation deficit on investment properties (W2)	(1,800)
Total gains and losses recognised since the last annual report	50,900

(c)   **Darius balance sheet at 31 March 20X6**

	£000	£000
Tangible fixed assets		
Land and building (63,000 – 3,200 (W1))		59,800
Plant and equipment (W4)		22,500
Investment property (W2)		13,500
		95,800
Current assets		
Stock (10,500 – 300 (W1))	10,200	
Trade debtors	13,500	
	23,700	
Creditors: amounts falling due within one year		
Trade creditors	11,800	
Taxation	8,000	
Bank overdraft	900	
	(20,700)	
Net current assets		3,000
Total assets less current liabilities		98,800
Creditors: amounts falling due after more than one year		
10% Redeemable preference shares of £1 each		(10,000)
Provisions for liabilities		
Deferred tax (W3)		(3,600)
		85,200
Capital and reserves		
Ordinary shares of 25p each		20,000
Revaluation reserve		21,000
Profit and loss reserve (15,700 + 31,700 – (20,000 × 4 × 4p ord div))		44,200
		85,200

Workings

(W1) **Cost of sales**

	£000
Per question	143,800
Stock write down (800 – (950 – 450))	300
Depreciation – building (48,000/15)	3,200
– plant (W3)	2,400
Write down of plant to be sold (6m × 95% – (12 – 4)m)	2,300
	152,000

(W2) Investment property revaluation

	£000
Carrying amount at 1 April 20X5	16,000
Valuation 31 March 20X6	13,500
Loss on revaluation	2,500
Balance on investment property revaluation reserve	1,800
Loss charged to profit and loss account	700

Tutorial note: Per SSAP 19 *Accounting for investment properties* any deficit on revaluation should be taken to the investment revaluation reserve, even if it creates a debit balance. The only exception is that if the deficit is expected to be permanent, it should be recognised in the profit and loss account. This answer assumes that the deficit is permanent, although it would be possible to treat it as temporary, making the reserve negative.

(W3) Tax

	£000
Deferred tax	
Balance b/f	5,200
Balance c/f (12,000 × 30%)	3,600
Written back	1,600
Charge on profits for the year	(8,000)
	(6,400)

(W4) Plant and equipment

	£000
Balance b/f	36,000
Accumulated depreciation b/f	(16,800)
Carrying amount	19,200
Depreciation charge for year – 12.5%	(2,400)
Carrying amount c/f	16,800
Asset to be sold (6,000 × 95%)	5,700
	22,500

Note: Preference shares that are redeemable have the substance of debt and under FRS 25 *Financial instruments: presentation* the preference dividend should be treated as a finance cost and the share capital itself treated as a liability.

38   TADEON

> ### Key answer tips
>
> Most of the work for this question is done in the profit and loss account and the adjustments there lead through to the balance sheet. So make sure that when you make an adjustment in the profit and loss account that you also remember to adjust the appropriate balance sheet figures.

(a)   **Tadeon – Profit and loss account – Year to 30 September 20X6**

	£000	£000
Turnover		277,800
Cost of sales (w (i))		(144,000)
Gross profit		133,800
Operating expenses (40,000 + 1,200 (w (ii)))		(41,200)
Investment income		2,000
Finance costs – finance lease (w (ii))	(1,500)	
– loan (w (iii))	(2,750)	(4,250)
Profit before tax		90,350
Tax (38,000 – 1,200) (w (iv))		(36,800)
Profit for the period		53,550

(b)   **Tadeon – Balance Sheet as at 30 September 20X6**

	£000	£000
Fixed assets		
Tangible fixed assets (w (v))		299,000
Investments at amortised cost		42,000
		341,000
Current assets		
Stock	33,300	
Trade debtors	53,500	
	86,800	
Creditors: amounts falling due within one year		
Trade creditors	18,700	
Finance lease obligation (w (ii))	6,000	
Bank overdraft	1,900	
Corporation tax payable (w (iv))	38,000	

		(64,600)
		————
Net current assets		22,200
Creditors: amounts falling due after more than one year		
2% Loan note (w (iii))	51,750	
Finance lease obligation (w (ii))	10,500	(62,250)
	————	
Provisions for liabilities		
Deferred tax (w (iv))		(14,800)
		————
		286,150
		————
Share capital and reserves:		
Equity shares of 20 pence fully paid (150,000 + 50 000 w (vi))		200,000
Reserves		
Share premium (w (vi))	28,000	
Revaluation reserve (w (v))	16,000	
Profit and loss account (w (vii))	42,150	86,150
	————	————
		286,150
		————

Workings (note figures in brackets are in £000)

(i)	Cost of sales:		£000
	Per trial balance		118,000
	Depreciation (12,000 + 5,000 + 9,000 w (v))		26,000
			————
			144,000
			————

(ii) Vehicle rentals/finance lease:

The total amount of vehicle rentals is £6.2 million of which £1.2 million are operating lease rentals and £5 million is identified as finance lease rentals. The operating rentals have been included in operating expenses.

Finance lease		£000
Fair value of vehicles		20,000
First rental payment – 1 October 20X5		(5,000)
		————
Capital outstanding to 30 September 20X6		15,000
Accrued interest 10% (current liability)		1,500
		————
Total outstanding 30 September 20X6		16,500
		————

In the year to 30 September 20X7 (i.e. on 1 October 20X6) the second rental payment of £6 million will be made, of this £1.5 million is for the accrued interest for the previous year, thus £4.5 million will be a capital repayment.

The remaining £10.5 million (16,500 − (4,500 + 1,500)) will be shown as a creditor payable after more than one year.

(iii)   Although the loan has a nominal (coupon) rate of only 2%, amortisation of the large premium on redemption, gives an effective interest rate of 5.5% (from question). This means the finance charge to the profit and loss account will be a total of £2.75 million (50,000 × 5.5%). As the actual interest paid is £1 million an accrual of £1.75 million is required. This amount is added to the £50 million carrying amount of the loan in the balance sheet to give a liability of £51.75 million.

(iv)   Tax and deferred tax

The profit and loss account charge is made up as follows:

	£000
Current year's provision	38,000
Deferred tax (see below)	(1,200)
	36,800

There are £74 million of timing differences at 30 September 20X6. With a corporation tax rate of 20%, this would require a deferred tax liability of £14.8 million (74,000 × 20%). The tax on the sale of the leasehold property will be £4 million (£20m × 20%). This forms a part of the deferred tax liability at 30 September 20X6. Therefore £4 million must be transferred to deferred tax and debited to the property revaluation reserve. The effect of deferred tax on the profit and loss account is therefore a credit of £1.2 million (14,800 − 4,000 − 12,000 b/f).

(v)   Fixed assets/depreciation:

Non-leased plant

This has a carrying amount of £96 million (181,000 − 85,000) prior to depreciation of £12 million at 12½% reducing balance to give a carrying amount of £84 million at 30 September 20X6.

The leased vehicles will be included in fixed assets at their fair value of £20 million and depreciated by £5 million (four years straight-line) for the year ended 30 September 20X6 giving a carrying amount of £15 million at that date.

The 25 year leasehold property is being depreciated at £9 million per annum (225,000/25 years). Prior to its revaluation on 30 September 20X6 there would be a further year's depreciation charge of £9 million giving a carrying amount of £180 million (225,000 − (36,000 + 9,000)) prior to its revaluation to £200 million. Thus £20 million would be transferred to a revaluation reserve. The question says the revaluation gives rise to £20 million of deductible temporary differences, at a tax rate of 20%, this would give a credit to deferred tax of £4 million which is debited to the revaluation reserve to give a net balance of £16 million. Summarising:

	Cost/valuation	Accumulated depreciation	Carrying amount
	£000	£000	£000
25 year leasehold property	200,000	nil	200,000
Non-leased plant	181,000	97,000	84,000
Leased vehicles	20,000	5,000	15,000
	401,000	102,000	299,000

(vi) Suspense account

The called up share capital of £150 million in the trial balance represents 750 million shares (150m/0.2) which have a market value at 1 October 20X5 of £600 million (750m × 80 pence). A yield of 5% on this amount would require a £30 million dividend to be paid.

A fully subscribed rights issue of one new share for every three shares held at a price of 32p each would lead to an issue of 250 million (150m/0.2 × 1/3). This would yield a gross amount of £80 million, and after issue costs of £2 million, would give a net receipt of £78 million. This should be accounted for as £50 million (250m × 20p) to equity share capital and the balance of £28 million to share premium.

The receipt from the share issue of £78 million less the payment of dividends of £30 million reconciles the suspense account balance of £48 million.

(vii) Profit and loss account

	£000
At 1 October 20X5	18,600
Year to 30 September 20X6	53,550
less dividends paid (w (vi))	(30,000)
	42,150

39 CANDEL   WALK IN THE FOOTSTEPS OF A TOP TUTOR

Key answer tips

Make sure you remember to complete all parts of the question – a statement of the movements in share capital and reserves is required as well as a profit and loss account and balance sheet. Be wary of the revaluation. The revaluation takes place at the end of the year, therefore a full year depreciation should be applied before you undertake the revaluation.

(a) Candel – Profit and loss account for the year ended 30 September 2008

	£000
Turnover (300,000 – 2,500)	297,500
Cost of sales (w (i))	(225,400)
Gross profit	72,100
Distribution costs	(14,500)
Administrative expenses (22,200 – 400 + 100 see note below)	(21,900)
Operating profit	35,700
Finance costs (200 + 1,200 (w (ii)))	(1,400)
Profit before tax	34,300
Taxation (11,400 + (6,000 – 5,800 deferred tax))	(11,600)
Profit for the year	22,700

Note: as it is considered that the outcome of the legal action against Candel is unlikely to succeed (only a 20% chance) it is inappropriate to provide for any damages. The potential damages are an example of a contingent liability which should be disclosed (at £2 million) as a note to the financial statements. The unrecoverable legal costs are a liability (the start of the legal action is a past event) and should be provided for in full.

(b) Candel – Statement of movements in shareholders' funds for the year ended 30 September 2008

	Share capital £000	Revaluation reserve £000	Profit and loss a/c £000	Total equity £000
Balances at 1 October 2007	50,000	10,000	24,500	84,500
Dividend			(6,000)	(6,000)
Revaluation loss		(4,500)		(4,500)
Profit for year			22,700	
Balances at 30 September 2008	50,000	5,500	41,200	96,700

(c)   Candel – Balance sheet as at 30 September 2008

	£000	£000
Fixed assets (w (iii))		
Intangible – development costs		14,800
Leasehold property		43,000
Plant and equipment		38,400
		96,200
Current assets		
Stock	20,000	
Trade debtors	43,100	
	63,100	
Creditors: amounts falling due within one year		
Trade creditors (23,800 – 400 + 100 – re legal action)	23,500	
Bank overdraft	1,300	
Corporation tax	11,400	
	(36,200)	
Net current assets		26,900
Total assets less current liabilities		123,100
Creditors: amounts falling due after more than one year		
8% redeemable preference shares (20,000 + 400 w (ii))		(20,400)
Provision for liabilities		
Deferred tax		(6,000)
		96,700
Capital and reserves		
Equity shares of 25 pence each (from b)		50,000
Revaluation reserve (from b)	5,500	
Profit and loss account (from b)	41,200	46,700
		96,700

Workings (figures in brackets in £000)

(i) Cost of sales:

	£000
Per trial balance	204,000
Depreciation (w (iii)) – leasehold property	2,500
– plant and equipment	9,600
Loss on disposal of plant (4,000 – 2,500)	1,500
Amortisation of development costs (w (iii))	4,000
Research and development expensed (1,400 + 2,400 (w (iii)))	3,800
	225,400

(ii) The finance cost of £1.2 million for the preference shares is based on the effective rate of 12% applied to £20 million issue proceeds of the shares for the six months they have been in issue (20m × 12% × 6/12). The dividend paid of £800,000 is based on the nominal rate of 8%. The additional £400,000 (accrual) is added to the carrying amount of the preference shares in the balance sheet. As these shares are redeemable they are treated as debt and their dividend is treated as a finance cost.

(iii) Fixed assets:

	£000
Leasehold property	
Valuation at 1 October 2007	50,000
Depreciation for year (20 year life)	(2,500)
Carrying amount at date of revaluation	47,500
Valuation at 30 September 2008	(43,000)
Revaluation deficit (to reserve)	4,500

Remember to write off the disposed asset, both cost and b/fwd accumulated depreciation before calculating the current year depreciation charge.

	£000
Plant and equipment per trial balance (76,600 – 24,600)	52,000
Disposal (8,000 – 4,000)	(4,000)
	48,000
Depreciation for year (20%)	(9,600)
Carrying amount at 30 September 2008	38,400

Capitalised/deferred development costs :

Carrying amount at 1 October 2007 (20,000 – 6,000)	14,000
Amortised for year (20,000 x 20%)	(4,000)
Capitalised during year (800 x 6 months)	4,800
Carrying amount at 30 September 2008	14,800

Note: development costs can only be treated as an asset from the point where they satisfy the deferment criteria in SSAP 13 *Accounting for research and development*. In this case this will be from when the directors became confident that the project would be successful and yield a profit. Thus only the development costs from 1 April to 30 September 2008 of £4.8 million (800 × 6 months) can be capitalised. These will not be amortised as the project is still in development. The research costs of £1.4 million plus three months' development costs of £2.4 million (800 × 3 months) (i.e. those incurred before 1 April 2008) are treated as an expense.

40 PRICEWELL

(a) **Pricewell – Profit and loss account for the year ended 31 March 2009:**

	£000
Turnover (310,000 + 22,000 (w (i)) – 6,400 (w (ii)))	325,600
Cost of sales (w (iii))	(255,100)
Gross profit	70,500
Distribution costs	(19,500)
Administrative expenses	(27,500)
Finance costs (4,160 (w (v)) + 1,248 (w (vi)))	(5,408)
Profit before tax	18,092
Corporation tax (4,500 +700 – (8,400 – 5,600) deferred tax)	(2,400)
Profit for the year	15,692

(b) **Pricewell – Balance sheet as at 31 March 2009:**

	£000	£000
Fixed assets (w (iv))		
Land and buildings		24,900
Plant and equipment		41,500
		66,400

Current assets		
Stock	28,200	
Contract stock (w (i))	800	
Debtors	33,100	
Amounts recoverable on contracts (w (i))	16,300	
Bank	5,500	
	———	
	83,900	
	———	
Creditors: amounts falling due within one year:		
Trade creditors	33,400	
Finance lease obligation (10,848 – 5,716 (w (vi)))	5,132	
Corporation tax	4,500	
	———	
	(43,032)	
	———	
Net current assets		40,868
		———
Total assets less current liabilities		107,268
Creditors: amounts falling due after more than one year		
Finance lease obligation (w (vi))	5,716	
6% redeemable preference shares (41,600 + 1,760 (w (v)))	43,360	(49,076)
	———	
Provision for liabilities		
Deferred tax		(5,600)
		———
		52,592
		———
Capital and reserves		
Equity shares of 50 pence each		40,000
Profit and loss account (w (vii))		12,592
		———
		52,592
		———

Workings (figures in brackets in £000)

		£000
(i)	Long-term contract:	
	Selling price	50,000
	Estimated cost	
	To date	(12,000)
	To complete	(10,000)
	Plant	(8,000)
		———
	Estimated profit	20,000

Work done is agreed at £22 million so the contract is 44% complete (22,000/50,000).

Revenue	22,000
Cost of sales (= balance)	(13,200)
Profit to date (44% × 20,000)	8,800
Cost incurred to date materials and labour	12,000
Plant depreciation (8,000 × 6/24 months)	2,000
Charged to cost of sales	(13,200)
Included in balance sheet stock	800
Recognised in turnover	22,000
Cash received	(5,700)
Amounts recoverable on contracts	16,300

(ii) Pricewell is acting as an agent (not the principal) for the sales on behalf of Trilby. Therefore the profit and loss account should only include £1·6 million (20% of the sales of £8 million). Therefore £6·4 million (8,000 – 1,600) should be deducted from turnover and cost of sales. It would also be acceptable to show agency sales (of £1·6 million) separately as other income.

	£000
(iii) Cost of sales	
Per question	234,500
Contract (w (i))	13,200
Agency cost of sales (w (ii))	(6,400)
Depreciation (w (iv)) – leasehold property	1,800
– owned plant ((46,800 – 12,800) × 25%)	8,500
– leased plant (20,000 × 25%)	5,000
Surplus on revaluation of leasehold property (w (iv))	(1,500)
	255,100

(iv) Fixed assets	
Leasehold property valuation at 31 March 2008	25,200
Depreciation for year (14 year life remaining)	(1,800)
Carrying amount at date of revaluation	23,400
Valuation at 31 March 2009	(24,900)
Revaluation surplus (to profit and loss account – see below)	1,500

The £1˙5 million revaluation surplus is credited to the profit and loss account as this is the partial reversal of the £2˙8 million impairment loss recognised as an expense in the previous period (i.e. year ended 31 March 2008).

Plant and equipment

– owned (46,800 – 12,800 – 8,500)	25,500
– leased (20,000 – 5,000 – 5,000)	10,000
– contract (8,000 – 2,000 (w (i)))	6,000
	———
Carrying amount at 31 March 2009	41,500
	———

(v) The finance cost of £4,160,000 for the preference shares is based on the effective rate of 10% applied to £41·6 million balance at 1 April 2008. The accrual of £1,760,000 (4,160 – 2,400 dividend paid) is added to the carrying amount of the preference shares in the balance sheet. As these shares are redeemable they are treated as debt and their dividend is treated as a finance cost.

(vi) Finance lease liability

Balance at 31 March 2008	15,600
Interest for year at 8%	1,248
Lease rental paid 31 March 2009	(6,000)
	———
Total liability at 31 March 2009	10,848
Interest next year at 8%	868
Lease rental due 31 March 2010	(6,000)
	———
Total liability at 31 March 2010	5,716
	———

(vii) Profit and loss account reserve

Balance at 1 April 2008	4,900
Profit for year	15,692
Equity dividend paid	(8,000)
	———
Balance at 31 March 2009	12,592
	———

ACCA marking scheme			
			Marks
(a)	Profit and loss account		
	Turnover		2
	Cost of sales		5
	Distribution costs		0.5
	Administrative expenses		0.5
	Finance costs		2
	Corporation tax		2
		Maximum	12
(b)	Balance sheet		
	Land and buildings		1
	Plant and equipment		1.5
	Stock		0.5
	Contract stock		1
	Debtors		0.5
	Amounts recoverable on contracts		1
	Bank		0.5
	Trade creditors		0.5
	Finance lease – creditor due within one year		1
	Corporation tax		1
	Finance lease – creditor due after one year		0.5
	Preference shares		1
	Deferred tax		1
	Equity shares		0.5
	Profit and loss account (1 for dividend)		1.5
		Maximum	13
Total			25

Examiner's comments

This was a familiar question of preparing financial statements from a trial balance with various adjustments. These involved a revaluation of a non-current asset, dealing with a finance lease agreement, accounting for a construction contract, a revenue recognition issue, an effective rate finance cost for a financial instrument and taxation.

This question was the second best answered question, but it was not as well answered as I have come to expect. The most common errors were:

- deducting from revenue the agency sales, without recognising the commission earned

- rather worryingly, a number of candidates deducted the closing inventory from the cost of sales (by definition it has already been deducted)

- basing calculations of the depreciation and impairment reversal of the leasehold property on the revaluation as if it had been at the beginning of the year (the question clearly stated it was at the end of the year)

- taking the reversal of the impairment to reserves rather than through the income statement as, on this occasion, this reversed a previous impairment loss recognised in the income statement

- also worryingly, a number of candidates depreciated the owned plant and equipment using cost rather than carrying value; the distinction between straight line and reducing balance depreciation should be very familiar to candidates at this stage

- a number of candidates decided that the leasehold property and the leased plant (and hence the finance lease payment) were the same asset; this produced some very unhelpful workings and balances

- many complex (and unnecessary) lease calculations were provided – if future payments are to be discounted, the appropriate factors will be provided as part of the question – the finance cost of the redeemable preference shares was incorrectly calculated at the nominal rate of its dividend rather than at the effective rate based on the carrying amount at the start of the period. Also the dividends are part of the finance cost in the income statement and the shares themselves are classified as debt on the statement of financial position; redeemable preference shares do not have the characteristics of an equity instrument

- there were errors in the treatment of the taxation in both the income statement and the statement of financial position, these included: crediting the under provision of tax from the previous year to the income statement (as a debit balance it should have been charged); treating the closing provision for deferred tax as the charge in the income statement (it should be the movement on the provision that appears in the income statement); showing the current tax net of the under-provision as a current liability (only the current year's tax is a current liability).

- many candidates made a fair attempt at the construction contract figures in the workings (credit was given for this), but often did not follow them through to the financial statements

- the treatment of the finance lease caused problems, many candidates based the finance cost and current/noncurrent liability on the carrying amount of the leased asset rather than on the opening liability for the lease obligation

- a number of candidates are still showing equity dividends in the income statement rather than as part of the retained earnings (or statement of changes in equity if it had been required).

- The statement of financial position was generally well done and most of the errors that were made generally related to the following through of errors from the income statement.

41 UPDATE PLC

Key answer tips

Consider what the diluted earnings per share figure actually tells (and does not tell) a prospective investor.

(i)   The ordinary dividends for the year to 31 March 20X3 are:

	£
Interim (12 million (3 million × £1/25p) × 3p)	360,000
Final (12 million × ((5 + 1)/5) for rights issue × 6p)	864,000
	1,224,000
Earnings attributable to ordinary shares (see (ii))	2,475,000
Dividend cover (2,475,000/1,224,000)	2.02 times

The dividend cover is the number of times the current year's ordinary dividends could have been paid out of the current year's profit attributable to ordinary shareholders. It is an indication of the company's dividend policy i.e. a company having a dividend cover of three has paid out one third of its profit as dividends. In terms of maintainable dividends, the dividend cover is a basic measure of risk; the higher the dividend cover the less is the risk that dividends would be reduced if profits suffer a downturn. Conversely, a low dividend cover means that future dividends are more vulnerable to a deterioration in profit. A dividend cover of less than one means the company has used previous years' retained earnings to pay the current year's dividend. This is not a good sign and is not sustainable in the long term.

(ii)   All items in arriving at the profit for the financial year are included in the calculation of the earnings per share.

Earnings attributable to the ordinary shares are after the deduction of the following dividends on irredeemable preference shares:

	£
8% on £1 million for full year	80,000
New issue 6% on £1 million for six months	30,000
	110,000
Earnings attributable to ordinary shares (2,585,000 − 110,000)	2,475,000

Weighted average number of shares in issue:
Calculation of theoretical ex rights price:

100 shares at £2.40 would be worth	240
Rights to 20 shares at £1.50 each costing	30
120 shares now worth	270

This gives a theoretical ex-rights value of £2.25 per share (£270/120)

Weighted average calculation:

12,000,000 × £2.4/£2.25 × $^3/_{12}$	3,200,000
14,400,000 (12 million × ((5 + 1)/5)) × $^9/_{12}$)	10,800,000
	————
Weighted average number	14,000,000
	————

Earnings per share is 17.7p (£2,475,000/14,000,000 × 100)

Restated earnings per share for the year to 31 March 20X2 is 22.5p (24 × 2.25/2.40)

(iii) **Fully diluted earnings per share**

On conversion the loan stock would create an extra 800,000 new shares (£2 million × 40/£100) The effect on earnings would be a saving of interest of £140,000 (£2 million × 7%) before tax and £98,000 after tax (140,000 × (100% − 30%))

The directors' warrants would create an additional 750,000 new shares without any effect on earnings. Fully diluted earnings per share is 16.5p ((2,475,000 + 98,000)/ (14,000,000 + 800,000 + 750,000))

The basic earnings per share is a measure of past performance. The diluted earnings per share figure is more forward looking and is intended to act as a warning to existing and prospective shareholders. Although it is still based on past performance, it does recognise the effect of potential ordinary shares outstanding during the period. Its disclosure is required where circumstances exist that would cause the EPS to be lower if those circumstances had crystallised. It is not a prediction of the future earnings per share figures, as these will be based on the future profits and the number of shares in issue in the future. The diluted EPS is more a 'theoretical' value, as it is unlikely that the profit in the period when the circumstances crystallise will be the same as the current year's profit.

The convertible loan stock in the question is a good example of a diluting circumstance. On conversion the share entitlement will cause the number of shares in issue in the future to be greater than the present (assuming loan stockholders opt for conversion). There will be a compensating increase in profit as a result of the non-payment of interest but overall the expected conversion will cause a dilution.

42 JKL

(a) Basic and diluted earnings per share

$$\text{Basic earnings per share} \quad \frac{2,763,000}{6,945,922\,(\text{W3})} = 39.8\text{p}$$

$$\text{Diluted EPS:} \quad \frac{2,858,200\,(\text{W4})}{9,045,922\,(\text{W5})} = 31.6\text{p}$$

(W1) Calculate the theoretical ex-rights price after the rights issue

	P
4 shares × 145p	580
1 share × 125p	125
Theoretical value of holding of 5 shares	705
Theoretical ex-rights price of 1 share after rights issue: 705/5	141

(W2) Calculate bonus fraction

$$\frac{\text{Fair value of one share before rights issue}}{\text{Theoretical ex - rights price of one share (W1)}} = \frac{145}{141}$$

(W3) Weighted average number of shares in issue in the year to 31 August 20X4

	Number of shares
1 September 20X3 – 1 February 20X4	
6,000,000 × 145/141 × 5/12	2,570,922
1 February 20X4 – 31 August 20X4	
6,000,000 × ((4 + 1)/4) × 7/12	4,375,000
	6,945,922

(W4) Adjustment to earnings for calculation of diluted EPS

	£
Earnings	2,763,000
Add: Interest after tax	
(2,000,000 × 7%) × (1 – 0.32)	95,200
	2,858,200

(W5) Adjustment to number of shares for calculation of diluted EPS

Note: Use the most advantageous (for loan stockholders) conversion rate.

	Number of shares
Weighted average shares in issue in year to 31 August 20X4 (W3)	6,945,922
Add: Dilutive effect 2,000,000/100 × 105	2,100,000
Diluted shares	9,045,922

$$\text{Diluted EPS: } \frac{2,858,200}{9,045,922} = 31.6p$$

(b)   Much of the information contained in financial statements refers to events that have occurred in the past, and so it is of relatively restricted usefulness in making decisions. Diluted earnings per share, however, can be quite useful to investors and potential investors in that it incorporates some information about likely future events. Where potentially dilutive financial instruments have been issued, it is helpful to investors to be able to appreciate the impact full dilution would have upon the earnings of the business. However, it should be appreciated that only some elements of the calculation relate to the future. One of the key elements of the calculation, the basic earnings for the period, relates to events that have already taken place and that may not be replicated in the future.

BUSINESS COMBINATIONS

43   HIGHMOOR

> **Key answer tips**
>
> Think carefully about the contingent consideration in part (a). It will be paid if Slowmoor reports a profit, but the directors are not confident that this will happen. The fact that part (b) deals with negative goodwill makes it probable that the balance sheet prepared in part (a) should include negative goodwill rather than positive goodwill.

(a)   **Consolidated balance sheet of Highmoor as at 30 September 20X3**

	£ million	£ million
Fixed assets		
Intangible		
Consolidated negative goodwill (40 – 11 (W2))		(29)
Software (W4)		24
Tangible (585 + 172)		757
Investments (225 – 160 shares – 50 loan (W3) + 13)		28
		———
		780
Current assets		
Stocks (85 + 42)	127	
Trade debtors (95 – 4 in transit (W3) + 36)	127	
Tax asset	80	
Bank (20 + 9 in transit (W3))	29	
	———	
	363	
	———	
Creditors: amounts falling due within one year		
Trade creditors (210 + 71)	281	
Overdraft	17	
Taxation	70	
	———	
	(368)	
Net current liabilities		(5)

Creditors: amounts falling due after more than one year

12% loan notes	(35)
	———
Net assets	740
	———

Share capital and reserves

Ordinary shares £1 each	400
Profit and loss account (W6)	297
	———
	697
Minority interest (W5)	43
	———
	740
	———

Workings (all figures in £ million)

(W1) **Net assets of subsidiary**

	At acquisition	At balance sheet date
	£	£
Share capital	100	100
Profit and loss reserve	150	115
	———	———
	250	215
	———	———

(W2) **Goodwill**

	£
Cost of investment (80% × 100) × £2	160
Net assets at acquisition 80% × 250 (W1)	200
	———
Negative goodwill	40
	———

The contingent consideration has not been included in the above calculation. FRS 7 *Fair Values in Acquisition Accounting* requires contingent consideration to be included in the cost of an acquisition at a reasonable estimate of the fair value of the amount that is expected to be paid. The additional £96 million (i.e. 100 × 80% × £1.20 per share) is only payable if Slowmoor makes a profit within two years of acquisition. In the year since acquisition the company made a loss of £35 million and the directors of Highmoor are now less confident of the future prospects of Slowmoor. This seems to indicate that it is unlikely that any further consideration will be paid and the above treatment is justified.

The negative goodwill of £40 million will be realised as follows:

Attributable to:		Proportion realised year to 30 September 20X3	Amounts
Stock	4	100%	4
Land	8	none until sold	Nil
Other non-monetary assets (balance)	28	25% (four year life)	7
Total negative goodwill	40		11

(W3) **Elimination of loan and accrued interest**

After removing the purchase consideration of £160 million (W2) for Slowmoor, the balance of Highmoor's investments will include an unadjusted amount of £50 million as a loan to Slowmoor. The cash in transit of £9 million from Slowmoor should be applied £4 million to cancel the accrued interest receivable and the balance of £5 million to the investment (loan). When this adjustment is made the remaining investment in Slowmoor and the loan will cancel each other out.

(W4) The net book value of the software in Slowmoor's books is £40 million (50 less 20%). If the software had been depreciated on its original cost of £30 million it would have a book value of £24 million (£30 less £6 million depreciation at 20% per annum). Thus there is an unrealised profit on the sale of the software by Highmoor of £16 million (£40 million – £24 million).

(W5) **Minority interest**

20% × net assets at balance sheet date (20% × 215) (W2) = 43

(W6) **Consolidated profit and loss account reserve**

	£
Highmoor	330
Slowmoor – post acquisition 80% × (35)	(28)
Unrealised profit in software (W4)	(16)
Negative goodwill realised (W2)	11
	297

(b) Negative goodwill arises in bookkeeping where the consideration given for a business is less than the fair value of the net assets acquired. Intuitively it does not make sense for a vendor to sell net assets for less than they are worth. This view is reflected by the ASB which is rather sceptical about the existence of negative goodwill. They say it should only rarely occur and FRS 7 *Fair Values in Acquisition Accounting* requires a careful check of the value of the assets acquired and whether any liabilities have been omitted where negative goodwill appears to arise.

Negative goodwill may arise for several reasons; the most obvious is that there has been a bargain purchase. This may occur through the vendor being in a poor financial position and needing to realise assets quickly, or it may be due to good negotiating skills on the part of the acquirer, or the vendor may not realise how much the assets are really worth.

A more controversial occasion where negative goodwill arises is where a company, in determining the amount of consideration it is willing to pay for a business, will take into account the cost of anticipated future losses and post acquisition reorganisation expenditure that it believes will be required. The effect of this is that it would reduce the consideration offered/paid. As these costs cannot generally be recognised as a liability at the date of purchase, this can lead to the consideration being lower than the recognisable net assets.

In relation to the acquisition of Slowmoor the following are questionable issues:

–   Highmoor may be trying to deliberately create losses at Slowmoor to avoid paying the further consideration. An example of this may be the transfer price of the software. The additional consideration of £96 million, if payable, would change the negative goodwill into positive goodwill of £56 million.

–   The tax asset of Slowmoor may be questionable. Accounting standards are quite restrictive over the recognition of tax assets.

44   HIGHVELDT

Key answer tips

Part (a) of this question requires the three standard workings for the consolidated balance – goodwill, minority interest and consolidated reserves. These should be well known to students but as the rest of the consolidated balance sheet is not required there are more complications than in a normal balance sheet question. Read carefully through each of the notes i) to vi) and think about how they will affect your figures. There are not only fair value adjustments to make but also an accounting policy adjustment with regard to the development expenditure. Note the deferred element of the consideration which should be discounted and the unwinding of the discount shown as a reduction of consolidated profits.

Leave enough time for part b) which is 5 easy marks on the advantages to users of consolidated financial statements.

(a)   (i)   **Goodwill**

	£m
Cost of investment	
Cash (75% × 80m × £3.50)	210
Deferred consideration (108 × 1/1.08)	100
	____
	310
Less: net assets at acquisition 75% × 296 (W2)	222
	____
Goodwill at 1 April 20X4	88
Amortisation (88 × 1/4)	(22)
	____
Goodwill at balance sheet date	66
	____

			£m
(ii)	**Minority interest**		
	Net assets at balance sheet date		
	25% × 350 (W2)		87.5
	Less: unrealised profit in stock 25% × 2m (W3)		(0.5)
			87.0

(iii) **Consolidated share premium**

	£m
Parent only	80

Consolidated revaluation reserve

	£m
Parent	45
Subsidiary – post-acquisition (75% × 4m)	3
	48

Consolidated profit and loss reserve

	£m
Parent	350.0
Add: interest receivable (60m × 10%)	6.0
Less: unwinding of discount on deferred consideration 100 × 8%	(8.0)
	348.0
Subsidiary – group share post-acquisition (ex 4 re land and buildings taken to revaluation reserve) 75% × ((350 – 296) – 4) (W2)	37.5
Less: unrealised profit in stock 75% × 2m (W3)	(1.5)
Less: amortisation of goodwill (part i)	(22.0)
	362.0

(W1) Group structure

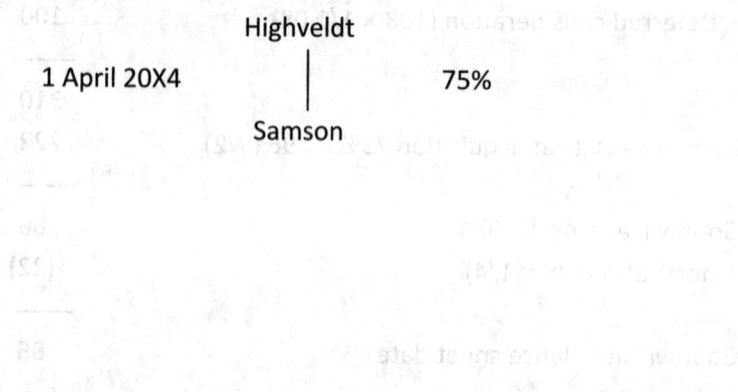

Highveldt

1 April 20X4   75%

Samson

(W2) **Net assets**

	At acquisition £m		At balance sheet date £m
Share capital	80		80
Share premium	40		40
Profit and loss	134		210
	254		330
Fair value adjustments:			
Land and buildings	20		24
Brand	40	× 9/10	36
Development costs	(18)		(40)
	296		350

The brand should be recognised in the consolidated balance sheet even though it is not included in Samson's own balance sheet. As the brand has been professionally valued then it can be 'reliably measured' and should be included in the consolidated balance sheet.

(W3) **Unrealised profit in stock**

Profit = £6m

Still in stock = 1/3 × £6m = £2m

(b)   The objective of consolidated financial statements is to show the financial performance and position of the group as if it was a single economic entity. There is a view that, as the entity financial statements of the parent company contain the investments in subsidiaries as fixed assets, they reflect the assets of the group as a whole. The more traditional view is that entity financial statements do not provide users with sufficient information about subsidiaries for them to make a reliable assessment of the performance of the group as a whole. The following illustrates the benefits of consolidated financial statements:

–   They identify the nature and classification of the subsidiary's assets. For example, the investment in a subsidiary may be almost entirely in intangible assets or conversely they may be substantially land and buildings. Such a distinction is of obvious importance to users.

–   The amount of the subsidiary's debt could not be assessed from the parent's entity financial statements. In effect the subsidiary's assets and liabilities are netted off when it is shown as an investment. This means group liquidity and gearing cannot be properly assessed.

–   The cost of the investment does not reflect the size of a company. For example a parent company may show an investment in a subsidiary at a cost of £10 million. This may represent the purchase of a subsidiary that has £10 million of assets and no liabilities. Alternatively this could be a subsidiary that has £100 million in assets and £90 million of liabilities. Clearly the latter subsidiary would be a much larger company than the former.

–   The cost of the investment may be a fair representation of its value at the date of purchase, but with the passage of time (assuming the subsidiary is profitable), its value will increase. This increase would not be reflected in the original cost, but it would be reflected in the consolidated net assets of the subsidiary (and the increase in group reserves).

– The cost of the investment might represent all of the ownership of the subsidiary or only just over half of it i.e. there would be no indication of the minority interest.

To summarise, in the absence of a consolidated balance sheet, users would have no information on the current value of a subsidiary, its size, the composition of its net assets and how much of it was owned by the group.

45   HILLUSION PLC

Key answer tips

Part (b) asks you why it is necessary to eliminate unrealised profits. You do not need to discuss the double entry techniques for dealing with intra-group adjustments, nor the reasons why they arise. You are also specifically asked to refer to the circumstances described in the question. These include the high level of related party sales and the fact that there is no charge for administration costs.

(a)   **Hillusion plc**

Consolidated profit and loss account for the year to 31 March 20X3

	£000	£000
Turnover ($60,000 + (24,000 \times {}^{9}/_{12}) - 12,000$ intra-group sales)		66,000
Cost of sales (W2)		(46,100)
Gross profit		19,900
Operating expenses ($6,000 + (200 \times {}^{9}/_{12}) + 300$ goodwill (W4))	(6,450)	
Loan interest (($200 \times {}^{9}/_{12}) - 75$ intra-group)	(75)	
		(6,525)
Profit before tax		13,375
Taxation ($3,000 + (600 \times {}^{9}/_{12})$)		(3,450)
Profit after tax		9,925
Minority interest ((($3,000 \times {}^{9}/_{12}) - 600$ depreciation adjustment (W2)) $\times$ 20%)		(330)
Profit for the year		9,595

Consolidated balance sheet at 31 March 20X3

	£000	£000
Intangible fixed assets:		
Goodwill (W4) (1,200 – 300)		900
Tangible fixed assets (19,320 + 8,000 + 3,200 – 600		
depreciation adjustment (W2))		29,920
		30,820
Current assets (W7)	21,750	
Creditors: amounts falling due within one year (W7)	(12,850)	8,900
		39,720
Creditors: amounts falling due after more than one year		
10% Loan notes (2,000 – 1,000 intra-group)		(1,000)
Net assets		38,720
Share capital and reserves:		
Ordinary shares of £1 each		10,000
Reserves:		
Profit and loss account (W6)		26,120
		36,120
Minority interest (W5)		2,600
		38,720

Workings (in £000)

(W1) Group structure

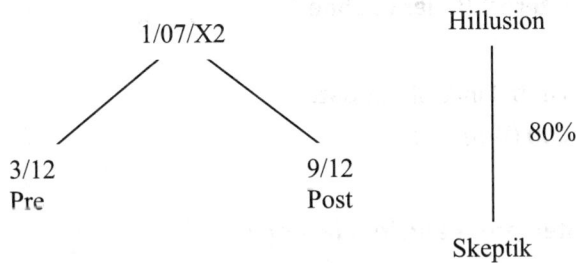

```
                    1/07/X2              Hillusion
                      /\                    |
                     /  \                   | 80%
                    /    \                  |
                3/12    9/12                |
                Pre     Post             Skeptik
```

(W2) Cost of sales

Hillusion plc	42,000
Skeptik plc (20,000 × $^9/_{12}$)	15,000
Intra-group sales	(12,000)
URP in stock	500
Additional depreciation	600
	46,100

The unrealised profit (URP) in stock is calculated as:

Intra-group sales are £12 million of which Skeptik plc has sold on £10 million leaving £2 million ($\frac{1}{6}$) still in stock at the year-end. The cost of the sales made by Hillusion plc to Skeptik plc was £9 million giving Hillusion plc a profit of £3 million (12m – 9m). The unrealised element of this is £500,000 (£3 million $\times \frac{1}{6}$).

The fair value adjustment to the tangible fixed assets is £3.2 million. At the date of acquisition they have a remaining life of four years. Additional depreciation would be £800,000 per annum which requires apportioning by $\frac{9}{12}$ = £600,000

(W3) Net assets in subsidiary

	At acquisition	At balance sheet date
	£000	£000
Share capital	2,000	2,000
Profit and loss reserve ((8,400 – 3,000) + (3/12 × 3,000))	6,150	8,400
Fair value adjustment – depreciation per (W2)	3,200	2,600
	11,350	13,000

(W4) Goodwill

Investment at cost	10,280
Net assets at acquisition 80% × 11,350 (W3)	(9,080)
Goodwill on consolidation	1,200
Goodwill amortisation will be £1,200/3 × $\frac{9}{12}$ =	300

(W5) Minority interest (balance sheet)

	£000
Net assets at balance sheet date 20% × 13,000 (W3)	2,600

(W6) Consolidated profit and loss reserves:

Hillusion plc's reserves	25,600
Skeptik plc's post acquisition (80% × 13,000 – 11,350 (W3))	1,320
URP in stock (see (W2))	(500)
Goodwill amortisation ((W4) above)	(300)
	26,120

(W7) Current assets and creditors payable within one year

Current assets:	
Hillusion plc	15,000
Skeptik plc	8,000
URP in stock (see (W2))	(500)
Intra-group balance	(750)
	21,750
Creditors payable within one year:	
Hillusion plc	10,000
Skeptik plc	3,600
Intra-group balance	(750)
	12,850

(b)   The main reason why intra-group unrealised profits must be eliminated on consolidation is to achieve the main objective of group financial statements which is to show the position of the group as if it were a single economic entity. As such, a group cannot really trade with itself, nor can it make a profit out of itself. In a similar way it cannot increase its sales or its net assets by transferring assets and liabilities between members of the group.

As a simple illustrative example, but for the requirement to eliminate intra-group profits, a group could buy an item of stock; sell it to another member of the group (at a profit), who in turn could sell it to another member of the group and so on. The result would be that each member of the group would make a profit which would then be combined to form a large group profit. This would be 'balanced' by an inflated stock value in the balance sheet (in practice this effect would be limited by the application of the lower of cost and net realisable value principle of valuing stock). Such accounting would not show a true and fair view.

The main problem with using Skeptik plc's entity financial statements to assess its performance is that it is a related party of its parent, Hillusion plc. Related party transactions can distort the true economic performance and financial position of a company. In this case, the related party relationship extends to control of Skeptik plc by Hillusion plc.

From the information in the question, it can be seen that most of Skeptik plc's trading is from goods it buys from Hillusion plc.) Sales of non-group sourced goods are only £9 million (out of £24 million).) It may be that these have been transferred at a favourable price allowing Skeptik plc to achieve a higher level of sales and make a higher than normal profit. Ultimately this course of action is no real detriment to the group as a whole as most of Skeptik plc's profits (and all of them if it were 100% owned) are consolidated into the group profit. In a similar manner the fact that Hillusion plc does not make any charge for Skeptik plc's administration costs acts to increase Skeptik plc's profit. If Skeptik plc was to be purchased by an external party, all these beneficial effects would cease and Skeptik plc's profit would then be much lower. It could be observed that Hillusion plc may be 'massaging' Skeptik plc's financial statements with a view to obtaining a favourable price on its future sale.

Hillusion plc's past record of success in selling previous businesses at a considerable profit after only a short period of ownership supports this view.

46 HAPSBURG

(a)   **Consolidated balance sheet of Hapsburg as at March 20X4**

	£000	£000
Fixed assets		
Intangible – Goodwill (W3)		12,800
Tangible		
Land and buildings (16,600 + 9,700)	26,300	
Plant (24,400 + 25,100 + 3,750 (fair value adj (W2)))	53,250	79,550
Investments:		
– in associate (W7)	15,150	
– other (3,000 + 1,500 fair value increase)	4,500	19,650
		112,000
Current assets		
Stock (9,900 + 4,800 – 300 (W4))	14,400	
Debtors (13,600 + 8,600)	22,200	
Cash (1,200 + 3,800)	5,000	
	41,600	
Creditors: amounts failing due within one year		
Trade creditors (16,500 + 6,900)	23,400	
Taxation (9,600 + 3,400)	13,000	
	(36,400)	
Net current assets		5,200

Creditors: amounts failing due after more than one year

10% Loan note (16,000 + 4,200)	20,200	
Deferred consideration (18,000 + 1,800 (W3))	19,800	
	———	
		(40,000)
		———
Net assets		77,200
		———

Share capital and reserves

Ordinary share capital (20,000 + 16,000)		36,000
Reserves:		
Share premium (8,000 + 16,000)	24,000	
Profit and loss reserve (W6)	8,050	
	———	
		32,050
		———
		68,050
Minority interest (W5)		9,150
		———
		77,200
		———

Workings (all working figures in £000)

(W1) **Group structure**

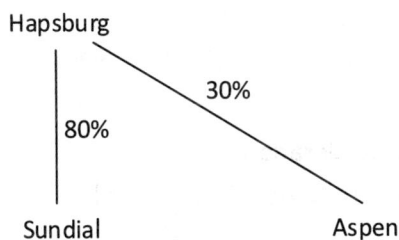

Hapsburg

80% Sundial

30% Aspen

(W2) **Net assets**

	At acquisition	At balance sheet date
	£000	£000
Sundial		
Share capital	30,000	30,000
Share premium	2,000	2,000
Profit and loss (8,500 – 4,500)	4,000	8,500
	———	———
	36,000	40,500

Fair value – Plant (15,000 – 10,000) 5,000 × ¾	5,000	3,750
Investment (4,500 – 3,000)	1,500	1,500
	42,500	45,750

Aspen

Share capital	20,000	20,000
Profit and loss reserve		
(8,000 – 6,000 + (6/12 × 6,000))	5,000	8,000
	25,000	28,000

(W3) **Goodwill/premium on acquisition**

Sundial

	£000
Cost of investment:	
Shares 24m × 2/3 × £2 (£1 share capital, £1 share premium)	32,000
Cash 24m × £1 × 0.75	18,000
	50,000
Net assets acquired 80% × 42,500 (W2)	34,000
Goodwill	16,000
Amortisation 16,000/5	(3,200)
	12,800

Unwind discount on deferred consideration

Debit Consolidated profit and loss reserve (18,000 × 10%)	1,800
Credit Deferred consideration	1,800

Aspen

Cost of investment (6m × £2.50)	15,000
Net assets acquired 30% × 25,000 (W2)	7,500
Premium	7,500
Amortisation (7,500 /5 × 6/12)	(750)
	6,750

(W4) **Unrealised profit in stock** £000

Aspen (associate) selling to Hapsburg (parent)

(2.5m × ((4m – 2.4m)/4m)) × 30% =	300,000

(W5) **Minority interest**

	£000
20% × 45,750 (W2)	9,150

(W6) **Consolidated profit and loss reserve**

	£000
Hapsburg	10,600
Post acquisition in Sundial	
(45,750 − 42,500 (W3)) × 80%	2,600
Post acquisition in Aspen	
(28,000 − 25,000 (W3)) × 30%	900
Less: amortisation (3,200 + 750) (W3)	(3,950)
Less: unwinding of discount (W3)	(1,800)
Less: unrealised profit in stock (W4)	(300)
	8,050

(W7) **Investment in associate**

	£000
Net assets at balance sheet date	
28,000 × 30% (W2)	8,400
Unamortised premium (W3)	6,750
	15,150

(b)   In recent years many companies have increasingly conducted large parts of their business by acquiring substantial minority interests in other companies. There are broadly three levels of investment. Below 20% of the equity shares would normally be classed as an ordinary financial asset investment, measured according to the FRS 26 *Financial Instruments: Recognition and Measurement* rules for the particular category of asset. A holding of above 50% normally gives control and would create subsidiary company status and consolidation is required.

Between these two, in the range of over 20% up to 50%, the investment would normally be deemed to be an associate (***note:*** the level of shareholdings is not the only determining criterion). The relevance of this level of shareholding is that it is presumed to give a degree of influence over the operating and financial policies of the investee (but this presumption can be rebutted). If such an investment were treated as an ordinary investment, the investing company would have the opportunity to manipulate its profit. The most obvious example of this would be by exercising influence over the size of the dividend the associate company paid. This would directly affect the reported profit of the investing company. Also, as companies tend not to distribute all of their earnings as dividends, over time the cost of the investment in the balance sheet may give very little indication of its underlying value.

Equity accounting for associated companies is an attempt to remedy these problems. In the profit and loss account any dividends received from an associate are replaced by the investor's share of the associates' underlying earnings, and in the balance sheet the investor's share of the associate's net assets replace the investment at cost. This treatment means that the investor would show the same profit irrespective of the size of the dividend paid by the associate and the balance sheet more closely reflects the worth of the investment.

The problem of off balance sheet finance relates to the fact that it is the net assets that are shown in the investor's balance sheet. Any share of the associate's liabilities is effectively hidden because they have been offset against the associate's assets. As a simple example, say a holding company owned 100% of another company that had assets of £100 million and debt of £80 million; both the assets and the debt would appear on the consolidated balance sheet. Whereas if this single investment was replaced by owning 50% each of the two companies that had the same balance sheets (i.e. £100 million assets and £80 million debt), then under equity accounting only £20 million (100 − 80) × 50% × 2) of net assets would appear on the balance sheet thus hiding the £80 million of debt. Because of this problem, it has been suggested that proportional consolidation is a better method of accounting for associated companies as both assets and debts would be included in the investor's balance sheet. FRS 9 requires disclosures of the major categories of balance sheet items where the investments in associates are material (the 15% and 25% rules). This goes some way to addressing the problem of off balance sheet finance, however it must be remembered that these are disclosures and are not incorporated as balance sheet items.

47   HEDRA

Key answer tips

Take care with the deferred consideration and the tax losses. Not only is the deferred consideration part of the cost of Salvador but it is also a creditor. The tax losses are a deferred tax asset of the group but this asset is only the tax losses at the tax rate. Remember also that Hedra has not yet recorded the acquisition of Aragon, therefore Hedra's share capital and share premium must be adjusted.

Consolidated balance sheet of Hedra as at 30 September 20X5:

	£m	£m
Fixed assets		
Intangible – Goodwill (W3)		80
Tangible		
Land and buildings (208 + 105 + 12 + 25) (W2)	350	
Plant (150 + 135 +15) (W2)	300	650
Investments		
Investment in associate (W4)		214
Other		45
		989

Current assets

Stocks (130 + 80)	210	
Debtors (142 + 97)	239	
Cash	4	
	453	

Creditors: amounts falling due within one year

Overdraft	12	
Trade creditors (118 + 141)	259	
Deferred consideration	49	
Taxation	50	
	(370)	

Net current assets		83
Total assets less current liabilities		1,072
Provisions for liabilities		
Deferred tax (45 − 10) (W2)		(35)
		1,037

Capital and reserves

Ordinary share capital (400 + (40 × 2)) (W4)		480
Reserves:		
Share premium (40 + (200 − (40 × 2)) (W4)	160	
Revaluation (15 + 12 + (5 × 60%)	30	
Profit and loss reserve	255	445
		925
Minority interest		112
		1,037

Workings

(W1) Group structure

Investment in Salvador =	72m/120m	=	60% – consolidate
Investment in Aragon =	40m/100m	=	40% – equity account

(W2) Net assets in Salvador

	At acquisition £m		At balance sheet date £m
Share capital	120		120
Share premium	50		50
Profit and loss account	20		60
Fair value adjustments:			
Land and buildings	20		25
Plant	20	× 3/4	15
Deferred tax asset (40 × 25%)	10		10
	240		280

(W3) Goodwill

	£m	£m
Cost of investment – cash		195
deferred		49
		244
Net assets acquired (60% × 240 (W1))		144
Goodwill at acquisition		100
Amortisation (100/5)		(20)
Goodwill in balance sheet		80

(W4) Investment in associate

	£m	£m
Cost of investment (40m × 2 × £2.50)		200
Net assets at acquisition		
Share capital	100	
Profit and loss account		
(200 + ((300 − 200) × 6/12)	250	
	350	
Group share 350 × 40%		140
Goodwill		60
Investment in associate		
Cost		200
Group share of post acquisition profit		
(40% × ((300 − 200) × 6/12))		20
Less : amortisation of goodwill		
(60/5 × 6/12		(6)
		214

OR

Investment in association		
Share of net assets (40% × 400)		160
Goodwill (60 − 6)		54
		214

(W5) Minority interest

Minority share of net assets at balance sheet date (40% × 280 (W2))	112

(W6) Consolidated profit and loss reserve

	£m	£m
Hedra		240
Salvador – post acquisition (60 – 20)	40	
Additional depreciation	(5)	
	35	
Group share 60%		21
Aragon (W4)		20
Amortisation of goodwill (20 (W3) + 6 (W4))		(26)
		255

48 HOLDRITE, STAYBRITE AND ALLBRITE

Key answer tips

Part (a) contains a routine calculation of goodwill, being the difference between the fair value of the consideration paid and the fair value of the net assets acquired. In part (b) note that both the subsidiary and the associate were acquired half-way into the current year, so only half a year's post-acquisition profits can be included in group profits in the consolidated profit and loss account.

(a) **Goodwill arising on purchase of Staybrite – at 1 April 20X4:**

	£000	£000
Consideration		
Shares (10,000 × 75% × 2/3 × £6)		30,000
8% loan notes (10,000 × 75% × £100/250)		3,000
		33,000
Less		
Equity shares	10,000	
Share premium	4,000	
Pre-acq reserves (7,500 + (9,000 × $^6/_{12}$))	12,000	
Fair value adjustment (3,000 + 5,000)	8,000	
	34,000 × 75%	(25,500)
Goodwill		7,500

Goodwill amortisation over five years for six months is £750,000.

Goodwill on the purchase of shares in Allbrite – at 1 April 20X4:

Consideration	
Shares (5,000 × 40% × 3/4 × £6)	9,000

Cash (5,000 × 40% × £1)		2,000
		11,000
Less		
Equity shares	5,000	
Share premium	2,000	
Pre acq reserves (6,000 + (4,000 × 6/12))	8,000	
	15,000 × 40%	(6,000)
Goodwill		5,000

Goodwill amortisation over five years for six months is £500,000.

(b) **Holdrite Group Consolidated profit and loss account for the year ended 30 September 20X4**

	£000	£000
Turnover (75,000 + (40,700 × 6/12) − 10,000)		85,350
Cost of sales (W1)		(48,750)
Gross profit		36,600
Operating expenses (W2)		(15,730)
Profit from operations		20,870
Income from associate (W3)		700
		21,570
Interest expense		(170)
Profit before tax		21,400
Taxation		
− Group (4,800 + (3,000 × 6/12))	(6,300)	
− Associate (W3)	(400)	(6,700)
Profit after tax		14,700
Minority interest (W4)		(1,000)
Net profit from ordinary activities		13,700

(c) **Holdrite Group Movement on consolidated profit and loss reserve for the year ended 30 September 20X4**

	£000
Net profit for the period	13,700
Dividend paid	(5,000)
	8,700
Retained profits b/f	18,000
Retained profits c/f	26,700

Workings (£000)

(W1)		**Cost of sales**
		£000
	Holdrite	47,400
	Staybrite (19,700 × 6/12)	9,850
	Additional depreciation of plant	500
	Intra group purchases	(10,000)
	Unrealised profit in stock (4,000 × 25%)	1,000
		48,750

(W2)	Operating expenses	
	Holdrite	10,480
	Staybrite (9,000 × 6/12)	4,500
	Amortisation of Staybrite's goodwill (see (a) above)	750
		15,730

(W3)	Associated company	
	Profit for the year (6,000 × 6/12 × 40%)	1,200
	Goodwill amortisation (see (a) above)	(500)
		700
	Taxation (2,000 × 6/12 × 40%)	400

(W4)	Minority interest	
	9,000 × 6/12	4,500
	Less additional depreciation	(500)
		4,000
	× 25%	1,000

Tutorial note: The retained profits c/f can be proved as:

	£000
Holdrite (18,000 + 12,150 – 5,000)	25,150
Staybrite ($75\% \times 9,000 \times \frac{6}{12}$)	3,375
Allbrite ($40\% \times 4,000 \times \frac{6}{12}$)	800
Additional depreciation of plant (75% × 500)	(375)
Unrealised profit in stock (W1)	(1,000)
Amortisation of goodwill: Staybrite	(750)
Amortisation of goodwill: Allbrite	(500)
	26,700

49 HOSTERLING

Key answer tips

Parts (a) and (b) are relatively easy marks. Note that in part (a) you are asked to calculate the goodwill at acquisition so before any impairment. When preparing the profit and loss account remember that you are dealing with losses in the associate.

(a) **Goodwill arising on purchase of Sunlee – at 1 October 20X5:**

	£000	£000
Consideration		
Shares (20,000 × 80% × 3/5 × £5)		48,000
Less		
Equity shares	20,000	
Pre acq reserves	18,000	
Fair value adjustments ((22,000 – 18,000) + (20,000 – 17,000) + (35,000 – 30,000))	12,000	
	50,000 × 80%	(40,000)
Goodwill at date of acquisition		8,000

(b) **Carrying amount of Amber 30 September 20X6:**

	£000	£000
Net assets other than goodwill ((15,000 + 35,000 – 20,000 loss) × 40%)		12,000
Goodwill (see below)		9,500
Carrying amount at 30 September 20X6		21,500

Goodwill:

Cost of investment

Cash (6,000 × £4)		24,000

Less

Net assets at 1 July 20X6:

Equity 1 October 20X5 (15,000 + 35,000)	50,000	
Losses to date of acquisition (20,000 × 9/12)	(15,000)	
	——	
	35,000 × 40%	(14,000)
		——
Goodwill		10,000
Amortisation (see (c) below)		(500)
		——
Goodwill at 30 September 20X6		9,500
		——

(c)   **Hosterling Group**

Consolidated profit and loss account for the year ended 30 September 20X6

	£000	£000
Turnover (105,000 + 62,000 − 18,000 intra group)		149,000
Cost of sales (see working)		(89,000)
		——
Gross profit		60,000
Distribution costs (4,000 + 2,000)		(6,000)
Administrative expenses (7,500 + 7,000)		(14,500)
Goodwill amortisation (see below)		(1,600)
		——
Group operating profit		37,900
Share of loss from associate (24,000 × 3/12 × 40%)	(2,400)	
Amortisation associate's goodwill (see below)	(500)	(2,900)
	——	——
		35,000
Finance costs (1,200 + 900)		(2,100)
		——
Profit before tax		32,900
Taxation − Group (8,700 + 2,600)	(11,300)	
− Associate (4,000 × 3/12 × 40%)	400	(10,900)
	——	——
Profit after tax		22,000
Minority Interest ((13,000 − 1,000 depreciation adjustment) × 20%)		(2,400)
		——
Profit for the financial year		19,600
		——

Note: The dividend from Sunlee is eliminated on consolidation.

Goodwill amortisation for year ended 30 September 20X6 is:

Sunlee – £1.6 million (8m/5 years)

Amber – £500,000 (10m/5 years × 3/12).

Working

	£000
Cost of sales	
Hosterling	68,000
Sunlee	36,500
Intra group purchases	(18,000)
Additional depreciation of plant ((35,000 – 30,000)/5 years)	1,000
Unrealised profit in stock (7,500 × 25%/125%)	1,500
	——
	89,000
	——

50 PARENTIS

Consolidated balance sheet of Parentis as at 31 March 2007

	£ million	£ million
Assets		
Fixed assets		
Intangible		
Consolidated goodwill (135 (w (i)) – 27)		108
Tangible (640 + 340 + 40 – 2)		1,018
		——
		1,126
Current assets		
Stock (76 + 22 – 2 URP)	96	
Trade debtors (84 + 44 – 11 intra-group)	117	
Debtor re intellectual property	10	
Bank	4	
	——	
	227	
	——	
Creditors: amounts falling due within one year		
Trade creditors (130 + 57 – 7 intra-group)	180	
Cash consideration due 1 April 2007 (60 + 6 interest)	66	
Overdraft (25 – 4 CIT)	21	
Taxation (45 + 23)	68	
	——	
	(335)	
	——	
Net current liabilities		(108)

Creditors: amounts falling due after more than one year

10% loan notes (120 + 20)		(140)
		878

Capital and reserves:

Equity shares 25p each (w (i))		375
Reserves:		
Share Premium (w (i))	150	
Profit and loss account (w (ii))	264	414
		789
Minority interest (w (iii))		89
		878

Workings (Note: all figures in £ million)

(i) **Goodwill**

The acquisition of 600 million shares represents 75% of Offspring's 800 million shares (£200m/25p). The share exchange of 300 million (i.e. 1 for 2) at £0.75 each will result in an increase in equity share capital of £75 million (the nominal value) and create a share premium balance of £150 million (i.e. £0.50 premium on 300 million shares).

Consideration:

Equity shares (600/2 × £0.75)		225
10% loan notes (see below)		120
Cash (600 × £0.11/1.1 i.e. discounted at 10%)		60
		405

Acquired:

Equity shares (600m × 25p)	150	
Pre acquisition profits (120 × 75%)	90	
Fair value adjustment to properties (40 × 75%)	30	(270)
Goodwill		135

Amortised over five years at £27 million per annum.

The issue of the 10% loan notes is calculated as 600 million/500 × £100 = £120 million.

(ii) **Retained profits**

Parentis		300
Interest on deferred consideration (60 × 10%)		(6)
Goodwill amortisation		(27)
Offspring	140	
URP in stock (see below)	(2)	
Additional depreciation (from question)	(2)	
Write down intellectual property (30 – 10)	(20)	
Pre acquisition	(120)	
	———	
	(4) × 75%	(3)
		———
		264
		———

The unrealised profit in stock (URP) is £5m/£15m of the profit of £6 million made by Offspring.

(iii) **Minority interest**

Offspring net assets at 31 March 2007	340	
Fair value adjustment	40	
URP in stock	(2)	
Additional depreciation	(2)	
Write down intellectual property (30 – 10)	(20)	
	———	
	356 × 25%	89
	———	———

51 **PLATEAU** 👣 *Walk in the footsteps of a top tutor*

🔑

Key answer tip

Part (a) required the preparation of a balance sheet that is relatively straightforward. Ensure that you do not include the associate on a line-by-line basis and equity account instead. One of the complications in this question is a negative fair value adjustment. The question also required your knowledge of FRS 25/26 to ensure the available-for-sale assets were accounted for at fair value. The highlighted words are key phrases that markers are looking for.

(a) **Consolidated balance sheet of Plateau as at 30 September 2007**

	£000	£000
Fixed assets		
Goodwill (w (ii))		3,600
Tangible assets (18,400 + 10,400 – 400 (w (i)))		28,400
Investments – associate (w (iii))		10,500
– other available for sale		9,000
		51,500
Current assets		
Stock (6,900 + 6,200 – 300 URP (w (iv)))	12,800	
Debtors (3,200 + 1,500)	4,700	
	17,500	
Creditors: amounts falling due within one year (8,000 + 4,200)	(12,200)	5,300
Creditors: amounts falling due after more than one year		
7% Loan notes (5,000 + 1,000)		(6,000)
		50,800
Capital and reserves		
Equity shares of £1 each (w (v))		11,500
Reserves:		
Share premium (w (v))	7,500	
Profit and loss account (w (vi))	28,650	36,150
		47,650
Minority interest (w (vii))		3,150
		50,800

Workings (figures in brackets are in '000)

(i)   Tangible fixed assets

The transfer of the plant creates an initial unrealised profit (URP) of £500,000. This is reduced by £100,000 for each year (straight-line depreciation over five years) of depreciation in the post-acquisition period. Thus at 30 September 2007 the net unrealised profit is £400,000. This should be eliminated from Plateau's retained profits and from the carrying amount of the plant. The fall in the fair value of the land has already been taken into account in Savannah's balance sheet.

(ii) Goodwill in Savannah:

	£000	£000
Investment at cost:		
Shares issued (3,000/2 × £6)		9,000
Cash (3,000 × £1)		3,000
		12,000
Less – equity shares of Savannah	(3,000)	
– pre-acquisition reserves (6,000 × 75% (see below))	(4,500)	(7,500)
Goodwill on consolidation		4,500

Goodwill is amortised over a five year life giving a charge of £900,000 and a carrying amount at 30 September 2007 of £3.6 million.

Savannah's pre-acquisition reserves of £6.5 million require an adjustment for a write down of £500,000 in respect of the fair value of its land being below its carrying amount. Thus the adjusted pre-acquisition reserves of Savannah are £6 million. A consequent effect is that the post-acquisition reserves which are reported as £2.4 million in Savannah's balance sheet will become £2.9 million. This is because the fall in the value of the land has effectively been treated by Savannah as a post-acquisition loss.

(iii) **Axle**

	£000
Cost (4,000 × 30% × £7.50)	9,000
Share of net assets at acquisition (30% × (20,000 – 5,000))	(4,500)
Goodwill (not amortised or impaired)	4,500
Carrying amount of Axle at 30 September 2007	
Cost	9,000
Share post-acquisition profit (5,000 × 30%)	1,500
	10,500

(iv) The unrealised profit (URP) in stock is calculated as: Intra-group sales are £2.7 million on which Savannah made a profit of £900,000 (2,700 × 50/150). One third of these are still in the stock of Plateau, thus there is an unrealised profit of £300,000.

(v) The 1.5 million shares issued by Plateau in the share exchange at a value of £6 each would be recorded as £1 per share as capital and £5 per share as share premium giving an increase in share capital of £1.5 million and a share premium of £7.5 million.

(vi)   Consolidated profit and loss:

	£000
Plateau's profit and loss	24,000
Savannah's post-acquisition ((2,900 – 300 URP) × 75%)	1,950
Axle's post-acquisition profits (5,000 × 30%)	1,500
URP in plant (see (i))	(400)
Gain on available-for-sale investment (9,000 – 6,500) see below	2,500
Goodwill amortisation – Savannah	(900)
	28,650

The gain on available-for-sale investments must be recognised directly in equity.

(vii)   Minority interest

Adjusted equity at 30 September 2007: (12,900 – 300 URP) = 12,600 × 25%
3,150

(b)   FRS 7 *Fair Values in Acquisition Accounting* requires the purchase consideration for an acquired entity to be allocated to the fair value of the net assets acquired with any residue being allocated to goodwill. This also means that those net assets will be recorded at fair value in the consolidated balance sheet. This is entirely consistent with the way other net assets are recorded when first transacted (i.e. the initial cost of an asset is normally its fair value). The purpose of this process is that it ensures that individual assets and liabilities are correctly classified (and valued) in the consolidated balance sheet. Whilst this may sound obvious, consider what would happen if say a property had a carrying amount of £5 million, but a fair value of £7 million at the date it was acquired. If the carrying amount rather than the fair value was used in the consolidation it would mean that tangible assets (property) would be understated by £2 million and intangible assets (goodwill) would be overstated by the same amount (note: in the consolidated balance sheet of Plateau the opposite effect would occur as the fair value of Savannah's land is below its carrying amount at the date of acquisition). There could also be a 'knock on' effect with incorrect depreciation/amortisation charges for both property and goodwill. Thus the use of carrying amounts rather than fair values would not give a 'true and fair view' as required by the *Statement of Principles for Financial Reporting*.

The assistant's comment regarding the inconsistency of value models in the consolidated balance sheet is a fair point, but it is really a deficiency of the historical cost concept rather than a flawed consolidation technique. Indeed the fair values of the subsidiary's net assets are the historical costs to the parent. To overcome much of the inconsistency, there would be nothing to prevent the parent company from applying the revaluation model to its tangible fixed assets.

Examiners Report

Required the preparation of a consolidated balance sheet for a parent, subsidiary and an associate (equity accounted) followed by a short 5 mark section requiring an explanation of why fair values are used for the subsidiary's assets on its acquisition. The consolidated

---

balance sheet was well answered, but few candidates got to grips with the written section and many did not attempt it at all.

The main areas where candidates went wrong were:

In part (a)

- most candidates incorrectly deducted a $500,000 reduction in the fair value of the land from the property, plant and equipment. This effectively double counted the fall in value as the question clearly stated that the land had already been written down in the post acquisition period. The point of the information is that the fall in the value of the land should have been treated as an adjustment between pre and post acquisition profits (affecting goodwill). Also many candidates failed to adjust for the $100,000 additional deprecation on the plant.

- some confusion existed over the value of the associate with many simply showing it in the balance sheet at cost rather than using equity accounting. A very small minority proportionally consolidated the associate (some even proportionately consolidated the subsidiary).

- many candidates did correctly calculate the unrealised profit on inventory (stock), but did not always eliminate it from retained earnings.

- surprisingly, many candidates failed to adjust share capital and premium for the share issue relating to the acquisition.

- generally candidates scored well in the calculation of retained earnings, but the most common errors were not adjusting the subsidiary's post acquisition profit for the revaluation of land (mentioned earlier), failing to adjust for the unrealised profit in the plant and not including the gain on investments (often incorrectly shown as a revaluation reserve).

In part (b) the answers were quite disappointing. Generally candidates stated that the use of fair values was simply a requirement of accounting standards or discussed, sometimes at length, the definition of fair values. Most answers did not even try to address the inconsistency between the value of the subsidiary's assets and those of the parent. Better answers did refer to fair presentation of the balance sheet and the effect that the use of fair values had on consolidated goodwill.

	ACCA marking scheme		
			Marks
(a)	Balance sheet:		
	Goodwill		4
	Tangible fixed assets		2
	Investments	– associate	2
		– other	1
	Current assets		2
	Creditors due within one year		1
	7% loan notes		1
	Equity shares		1
	Share premium		1
	Profit and loss account		4
	Minority interest		1
			20
(b)	1 mark per relevant point		5
Total			25

52   PATRONIC   *Walk in the footsteps of a top tutor*

Key answer tip

Part (a) requires the calculation of goodwill considering fair value adjustments to both the purchase consideration and the subsidiaries net assets. Part (b) requires the preparation of a consolidated P&L – be careful to ensure that you pro-rate the subsidiaries results to take into account that they have only been a subsidiary for eight months. Part (c) requires you to discuss the criteria of an associate company and to identify that Acerbic is no longer an associate. The highlighted words are key phrases that markers are looking for.

(a)	Cost of control in Sardonic:	£000	£000
	Consideration		
	Shares (18,000 × 2/3 × £5·75)		69,000
	Deferred payment (18,000 × 2·42/1·21 (see below))		36,000
			―――――
			105,000
	Less		
	Equity shares	24,000	
	Pre-acquisition reserves:		
	At 1 April 2007	69,000	
	To date of acquisition (13,500 × 4/12)	4,500	
	Fair value adjustments (4,100 + 2,400)	6,500	
		―――――	
		104,000 × 75%	(78,000)
			―――――
	Goodwill		27,000
			―――――

£1 compounded for two years at 10% would be worth £1·21.

The acquisition of 18 million out of a total of 24 million equity shares is a 75% interest.

(b)   **Patronic Group**

Consolidated profit and loss account for the year ended 31 March 2008

	£000	£000
Turnover (150,000 + (78,000 × 8/12) − (1,250 × 8 months intra group))		192,000
Cost of sales (w (i))		(119,100)
Gross profit		72,900
Distribution costs (7,400 + (3,000 × 8/12))		(9,400)
Administrative expenses (12,500 + (6,000 × 8/12))		(16,500)
Amortisation of goodwill (27,000/9 years × 8/12)		(2,000)
Operating profit		45,000
Finance costs (w (ii))		(5,000)
Share of profit from associate (10,000 × 30%)		3,000
Profit before tax		43,000
Tax − group (10,400 + (3,600 × 8/12))	(12,800)	
− associate (4,000 × 30%)	(1,200)	(14,000)
Profit after tax		29,000
Minority interest (w (iii))		(2,100)
Profit for the year		26,900

(c)   An associate is defined by FRS 9 *Associates and Joint Ventures* as an investment over which an investor has significant influence. There are several indicators of significant influence, but the most important are usually considered to be a holding of 20% or more of the voting shares and board representation. Therefore it was reasonable to assume that the investment in Acerbic (at 31 March 2008) represented an associate and was correctly accounted for under the equity accounting method.

The current position (from May 2008) is that although Patronic still owns 30% of Acerbic's shares, Acerbic has become a subsidiary of Spekulate as it has acquired 60% of Acerbic's shares. Acerbic is now under the control of Spekulate (part of the definition of being a subsidiary), therefore it is difficult to see how Patronic can now exert significant influence over Acerbic. The fact that Patronic has lost its seat on Acerbic's board seems to reinforce this point. In these circumstances the investment in Acerbic falls to be treated under FRS 26 *Financial Instruments: Recognition and Measurement*. It will cease to be equity accounted from the date of loss of significant influence. Its carrying amount at that date will be its initial recognition value under FRS 26 and thereafter it will be carried at fair value.

Workings

(i)

		£000	£000
Cost of sales			
Patronic			94,000
Sardonic (51,000 × 8/12)			34,000
Intra group purchases (1,250 × 8 months)			(10,000)
Additional depreciation: plant (2,400/ 4 years × 8/12)		400	
property (per question)		200	600
Unrealised profit in stock (3,000 × 20/120)			500
			119,100

Note: for both sales and cost of sales, only the post acquisition intra group trading should be eliminated.

(ii)

	£000
Finance costs	
Patronic per question	2,000
Unwinding interest – deferred consideration (36,000 × 10% × 8/12)	2,400
Sardonic (900 × 8/12)	600
	5,000

(iii)

	£000
Minority interest	
Sardonic's post acquisition profit (13,500 × 8/12)	9,000
Less post acquisition additional depreciation (w (i))	(600)
	8,400
	× 25% = 2,100

Examiners Report

Required the calculation of goodwill and the preparation of a consolidated income statement for a parent, subsidiary and an associate (equity accounted) followed by a short 4 mark section requiring an explanation of how an investment in an associate should be treated after it became a subsidiary of another company. The consolidation was generally well answered, but answers to the written section were more 'patchy'.

The main areas where candidates went wrong were:

In part (a) – goodwill calculation

– most candidates correctly calculated the share exchange consideration, but failed to discount (for two years) the deferred cash consideration correctly. The calculation of the pre-acquisition equity was also done quite well, but the most common mistakes were not including an apportionment (4 months) of the current year's profit as part of the pre-acquisition figure and incorrectly including post acquisition adjustments for additional depreciation and unrealised profits as pre-acquisition items. It was also common for candidates to forget to include the subsidiary's share capital in the calculation of equity.

Part (b) – consolidated income statement

- a surprisingly common error was not time apportioning (for 8 months) the subsidiary's results, instead a full year's results were often included. This is a fundamental error showing a lack of understanding of the principle that a subsidiary's results are only included the consolidated accounts from date it becomes a member of the group. A small minority of candidates proportionally consolidated, rather than equity accounted, the associate (some even proportionately consolidated the subsidiary), however this error is now becoming much less common.

- many candidates did not correctly eliminate the intra-group trading; either no adjustment at all or eliminating pre-acquisition trading as well.

- the unrealised profit in inventory was often calculated as a gross profit percentage, whereas the question stated it was a mark up was on cost. It was also common for this adjustment to be deducted from cost of sales rather than added.

- impairment/amortisation of goodwill was often omitted.

- the finance cost relating to the unwinding of the deferred consideration was omitted by most candidates.

- the calculation of the minority interest (now called non-controlling interest) was sometimes ignored or did not take account the post acquisition additional depreciation adjustment or time apportionment.

In part (c) the answers were very disappointing; many not attempting it all. The question was based on how an associate, that had previously been equity accounted, would be treated in the following year when it had lost its 'significant influence' due to the associate becoming a subsidiary of another entity. Of those that did attempt this section many wasted time by reproducing (as an answer) the scenario given in the question rather than actually answering the question. Others did not think the investment should be treated any differently in the following year saying that the percentage of share ownership is all that matters (despite the loss of a seat on the board). Some candidates thought the question asked for an explanation of how the investment should be treated in the current year. The correct answer is that it should be treated as an 'ordinary investment' (no longer an associate) under IAS 39.

	ACCA marking scheme	
		Marks
(a)	Goodwill of Sardonic:	
	consideration	2
	net assets acquired calculated as:	
	equity shares	1
	pre acquisition reserves	2
	fair value adjustments	1
	Maximum	6
(b)	Profit and loss account:	
	turnover	2
	cost of sales	5
	distribution costs and administrative expenses	1
	amortisation of goodwill	1
	finance costs	2
	share of associate's profit	½
	tax – group	1

	tax – associate	½
	minority interest	2
	Maximum	15
(c)	1 mark per relevant point to	4
Total		**25**

53   PEDANTIC   *Walk in the footsteps of a top tutor*

Key answer tips

This question requires the preparation of a fairly straightforward consolidated profit and loss account and a consolidated balance sheet. The biggest problem for candidates is to complete the tasks in the exam time available. Ensure you pro-rate the subsidiary's results in part (a) to gain the easy marks available.

(a)   **Consolidated profit and loss account for the year ended 30 September 2008**

	£000	£000
Turnover		
(85,000 + (42,000 × 6/12) – 8,000 intra-group sales)		98,000
Cost of sales (w (i))		(72,000)
		———
Gross profit		26,000
Distribution costs (2,000 + (2,000 × 6/12))		(3,000)
Administrative expenses		
(6,000 + (3,200 × 6/12) – 300 acquisition costs)		(7,300)
		———
Operating profit		15,700
Finance costs (300 + (400 × 6/12))		(500)
		———
Profit before tax		15,200
Taxation (4,700 + (1,400 × 6/12))		(5,400)
		———
Profit after tax		9,800
Minority interest		
(((3,000 × 6/12) – (800 URP + 200 depreciation)) × 40%)		(200)
		———
Profit for the year		9,600
		———

(b)   Consolidated balance sheet as at 30 September 2008

Fixed assets

Intangible – goodwill (w (ii))	3,300
Tangible	
(40,600 + 12,600 + 2,000 – 200 depreciation adjustment (w (i)))	55,000
	58,300
Current assets (w (iii))	21,400
Creditors: amounts falling due within one year	
(8,200 + 4,700 – 400 intra-group balance)	(12,500)
Net current assets	8,900
Total assets less current liabilities	67,200
Creditors: amounts falling due after more than one year	
10% loan notes (4,000 + 3,000)	(7,000)
Net assets	60,200
Capital and reserves	
Equity shares of £1 each ((10, 000 + 1,600) w (ii))	11,600
Share premium (w (ii))	8,000
Profit and loss account (w (iv))	36,000
	55,600
Minority interest (w (v))	4,600
	60,200

Workings (figures in brackets in £000)

(W1) Group structure

Pedantic

60%   Investments occurred on 1 April 2008 so has been
          held for 6 months.

Sophistic

(W2) Net assets of Sophistic

	At acquisition	At b/s date
	$000	$000
Share capital	4,000	4,000
Retained earnings	5,000	6,500
Fair value adjustment:		
Plant	2,000	2,000
Depreciation (2,000 / 5 years) x 6 months		(200)
PURP on inventory (W6)		(800)
	11,000	11,500

(W3) Goodwill

	Sophistic
	$000
Cost of investment	
Shares ((4,000 × 60%) x 2/3 × $6)	9,600
Acquisition costs	300
	9,900
Share of net assets	(6,600)
(60% × 11,000)	
Goodwill on consolidation	3,300

The share consideration given on the acquisition of Sophistic has not been recorded. Therefore share capital should be increased by ((4,000 x60%) x 2/3 × $1) $1,600 and share premium should be increased by ((4,000 × 60%) x 2/3 × $5) $8,000.

(W4) Minority interest

	$000
Share of net assets (40% x 11,500)	4,600

(W5) Consolidated reserves

	$000
Pedantic	35,400
Acquisition costs	300
Sophistic (60% × (11,500 − 11,000))	300
	36,000

(W6) Provision for unrealised profit on inventory

The unrealised profit (URP) in inventory is calculated as ($8 million − $5.2 million) × 40/140 = $800,000.

(W7) Cost of sales	$000
Pedantic	63,000
Sophistic (32,000 × 6/12)	16,000
Intra-group sales	(8,000)
URP in inventory	800
Additional depreciation (2,000/5 years × 6/12)	200
	72,000

(W8) Current assets	$000
Pedantic	16,000
Sophistic	6,600
URP in inventory	(800)
Cash in transit	200
Intra-group balance	(600)
	21,400

54 PACEMAKER

Consolidated balance sheet of Pacemaker as at 31 March 2009:

	£million	£million
Fixed assets		
Intangible		
Goodwill (20 – 8) (w (i))		12
Brand (25 – 5 (25/10 × 2 years post-acq. amortisation))		20
Tangible (w (ii))		818
Investments		
Investment in associate (w (iii))		144
Other available-for-sale investments (82 + 37)		119
		1,113
Current assets		
Stock (142 + 160 – 16 URP (w (iv)))	286	
Debtors (95 + 88)	183	
Cash and bank (8 + 22)	30	
	499	

Creditors: amounts falling due within one year (200 + 165)	(365)	
	———	
Net current assets		134
		———
Total assets less current liabilities		1,247
Creditors: amounts falling due after more than one year		
10% loan notes (180 + 20)		(200)
		———
		1,047
		———
Capital and reserves		
Equity shares (500 + 75 (w (iii)))		575
Share premium (100 + 45 (w (iii)))	145	
Profit and loss account (w (iv))	239	384
	———	———
		959
Minority interest (w (v))		88
		———
		1,047
		———

Workings (all figures in £ million)

The investment in Syclop represents 80% (116/145) of its equity and is likely to give Pacemaker control thus Syclop should be consolidated as a subsidiary. The investment in Vardine represents 30% (30/100) of its equity and is normally treated as an associate that should be equity accounted.

(i) Goodwill in Syclop:

Investment at cost – cash		210
– loan note (116/200 × £100)		58
		———
		268
Equity shares	145	
Pre-acquisition profit	120	
Fair value adjustments – property (w (ii))	20	
– brand	25	
	———	
Fair value of net assets at acquisition	310 × 80%(248)	
	———	———
Goodwill		20
		———

At 31 March 2009 there will be two years amortisation of goodwill = 8 (20/5 years × 2)

(ii) Tangible fixed assets:

Pacemaker	520
Syclop	280

Fair value property (82 – 62)	20
Post-acquisition depreciation (2 years) (20 × 2/20 years)	(2)
	———
	818
	———

		£million
(iii)	Investment in associate:	
	Investment at cost (30 × 5/2 × £1·60)	120
	Share of post-acquisition profit (100 – 20 × 30%)	24
		———
		144
		———

The purchase consideration by way of a share exchange (75 million shares in Pacemaker for 30 million shares in Vardine) would be recorded as an increase in share capital of £75 million (£1 nominal value) and an increase in share premium of £45 million (75 million × £0·60).

As the goodwill of Vardine has an indefinite life, it will not be amortised and therefore it does not need to be calculated.

(iv)	Consolidated profit and loss account reserve:	
	Pacemaker's profits	130
	Syclop's post-acquisition profits (130 × 80% see below)	104
	Goodwill amortisation (w (i))	(8)
	Gain on investments – Pacemaker (see below)	5
	Vardine's post-acquisition profits (w (iii))	24
	URP in stocks (56 × 40/140)	(16)
		———
		239
		———

Syclop's profits:		
Pre-acquisition		120
Post-acquisition (260 – 120)	140	
Additional depreciation/amortisation (5 + 2) (w (i) and (ii))	(7)	
Loss on available-for-sale investments (40 – 37)	(3)	
	———	
Adjusted post-acquisition profits		130
		———
Adjusted profits		250
		———

Gain on the value of Pacemaker's available-for-sale investments:	
Carrying amount at 31 March 2008 (345 – 210 cash – 58 loan note)	77
Carrying amount at 31 March 2009	82
	———
Gain to profit and loss account reserve (or 'other components of equity')	5
	———

(v)   Minority interest

Equity shares (145 × 20%)	29
Adjusted profits (250 × 20% (w (iv)))	50
Fair value adjustments for brand and property ((25 + 20) × 20%)	9
	88

ACCA marking scheme	
	Marks
goodwill	4.5
brand	1
tangible fixed assets	2
investment in associate	2
other investments	1
stock	2
debtors, cash and bank	1
creditors due within one year	0.5
loan notes	0.5
equity shares	1
share premium	1
profit and loss account	6.5
minority interest	2
Total	25

Examiner's comments

This question required the preparation of a consolidated statement of financial position (balance sheet) for a parent, a subsidiary (line-by-line consolidation) and an associate (equity accounted). The question required the calculation of goodwill with the consideration based on a cash payment and loan note issue (that had already been accounted for) and included some fair value adjustments. This was the best answered question demonstrating that most candidates have a sound knowledge of consolidation techniques. The main areas where candidates went wrong were:

- goodwill calculation: a failure to account for loan note element of the consideration and/or the non-controlling interest element of the goodwill (not applicable to UK stream) and incorrectly accounting for the new property by using its fair value rather than the excess of fair value over cost

- not realising the post-acquisition period was two years, many candidates only accounted for one year's additional depreciation on the new property and amortisation of the brand

- the detailed components of the consolidated retained earnings were often missed; depreciation adjustments, unrealised profit (URP) in inventory (often calculated wrongly as well - see below), gain/loss on available-for-sale investments

- the URP was often calculated as a gross profit percentage, whereas the question stated it was a mark up was on cost. Some candidates eliminated the cost of the

> inventory rather than the URP in the inventory and many incorrectly split the URP between the parent and the subsidiary even though the parent had made the sale
>
> • a small minority of candidates are still proportionally consolidating the associate (some even proportionally consolidated the subsidiary); others fully consolidated the associate and computed a non-controlling interest of 70%
>
> • many candidates did not account for the effect of the share exchange on acquisition of the interest in the associate on the share capital and share premium.

ANALYSING AND INTERPRETING FINANCIAL STATEMENTS

55 COMPARATOR 🔑 *Walk in the footsteps of a top tutor*

Key answer tips

Be careful with your time allocation for answering this question. The bulk of your time should be spent in writing the report required in part (c). Only 6 marks are offered for calculating ratios. All the remaining marks are for explanation and interpretation. The highlighted words are key phrases that markers are looking for.

(a) Ratios are used to assess the financial performance of a company by comparing the calculated figures to various other sources. This may be to previous years' ratios of the same company, to the ratios of a similar rival company, to accepted norms (say of liquidity ratios) or, as in this example, to industry averages. The problems inherent in these processes are several. Probably the most important aspect of using ratios is to realise that they do not give the answers to the assessment of how well a company has performed; they merely raise the questions and direct the analyst into trying to determine what has caused favourable or unfavourable indicators. In many ways it can be said that ratios are only as useful as the skills of the person using them. It is also true that any assessment should also consider other information that may be available including non-financial information.

More specific problem areas are:

– Accounting policies: if two companies have different accounting policies, it can invalidate any comparison between their ratios. For example return on capital employed is materially affected by revaluations of fixed assets. Comparing this ratio for two companies where one has revalued its fixed assets and the other carries them at depreciated historic cost would not be very meaningful. Similar examples may involve depreciation methods, stock valuation policies, etc.

– Accounting practices: this is similar to differing accounting policies in its effects. An example of this would be the use of debtor factoring. If one company collects its debts in the normal way, then the calculation of debtor days would be a reasonable indication of the efficiency of its credit control department. However if a company chose to factor its debtors (i.e. 'sell' them to a finance company) then the calculation of its debtor days would be meaningless. A more controversial example would be the engineering of a lease such that it fell to be treated as an operating lease rather than a finance lease.

– Balance sheet averages: many ratios are based on comparing profit and loss account items with balance sheet items. The ratio of debtors days is a good example of this. For such ratios to have meaning, there is an assumption that the year-end balance sheet figures are representative of annual norms. Seasonal trading and other factors may invalidate this assumption. For example the level of debtors and stock of a toy manufacturer could vary largely due to the nature of its seasonal trading.

– Inflation can distort comparisons over time.

– The definition of an accounting ratio. If a ratio is calculated by two companies using different definitions, then there is an obvious problem. Common examples of this are gearing ratios (some use debt/equity, others may use debt/debt + equity). Also where a ratio is partly based on a profit figure, there can be differences as to what is included and what is excluded from the profit figure. Problems of this type include the treatment of exceptional items and finance costs.

– The use of norms can be misleading. A desirable range for the current ratio may be say between 1.5 and 2 : 1, but all businesses are different. This would be a very low ratio for a supermarket (with few debtors), but a high figure for a construction company (with high levels of work in progress).

– Looking at a single ratio in isolation is rarely useful. It is necessary to form a view when considering ratios in combination with other ratios.

A more controversial aspect of ratio analysis is that management have sometimes indulged in creative accounting techniques in order that the ratios calculated from published financial statements will show a more favourable picture than the true underlying position. Examples of this are sale and repurchase agreements, which manipulate liquidity figures, and off balance sheet finance which distorts return on capital employed.

Inter-firm comparisons:

Of particular concern with this method of using ratios is:

– They are themselves averages and may incorporate large variations in their composition. Some inter-firm comparison agencies produce the ratios analysed into quartiles to attempt to overcome this problem.

– It may be that the sector in which a company is included may not be sufficiently similar to the exact type of trade of the specific company. The type of products or markets may be different.

– Companies of different sizes operate under different economies of scale, this may not be reflected in the industry average figures.

– The year end accounting dates of the companies included in the averages are not going to be all the same. This highlights issues of balance sheet averages and seasonal trading referred to above. Some agencies try to minimise this by grouping companies with approximately similar year-ends together as in the example of this question, but this is not a complete solution.

(b)   Calculation of specified ratios:

	Comparator	Sector average
Return on capital employed (186 +34 loan interest/(335 + 300))	34.6%	22.1%
Net assets turnover (2,425/(335 + 300))	3.8 times	1.8 times
Gross profit margin (555/2,425 × 100)	22.9%	30%
Net profit (excluding exceptionals) margin (306/2,425 × 100)	12.6%	not available
Net profit (before tax) margin (186/2,425 × 100)	7.7%	12.5%
Current ratio (595/500)	1.19 : 1	1.6 : 1
Quick ratio (320/500)	0.64 : 1	0.9 : 1
Stock holding period (275/1,870 × 365)	54 days	46 days
Debtors' collection period (320/2,425 × 365)	48 days	45 days
Creditor payment period (350/1,870 × 365) (based on cost of sales)	68 days	55 days
Debt to equity (300/335 × 100)	90%	40%
Dividend yield (see below)	2.5%	6%
Dividend cover (96/90)	1.07 times	3 times

The workings are in £000 (unless otherwise stated) and are for Comparator's ratios.

The dividend yield is calculated from a dividend per share figure of 15p (£90,000/(150,000 × 4)) and a share price of £6.00.

Thus the yield is 2.5% (15p/£6.00 × 100%).

(c)   Analysis of Comparator's financial performance compared to sector average for the year to 30 September 20X3:

To:

From:

Date:

Operating performance

The return on capital employed of Comparator is impressive being more than 50% higher than the sector average. The components of the return on capital employed are the asset turnover and profit margins. In these areas Comparator's asset turnover is much higher (nearly double) than the average, but the net profit margin after exceptionals is considerably below the sector average. However, if the exceptionals are treated as one off costs and excluded, Comparator's margins are very similar to the sector average.

This short analysis seems to imply that Comparator's superior return on capital employed is due entirely to an efficient asset turnover i.e. Comparator is making its assets work twice as efficiently as its competitors. A closer inspection of the underlying figures may explain why its asset turnover is so high. It can be seen from the note to the balance sheet that Comparator's fixed assets appear quite old. Their net book value is only 15% of their original cost. This has at least two implications; they will need replacing in the near future and the company is already struggling for funding; and their low net book value gives a high figure for asset turnover. Unless Comparator has underestimated the life of its assets in its depreciation calculations, its fixed assets will need replacing in the near future. When this occurs its asset turnover and return on capital employed figures will be much lower.

This aspect of ratio analysis often causes problems and to counter this anomaly some companies calculate the asset turnover using the cost of fixed assets rather than their net book value as this gives a more reliable trend. It is also possible that Comparator is using assets that are not on its balance sheet. It may be leasing assets that do not meet the definition of finance leases and thus the assets and corresponding obligations are not recognised on the balance sheet.

A further issue is which of the two calculated margins should be compared to the sector average (i.e. including or excluding the effects of the exceptionals). The gross profit margin of Comparator is much lower than the sector average. If the exceptional losses were taken in at trading account level, which they should be as they relate to obsolete stock, Comparator's gross margin would be even worse. As Comparator's net margin is similar to the sector average, it would appear that Comparator has better control over its operating costs. This is especially true as the other element of the net profit calculation is finance costs and as Comparator has much higher gearing than the sector average, one would expect Comparator's interest to be higher than the sector average.

Liquidity

Here Comparator shows real cause for concern. Its current and quick ratios are much worse than the sector average, and indeed far below expected norms. Current liquidity problems appear to be due to high levels of trade creditors and a high bank overdraft. The high levels of stock contribute to the poor quick ratio and may be indicative of further obsolete stock (the exceptional item is due to obsolete stock). The debtors' collection figure is reasonable, but at 68 days, Comparator takes longer to pay its creditors than its competitors do. Whilst this is a source of 'free' finance, it can damage relations with suppliers and may lead to a curtailment of further credit.

Gearing

As referred to above, gearing (as measured by debt/equity) is more than twice the level of the sector average. Whilst this may be an uncomfortable level, it is currently beneficial for shareholders. The company is making an overall return of 34.6%, but only paying 8% interest on its loan notes. The gearing level may become a serious issue if Comparator becomes unable to maintain the finance costs. The company already has an overdraft and the ability to make further interest payments could be in doubt.

Investment ratios

Despite reasonable profitability figures, Comparator's dividend yield is poor compared to the sector average. From the profit and loss account reserve movements it can be seen that total dividends are £90,000 out of available profit for the year of only £96,000 (hence the very low dividend cover). The interim dividend was £60,000 but the final is only £30,000. Perhaps this indicates a worsening performance during the year, as normally final dividends are higher than interim dividends. Considering these factors it is surprising the company's share price is holding up so well.

Summary

The company compares favourably with the sector average figures for profitability, however the company's liquidity and gearing position are quite poor and give cause for concern. If it is to replace its old fixed assets in the near future, it will need to raise further finance. With already high levels of borrowing and poor dividend yields, this may be a serious problem for Comparator.

Yours faithfully

56   RYTETREND PLC

Key answer tips

The note reconciling net cash flow to net debt is not required in part (a).

Although you are specifically asked for ratios in part (b), most of the marks can be gained through observation and analysis. As well as the profit and loss account and balance sheet, you should refer to the cash flow statement that you prepared in part (a). This highlights a central issue: the heavy expenditure on fixed assets during the year.

(a)   **Rytetrend plc – Cash flow statement for the year to 31 March 20X3**

Reconciliation of operating profit to net cash inflow from operating activities

(*Note:* figures in brackets are in £000)	£000	£000
Operating profit per question		3,860
Capitalisation of installation costs		
less depreciation (300 – 20%) (W1)		240
Adjustments for:		
Depreciation of fixed assets (W1)	7,410	
Loss on disposal of plant (W1)	700	
		8,110
Increase in warranty provision (500 – 150)		350
Decrease in stock (3,270 – 2,650)		620
Decrease in debtors (1,950 – 1,100)		850
Increase in creditors (3,300 – 2,260)		1,040
Net cash flow from operating activities		15,070

Cash Flow Statement

Net cash flow from operating activities (above)	15,070
Servicing of finance: interest paid	(460)
Taxation paid (W2)	(910)
Capital expenditure: purchase of fixed assets (W1)	(15,550)
	(1,850)
Ordinary dividends paid	(600)
	(2,450)

Financing:

Issue of ordinary shares (1,500 + 1,500)	3,000	
Issue of 6% loan note	2,000	
Repayment of 10% loan notes	(4,000)	
	———	1,000
		———
Decrease in cash (400 + 1,050)		(1,450)
		———

Workings

(W1) **Fixed assets – cost**

	£000
Balance b/f	27,500
Disposal	(6,000)
Balance c/f (37,250 + 300 re installation)	(37,550)
	———
Cost of assets acquired	(16,050)
Trade in allowance	500
	———
Cash flow for acquisitions	(15,550)
	———
Depreciation	
Balance b/f	(10,200)
Disposal (6,000 × 20% × 4 years)	4,800
Balance c/f (12,750 + (300 × 20%))	12,810
	———
Difference – charge for year	7,410
	———
Disposal	
Cost	6,000
Depreciation	(4,800)
	———
Net book value	1,200
Trade in allowance	(500)
	———
Loss on sale	700
	———

(W2) **Tax paid:**

Tax provision b/f	(630)
Profit and loss account tax charge	(1,000)
Tax provision c/f	720
	———
Difference cash paid	(910)
	———

(b)   Report on the financial performance of Rytetrend plc for the year ended 31 March 20X3

To:

From:

Date:

Operating performance

(i)   Turnover up £8.3 million representing an increase of 35.3% on 20X2 figure of £23.5 million.

(ii)   Costs of sales up by £6.5 million (40.6% increase on 20X2 figure of £16 million)

Overall the increase in activity has led to an increase in gross profit of £1.8 million, however the gross profit margin has eased slightly from 31.9% in 20X2 to 29.2% in 20X3. Perhaps the slight reduction in margins gave a boost to sales.

(iii)   Operating expenses have increased by £840,000, an increase of 18.3% on 20X2 figure of £4.6 million but this is considerably lower than the increase in turnover.

(iv)   Interest costs reduced by £40,000. It is worth noting that the composition of them has changed. It appears that Rytetrend plc has taken advantage of a cyclic reduction in borrowing cost and redeemed its 10% loan notes and (partly) replaced these with lower cost 6% loan notes. From the interest cost figure, this appears to have taken place half way through the year. Although borrowing costs on long-term finance have decreased, other factors have led to a substantial overdraft which has led to further interest of £200,000.

(v)   The accumulated effect is an increase in profit before tax of £1 million (up 41.7% on 20X2) which is reflected by an increase in dividends of £200,000.

(vi)   The company has invested heavily in acquiring new fixed assets (over £15 million – see cash flow statement). The refurbishment of the equipment may be responsible for the increase in the company's sales and operating performance.

Analysis of financial position

(vii)   Stock and debtors have both decreased markedly. Stock is now at 43 days (2,650/22,500 × 365) from 75 days (3,270/16,000 × 365), this may be due to new arrangements with suppliers or that the different range of equipment that Rytetrend plc now sells may offer less choice requiring lower stocks. Debtors are only 13 days (1,100/31,800 × 365) (from 30 days (1,950/23,500 × 365)).

(viii) Although creditors have increased significantly, they still represent only 54 days ((3,300/22,500 × 365) based on cost of sales) which is almost the same as in 20X2 (2,260/16,000 × 365).

(ix)   A very worrying factor is that the company has gone from net current assets of £2,580,000 to net current liabilities of £1,820,000. This is mainly due to a combination of the above mentioned items; decreased stock and debtors, increased creditors leading to a fall in cash balances of £1,450,000. That said, traditionally acceptable norms for liquidity ratios are not really appropriate to a mainly retailing business.

(x) Long-term borrowing has fallen by £2 million; this has lowered gearing from 20% (4,000/(4,000 + 15,880)) to only 9% (2,000/(2,000 + 20,680)). This is a very modest level of gearing.

The cash flow statement

This indicates very healthy operating cash flows of £15,070, more than sufficient to pay interest costs, taxation and dividends. The main reason why the overall cash balance has fallen is that new fixed assets (costing over £15 million) have largely been financed from operating cash flows (only £1 million net of new capital has been raised). If Rytetrend plc continues to generate operating cash flows in the order of the current year, its liquidity will soon get back to healthy levels.

57 BIGWOOD

> **Key answer tips**
>
> Be sure that you know the FRS 1 format for the cash flow statement before the exam, so that you can quickly slot in the required figures to earn full marks. Part (b) tells you exactly what is required. Make sure that you refer to your cash flow statement from part (a) as instructed.

(a) **Bigwood – Cash Flow Statement for the year to 30 September 20X4**

Reconciliation of operating profit to net cash inflow from operating activities

Note: figures in brackets are in £000	£000	£000
Operating profit		1,000
Adjustments for:		
Depreciation – fixed assets (W1)	3,800	
Loss on disposal of fixtures (W1)	1,250	5,050
Increase in stock (2,900 – 1,500)		(1,400)
Increase in debtors (100 – 50)		(50)
Increase in creditors (3,100 – 2,150)		950
Net cash flow from operating activities		5,550
Cash flow statement		
Net cash flow from operating activities (above)		5,550
Servicing of finance: interest paid		(300)
Taxation paid (W2)		(480)
Capital expenditure – purchase of fixed assets (W1)	(10,500)	
– disposal costs of fixtures (W1)	(50)	(10,550)
		(5,780)

Equity dividends paid		(600)
		(6,380)
Financing:		
Issue of ordinary shares (2,000 + 1,000)	3,000	
Long-term loans (3,000 – 1,000)	2,000	5,000
Decrease in cash (450 + 930)		(1,380)

Workings (all figures in £000)

(W1)   **Fixed assets – cost**

Balance b/f	9,500
Disposal	(3,000)
Balance c/f	(17,000)
Difference cash purchase	(10,500)

Depreciation

Balance b/f	(3,000)
Disposal (3,000 – 1,200)	1,800
Balance c/f	5,000
Difference charge for year	3,800

Disposal

Cost	3,000
Depreciation	(1,800)
Net book value	1,200
Cost of disposal	50
Total loss on disposal	(1,250)

(W2)   **Tax paid:**

Tax provision b/f	(450)
Profit and loss account tax charge	(250)
Tax provision c/f	220
Difference cash paid	(480)

(b) **Report on the financial performance of Bigwood for the two years ended 30 September 20X4**

To:

From:

Date:

Operating performance

Bigwood's overall performance as measured by the return on capital employed has deteriorated markedly. This ratio is a composite of the company's profit margins and its asset utilisation. The expansion represented by the acquisition of the five new stores has considerably increased investment in net assets. The asset turnover (a measure of asset utilisation) has fallen from 3.3 times to just 2.1 times. This is a relatively large fall and is partly responsible for the deteriorating performance. However, it should be borne in mind that it often takes some time before new investment generates the same level of sales as existing capacity so it may be that the situation will improve in future years.

Of more concern in the current year is the deteriorating gross profit margin of the company's clothing sales. This has fallen from 18.6% to 9.4%. The effect of this is all the more marked because sales of clothing (in the current year) represents nearly 70% (16,000 as % of 23,000) of turnover. It should also be noted that the stock holding period of clothing has also increased significantly from 39 days in 20X3 to 68 days in the current year. This may be a reflection of a company policy to increase stock levels in order to attract more sales, but it may also be an indication that there is some slow-moving or obsolete stock. The clothing industry is notoriously susceptible to fashion changes; the new designs may not have gone down well with the buying public. By contrast the profit margin on food sales has increased substantially (from 25% to 32.1%) as indeed have the sales themselves (up 75% on last year). These improvements have helped to offset the weaker performance of clothing sales.

A more detailed analysis shown by the ratios in the appendix confirms the position. The expansion has created a 35% increase in the sales floor area, but the proportionate increase in turnover is only 17.3%. Breaking this down between the two sectors shows that the clothing sector is responsible for this deterioration; an increase in capacity of 37% has led to an increase in sales of only 2.6%, whereas a more modest increase of 20% in the food floor area has led to a remarkable increase of 75% in food sales. In the current year food retailing has generated a turnover of £1,167,000 per square metre, whereas clothing sales per square metre has fallen from £446,000 to £333,000. When the relative profit margins of clothing and food are considered, it can be seen that food retailing has been far more profitable than clothing retailing and this gap in margins has increased during the current year.

This deterioration in trading margins has continued through to net profit margins (falling from 7.1% to only 2.0%). It can be observed that operating expenses have increased considerably, but this is to be expected and is probably in line with the increase in the number of stores.

In summary, the increase in capacity has focused on clothing rather than food retailing. On reflection this seems misguided as the performance of food retailing was superior to that of clothing (in 20X3) and this has continued (even more so) during the current year.

Liquidity/solvency

The increase in the investment in new stores and the refurbishment of existing stores has been largely financed by increasing long-term loans by £2 million and issuing £3 million of equity. The effect of this is an increase in gearing from 17% to 28%. Although the level of gearing is still modest, the interest cover has fallen from a very healthy 25 times to a worrying low 3.3 times. The investment has also taken its toll on the bank balance falling from £450,000 in hand to an overdraft of £930,000. This probably explains why the company has stretched its payment of creditors to 59 days in 20X4 from 50 days in 20X3.

The company's current liquidity position has deteriorated slightly from 0.77 : 1 to 0.71 : 1. No quick ratios have been given, nor would they be useful. Liquidity ratios are difficult to assess for retailing companies. Most of the sales generated by such companies are for cash (thus there will be few debtors) and normal liquidity benchmarks are not appropriate. The cash flow statement reveals net cash flows from operating activities of £5,550,000. This is a far more reliable indicator of the company's liquidity position. The £5,550,000 is more than adequate to service the finance costs, taxation and the dividend payments. Indeed the operating cash flows have contributed significantly to the financing of the expansion programme.

Share price and dividends

Bigwood's share price has halved from £6.00 to £3.00 during the current year. The dilution effect of the share issue at £1.50 per share (2 million shares for £3 million) would account for some of this fall (to approximately £4.20), but the further fall probably represents the market's expectations of the company's performance. It is worth noting that the company has maintained its dividends at £600,000 despite an after tax profit of only £450,000. Whilst this dividend policy cannot be maintained indefinitely (at the current level of profits), the directors may be trying to convey to the market a feeling of confidence in the future profitability of the company. It may also be a reaction designed to support the share price. It should also be noted that although the total dividend has been maintained, the dividend per share will have decreased due to the share issue during the year.

Summary

The above analysis of performance seems to give mixed messages. The company has invested heavily in new and upgraded stores, but operating performance has deteriorated and the expansion may have been mis-focused. This appears to have affected the share price adversely. Alternatively, it may be that the expansion will take a little time to bear fruit and the deterioration may be a reflection of the current state of the economy. Cash generation remains sound and if this continues, the poor current liquidity position will soon be reversed.

Signed A N Other

Appendix

The following additional ratios can be calculated:

	Clothing		Food		Overall	
Increase in sales area	(13,000/35,000)	37%	(1,000/5,000)	20%	(14,000/40,000)	35%
Increase in turnover	(400/15,600)	2.6%	(3,000/4,000)	75%	(3,400/19,600)	17.3%

	Sales per sq mtr 20X4		Sales per sq mtr 20X3	
		£000		£000
Overall	(23,000/54)	426	(19,600/40)	490
Clothing	(16,000/48)	333	(15,600/35)	446
Food	(7,000/6)	1,167	(4,000/5)	800

58 MINSTER

> **Key answer tips**
>
> The question asks you to analyse the performance of the company from the cash flow statement you have prepared and the financial statements given. There is therefore no need to calculate any ratios.

(a) **Cash Flow Statement of Minster for the Year ended 30 September 20X6:**

Reconciliation of operating profit to net cash inflow from operating activities

	£000	£000
Operating profit (before interest, investment gains and tax)		162
Adjustments for:		
Depreciation of tangible fixed assets	255	
Amortisation of software (180 – 135)	45	300
		462
Working capital adjustments		
Decrease in stock (510 – 480)	30	
Decrease in debtors (380 – 270)	110	
Increase in amounts due from long-term contracts (80 – 55)	(25)	
Decrease in trade creditors (555 – 350)	(205)	(90)
Net cash inflow from operating activities		372

Cash Flow Statement for Minster year ended 30 September 20X6

Net cash inflow from operating activities		372
Returns on investments and servicing of finance (note 1)		(23)
Taxation (w (ii))		(54)
Capital expenditure (note 1)		(600)
Equity dividends paid (500 × 4 × 5 pence)		(100)
		____
Cash outflow before use of liquid resources and financing		(405)
Financing (note 1)		385
		____
Decrease in cash ((35 − 40) − 25)		(20)
		____

Note 1

Returns on investment and servicing of finance		
Investment income received (20 − 15 gain on investments)	5	
Finance costs paid (40 − 12 (150 × 8%) re unwinding of environmental provision)	(28)	(23)
	____	
Capital expenditure		
Purchase of − tangible fixed assets (w (i))	(410)	
− software	(180)	
− investments (150 − (15 + 125))	(10)	(600)
	____	
Financing		
Issue of equity shares (w (iii))	265	
Issue of 9% loan note	120	385
	____	____

Workings (in £000)

(i)	Tangible fixed assets:	
	Carrying amount b/f	940
	Non-cash environmental provision	150
	Revaluation	35
	Depreciation for period	(255)
	Carrying amount c/f	(1,280)
		____
	Difference is cash acquisitions	(410)
(ii)	Taxation:	
	Tax provision b/f	(50)
	Deferred tax b/f	(25)
	Profit and loss account charge	(57)
	Provision c/f	60
	Deferred tax c/f	18
		____
	Difference is cash paid	(54)

(iii)   Equity shares

Balance b/f	(300)
Bonus issue (1 for 4)	(75)
Balance c/f	500
Difference is cash issue	125

Share premium

Balance b/f	(85)
Bonus issue (1 for 4)	75
Balance c/f	150
Difference is cash issue	140

Therefore the total proceeds of cash issue of shares are £265,000 (125 + 140).

(b)   Report on the financial position of Minster for the year ended 30 September 20X6

To:

From:

Date:

Operating cash flows:

Minster shows healthy cash inflows of £372,000 from operating activities. This is considered by many commentators as a very important figure as it is often used as the basis for estimating the company's future maintainable cash flows. Subject to (inevitable) annual expected variations and allowing for any changes in the company's structure this figure is more likely to be repeated in the future than most other figures in the cash flow statements which are often 'one-off' cash flows such as raising loans or purchasing fixed assets. The operating cash inflow compares well with the underlying operating profit of £162,000. This is mainly due to depreciation charges of £300,000 being added back to the profit as they are a non-cash expense. The operating cash inflow of £372,000 after the reduction in net working capital of £90,000 is more than sufficient to cover the company's taxation payments of £54,000, finance payments of £28,000 and the dividend of £100,000 and leaves an amount to contribute to the funding of the increase in fixed assets. It is important that these short-term costs are funded from operating cash flows; it would be of serious concern if, for example, interest or tax payments were having to be funded by loan capital or the sale of fixed assets.

There are a number of points of concern. The dividend of £100,000 gives a dividend cover of less than one (85/100 = 0.85) which means the company has distributed previous year's profits. This is not a tenable situation in the long-term. The size of the dividend has also contributed to the lower cash balances (see below). There is less investment in both stock levels and trade debtors. This may be the result of more efficient stock control and better collection of debtors, but it may also indicate that trading volumes may be falling. Also of note is a large reduction in trade creditor balances of £205,000. This too may be indicative of lower trading (i.e. less stock purchased on credit) or pressure from suppliers to pay earlier. Without more detailed information it is difficult to come to a conclusion in this matter.

Capital expenditure:

The cash flow statement shows considerable investment in fixed assets, in particular £410,000 in tangible fixed assets. These acquisitions represent an increase of 44% of the carrying amount of the tangible fixed assets as at the beginning of the year. As there are no disposals, the increase in investment must represent an increase in capacity rather than the replacement of old assets. Assuming that this investment has been made wisely, this should bode well for the future (most analysts would prefer to see increased investment rather than contraction in operating assets). An unusual feature of the required treatment of environmental provisions is that the investment in fixed assets as portrayed by the cash flow statement appears less than if balance sheet figures are used. The balance sheet at 30 September 20X6 includes £150,000 of fixed assets (the discounted cost of the environmental provision), which does not appear in the cash flow figures as it is not a cash 'cost'. A further consequence is that the 'unwinding' of the discounting of the provision causes a financing expense in the profit and loss account which is not matched in the cash flow statement as the unwinding is not a cash flow. Many commentators have criticised the required treatment of environmental provisions because they cause financing expenses which are not (immediate) cash costs and no 'loans' have been taken out. Viewed in this light, it may be that the information in the cash flow statement is more useful than that in the profit and loss account and balance sheet.

Financing:

The total capital expenditure of £600,000 has been largely funded by an issue of shares at £265,000 and raising a 9% £120,000 loan note. This indicates that the company's shareholders appear reasonably pleased with the company's past performance (or they would not be very willing to purchase further shares). The interest rate of the loan at 9% seems quite high, and virtually equal to the company's overall return on capital employed of 9.1% (162/(1,660 + 120)). Provided current profit levels are maintained, it should not reduce overall returns to shareholders.

Cash position:

The overall effect of the year's cash flows has worsened the company's cash position by an increased net cash liability of £20,000. Although the company's overdraft has reduced by £15,000, the cash at bank of £35,000 at the beginning of the year has now gone. In comparison to the cash generation ability of the company and considering its large investment in fixed assets, this £20,000 is a relatively small amount and should be relieved by operating cash inflows in the near future.

Summary

The above analysis shows that Minster has invested substantially in new fixed assets suggesting expansion. To finance this, the company appears to have no difficulty in attracting further long-term funding. At the same time there are indications of reduced stock, trade debtors and creditors which may suggest the opposite i.e. contraction. It may be that the new investment is a change in the nature of the company's activities (e.g. mining) which has different working capital characteristics. The company has good operating cash flow generation and the slight deterioration in short-term net cash balance should only be temporary.

59 PENDANT LTD

> **Key answer tips**
>
> (a) You are given two balance sheets but no profit and loss account. You must therefore reconstruct the profit and loss account from the information you are given, in order to derive the first figure in the cash flow statement, the profit for the year.
>
> (b) Don't calculate any ratios, as told. Just identify the important features of the cash flow statement you have produced in part (a)

(a) **Cash flow statement of Pendant Ltd for the year to 31 March 20X1**

Reconciliation of operating profit to net cash inflow from operating activities

		£000	£000
Operating profit (profit before interest and tax (W1))			176
Adjustments for:			
Depreciation	– leasehold buildings	20	
	– 'purchased' plant (W3)	193	
	– leased plant (140 – 30)	110	323
Profit on disposal of	– freehold (800 – 580)	(220)	
	– plant (from question)	(18)	
			(238)
Decrease in stock (540 – 490)			50
Increase in debtors (787 – 584)			(203)
Increase in creditors (663 – 602)			61
Net cash inflow from operating activities			169

Cash flow statement

	£000
Net cash flow from operating activities	169
Returns on investments and servicing of finance (note 1)	(30)
Taxation (W2)	(321)
Capital expenditure – net receipt (note 1)	45
Equity dividends paid	(150)
Cash outflow before use of liquid resources and financing	(287)
Management of liquid resources (note 1)	177
Financing (note 1)	(60)
Decrease in cash (125 + 45)	(170)

Note 1

Returns on investments and servicing of finance

Interest received (from question)	15	
Interest element of finance lease (from question)	(35)	
Bank interest paid (from question)	(10)	(30)

Capital expenditure

Purchase of – leasehold land and buildings	(500)	
– plant (W3)	(130)	
Software development (300 – 100)	(200)	
Sale of – freehold land and buildings	800	
– plant	75	45

Management of liquid resources

Sale of government securities (180 – 30 + 27 profit)	177

Financing

Issue of ordinary shares (100 + 70)	170	
Repayments of finance leases (W4)	(230)	(60)

Workings (in $000)

(W1) In the absence of a profit and loss account the figure for the operating profit before interest and tax has to be derived from the balance sheets plus the information given in the notes. The basic technique is to start with the change in the profit and loss account reserve, which would be the retained profit or loss for the year, and work back to the profit before interest and tax. In this instance there is a decrease in the profit and loss reserve indicating a small retained loss for the year.

Decrease in profit and loss account reserve (1,084 – 1,092)	(8)
Dividends paid	150
Tax (from note in question)	31
Interest – payable on finance lease (from question)	35
– bank overdraft (from question)	10
– receivable (from question)	(15)
Profit on sale of Government securities (from question)	(27)
Profit before investment gains, interest and tax	176

(W2) **Taxation**

Tax provision b/f	(213)
Deferred tax b/f	(172)
Profit and loss account charge (from note in question)	(31)
Tax provision c/f	83
Deferred tax c/f	12
Difference is cash paid	(321)

(W3) 'Purchased' plant

Cost b/f	620
Disposals	(200)
Balance c/f	(550)
Difference is cash purchases	(130)

Cost of disposal	200
Proceeds	(75)
Profit on disposal	18
Difference is accumulated depreciation on disposal	143
Depreciation b/f	200
Less – disposal (above)	(143)
Depreciation c/f	(250)
Depreciation charge for year	(193)

(W4) Lease obligation

Balances b/f (30 + 60)	(90)
Additions (650 – 150)	(500)
Balances c/f (70 + 290)	360
Difference – capital repayment (or £265,000 – £35,000 interest)	(230)

(b) From the information in the question and the above cash flow statement, the following observations can be made:

(i) The (derived) operating profit of £176,000 is much the same as the cash generated from operations of £169,000. A closer inspection of the figures reveals a more worrying picture. The operating profit has been boosted by some non-recurring items; a large profit of £220,000 on the sale of the company's freehold and a profit of £18,000 on the sale of some plant. Without these items the operating profit of £176,000 would have been an operating loss of £62,000.

Overall the company's profitability should cause concern over the future prospects of the company.

(ii) Despite there being positive cash flows from operations of £169,000, this figure is inadequate for the continued liquidity of the company. It is woefully insufficient to pay net interest costs of £30,000, a tax bill of £321,000 and the dividends to shareholders of £150,000. If the company had not sold its freehold for £800,000 and some investments for £177,000 its liquidity and solvency position would be very serious. Even with these sales the company's bank account has gone from a balance of £125,000 to an overdraft of £45,000.

(iii) Other factors that may also be an indication of cash flow difficulties are a move towards leasing rather than purchasing plant, a sizeable reduction in stock levels (this may be welcomed provided it does not jeopardise future sales) and an increase in the level of trade creditors.

In summary Pendant Ltd seems to have undertaken a number of measures that have improved both the current year's profit and cash flows, but most of these are unsustainable and do not bode well for the future.

60 CHARMER

Key answer tips

Read the question carefully. You may find it helpful to tick off items of information as you deal with them. Set out your workings clearly and cross reference them to your main answer. Although the answer shows gross cash flows as a note (Note 1) it would be equally acceptable to show them as part of the main cash flow statement.

Charmer plc cash flow statement for the year to 30 September 20X1:

Reconciliation of operating profit to net cash inflow from operating activities

(Note figures in brackets are in £000)	£000	£000
Net profit before interest and tax (3,198 – 1,479)		1,719
Adjustments for:		
Depreciation – buildings (W1)	80	
– plant (W1)	276	
Loss on disposal of plant (W1)	86	442
Amortisation of government grants (W2)		(125)
Negligence claim previously provided		(120)
Increase in stock (1,046 – 785)		(261)
Increase in debtors (935 – 824)		(111)
Decrease in creditors (760 –644)		(116)
Net cash inflow from operating activities		1,428

Cash flow statement	£000
Net cash flow from operating activities (above)	1,428
Returns on investments and servicing of finance – Note 1	(125)
Taxation (W4)	(368)
Capital expenditure – Note 1	(1,243)
	(308)
Equity dividends paid	(180)
	(488)

Management of liquid resources (120 – 50)		(70)
Financing – Note 1		300
Decrease in cash (122 + 136)		(258)

Note 1

Returns on investments and servicing of finance

Interest paid (260 + 25 – 40)	(245)	
Investment income	120	(125)

Capital expenditure		
Purchase of land and buildings (W1)	(50)	
Purchase of plant (W1)	(848)	
Proceeds of sale of plant (W1)	170	
Purchase of investments	(690)	
Receipt of government grant (W2)	175	(1,243)

Financing		
Issue of ordinary shares (W3)		300

Workings

(W1) **Fixed assets**

Land and buildings – cost/valuation	
Balance b/f	1,800
Revaluation surplus	150
Balance c/f	(2,000)
Difference cash purchase	(50)

Plant – cost	
Balance b/f	1,220
Disposal	(500)
Balance c/f	(1,568)
Difference cash purchase	(848)

Depreciation of fixed assets	
Building (760 – 680)	80
Plant (464 – (432 – 244))	276

The plant had a carrying value of £256,000 at the date of its disposal (500 cost – 244 depreciation). As there was a loss on sale of £86,000 (given in question), the sale proceeds must have been £170,000 (i.e. 256 – 86).

(W2) Government grant

Balances b/f – current	(125)
– non-current	(200)
Amortisation credited to cost of sales	125
Balances c/f – current	100
– non-current	275
Difference cash receipt	175

(W3) Share capital and convertible loan stock. A reconciliation of share capital, share premium and the revaluation reserve shows the shares issued for cash.

	Share capital £000	Share premium £000	Revaluation reserve £000
Opening balance	(1,000)	(160)	(40)
Revaluation of land	Nil	Nil	(150)
Bonus issue 1 for 10	(100)	100	Nil
Conversion of loan stock (see below)	(100)	(300)	Nil
Closing balance	1,400	460	190
Difference issued for cash	200	100	nil

The 10% convertible loan stock had a carrying value of £400,000 at the date of conversion to equity shares. This would be taken as the consideration for the shares issued which would be 100,000 £1 shares (i.e. 400,000/100 × 25). This would increase issued share capital by £100,000 and share premium by £300,000.

(W4) Taxation

	£000
Tax provision b/f	(367)
Deferred tax b/f	(400)
Profit and loss account tax charge	(520)
Tax provision c/f	480
Deferred tax c/f	439
Difference cash paid	(368)

61 PLANTER

> **Key answer tips**
>
> This is slightly different to the normal cash flow statement question, but the trial balance provided includes the operating profit for the year, to go at the top of the cash flow statement, so you should have no major problems in slotting the correct figures into the cash flow pro forma.

Cash flow statement of Planter for the Year to 31 March 20X4

Reconciliation of operating profit to net cash inflow from operating activities

	£	£
Operating profit per question		15,600
Adjustments for:		
Depreciation – buildings (W1)	1,800	
– plant (W1)	26,600	28,400
Loss of sale of plant (W1)		4,200
Decrease in stock (57,400 – 43,300)		14,100
Increase in debtors (50,400 – 28,600)		(21,800)
Decrease in creditors (31,400 – 26,700)		(4,700)
Net cash flow from operating activities		35,800

Cash Flow Statement

	£
Net cash flow from operating activities	35,800
Returns on investments and servicing of finance (note 1)	(1,000)
Taxation (8,900 + 1,100)	(10,000)
Capital expenditure (note 2)	(26,400)
	(1,600)
Equity dividends paid	(26,100)
	(27,700)
Management of liquid resources	nil
Financing (note 3)	24,600
Decrease in cash (1,200 + 1,900)	(3,100)

Notes

1   Returns on investments and servicing of finance

Interest paid (1,700 – 300 accrued)	(1,400)	
Investment income	400	
		(1,000)

2   Capital expenditure

Purchase of plant (W1)	(38,100)	
Purchase of land and buildings (W1)	(7,100)	
Sales of plant (W1)	7,800	
Sale of investments	11,000	
		(26,400)

3   Financing

Issue of ordinary shares (W2)	28,000	
Redemption of 8% loan notes (43,200 – 39,800)	(3,400)	
		24,600

Workings

(W1) **Fixed assets:**

	£
Land and buildings	
Valuation b/f	49,200
Revaluation surplus (18,000 – 12,000)	6,000
Acquisitions – balancing figure	7,100
Valuation c/f	62,300
Depreciation b/f	5,000
Charge for year – balancing figure	1,800
Depreciation c/f	6,800
Plant	
Cost b/f	70,000
Disposals at cost	(23,500)
Acquisitions – balancing figure	38,100
Cost c/f	84,600
Depreciation b/f	22,500
Disposals	(11,500)
Charge for year – balancing figure	26,600
Depreciation c/f	37,600

Disposal of plant:

Net book value	12,000
Proceeds from question	(7,800)
	———
Loss on sale	4,200
	———

(W2) Share capital and share premium:

Ordinary shares b/f	25,000
Bonus issue 1 for 10 (from share premium)	2,500
Ordinary shares c/f	(50,000)
	———
Difference issue for cash	22,500
	———
Share premium b/f	5,000
Bonus issue	(2,500)
Share premium c/f	(8,000)
	———
Increase is premium on cash issue	5,500
	———
Total proceeds of issue is (22,500 + 5,500)	28,000
	———

(W3) Reconciliation of revaluation reserve

Balance b/f	12,000
Difference revaluation of land	6,000
	———
Balance c/f	18,000
	———

62 CASINO

Key answer tips

Part (a) is a standard, although quite long, cash flow statement question. Note that the starting point is an operating loss which then becomes a net cash outflow from operating activities. Take care when calculating the tax cash flow as you will need to include the opening and closing deferred tax balances as well as the balances for current tax.

(a) **Cash flow statement of Casino for the Year to 31 March 20X5:**

Reconciliation of operating profit to net cash inflows from operating activities

	£ million	£ million
Operating loss		(32)
Adjustments for:		
Depreciation – buildings (W1)	12	
– plant (W2)	81	
– intangibles (510 – 400)	110	
Loss on disposal of plant (from question)	12	215
		183
Working capital adjustments		
Decrease in stock (420 – 350)		70
Increase in debtors (808 – 372)		(436)
Increase in creditors (530 – 515)		15
Net cash outflow from operating activities		(168)

	£ million	£ million
Cash flow statement		
Net cash outflow from operating activities (from above)		(168)
Returns on investments and servicing of finance (note 1)		(8)
Taxation (W3)		(81)
Capital expenditure (note 1)		(155)
Equity dividends paid		(25)
Cash outflow before use of liquid resources and financing		(437)
Management of liquid resources (120 – 32)		88
Financing (note 1)		164
Decrease in cash (75 + (125 – 15))		(185)

Note 1		
Returns on investment and servicing of finance		
Interest received (12 – 5 + 3)	10	
Interest paid	(18)	(8)
Capital expenditure		
Purchase of – land and buildings (W1)	(110)	
– plant (W2)	(60)	
Sale of plant (W2)	15	(155)
Financing		
Issue of ordinary shares (100 + 60)	160	
Issue of 8% variable rate loan	160	
Repayments of 12% fixed rate loan (150 + 6 penalty)	(156)	164

Workings (in £ million)

(W1) Land and buildings

Net book value b/f	420
Revaluation gains	70
Depreciation for year (balance after revaluation)	(12)
Net book value c/f	(588)
Difference is cash purchases	(110)

(W2) Plant

Cost b/f	445
Additions from question	60
Balance c/f	(440)
Difference is cost of disposal	65
Loss on disposal	(12)
Proceeds	(15)
Difference accumulated depreciation of plant disposed of	38
Depreciation b/f	105
Less – disposal (above)	(38)
Depreciation c/f	(148)
Charge for year	(81)

(W3) Taxation

Tax provision b/f	(110)
Deferred tax b/f	(75)
Income statement net charge	(1)
Tax provision c/f	15
Deferred tax c/f	90
Difference is cash paid	(81)

(W4) Revaluation reserve

Balance b/f	45
Revaluation gains	70
Transfer to retained earnings	(3)
Balance c/f	112

(W5) Profit and loss reserve

Balance b/f	1,165
Loss for period	(45)
Dividends paid	(25)
Transfer from revaluation reserve	3
Balance c/f	1,098

(b)   The accruals/matching concept applied in preparing a profit and loss account has the effect of smoothing cash flows for reporting purposes. This practice arose because interpreting 'raw' cash flows can be very difficult and the accruals process has the advantage of helping users to understand the underlying performance of a company. For example, if an item of plant with an estimated life of five years is purchased for £100,000, then in the cash flow statement for the five year period there would be an outflow in year 1 of the full £100,000 and no further outflows for the next four years. Contrast this with the profit and loss account where by applying the accruals principle, depreciation of the plant would give a charge of £20,000 per annum (assuming straight-line depreciation). Many would see this example as an advantage of a profit and loss account, but it is important to realise that profit is affected by many items requiring judgements. This has led to accusations of profit manipulation or creative accounting, hence the disillusionment of the usefulness of the profit and loss account. Another example of the difficulty in interpreting cash flows is that counter-intuitively a decrease in overall cash flows is not always a bad thing (it may represent an investment in increasing capacity which would bode well for the future), nor is an increase in cash flows necessarily a good thing (this may be from the sale of fixed assets because of the need to raise cash urgently).

The advantages of cash flows are:

–   it is difficult to manipulate cash flows, they are real and possess the qualitative characteristic of objectivity (as opposed to profits affected by judgements);

–   cash flows are an easy concept for users to understand; indeed many users misinterpret profit and loss account items as being cash flows;

–   cash flows help to assess a company's liquidity, solvency and financial adaptability. Healthy liquidity is vital to a company's going concern;

–   many business investment decisions and company valuations are based on projected cash flows;

–   the 'quality' of a company's operating profit is said to be confirmed by closely correlated cash flows. Some analysts take the view that if a company shows a healthy operating profit, but has low or negative operating cash flows, there is a suspicion of profit manipulation or creative accounting.

63   TABBA   *Walk in the footsteps of a top tutor*

Key answer tips

The cash flow statement has the usual standard calculations but take care with the government grant and finance lease which both have balances in both current and long-term liabilities. Part (b) requires an analysis of the company based on the information revealed in the cash flow statement rather than by standard ratio analysis. The highlighted words are key phrases that markers are looking for.

(a)   **Cash flow statement of Tabba for the year ended 30 September 20X5:**

Reconciliation of operating profit to net cash outflow from operating activities

	£000
Net profit before interest and tax (per question)	270
Adjustments for:	
Depreciation (W1)	2,200
Amortisation of government grant (W3)	(250)
Profit on sale of factory (W1)	(4,600)
Increase in insurance claim provision (1,500 – 1,200)	(300)
Working capital adjustments:	
Increase in stocks (2,550 – 1,850)	(700)
Increase in debtors (3,100 – 2,600)	(500)
Increase in creditors (4,050 – 2,950)	1,100
	———
Net cash outflow from operating activities	(2,780)
	———

Cash Flow Statement

	£000
Net cash outflow from operating activities	(2,780)
Returns on investments and servicing of finance (note 1)	(220)
Taxation (W4)	(1,350)
Capital expenditure (note 2)	10,050
	———
	5,700
Management of liquid resources	nil
Financing (note 3)	(4,300)
	———
Increase in cash (850 + 550)	1,400
	———

Notes:

1   Returns on investments and servicing of finance

Interest paid	(260)	
Interest received	40	(220)
	———	

2   Capital expenditure

Sale of factory	12,000	
Purchase of fixed assets (W1)	(2,900)	
Receipt of government grant (from question)	950	10,050
	———	

3   Financing

Issue of 6% loan notes	800	
Redemption of 10% loan notes	(4,000)	
Repayment of finance leases (W2)	(1,100)	(4,300)
	———	

Workings (in £000)

(W1) **Tangible fixed assets:**

Cost/valuation b/f	20,200
New finance leases (from question)	1,500
Disposals	(8,600)
Acquisitions – balancing figure	2,900
Cost/valuation c/f	16,000

Depreciation b/f	4,400
Disposal	(1,200)
Depreciation c/f	(5,400)
Charge for year – balancing figure	(2,200)

Sale of factory:	
Net book value	7,400
Proceeds (from question)	(12,000)
Profit on sale	(4,600)

(W2) **Finance lease obligations**

Balance b/f	– current	800
	– over 1 year	1,700
New leases (from question)		1,500
Balance c/f	– current	(900)
	– over 1 year	(2,000)
Cash repayments – balancing figure		1,100

(W3) **Government grant:**

Balance b/f	– current	400
	– over 1 year	900
Grants received in year (from question)		950
Balance c/f	– current	(600)
	– over 1 year	(1,400)
Difference – amortisation credited to profit and loss account		250

(W4) **Taxation:**

Current provision b/f	1,200
Deferred tax b/f	500
Tax credit in profit and loss account	(50)
Current provision c/f	(100)
Deferred tax c/f	(200)
Tax paid – balancing figure	1,350

(W5) **Reconciliation of profit and loss reserve**

Balance b/f	850
Transfer from revaluation reserve	1,600
Profit for period	100
	———
Balance c/f	2,550
	———

(b) Consideration of the cash flow statement reveals some important information in assessing the change in the financial position of Tabba in the year ended 30 September 20X5. The reconciliation of operating profit to the operating cash flows shows that there is a huge net outflow of cash from operating activities of £2,780,000 despite Tabba reporting a modest operating profit of £270,000. More detailed analysis of this reconciliation reveals some worrying concerns for the future. Many companies experience higher operating cash flows than the underlying operating profit mainly due to depreciation charges being added back to profits to arrive at the cash flows. This is certainly true in Tabba's case, where operating profits have been 'improved' by £2.2 million during the year in terms of the underlying cash flows. However, the major reconciling difference is the profit on the sale of Tabba's factory of £4.6 million. By including this in operating profit, it has dramatically distorted operating performance. This treatment is also very questionable under the rules of FRS 3 *Reporting financial performance*. It states profits (and losses) on the disposal of fixed assets are exceptional items that should be separately disclosed after operating profit. If the sale and lease back of the factory had not taken place, Tabba's operating profits would be in a sorry state showing losses of £4.33 million (4,600 – 270 ignoring any possible tax effects). When Tabba publishes its financial statements this profit will almost certainly require separate disclosure which should make the effects of the transaction more transparent to the users of the financial statements. A further indication of poor operating profits is that they have been boosted by £300,000 due to an increase in the insurance claim provision (again this is not a cash flow) and £250,000 amortisation of government grants.

Many commentators believe that the net cash flow from operating activities is the most important figure in the cash flow statement. This is because it is a measure of expected or maintainable future cash flows. In Tabba's case this highlights a very important point; although Tabba has increased its cash position during the year by £1.4 million, £12 million has come from the sale of its factory. Clearly this is a one-off transaction that cannot be repeated in future years. If the drain on the operating cash flows continues at the current rates, the company will not survive for very long.

The tax position is worthy of comment. There is a small tax credit in the profit and loss account, whereas the cash flow statement shows that tax of £1.35 million has been paid during the year. This payment of tax is on what must have been a substantial profit for the previous year. This seems to confirm the deteriorating position of the company.

Another relevant point is that there has been a very small increase in working capital of £100,000 (700 + 500 – 1,100). However, underlying this is the fact that both stocks and debtors are showing substantial increases (despite the profit deterioration), which may indicate the presence of bad debts or obsolete stock, and trade creditors have also increased substantially (by £1.1 million) which may be a symptom of liquidity problems prior to the sale of the factory.

On the positive side there has been substantial investment in fixed assets (after stripping out the sale of the factory), but even this is partly due to leasing assets of £1.5 million (companies often lease assets when they do not have the resources to purchase them outright) and finance from a government grant of £950,000.

The company appears to have taken advantage of the proceeds from the sale of the factory to redeem the expensive 10% £4 million loan note (this has partly been replaced by a less expensive 6% £800,000 loan note).

In conclusion the cash flow statement reveals some interesting and worrying issues that may indicate a bleak future for Tabba and serves as an illustration of the importance of a cash flow statement to the users of financial statements.

64 PINTO *Walk in the footsteps of a top tutor*

Key answer tip

Part (a) - Many easy marks to gain from the cash flow statement. Set up the proforma and build up the cash flow ticking off from the face of the question every time a figure is used. Get the easy marks first such as movement in working capital, share capital and loans. The loan penalty is an additional cost incurred in repaying the loan notes early. Part (b) specifically asks for the cash flow statement to be analysed. The examiner specifically stated that ratio calculations will not be awarded any marks so do not waste time preparing such calculations. Ensure that you comment on the overall movement in cash and the sources and uses of cash during the year. The highlighted words are key phrases that markers are looking for.

(a)   **Cash flow statement of Pinto for the Year ended 31 March 2008:**

Reconciliation of operating profit to net cash inflow from operating activities

	£000	£000
Operating profit		430
Adjustments for:		
Redemption penalty costs included in administrative expenses		20
Depreciation charges	280	
Loss on sale of tangible fixed assets	90	370
Working capital adjustments		
Increase in stock (1,210 – 810)	(400)	
Decrease in debtors (540 – 480)	60	
Increase in warranty provision (200 – 100)	100	
Increase in creditors (1,410 – 1,050)	360	120
Net cash inflow from operating activities		940

Cash Flow Statement

Net cash inflow from operating activities		940
Returns on investments and servicing of finance (note 1)		(10)
Tax refund (w (i))		60
Capital expenditure (note 1)		(1,290)
Equity dividends paid (1,000 × 5 × 3 pence)	(150)	
		_____
Cash outflow before financing		(450)
Financing (note 1)		580
		_____
Increase in cash (120 + 10)		130
		_____

Note 1 Gross cash flows

Returns on investment and servicing of finance

Investment income received (60 – 20 gain on investment property)	40	
Finance costs paid	(50)	(10)
	_____	

Capital expenditure

Purchase of tangible fixed assets (w (ii))	(1,440)	
Sale of tangible fixed assets (240 – 90)	150	(1,290)
	_____	_____

Financing

Proceeds from issue of equity shares (400 + 600)	1,000	
Redemption of loan notes (400 plus 20 penalty)	(420)	580
	_____	_____

Workings (in £000)

(i)   Tax:

tax asset b/f	50
deferred tax b/f	(30)
profit and loss account charge	(160)
tax provision c/f	150
deferred tax c/f	50
	_____
difference is cash received	60
	_____

(ii)   Tangible fixed assets:

carrying amount b/f	1,860
revaluation	100
depreciation for period	(280)
disposal	(240)
carrying amount c/f	(2,880)
	_____
difference is cash acquisitions	(1,440)
	_____

(b)   Comments on the cash management of Pinto

Operating cash flows:

Pinto's operating cash inflows at £940,000 are considerably higher than operating profit of £430,000. This shows a satisfactory cash generating ability and is more than sufficient to cover finance costs, taxation (see later) and dividends. The major reasons for the cash flows being higher than the operating profit are due to the (non-cash) increases in the depreciation and warranty provisions. Working capital changes are relatively neutral; a large increase in stock appears to be being financed by a substantial increase in creditors and a modest reduction in debtors. The reduction in debtors is perhaps surprising as other indicators point to an increase in operating capacity which has not been matched with an increase in debtors. This could be indicative of good control over the cash management of the debtors (or a disappointing sales performance).

An unusual feature of the cash flow is that Pinto has received a tax refund of £60,000 during the current year. This would indicate that in the previous year Pinto was making losses (hence obtaining tax relief). Whilst the current year's profit performance is an obvious improvement, it should be noted that next year's cash flows are likely to suffer a tax payment (estimated at £150,000 in the balance sheet at 31 March 2008) as a consequence. In any forward planning, Pinto should be aware that the tax reversal position will create an estimated total incremental outflow of £210,000 in the next period.

Capital expenditure:

There has been a dramatic investment/increase in tangible fixed assets. Their carrying amount at 31 March 2008 is substantially higher than a year earlier (admittedly £100,000 is due to revaluation rather than a purchase). It is difficult to be sure whether this represents an increase in operating capacity or is the replacement of assets disposed of. However, the net expenditure of £1,290,000 is much higher than the depreciation of the tangible fixed assets and, coupled with the (apparent) overall improvement in profit position, it seems likely that there has been a successful increase in capacity. It is not unusual for there to be a time lag before increased investment reaches its full beneficial effect and in this context it could be speculated that the investment occurred early in the accounting year (because its effect is already making an impact) and that future periods may show even greater improvements.

The investment property is showing a good return which is composed of rental income (presumably) of £40,000 and a valuation gain of £20,000.

Financing:

It would appear that Pinto's financial structure has changed during the year. Debt of £400,000 has been redeemed (for £420,000) and there has been a share issue raising £1 million. The company is now nil geared compared to modest gearing at the end of the previous year. The share issue has covered the cost of redemption and contributed to the investment in tangible fixed assets. The remainder of the finance has come from the very healthy operating cash flows. If ROCE is higher than the finance cost of the loan note at 6% (nominal) it may call into question the wisdom of the early redemption especially given the penalty cost (which has been classified within financing) of the redemption.

Cash position:

The overall effect of the year's cash flows is that they have improved the company's cash position dramatically. A sizeable overdraft of £120,000, which may have been a consequence of the (likely) losses in the previous year, has been reversed to a modest bank balance of £10,000 even after the payment of a £150,000 dividend.

Summary

The above analysis indicates that Pinto has invested substantially in renewing and/or increasing its tangible fixed assets. This has been financed largely by operating cash flows, and appears to have brought a dramatic turnaround in the company's fortunes. All the indications are that the future financial position and performance will continue to improve.

Examiners Report

Part (a) required the preparation of a cash flow statement followed by an interpretation of the company's cash flow management. Cash flows are generally a popular question and this one proved no exception with many candidates scoring well. A significant number of candidates had very little idea of which item should be included in which section of the statement (poor format knowledge).

A number of candidates had difficulty with the fact that the tax cash flow was a refund rather than the usual payment and the revaluation of a property was often not taken into account when calculating the cash outflow on non-current assets.

Weaker answers did not seem to know the difference between cash and non-cask flows, for example reserve movements, provisions (for a warranties) and the loss on the disposal of plant were treated as cash flows. Other common errors included getting the cash movements the wrong way round and incorrectly calculating the dividend as $30,000 instead of $150,000 by not realising the shares were 20 cents each.

Part (b), the interpretive part of the question, often lacked depth by failing to draw valid conclusions from correctly calculated figures and not really making any attempt to analyse/interpret the cash flow statement. Many candidates calculated and commented on ratios, even though the question specifically gave instructions not to calculate ratios and that no marks would be awarded for them. This led to discussion of many aspects of performance such as return on capital employed, asset utilisation and profit margins that are not part of cash management which was the topic of the question that was asked, thus illustrating the dangers of 'question spotting'. Many important issues were not mentioned at all such as the good operating cash flow generating capacity of the company, the effects of a huge investment in non-current assets, the changes in the capital structure due to issuing new shares and redeeming a loan. Hardly anyone mentioned that the company had benefited from a tax refund of $60,000 (implying losses in the previous year) and that a tax payment estimated at $160,000 would be expected next year.

Very weak answers simply described the figures in the cash flow statement such as inventories have increased by $400,000 or finance cost incurred were $50,000 – this is not interpretation.

	ACCA marking scheme	Marks
(a)	operating activities	
	operating profit	1
	adjustment for redemption penalty	1
	depreciation/loss on sale	1
	working capital items (including warranty provision)	2
	returns on investment and servicing of finance	2
	tax received	2
	capital expenditure	2
	dividend paid	1
	financing	2
	increase in cash	1
	Maximum	15
(b)	1 mark per relevant point	10
		—
	Total	25
		—

65 HARBIN *Walk in the footsteps of a top tutor*

Key answer tip

Part (a) required the calculation of standard ratios for one accounting year – be careful with ratios like net profit margin as the examiner specifically tells you to use profit before tax which might contradict with the formula learned during your studies. Part (b) requires that the financial position and performance is analysed using the ratios calculated in part (a). Be aware that the examiner specifically asks you to draw your attention to the chief executives report and the purchase of Fatima – if you do not discuss this at all you will be limited in the overall marks that you can achieve. You may choose to calculate further ratios to support your analysis (marks would be awarded where relevant). The highlighted words are key phrases that markers are looking for.

(a)   Note: figures in the calculations of the ratios are in £million

	2007	Workings	2006	2007 re Fatima (b)
Return on year end capital employed	11.2%	24/(114 + 100) × 100	7.1%	18.9%
Net asset turnover	1.2 times	250/214	1.6	0.6
Gross profit margin (given in question)	20%		16.7%	42.9%
Net profit (before tax) margin	6.4%	16/250	4.4%	31.4%
Current ratio	0.9:1	38/44	2.5	
Closing stock holding period	46 days	25/200 × 365	37	
Debtors' collection period	19 days	13/250 × 365	16	
Creditors' payment period	42 days	23/200 × 365	32	
Gearing	46.7%	100/214 × 100	Nil	

The gross profit margins and relevant ratios for 2006 are given in the question, and some additional ratios for Fatima are included above to enable a clearer analysis in answering part (b) (references to Fatima should be taken to mean Fatima's net assets).

(b)   Analysis of the comparative financial performance and position of Harbin for the year ended 30 September 2007. Note: references to 2007 and 2006 should be taken as the years ended 30 September 2007 and 2006.

Introduction

The figures relating to the comparative performance of Harbin 'highlighted' in the Chief Executive's report may be factually correct, but they take a rather biased and one dimensional view. They focus entirely on the performance as reflected in the profit and loss account without reference to other measures of performance (notably the ROCE); nor is there any reference to the purchase of Fatima at the beginning of the year which has had a favourable effect on profit for 2007. Due to this purchase, it is not consistent to compare Harbin's profit and loss account results in 2007 directly with those of 2006 because it does not match like with like. Immediately before the £100 million purchase of Fatima, the carrying amount of the net assets of Harbin was £112 million. Thus the investment represented an increase of nearly 90% of Harbin's existing capital employed. The following analysis of performance will consider the position as shown in the reported financial statements (based on the ratios required by part (a) of the question) and then go on to consider the impact the purchase has had on this analysis.

Profitability

The ROCE is often considered to be the primary measure of operating performance, because it relates the profit made by an entity (return) to the capital (or net assets) invested in generating those profits. On this basis the ROCE in 2007 of 11.2% represents a 58% improvement (i.e. 4.1% on 7.1%) on the ROCE of 7.1% in 2006. Given there were no disposals of fixed assets, the ROCE on Fatima's net assets is 18.9% (22m/100m + 16.5m). Note: the net assets of Fatima at the year end would have increased by profit after tax of £16.5 million (i.e. 22m × 75% (at a tax rate of 25%)). Put another way, without the contribution of £22 million to profit before tax, Harbin's 'pre tax' profit would have been a loss of £6 million which would give a negative ROCE. The principal reasons for the beneficial impact of Fatima's purchase is that its profit margins at 42.9% gross and 31.4% net (before tax) are far superior to the profit margins of the combined business at 20% and 6.4% respectively. It should be observed that the other contributing factor to the ROCE is the net asset turnover and in this respect Fatima's is actually inferior at 0.6 times (70m/116.5m) to that of the combined business of 1.2 times.

It could be argued that the finance costs should be allocated against Fatima's results as the proceeds of the loan note appear to be the funding for the purchase of Fatima. Even if this is accepted, Fatima's results still far exceed those of the existing business.

Thus the Chief Executive's report, already criticised for focussing on the profit and loss account alone, is still highly misleading. Without the purchase of Fatima, underlying turnover would be flat at £180 million and the gross margin would be down to 11.1% (20m/180m) from 16.7% resulting in a loss before tax of £6 million. This sales performance is particularly poor given it is likely that there must have been an increase in spending on tangible fixed assets beyond that related to the purchase of Fatima's net assets as the increase in tangible fixed assets is £120 million (after depreciation).

Liquidity

The company's liquidity position as measured by the current ratio has deteriorated dramatically during the period. A relatively healthy 2.5:1 is now only 0.9:1 which is rather less than what one would expect from the quick ratio (which excludes stock) and is a matter of serious concern. A consideration of the component elements of the current ratio suggests that increases in the stock holding period and creditors' payment period have largely offset each other. There is a small increase in the collection period for debtors (up from 16 days to 19 days) which would actually improve the current ratio. This ratio appears unrealistically low, it is very difficult to collect credit sales so quickly and may be indicative of factoring some of the debtors or a proportion of the sales being cash sales. Factoring is sometimes seen as a consequence of declining liquidity, although if this assumption is correct it does also appear to have been present in the previous year. The changes in the above three ratios do not explain the dramatic deterioration in the current ratio, the real culprit is the cash position, Harbin has gone from having a bank balance of £14 million in 2006 to an overdraft of £17 million in 2007.

A cash flow statement would give a better appreciation of the movement in the cash position.

It is not possible to assess, in isolation, the impact of the purchase of Fatima on the liquidity of the company.

Dividends

A dividend of 10 pence per share in 2007 amounts to £10 million (100m × 10 pence), thus the dividend in 2006 would have been £8 million (the dividend in 2007 is 25% up on 2006). It may be that the increase in the reported profits led the Board to pay a 25% increased dividend, but the dividend cover is only 1.2 times (12m/10m) in 2007 which is very low. In 2006 the cover was only 0.75 times (6m/8m) meaning previous years' reserves were used to facilitate the dividend. The low profit and loss reserve indicates that Harbin has historically paid a high proportion of its profits as dividends, however in times of declining liquidity, it is difficult to justify such high dividends.

Gearing

The company has gone from a position of nil gearing (i.e. no long-term borrowings) in 2006 to a relatively high gearing of 46.7% in 2007. This has been caused by the issue of the £100 million 8% loan note which would appear to be the source of the funding for the £100 million purchase of Fatima's net assets. At the time the loan note was issued, Harbin's ROCE was 7.1%, slightly less than the finance cost of the loan note. In 2007 the ROCE has increased to 11.2%, thus the manner of the funding has had a beneficial effect on the returns to the equity holders of Harbin. However, it should be noted that high gearing does not come without risk; any future downturn in the results of Harbin would expose the equity holders to much lower proportionate returns and continued poor liquidity may mean payment of the loan interest could present a problem. Harbin's gearing and liquidity position would have looked far better had some of the acquisition been funded by an issue of equity shares.

Conclusion

There is no doubt that the purchase of Fatima has been a great success and appears to have been a wise move on the part of the management of Harbin. However, it has disguised a serious deterioration of the underlying performance and position of Harbin's existing activities which the Chief Executive's report may be trying to hide. It may be that the acquisition was part of an overall plan to diversify out of what has become existing loss making activities. If such a transition can continue, then the worrying aspects of poor liquidity and high gearing may be overcome.

Examiners Report

Part (a) required the calculation of eight ratios for 2007 equivalent to given ratios for 2006 and part (b) required candidates to assess the performance of the company in light of the given financial statements and calculated ratios.

In general candidates did well in the calculation of the ratios typically gaining six to eight marks (the maximum). The ROCE and gearing calculations were the most troublesome for candidates. Unfortunately the performance assessment report that followed was usually quite poor. Many candidates did not take sufficient notice of the question's requirement which specifically asked candidates to refer to the Chief Executive's comments and the effect of the acquisition of the net assets of a separate business (Fatima). Weaker answers did not even point out the rather obvious issues below;

- whilst the Chief Executive's comments may have been factually correct, they were very selective (biased) and potentially misleading. Few candidates recognised the fact that the focus of the Chief Executive's report hid the underlying poor performance; some candidates even said the company was doing well

- without the favourable purchase of Fatima, the underlying business would have made a loss

- the payment of the high (cover only 1.2 times) and increased dividend (calculated as $10 million) exacerbated the poor liquidity position

- the purchase of Fatima has left the company with high gearing (46.7%) and its subsequent risks including much increased finance costs

As with similar questions in the past, many candidates' attempt at interpretation was simply to reiterate in words what the movement in the ratios had been, without any attempt to suggest what may have caused the change in the ratio or what it may indicate for the company's future prospects.

Interpretation is an area where the majority of candidates need to improve their understanding and technique.

ACCA marking scheme		
		Marks
(a)	One mark per required ratio	8
(b)	For consideration of Chief Executive's report	3
	Impact of purchase	6
	Remaining issues 1 mark per valid point	8
		17
Total		**25**

66 GREENWOOD

Profitability/utilisation of assets An important feature of the company's performance in the year to 31 March 2007 is to evaluate the effect of the discontinued operation. When using an entity's recent results as a basis for assessing how the entity may perform in the future, emphasis should be placed on the results from continuing operations as it is these that will form the basis of future results. For this reason most of the ratios calculated in the appendix are based on the results from continuing operations and ratio calculations involving net assets/capital employed generally exclude the value of the assets of the discontinuing operation.

On this basis, it can be seen that the overall efficiency of Greenwood (measured by its ROCE) has declined considerably from 33.5% to 29.7% (a fall of 11.3%). The fall in the asset turnover (from 1.89 to 1.67 times) appears to be mostly responsible for the overall decline in efficiency. In effect the company's assets are generating less sales per £ invested in them. The other contributing factors to overall profitability are the company's profit margins. Greenwood has achieved an impressive increase in headline sales of nearly 30% (6.3m on 21.2m) whilst being able to maintain its gross profit margin at around 29% (no significant change from 2006). This has led to a substantial increase in gross profit, but this has been eroded by an increase in operating expenses. As a percentage of sales, operating expenses were 10.5% in 2007 compared to 11.6% in 2006 (they appear to be more of a variable than a fixed cost). This has led to a modest improvement in the profit before interest and tax margin which has partially offset the deteriorating asset utilisation.

The decision to sell the activities which are classified as a discontinued operation is likely to improve the overall profitability of the company. In the year ended 31 March 2006 the discontinued operation made a modest pre tax profit of £450,000 (this represented a return of around 7% on the activity's assets of £6.3 million).This poor return acted to reduce the company's overall profitability (the continuing operations yielded a return of 33.5%). The performance of the discontinued operation continued to deteriorate in the year ended 31 March 2007 making a pre tax operating loss of £1.4 million which creates a negative return on the relevant assets. Despite incurring losses on the measurement to fair value of the discontinued operation's assets, it seems the decision will benefit the company in the future as the discontinued operation showed no sign of recovery.

Liquidity and solvency

Superficially the current ratio of 2.11 in 2007 seems reasonable, but the improvement from the alarming current ratio in 2006 of 0.97 is more illusory than real. The ratio in the year ended 31 March 2007 has been distorted (improved) by the inclusion of assets of the discontinued operation as current assets. These have been included at fair value which should be a realistic expectation of their sale proceeds. However, it is not clear whether the sale will be for cash (they may be exchanged for shares or other assets) or how Greenwood intends to use the disposal proceeds. What can be deduced is that without these assets being classified as current, the company's liquidity ratio would be much worse than at present (at below 1 for both years). Against an expected norm of 1, quick ratios (acid test) calculated on the normal basis of excluding stock (and in this case the assets of the discontinued operation) show an alarming position; a poor figure of 0.62 in 2006 has further deteriorated in 2007 to 0.44. Without the proceeds from the sale of the discontinued operation (assuming they will be for cash) it is difficult to see how Greenwood would pay its creditors (and tax liability), given a year end overdraft of £1,150,000.

Further analysis of the current ratios shows some interesting changes during the year. Despite its large overdraft Greenwood appears to be settling its trade creditors quicker than in 2006. At 68 days in 2006 this was rather a long time and the reduction in credit period may be at the insistence of suppliers – not a good sign. Perhaps to relieve liquidity pressure, the company appears to be pushing its customers to settle early. It may be that this has been achieved by the offer of early settlement discounts, if so the cost of this would have impacted on profit. Despite holding a higher amount of stock at 31 March 2007 (than in 2006), the company has increased its stock turnover; given that margins have been held, this reflects an improved performance.

Gearing

The additional borrowing of £3 million in loan notes (perhaps due to liquidity pressure) has resulted in an increase in gearing from 28.6% to 35.6% and a consequent increase in finance costs. Despite the increase in finance costs the borrowing is acting in the shareholders' favour as the overall return on capital employed (at 29.7%) is well in excess of the 5% interest cost.

Summary

Overall the company's performance has deteriorated in the year ended 31 March 2007. Management's action in respect of the discontinued operation is a welcome measure to try to halt the decline, but more needs to be done. The company's liquidity position is giving cause for serious concern and without the prospect of realising £6 million from the discontinuing operation's assets it would be difficult to envisage any easing of the company's liquidity pressures.

Appendix

	2007		2006
ROCE: continuing operations			
		(3,500 + 250)/(12,500 +	
(4,500 + 400)/(14,500 + 8,000 – 6,000)	29.7%	5,000 – 6,300)	33.5%

The return has been taken as the profit before interest (on loan notes only) and tax from continuing operations. The capital employed is the normal equity plus loan capital (as at the year end), but less the value of the assets of the discontinuing operations. This is because they have not contributed to the return from continuing operations.

Gross profit percentage (8,000/27,500)	29.1%	(6,200/21,200)	29.2%
Operating expense percentage of sales (2,900/27,500)	10.5%	(2,450/21,200)	11.6%
Profit before interest and tax margin (5,100/27,500)	18.5%	(3,750/21,200)	17.7%
Asset turnover (27,500/16,500)	1.67	(21,200/11,200)	1.89
Current ratio (9,500:4,500)	2.11	(3,700:3,800)	0.97
Current ratio (excluding discontinuing) (3,500:4,500)	0.77	Not applicable	
Quick ratio (excluding discontinuing) (2,000:4,500)	0.44	(2,350:3,800)	0.62
Stock (closing) turnover (19,500/1,500)	13.0	(15,000/1,350)	11.1
Debtors (in days) (2,000/27,500) $\times$ 365	26.5	(2,300/21,200) $\times$ 365	39.6
Creditors/cost of sales (in days) (2,400/19,500) $\times$ 365	44.9	(2,800/15,000) $\times$ 365	68.1
Gearing (8,000/8,000 + 14,500)	35.6%	(5,000/5,000 + 12,500)	28.6%

67 VICTULAR   👣 WALK IN THE FOOTSTEPS OF A TOP TUTOR

🔑

Key answer tips

This style of question is naturally time consuming – ensure you answer all parts of the question and do not spend too much time calculating ratios. Part (c) offers easy marks and is independent of the rest of the question – try doing part (c) first to ensure you do not miss out on such easy marks. When interpreting the results in part (b) be wary of making generalisations – you must ensure that you relate it to the information given in the question. Presentation is also crucial in part (b) the marker cannot award you any marks if they cannot read what you have written.

(a)   **Equivalent ratios from the financial statements of Merlot (workings in £000)**

Return on year end capital employed (ROCE)	20.9%	$(1,400 + 590)/(2,800 + 3,200$
		$+ 500 + 3,000) \times 100$
Pre tax return on equity (ROE)	50%	$1,400/2,800 \times 100$
Net asset turnover	2.3 times	$20,500/(14,800 - 5,700)$
Gross profit margin	12.2%	$2,500/20,500 \times 100$
Operating profit margin	9.8%	$2,000/20,500 \times 100$
Current ratio	1.3:1	$7,300/5,700$
Closing stock holding period	73 days	$3,600/18,000 \times 365$
Trade debtors' collection period	66 days	$3,700/20,500 \times 365$
Trade creditors' payment period	77 days	$3,800/18,000 \times 365$
Gearing	71%	$(3,200 + 500 + 3,000)/$
		$9,500 \times 100$
Interest cover	3.3 times	$2,000/600$
Dividend cover	1.4 times	$1,000/700$

As per the question, Merlot's obligations under finance leases (3,200 + 500) have been treated as debt when calculating the ROCE and gearing ratios.

(b)   **Assessment of the relative performance and financial position of Grappa and Merlot for the year ended 30 September 2008**

Introduction

This report is based on the draft financial statements supplied and the ratios shown in (a) above. Although covering many aspects of performance and financial position, the report has been approached from the point of view of a prospective acquisition of the entire equity of one of the two companies.

Profitability

The ROCE of 20·9% of Merlot is far superior to the 14·8% return achieved by Grappa. ROCE is traditionally seen as a measure of management's overall efficiency in the use of the finance/assets at its disposal. More detailed analysis reveals that Merlot's superior performance is due to its efficiency in the use of its net assets; it achieved a net asset turnover of 2.3 times compared to only 1.2 times for Grappa. Put another way, Merlot makes sales of £2.30 per £1 invested in net assets compared to sales of only £1.20 per £1 invested for Grappa. The other element contributing to the ROCE is profit margins. In this area Merlot's overall performance is slightly inferior to that of Grappa, gross profit margins are almost identical, but Grappa's operating profit margin is 10.5% compared to Merlot's 9.8%. In this situation, where one company's ROCE is superior to another's it is useful to look behind the figures and consider possible reasons for the superiority other than the obvious one of greater efficiency on Merlot's part.

A major component of the ROCE is normally the carrying amount of the fixed assets. Consideration of these in this case reveals some interesting issues. Merlot does not own its premises whereas Grappa does. Such a situation would not necessarily give a ROCE advantage to either company as the increase in capital employed of a company owning its factory would be compensated by a higher return due to not having a rental expense (and *vice versa*). If Merlot's rental cost, as a percentage of the value of the related factory, was less than its overall ROCE, then it would be contributing to its higher ROCE. There is insufficient information to determine this. Another relevant point may be that Merlot's owned plant is nearing the end of its useful life (carrying amount is only 22% of its cost) and the company seems to be replacing owned plant with leased plant. Again this does not necessarily give Merlot an advantage, but the finance cost of the leased assets at only 7.5% is much lower than the overall ROCE (of either company) and therefore this does help to improve Merlot's ROCE. The other important issue within the composition of the ROCE is the valuation basis of the companies' fixed assets. From the question, it appears that Grappa's factory is at current value (there is a property revaluation reserve) and note (ii) of the question indicates the use of historical cost for plant. The use of current value for the factory (as opposed to historical cost) will be adversely impacting on Grappa's ROCE. Merlot does not suffer this deterioration as it does not own its factory.

The ROCE measures the overall efficiency of management; however, as Victular is considering buying the equity of one of the two companies, it would be useful to consider the return on equity (ROE) – as this is what Victular is buying. The ratios calculated are based on pre-tax profits; this takes into account finance costs, but does not cause taxation issues to distort the comparison. Clearly Merlot's ROE at 50% is far superior to Grappa's 19.1%. Again the issue of the revaluation of Grappa's factory is making this ratio appear comparatively worse (than it would be if there had not been a revaluation). In these circumstances it would be more meaningful if the ROE was calculated based on the asking price of each company (which has not been disclosed) as this would effectively be the carrying amount of the relevant equity for Victular.

Gearing

From the gearing ratio it can be seen that 71% of Merlot's assets are financed by borrowings (39% is attributable to Merlot's policy of leasing its plant). This is very high in absolute terms and double Grappa's level of gearing. The effect of gearing means that all of the profit after finance costs is attributable to the equity even though (in Merlot's case) the equity represents only 29% of the financing of the net assets. Whilst this may seem advantageous to the equity shareholders of Merlot, it does not come without risk. The interest cover of Merlot is only 3.3 times whereas that of Grappa is 6 times. Merlot's low interest cover is a direct consequence of its high gearing and makes its profits vulnerable to relatively small changes in operating activity. For example, small reductions in sales, profit margins or small increases in operating expenses could result in losses and mean that interest charges would not be covered.

Another observation is that Grappa has been able to take advantage of the receipt of government grants; Merlot has not. This may be due to Grappa purchasing its plant (which may then be eligible for grants) whereas Merlot leases its plant. It may be that the lessor has received any grants available on the purchase of the plant and passed some of this benefit on to Merlot via lower lease finance costs (at 7.5% per annum, this is considerably lower than Merlot has to pay on its 10% loan notes).

Liquidity

Both companies have relatively low liquid ratios of 1.2 and 1.3 for Grappa and Merlot respectively, although at least Grappa has £600,000 in the bank whereas Merlot has a £1.2 million overdraft. In this respect Merlot's policy of high dividend payouts (leading to a low dividend cover and a low profit and loss account reserve) is very questionable. Looking in more depth, both companies have similar stock holding periods; Merlot collects its debtors one week earlier than Grappa (perhaps its credit control procedures are more active due to its large overdraft), and of notable difference is that Grappa receives (or takes) a lot longer credit period from its suppliers (108 days compared to 77 days). This may be a reflection of Grappa being able to negotiate better credit terms because it has a higher credit rating.

Summary

Although both companies may operate in a similar industry and have similar profits after tax, they would represent very different purchases. Merlot's turnover is over 70% more than that of Grappa, it is financed by high levels of debt, it rents rather than owns property and it chooses to lease rather than buy its replacement plant. Also its remaining owned plant is nearing the end of its life. Its replacement will either require a cash injection if it is to be purchased (Merlot's overdraft of £1.2 million already requires serious attention) or create even higher levels of gearing if it continues its policy of leasing. In short although Merlot's overall return seems more attractive than that of Grappa, it would represent a much more risky investment. Ultimately the investment decision may be determined by Victular's attitude to risk, possible synergies with its existing business activities, and not least, by the asking price for each investment (which has not been disclosed to us).

(c) The generally recognised potential problems of using ratios for comparison purposes are:

- inconsistent definitions of ratios

- financial statements may have been deliberately manipulated (creative accounting)

- different companies may adopt different accounting policies (e.g. use of historical costs compared to current values)

- different managerial policies (e.g. different companies offer customers different payment terms)

- balance sheet figures may not be representative of average values throughout the year (this can be caused by seasonal trading or a large acquisition of fixed assets near the year end)

- the impact of price changes over time/distortion caused by inflation

When deciding whether to purchase a company, Victular should consider the following additional useful information:

- in this case the analysis has been made on the draft financial statements; these may be unreliable or change when being finalised. Audited financial statements would add credibility and reliance to the analysis (assuming they receive an unqualified Auditors' Report).

- forward looking information such as profit and balance sheet forecasts, capital expenditure and cash budgets and the level of orders on the books.

- the current (fair) values of assets being acquired.

- the level of risk within a business. Highly profitable companies may also be highly risky, whereas a less profitable company may have more stable 'quality' earnings.

- not least would be the expected price to acquire a company. It may be that a poorer performing business may be a more attractive purchase because it is relatively cheaper and may offer more opportunity for improving efficiencies and profit growth.

68 COALTOWN

(a) **Coaltown – Cash flow statement for the year ended 31 March 2009:**

Note: figures in brackets in £000

Reconciliation of operating profit to net cash inflow from operating activities.

	£000	£000
Operating profit		10,800
Adjustments for:		
depreciation of fixed assets (w (i))	6,000	
loss on disposal of displays (w (i))	1,500	7,500
increase in warranty provision (1,000 – 300)		700
Working capital adjustments:		
increase in stock (5,200 – 4,400)		(800)
increase in debtors (7,800 – 2,800)		(5,000)
decrease in creditors (4,500 – 4,200)		(300)
Net cash inflow from operating activities		12,900

Cash flow statement		
Net cash inflow from operating activities		12,900
Servicing of finance – interest paid		(600)
Tax paid (w (ii))		(5,500)
Capital expenditure (note 1)		(21,000)

Equity dividends paid			(4,000)
			——
Cash outflow before financing			(18,200)
Financing (note 1)			13,900
			——
Decrease in cash (700 + 3,600)			(4,300)
			——

Note 1
Capital expenditure

Purchase of fixed assets (w (i))		(20,500)	
Disposal costs of fixed assets		(500)	(21,000)
		——	

Financing

Issue of equity shares (8,600 capital + 4,300 premium)		12,900	
Issue of 10% loan notes		1,000	13,900
		——	——

Workings   £000

(i) Fixed assets
Cost

Balance b/f	80,000
Revaluation (5,000 – 2,000 depreciation)	3,000
Disposal	(10,000)
Balance c/f	(93,500)
	———
Cash flow for acquisitions	20,500
	———

Depreciation

Balance b/f	48,000
Revaluation	(2,000)
Disposal	(9,000)
Balance c/f	(43,000)
	———
Difference – charge for year	6,000
	———

Disposal of displays

Cost	10,000
Depreciation	(9,000)
Cost of disposal	500
	———
Loss on disposal	1,500
	———

(ii)

Taxation	£000
Provision b/f	(5,300)
Profit and loss account charge	(3,200)
Provision c/f	3,000
Difference – cash paid	(5,500)

(b) (i) **Workings** – all monetary figures in £000

(Note: references to 2008 and 2009 should be taken as to the years ended 31 March 2008 and 2009)

The effect of a reduction in purchase costs of 10% combined with a reduction in selling prices of 5%, based on the figures from 2008, would be:

Sales (55,000 × 95%)	52,250
Cost of sales (33,000 × 90%)	(29,700)
Expected gross profit	22,550

This represents an expected gross profit margin of 43·2% (22,550/52,250 × 100)

The actual gross profit margin for 2009 is 33·4% (22,000/65,800 × 100)

(ii) The directors' expression of surprise that the gross profit in 2009 has not increased seems misconceived.

A change in the gross profit margin does not necessarily mean there will be an equivalent change in the absolute gross profit. This is because the gross profit figure is the product of the gross profit margin and the volume of sales and these may vary independently of each other. That said, in this case the expected gross profit margin in 2009 shows an increase over that earned in 2008 (to 43·2% from 40·0%) and the sales have also increased, so it is understandable that the directors expected a higher gross profit. As the actual gross profit margin in 2009 is only 33·4% something other than the changes described by the directors must have occurred. Possible reasons for the reduction are:

The opening stock being at old (higher) cost and the closing stock is at the new (lower) cost will have caused slight distortion.

Stock write downs due to damage/obsolescence.

A change in the sales mix (i.e. from higher margin sales to lower margin sales). New (lower margin) products may have been introduced from other new suppliers. Some selling prices may have been discounted because of sales promotions.

Import duties (perhaps not allowed for by the directors) or exchange rate fluctuations may have caused the actual purchase cost to be higher than the trade prices quoted by the new supplier.

Change in cost classification: some costs included as operating expenses in 2008 may have been classified as cost of sales in 2009 (if intentional and material this should be treated as a change in accounting policy) – for example it may be worth checking that depreciation has been properly charged to operating expenses in 2009.

The new supplier may have put his prices up during the year; due to market conditions the company may have felt it could not pass these increases on to its customers.

(iii) **Note** – all monetary figures in £000

Debtors' collection period in 2008:

2,800/28,500 × 365 = 35·9 days

Applying the 35·9 days collection period to the credit sales made in 2009:

53,000 × 35·9/365 = 5,213, the actual debtors are 7,800 thus potentially increasing the bank balance by 2,587

A similar exercise with the trade creditors' payment period in 2008:

4,500/33,000 × 365 = 49·8 days

Note the 33,000 above is the cost of sales for 2008. This was the same as the credit purchases as there was no change in the value of stock. However, in 2009 the credit purchases will be 44,600 (43,800 + 5,200 closing stock − 4,400 opening stock).

Applying the 49·8 days payment period to purchases made in 2009 gives:

44,600 × 49·8/365 = 6,085, the actual creditors are 4,200 thus potentially increasing the bank balance by

1,885.Inevitably a shortening of the period of credit offered by suppliers and lengthening the credit offered to customers will put a strain on cash resources. For Coaltown the combination of maintaining the same credit periods for both trade receivables and payables would have led to a reduction in cash outflows of 4,472 (2,587 + 1,885), which would have eliminated the overdraft of 3,600 leaving a balance in hand of 872.

ACCA marking scheme		Marks
(a)	operating activities	
	operating profit	1
	depreciation	2
	loss on disposal	1
	warranty adjustment	0.5
	working capital items	1.5
	servicing of finance	1
	tax paid	1
	purchase of fixed assets	2
	disposal cost of fixed assets	1
	dividend paid	1
	issue of equity shares	1
	issue of 10% loan note	1
	decrease in cash	1
	Maximum	15

(b)	(i)	calculation of expected gross profit margin for 2009 Maximum	2
	(ii)	comments on directors' surprise and other factors Maximum	4
	(iii)	calculate credit periods (debtors and creditors) in 2008	2
		apply to 2009 credit sales/purchases	1
		calculate 'savings' and effect on closing bank balance	1
			___
	Maximum		4
			___
Total			25

Examiner's comments

Part (a) required the preparation of a statement of cash flows for 15 marks followed by some 'targeted' interpretation for 10 marks. Cash flows are generally popular with candidates and many scored well, however, again the overall performance was not as good as I would have expected with surprisingly few candidates earning the maximum marks. Less well-prepared candidates showed poor format knowledge with little idea of which items should appear in which section of the statement nor did they know the difference between cash and noncash flows, for example reserve movements, provisions (for warranties) and the loss on the disposal of the displays were sometimes treated as cash flows. A number of candidates had difficulty with the accumulated depreciation being reset to zero after a revaluation and the cost of the disposal of an asset was often treated as the sale proceeds. Many candidates could not work out the movement on the accumulated depreciation as they could not follow the impact of the disposal of the displays which gave them a depreciation amount to be credited to the income statement. An area causing many marks to be lost was getting the cash movements the wrong way round (signing errors). For example, the marks for the movement in working capital items are normally for correctly identifying them as inflows or outflows rather than for correct arithmetic. Some candidates split the two finance costs both within the adjustments and the cash outflows (often in different sections of the statement) which was not necessary.

Part (b), gave information about percentage changes in the sales and the cost of sales instigated by the directors actions which was accompanied by information on changes in credit periods. Part (b)(i) required candidates to calculate the gross profit margin that should have resulted from the cost and revenue changes. Many candidates got this correct, but a number did not seem to read the requirement correctly and calculated the actual profit margin (rather than the 'theoretical margin'). A number of candidates made the adjustments to the 2008 revenue and cost of sales figures rather than to the 2009 figures, which may have been caused by not reading the question carefully enough.

Part (ii) was a written section effectively requiring candidates to identify other factors (apart from the cost and revenue changes) that could have caused the change in gross profit margin. This was generally very badly answered; many candidates discussed exclusively the cost changes instigated by the directors as being solely responsible for the overall change in the margin, despite the previous section having already identified the effect of those changes. The same candidates were usually convinced that the changed credit periods were the cause of the changes in the gross margin which shows a lack of understanding between profit and cash. Those candidates that did realise the question required other examples of causes of changes in gross profit margin often gave examples of items that do not affect gross profit such as higher bad debt charges, cash discounts and additional finance costs –

these do affect net profit, but not gross profit. A number of candidates did refer to quality issues and returns of goods to suppliers and from customers, with a small number of very perceptive candidates even noting the latter was reinforced by the disproportionate increase in the warranty provision. Part (iii) was again a targeted area of ratio understanding related to the changes in the credit periods (for payables and receivables). The question wanted candidates to quantify the effect it would have had on the bank balance if the previous year's (2008) credit periods been maintained in the current year (2009). This involved calculating 2008's credit periods and then applying those to the credit sales and credit purchases of 2009 to give 'theoretical' receivables and payables balances for 2009. These could then be compared to the actual payables and receivables balances of 2009 to identify the 'theoretical' effect on the bank balance. Many candidates presented a simple comparison of this year's credit periods with those of the previous year; either those candidates did not read the requirement properly or they only have a 'mechanical' understanding of the ratios and cannot adapt to a different scenario. Weaker candidates decided to calculate the inventory turnover figures for both years and then compute the working capital cycle which was of no relevance to the question set.

Section 3

PILOT PAPER EXAM QUESTIONS

1 PUMICE

On 1 October 2005 Pumice acquired the following fixed asset investments:

- 80% of the equity share capital of Silverton at a cost of £13.6 million
- 50% of Silverton's 10% loan notes at par
- 1.6 million equity shares in Amok at a cost of £6.25 each.

The summarised draft balance sheets of the three companies at 31 March 2006 are:

	Pumice		Silverton		Amok	
	£000	£000	£000	£000	£000	£000
Tangible fixed assets		20,000		8,500		16,500
Investments		26,000		Nil		1,500
		——		——		——
		46,000		8,500		18,000
Current assets	15,000		8,000		11,000	
Creditors: amounts falling due within one year	(10,000)		(3,500)		(5,000)	
	——		——		——	
Net current assets		5,000		4,500		6,000
		——		——		——
Total assets less current liabilities		51,000		13,000		24,000
Creditors: amounts falling after more than one year						
8% Loan note		(4,000)		Nil		Nil
10% Loan note		Nil		(2,000)		Nil
		——		——		——
		47,000		11,000		24,000
		——		——		——
Capital and reserves						
Equity shares of £1 each		10,000		3,000		4,000
Profit and loss account		37,000		8,000		20,000
		——		——		——
		47,000		11,000		24,000
		——		——		——

The following information is relevant:

(i)   The fair values of Silverton's assets were equal to their carrying amounts with the exception of land and plant. Silverton's land had a fair value of £400,000 in excess of its carrying amount and plant had a fair value of £1.6 million in excess of its carrying amount. The plant had a remaining life of four years (straight-line depreciation) at the date of acquisition.

(ii)   In the post acquisition period Pumice sold goods to Silverton at a price of £6 million. These goods had cost Pumice £4 million. Half of these goods were still in the stock of Silverton at 31 March 2006. Silverton had a balance of £1.5 million owing to Pumice at 31 March 2006 which agreed with Pumice's records.

(iii)   The net profit after tax for the year ended 31 March 2006 was £2 million for Silverton and £8 million for Amok. Assume profits accrued evenly throughout the year.

(iv)   Consolidated goodwill is to be written off over a five-year life using time apportionment in the year of acquisition.

(v)   No dividends were paid during the year by any of the companies.

Required:

(a)   Discuss how the investments purchased by Pumice on 1 October 2005 should be treated in its consolidated financial statements.   **(5 marks)**

(b)   Prepare the consolidated balance sheet for Pumice as at 31 March 2006.   **(20 marks)**

(Total: 25 marks)

2   KALA

The following trial balance relates to Kala, a publicly listed company, at 31 March 2006:

	£000	£000
Land and buildings at cost (note (i))	270,000	
Plant – at cost (note (i))	156,000	
Investment properties – valuation at 1 April 2005 (note (i))	90,000	
Purchases	78,200	
Operating expenses	15,500	
Loan interest paid	2,000	
Rental of leased plant (note (ii))	22,000	
Dividends paid	15,000	
Stock at 1 April 2005	37,800	
Trade debtors	53,200	
Turnover		278,400
Income from investment property		4,500
Equity shares of £1 each fully paid		150,000
Profit and loss reserve at 1 April 2005		112,500
Investment property revaluation reserve at 1 April 2005		7,000
8% (actual and effective) loan note (note (iii))		50,000
Accumulated depreciation at 1 April 2005 – buildings		60,000
– plant		26,000

Trade creditors		33,400
Deferred tax		12,500
Bank		5,400
	739,700	739,700

The following notes are relevant:

(i)　The land and buildings were purchased on 1 April 1990. The cost of the land was £70 million. No land and buildings have been purchased by Kala since that date. On 1 April 2005 Kala had its land and buildings professionally valued at £80 million and £175 million respectively. The directors wish to incorporate these values into the financial statements. The estimated life of the buildings was originally 50 years and the remaining life has not changed as a result of the valuation.

Later, the valuers informed Kala that investment properties of the type Kala owned had increased in value by 7% in the year to 31 March 2006.

Plant, other than leased plant (see below), is depreciated at 15% per annum using the reducing balance method. Depreciation of buildings and plant is charged to cost of sales.

(ii)　On 1 April 2005 Kala entered into a lease for an item of plant which had an estimated life of five years. The lease period is also five years with annual rentals of £22 million payable in advance from 1 April 2005. The plant is expected to have a nil residual value at the end of its life. If purchased this plant would have a cost of £92 million and be depreciated on a straight-line basis. The lessor includes a finance cost of 10% per annum when calculating annual rentals. (**Note:** you are not required to calculate the present value of the minimum lease payments.)

(iii)　The loan note was issued on 1 July 2005 with interest payable six monthly in arrears.

(iv)　The provision for corporation tax for the year to 31 March 2006 has been estimated at £28.3 million. The deferred tax provision at 31 March 2006 is to be adjusted to a credit balance of £14.1 million.

(v)　Stock at 31 March 2006 was valued at £43.2 million.

Required:

Prepare for Kala:

(a)　A profit and loss account for the year ended 31 March 2006.　**(9 marks)**

(b)　A statement of the movement in share capital and reserves for the year ended 31 March 2006.　**(5 marks)**

(c)　A balance sheet as at 31 March 2006.　**(11 marks)**

(Total: 25 marks)

Note: A statement of total recognised gains and losses is NOT required.

3   REACTIVE

Reactive is a publicly listed company that assembles domestic electrical goods which it then sells to both wholesale and retail customers. Reactive's management were disappointed in the company's results for the year ended 31 March 2005. In an attempt to improve performance the following measures were taken early in the year ended 31 March 2006:

–   a national advertising campaign was undertaken,

–   rebates to all wholesale customers purchasing goods above set quantity levels were introduced,

–   the assembly of certain lines ceased and was replaced by bought in completed products. This allowed Reactive to dispose of surplus plant.

Reactive's summarised financial statements for the year ended 31 March 2006 are set out below:

Profit and loss account	£million
Turnover (25% cash sales)	4,000
Cost of sales	(3,450)
Gross profit	550
Operating expenses	(370)
Operating profit	180
Profit on disposal of plant (note (i))	40
Finance costs	(20)
Profit before taxation	200
Taxation	(50)
Profit for the financial year	150

Balance Sheet	£million	£million
Tangible fixed assets		
Property		300
Plant and equipment (note (i))		250
		550
Current assets		
Stock	250	
Debtors	360	
Bank	Nil	
	610	
Creditors: amounts falling due within one year		
Bank overdraft	10	
Trade creditors	430	
Taxation	40	
	(480)	130

Creditors: amounts falling due after more than one year

8% loan note   (200)
                                                                                      ———
                                                                                       480
                                                                                      ———

Capital and reserves

Equity shares of 25 pence each   100

Profit and loss account reserve   380
                                                                                      ———
                                                                                       480
                                                                                      ———

Below are ratios calculated for the year ended 31 March 2005.

Return on year end capital employed (profit before interest and tax over total assets less current liabilities)   28.1%

Net asset (equal to capital employed) turnover   4 times

Gross profit margin   17 %

Net profit (before tax) margin   6.3 %

Current ratio   1.6:1

Closing stock holding period   46 days

Debtors' collection period   45 days

Creditors' payment period   55 days

Dividend yield   3.75%

Dividend cover   2 times

Notes:

(i)   Reactive received £120 million from the sale of plant that had a carrying amount of £80 million at the date of its sale.

(ii)   The market price of Reactive's shares throughout the year averaged £3.75 each.

(iii)   There were no issues or redemption of shares or loans during the year.

(iv)   Dividends paid during the year ended 31 March 2006 amounted to £90 million, maintaining the same dividend paid in the year ended 31 March 2005.

Required:

(a)   Calculate ratios for the year ended 31 March 2006 (showing your workings) for Reactive, equivalent to those provided.   **(10 marks)**

(b)   Analyse the financial performance and position of Reactive for the year ended 31 March 2006 compared to the previous year.   **(10 marks)**

(c)   Explain in what ways your approach to performance appraisal would differ if you were asked to assess the performance of a not-for-profit organisation.   **(5 marks)**

(Total: 25 marks)

4   PORTO

(a)   The qualitative characteristics of relevance, reliability and comparability identified in the ASB's *Statement of principles for financial reporting* are some of the attributes that make financial information useful to the various users of financial statements.

Required:

Explain what is meant by relevance, reliability and comparability and how they make financial information useful.   **(9 marks)**

(b)   During the year ended 31 March 2006, Porto experienced the following transactions or events:

(i)   entered into a finance lease to rent an asset for substantially the whole of its useful economic life.

(ii)   a decision was made by the Board to change the company's accounting policy from one of expensing the finance costs on building new retail outlets to one of capitalising such costs.

(iii) the company's profit and loss account prepared using historical costs showed a loss from operating its hotels, but the company is aware that that the increase in the value of its properties during the period far outweighed the operating loss.

Required:

Explain how you would treat the items in (i) to (iii) above in Porto's financial statements and indicate on which of the Statement's qualitative characteristics your treatment is based.   **(6 marks)**

(Total: 15 marks)

5   BEETIE

SSAP 9 *Stocks and long-term contracts* deals with accounting for long-term contracts whose durations usually span at least two accounting periods.

Required:

(a)   Describe the issues of revenue and profit recognition relating to long-term contracts.
                                                                                     (4 marks)

(b)   Beetie is a construction company that prepares its financial statements to 31 March each year. During the year ended 31 March 2006 the company commenced two construction contracts that are expected to be completed in the accounting period ended 31 March 2007. The position of each contract at 31 March 2006 is as follows:

Contract	*1*	*2*
	£000	£000
Agreed contract price	5,500	1,200
Estimated total cost of contract at commencement	4,000	900
Estimated total cost at 31 March 2006	4,000	1,250
Certified value of work completed at 31 March 2006	3,300	840
Contract billings invoiced and received at 31 March 2006	3,000	880
Contract costs incurred to 31 March 2006	3,900	720

The certified value of the work completed at 31 March 2006 is considered to be equal to the revenue earned in the year ended 31 March 2006. The percentage of completion is calculated as the value of the work completed to the agreed contract price.

Required:

Calculate the amounts which should appear in the profit and loss account and balance sheet of Beetie at 31 March 2006 in respect of the above contracts.

(6 marks)

(Total: 10 marks)

Section 4

ANSWERS TO PILOT PAPER EXAM QUESTIONS

1 PUMICE

(a) As the investment in shares represents 80% of Silverton's equity shares it is likely to give Pumice control of that company. Control is the ability to direct the operating and financial policies of an entity. This would make Silverton a subsidiary of Pumice and require Pumice to prepare group financial statements which would require the consolidation of the results of Silverton from the date of acquisition (1 October 2005). Consolidated financial statements are prepared on the basis that the group is a single economic entity.

The investment of 50% (£1 million) of the 10% loan note in Silverton is effectively a loan from a parent to a subsidiary. On consolidation Pumice's asset of the loan (£1 million) is cancelled out with £1 million of Silverton's total loan note liability of £2 million. This would leave a net liability of £1 million in the consolidated balance sheet.

The investment in Amok of 1.6 million shares represents 40% of that company's equity shares. This is generally regarded as not being sufficient to give Pumice control of Amok, but is likely to give it significant influence over Amok's policy decisions (e.g. determining the level of dividends paid by Amok). Such investments are generally classified as associates and FRS 9 *Associates and joint ventures* requires the investment to be included in the consolidated financial statements using equity accounting.

(b) **Consolidated balance sheet of Pumice at 31 March 2006**

	£000	£000
Intangible fixed assets:		
Goodwill (4,000 – 400 (w (ii)))		3,600
Tangible fixed assets (w (i))		30,300
Investments — associate (w (iii))		11,400
— other ((26,000 – 13,600 – 10,000 – 1,000 intra-group loan note))		1,400
		46,700
Current assets (15,000 + 8,000 – 1,000 (w (iv)) – 1,500 current account)	20,500	
Creditors: amounts falling due within one year (10,000 + 3,500 – 1,500 current account)	(12,000)	
Net current assets		8,500

Total assets less current liabilities			55,200
Creditors: amounts falling due after more than one year			
8% Loan note		(4,000)	
10% Loan note (2,000 – 1,000 intra-group)		(1,000)	(5,000)
			50,200
Capital and reserves:			
Equity shares of £1 each			10,000
Reserves:			
Profit and loss account (w (v))			37,640
			47,640
Minority interest (w (vi))			2,560
			50,200

Workings in £000

(i)	Tangible fixed assets			
	Pumice			20,000
	Silverton			8,500
	Fair value – land		400	
	– plant		1,600	2,000
	Additional depreciation (see below)			(200)
				30,300

The fair value adjustment to plant will create additional depreciation of £400,000 per annum (1,600/4 years) and in the post acquisition period of six months this will be £200,000.

		£000	£000
(ii)	Goodwill in Silverton:		
	Investment at cost		13,600
	Less – equity shares of Silverton (3,000 × 80%)	(2,400)	
	– pre-acquisition reserves (7,000 × 80% (see below))	(5,600)	
	– fair value adjustments (2,000 (w (i)) × 80%)	(1,600)	(9,600)
	Goodwill on consolidation		4,000
	Goodwill amortisation will be £4,000/5 years × 6/12 =		400

The pre-acquisition reserves are:		
At 31 March 2006		8,000
Post acquisition (2,000 × 6/12)		(1,000)
		7,000

(iii) Purchase of Amok

Cost of investment (1,600 × £6.25)		10,000
Less		
Net assets at 1 October 2005:		
Equity 31 March 2006	24,000	
Profit 1 October 2005 to 31 March 2006 (8,000 × 6/12)	(4,000)	
	20,000 × 40%	(8,000)
Goodwill		2,000
Carrying amount at 31 March 2006		
Cost		10,000
Share post acquisition profit (8,000 × 6/12 × 40%)		1,600
Less goodwill amortisation (2,000/5 years × 6/12)		(200)
Carrying amount		11,400

(iv) The unrealised profit (URP) In stock is calculated as:

Intra-group sales are £6 million of which Pumice made a profit of £2 million. Half of these are still in stock, thus there is an unrealised profit of £1 million.

(v) Consolidated reserves:

	£000	£000
Pumice's reserves		37,000
Silverton's post acquisition (((2,000 × 6/12) − 200 depreciation) × 80%)		640
Amok's post acquisition profits (8,000 × 6/12 × 40%)		1,600
URP in stock (see (iv))		(1,000)
Goodwill amortisation (w (ii)) – Silverton	400	
(w (iii)) – Amok	200	(600)
		37,640

(vi) Minority interest

Equity shares of Silverton (3,000 × 20%)	600
Profit and loss reserve ((8,000 − 200 depreciation) × 20%)	1,560
Fair value adjustments (2,000 × 20%)	400
	2,560

ACCA marking scheme		Marks
(a)	1 mark per relevant point	5
(b)	Balance sheet:	
	Goodwill	3½
	Tangible fixed assets	2½
	Investments – associate	3
	– other	1
	Current assets	2
	Creditors – 1 year	1
	8% Loan notes	½
	10% Loan notes	1
	Equity shares	1
	Profit and loss account	3
	Minority interest	1½
	Maximum	20
Total		25

2 KALA

(a) **Kala – Profit and loss account – Year ended 31 March 2006**

	£000	£000
Turnover		278,400
Cost of sales (w (i))		(115,700)
Gross profit		162,700
Operating expenses		(15,500)
Operating profit		147,200
Investment income – property rental		4,500
Finance costs – loan (w (ii))	(3,000)	
– lease (w (iii))	(7,000)	(10,000)
Profit on ordinary activities before tax		141,700
Taxation (28,300 + (14,100 – 12,500))		(29,900)
Profit for the financial year		111,800

(b) **Kala –Statement of movement in share capital and reserves – Year ended 31 March 2006**

	Equity shares £000	Investment property resv £000	Land and building revin reserve £000	Profit and loss account £000	Total £000
At 1 April 2005	150,000	7,000	Nil	112,500	269,500
Profit for period (see (a))				111,800	111,800
Revaluation (w (iv))		6,300	45,000		51,300
Equity dividends paid				(15,000)	(15,000)
At 31 March 2006	150,000	13,300	45,000	209,300	417,600

(c)   **Kala – Balance sheet as at 31 March 2006**

	£000	£000
Tangible fixed assets		
Land and buildings (w (iv))	250,000	
Plant (w (iv))	184,100	434,100
Investment properties (90,000 + (90,000 × 7%))		96,300
		530,400
Current assets		
Stock	43,200	
Trade debtors	53,200	
	96,400	
Creditors: amounts falling due within one year		
Trade creditors	33,400	
Accrued loan interest (w (ii))	1,000	
Bank overdraft	5,400	
Lease obligation (w (iii)) – accrued interest	7,000	
– capital	15,000	
Corporation tax	28,300	
	(90,100)	
Net current assets		6,300
Total assets less current liabilities		536,700
Creditors: amounts falling due after more than one year		
8% loan note	(50,000)	
Lease obligation (w (iii))	(55,000)	(105,000)
Provisions for liabilities		
Deferred tax		(14,100)
		417,600
Capital and reserves (see (b) above):		
Equity shares of £1 each		150,000
Reserves:		
Revaluation reserves – land and buildings	45,000	
– Investment property	13,300	
Profit and loss account	209,300	267,600
		417,600

Workings in brackets in £'000

(i) **Cost of sales:**

	£000
Opening stock	37,800
Purchases	78,200
Depreciation (w (iv)) – buildings	5,000
– plant: owned	19,500
leased	18,400
Closing stock	(43,200)
	115,700

(ii) The loan has been in issue for nine months. The total finance cost for this period will be £3 million (50,000 × 8% × 9/12). Kala has paid six months interest of £2 million, thus accrued interest of £1 million should be provided for.

(iii) **Finance lease:**

	£000
Net obligation at inception of lease (92,000 – 22,000)	70,000
Accrued interest 10% (current liability)	7,000
Total outstanding at 31 March 2006	77,000

The second payment in the year to 31 March 2007 (made on 1 April 2006) of £22 million will be £7 million for the accrued interest (at 31 March 2006) and £15 million paid of the capital outstanding. Thus the amount outstanding as an obligation over one year is £55 million (77,000 – 22,000).

(iv) **Fixed assets/depreciation:**

Land and buildings:

At the date of the revaluation the land and buildings have a carrying amount of £210 million (270,000 – 60,000). With a valuation of £255 million this gives a revaluation surplus (to reserves) of £45 million. The accumulated depreciation of £60 million represents 15 years at £4 million per annum (200,000/50 years) and means the remaining life at the date of the revaluation is 35 years. The amount of the revalued building is £175 million, thus depreciation for the year to 31 March 2006 will be £5 million (175,000/35 years). The carrying amount of the land and buildings at 31 March 2006 is £250 million (255,000 – 5,000).

Plant: owned

The carrying amount prior to the current year's depreciation is £130 million (156,000 – 26,000). Depreciation at 15% on the reducing balance basis gives an annual charge of £19.5 million. This gives a carrying amount at 31 March 2006 of £110.5 million (130,000 – 19,500).

Plant: leased

The fair value of the leased plant is £92 million. Depreciation on a straight-line basis over five years would give a depreciation charge of £18.4 million and a carrying amount of £73.6 million.

The carrying amount of all plant in the balance sheet at 31 March 2006 is therefore £184.1 million (110,500 + 73,600).

ACCA marking scheme		Marks
(a)	**Profit and loss account**	
	Turnover	½
	Cost of sales	4½
	Operating expenses	½
	Investment income	½
	Finance costs	1½
	Taxation	1½
	Maximum	9
(b)	**Movement in share capital and reserves**	
	Brought forward figures	1
	Profit for period	1
	Revaluation gains	2
	Dividends paid	1
	Maximum	5
(c)	**Balance sheet**	
	Land and buildings	2
	Plant and equipment	2
	Investment property	1
	Stocks and trade debtors	1
	Trade creditors and overdraft	1
	Accrued interest	½
	Lease obligation: interest and capital one year	1
	Capital over one year	1
	Corporation tax provision	½
	8% Loan	½
	Deferred tax	½
	Maximum	11
Total		**25**

3   REACTIVE

(a)   *Note:* figures in the calculations are in £million

Return on year end capital employed	32.3%	220/(550 + 130) × 100
Net assets turnover	5.9 times	4,000/680
Gross profit margin	13.8%	(550/4,000) × 100
Net profit (before tax) margin	5.0%	(200/4,000) × 100
Current ratio	1.3:1	610:480
Closing stock holding period	26 days	250/3,450 × 365
Debtors' collection period	44 days	360/(4,000 − 1,000) × 365
Creditors' payment period (based on cost of sales)	45 days	(430/3,450) × 365
Dividend yield	6.0%	(see below)
Dividend cover	1.67 times	150/90

The dividend per share is 22.5p (90,000/(100,000 × 4 i.e. 25p shares). This is a yield of 6.0% on a share price of £3.75.

(b)   Analysis of the comparative financial performance and position of Reactive for the year ended 31 March 2006

Profitability

The measures taken by management appear to have been successful as the overall ROCE (considered as a primary measure of performance) has improved by 15% (32.3 − 28.1)/28.1). Looking in more detail at the composition of the ROCE, the reason for the improved profitability is due to increased efficiency in the use of the company's assets (asset turnover), increasing from 4 to 5.9 times (an improvement of 48%). The improvement in the asset turnover has been offset by lower profit margins at both the gross and net level. On the surface, this performance appears to be due both to the company's strategy of offering rebates to wholesale customers if they achieve a set level of orders and also the beneficial impact on sales revenue of the advertising campaign. The rebate would explain the lower gross profit margin, and the cost of the advertising has reduced net profit margin (presumably management expected an increase in sales volume as a compensating factor). The decision to buy complete products rather than assemble them in house has enabled the disposal of some plant which has reduced the asset base. Thus possible increased sales and a lower asset base are the cause of the improvement in the asset turnover which in turn, as stated above, is responsible for the improvement in the ROCE.

The effect of the disposal needs careful consideration. The profit (before tax) includes a profit of £40 million from the disposal. As this is a 'one-off' profit, recalculating the ROCE without its inclusion gives a figure of only 23.7% (180m/(550m + 130m + 80m (the 80m is the carrying amount of plant)) and the fall in the net profit percentage (before tax) would be down even more to only 4.0% (160m/4,000m). On this basis the current year performance is worse than that of the previous year and the reported figures tend to flatter the company's real underlying performance.

Liquidity

The company's liquidity position has deteriorated during the period. An acceptable current ratio of 1.6 has fallen to a worrying 1.3 (1.5 is usually considered as a safe minimum). With the debtors collection period at virtually a constant (45/44 days), the change in liquidity appears to be due to the levels of stock and trade creditors. These give a contradictory picture. The closing stock holding period has decreased markedly (from 46 to 26 days) indicating more efficient stock holding. This is perhaps due to short lead times when ordering bought in products. The change in this ratio has reduced the current ratio, however the creditors' payment period has decreased from 55 to 45 days which has increased the current ratio. This may be due to different terms offered by suppliers of bought in products.

Importantly, the effect of the plant disposal has generated a cash inflow of £120 million, and without this the company's liquidity would look far worse.

Investment ratios

The current year's dividend yield of 6.0% looks impressive when compared with that of the previous year's yield of 3.75%, but as the company has maintained the same dividend (and dividend per share as there is no change in share capital), the 'improvement' in the yield is due to a falling share price. Last year the share price must have been £6.00 to give a yield of 3.75% on a dividend per share of 22.5 pence. It is worth noting that maintaining the dividend at £90 million from profits of £150 million gives a cover of only 1.67 times whereas on the same dividend last year the cover was 2 times (meaning last year's profit (after tax) was £180 million).

Conclusion

Although superficially the company's profitability seems to have improved as a result of the directors' actions at the start of the current year, much, if not all, of the apparent improvement is due to the change in supply policy and the consequent beneficial effects of the disposal of plant. The company's liquidity is now below acceptable levels and would have been even worse had the disposal not occurred. It appears that investors have understood the underlying deterioration in performance as there has been a marked fall in the company's share price.

(c)   It is generally assumed that the objective of stock market listed companies is to maximise the wealth of their shareholders. This in turn places an emphasis on profitability and other factors that influence a company's share price. It is true that some companies have other (secondary) aims such as only engaging in ethical activities (e.g. not producing armaments) or have strong environmental considerations. Clearly by definition not-for-profit organisations are not motivated by the need to produce profits for shareholders, but that does not mean that they should be inefficient. Many areas of assessment of profit oriented companies are perfectly valid for not-for-profit organisations: efficient stock holdings, tight budgetary constraints, use of key performance indicators, prevention of fraud etc.

There are a great variety of not-for-profit organisations; e.g. public sector health, education, policing and charities. It is difficult to be specific about how to assess the performance of a not-for-profit organisation without knowing what type of organisation it is. In general terms an assessment of performance must be made in the light of the stated objectives of the organisation. Thus for example in a public health service one could look at measures such as treatment waiting times, increasing life expectancy etc, and although such organisations do not have a profit motive requiring efficient operation, they should nonetheless be accountable for the resources they use. Techniques such as 'value for money' and the three Es (economy, efficiency and effectiveness) have been developed and can help to assess the performance of such organisations.

ACCA marking scheme		Marks
(a)	1 mark per ratio	10
(b)	1 mark per valid point	10
(c)	1 mark per valid point	5
Total		**25**

4   PORTO

(a)   Relevance

Information has the quality of relevance when it can influence users' economic decisions on a timely basis. It helps to evaluate past, present and future events by confirming, or perhaps correcting, past evaluations of economic events. There are many ways of interpreting and applying the concept of relevance, for example, only material information is considered relevant as, by definition, information is material only if its omission or misstatement could influence users. Other common aspects of relevance are the debate as to whether current value information is more relevant than that based on historical cost. An interesting emphasis placed on relevance within the Statement is that relevant information assists in the predictive ability of financial statements. That is not to say the financial statements should be predictive in the sense of forecasts, but that (past) information should be presented in a manner that assists users to assess an entity's ability to take advantage of opportunities and react to adverse situations. A good example of this is the separate presentation of discontinued operations in the profit and loss account. From this users will be better able to assess the parts of the entity that will produce future profits (the continuing operations) and users can judge the merits of the discontinuation i.e. has the entity sold a profitable part of the business (which would lead users to question why), or has the entity acted to curtail the adverse affect of a loss-making operation.

Reliability

The Statement states that for information to be useful it must be reliable. The quality of reliability is described as being free from material error (accurate) and representing faithfully that which it purports to portray (i.e. the financial statements are a faithful representation of the entities' underlying transactions). There can be occasions where the legal form of a transaction can be engineered to disguise the economic reality of the transaction. A cornerstone of faithful representation is that transactions must be accounted for according to their substance (i.e. commercial intent or economic reality) rather than their legal or contrived form. To be reliable information must be free from deliberate or systematic bias (i.e. it is neutral). Biased information attempts to influence users (to perhaps come to a predetermined decision) by the manner in which it is presented. It is recognised that financial statements cannot be absolutely accurate due to inevitable uncertainties surrounding their preparation. A typical example would be estimating the useful economic lives of fixed assets. This is addressed by the use of prudence which is the exercise of a degree of caution in matters of uncertainty. However, prudence cannot be used to deliberately understate profit or create excessive provisions (this would break the neutrality principle). Reliable information must also be complete; omitted information (that should be reported) will obviously mislead users.

Comparability

Comparability is fundamental to assessing an entity's performance. Users will compare an entity's results over time and also with other similar entities. This is the principal reason why financial statements contain corresponding amounts for previous period(s). Comparability is enhanced by the use (and disclosure) of consistent accounting policies such that users can confirm that comparative information (for calculating trends) is comparable and the disclosure of accounting policies at least informs users if different entities use different policies. That said, comparability should not stand in the way of improved accounting practices (usually through new Standards); it is recognised that there are occasions where it is necessary to adopt new accounting policies if they enhance relevance and reliability.

(b) (i) This item involves the characteristic of reliability and specifically the use of substance over form. As the lease agreement is for substantially the whole of the asset's useful economic life, Porto will experience the same risks and rewards as if it owned the asset. Although the legal form of this transaction is a rental, its substance is the equivalent to acquiring the asset and raising a loan. Thus, in order for the financial statements to be reliable (and comparable to those where an asset is bought from the proceeds of a loan), the transaction should be shown as an asset on Porto's balance sheet with a corresponding liability for the future lease rental payments. The profit and loss account should be charged with depreciation on the asset and a finance charge on the 'loan'.

(ii) This item involves the characteristic of comparability. Changes in accounting policies should generally be avoided in order to preserve comparability. Presumably the directors have good reason to believe the new policy presents a more reliable and relevant view. In order to minimise the adverse effect a change in accounting policy has on comparability, the financial statements (including the corresponding amounts) should be prepared on the basis that the new policy had always been in place (retrospective application). Thus the assets (retail outlets) should include the previously expensed finance costs and profit and loss accounts will no longer show a finance cost (in relation to these assets whilst under construction). Any finance costs relating to periods prior to the policy change (i.e. for two or more years ago) should be adjusted for by increasing profits brought forward in the profit and loss reserve (equity).

(iii) This item involves the characteristic of relevance. This situation questions whether historical cost accounting is more relevant to users than current value information. Porto's current method of reporting these events using purely historical cost based information (i.e. showing an operating loss, but not reporting the increases in property values) is perfectly acceptable. However, the company could choose to revalue its hotel properties (which would subject it to other requirements). This option would still report an operating loss (probably an even larger loss than under historical cost if there are increased depreciation charges on the hotels), but the increases in value would also be reported (in equity) arguably giving a more complete picture of performance.

ACCA marking scheme		
		Marks
(a)	3 marks each for relevance, reliability and comparability	9
(b)	2 marks for each transaction ((i) to (iii)) or event	6
Total		15

5   BEETIE

(a)   The correct timing of when revenue (and profit) should be recognised is an important aspect of a profit and loss account showing a true and fair view. Only realised profits should be included in the profit and loss account. For most types of supply and sale of goods it is generally accepted that a profit is realised when the goods have been manufactured (or obtained) by the supplier and satisfactorily delivered to the customer. The issue with long-term contracts is that the process of completing the project takes a relatively long time and, in particular, will spread across at least one accounting period-end. If such contracts are treated like most sales of goods, it would mean that revenue and profit would not be recognised until the contract is completed (the 'completed contracts' basis). This is often described as following the prudence concept. The problem with this approach is that it may not show a true and fair view as all the profit on a contract is included in the period of completion, whereas in reality (a true and fair view), it is being earned, but not reported, throughout the duration of the contract. SSAP 9 remedies this by requiring the recognition of profit on uncompleted contracts in proportion to some measure of the percentage of completion applied to the estimated total contract profit. This is sometimes said to reflect the accruals concept, but it should only be applied where the outcome of the contract is reasonably foreseeable. In the event that a loss on a contract is foreseen, the whole of the loss must be recognised immediately, thereby ensuring the continuing application of prudence.

(b)   **Beetie**

	Contract 1	Contract 2	Total
Profit and loss account	£000	£000	£000
Turnover	3,300	840	4,140
Cost of sales (balancing figure)	(2,400)	(890)	(3,290)
Attributable profit/(loss) (see working)	900	(50)	850
Balance sheet			
Stock: long-term contract balances			
Costs to date	3,900	720	4,620
Transferred to cost of sales	(2,400)	(720)	(3,120)
	1,500	Nil	1,500

Debtors: amounts recoverable

Turnover	3,300	3,300
Payments on account	(3,000)	(3,000)
	300	300
Creditors: amounts falling due within one year		
Payments on account (880 – 840)	40	40
Provisions		
Cost incurred and losses to date (890 – 720)	170	170

Workings in £000

Estimated total profit:

Agreed contract price	5,500	1,200
Estimated contract cost	(4,000)	(1,250)
Estimated total profit/(loss)	1,500	(50)

Percentage complete:

Work certified at 31 March 2006	3,300
Contract price	5,500
Percentage complete at 31 March 2006 (3,300/5,500 × 100)	60%
Profit to 31 March 2006 (60% × 1,500)	900

At 31 March 2006 the increase in the expected total costs of contract 2 mean that a loss of £50,000 is expected on this contract. In these circumstances, regardless of the percentage completed, the whole of this loss should be recognised immediately.

ACCA marking scheme		
		Marks
(a)	1 mark per valid point to maximum	4
(b)	Turnover (½ mark for each contract)	1
	Profit/loss (½ mark for each contract)	1
	Stocks	1
	Debtors	1
	Payment on account	1
	Provision	1
	Maximum	6
Total		**10**